THE SPIRIT IN LUKE-ACTS

Odette Mainville's translated book, *The Spirit in Luke-Acts*, is a most careful, enlightening, and fresh interpretation of the Holy Spirit's role in Luke and Acts, from the surprising starting point of a single verse, Acts 2:33. Mainville's diligent exegesis demonstrates the Lukan explanation that grounds the gift of the Holy Spirit at Pentecost in the Father's giving of the Spirit to the exalted Christ, who then pours out the Spirit upon Christians.

After two introductory chapters, Mainville's exegetical chapters painstakingly study Luke's theology of the Father's gift of the Spirit through the exalted Christ and provide many insights innovative even for contemporary scholars and readers. I wholeheartedly endorse this book and congratulate The Foundation for Pentecostal Scholarship for making this important older scholarship available to contemporary readers.

—William S. Kurz, S.J., *Emeritus Professor of New Testament,
Marquette University
Author of* Reading Luke-Acts: Dynamics of Biblical Narrative

How good to see a book that takes Acts 2:33 seriously as a key for unlocking Luke's themes and emphases! As someone who has devoted a whole book to a theological exposition of Acts 2:33, I regard this as a most worthwhile endeavor. What emerges is a work that engages fully with the Spirit's vitality in the life of Jesus and in the mission of the church. I am most pleased that Odette Mainville's book now comes to English-speaking audiences.

—William P. Atkinson, PhD, *Academic Vice Principal, Director of
Research, and Senior Lecturer in Pentecostal and
Charismatic Studies, London School of Theology
Author of* Trinity After Pentecost

From the Foreword: . . . I warmly recommend this insightful reading of Luke-Acts to you. It is filled with interesting exegesis and challenging observations. It affirms, perhaps unconsciously, a Pentecostal reading of Luke-Acts, but does so from a fresh perspective that interacts with a wide range of scholarship, including works from French-speaking authors that may be largely unknown to many North American readers. I trust that you will find this book as enjoyable, enriching, and edifying as I did.

—Robert P. Menzies, PhD, *Missionary-Scholar (China),
Author of* Empowered to Witness: The Spirit in Luke-Acts

Mainville's work is helpful both for its engagement with traditional approaches and for its fresh contributions and insights into Luke's internal narrative connections, Old Testament intertextuality, the exegesis of Acts 2:33, and the strongly charismatic/prophetic dimension of Luke's pneumatology. This is surely a welcome study.

—*Craig S. Keener, PhD, Professor of Biblical Studies,*
Asbury Theological Seminary
Author of Acts an Exegetical Commentary

Dr. Odette Mainville's revised and translated PhD thesis, marks a significant milestone in the journey toward a truly biblical theology. Her work, *The Spirit in Luke-Acts*, sees the culmination of Jesus's ministry in Acts 2:33, which she regards as the culminating summary statement of Luke-Acts. This is a crucial insight; it integrates the central theme in Luke-Acts, in a way that traditional systematic theology does not, *viz*, Jesus's experiences with the Spirit toward the end of creating a "community of prophets" to "perpetuate Jesus's missionary work." The Foundation for Pentecostal Scholarship is to be commended for translating this work for a much broader English audience. Dr. Mainville's contribution provides many valuable and original insights for the ongoing project that is Pentecostal/charismatic theology.

—*Jon Mark Ruthven, PhD, Professor Emeritus,*
Regent University School of Divinity
Author of What's Wrong with Protestant Theology?

I am delighted that Mainville's work has been made available to a wider, English-speaking audience. Her work presents Luke's understanding of the Holy Spirit in a broader, global perspective. Using a redactional and literary approach, she demonstrates that the role of the Holy Spirit is not to be relegated to a mere appendage of Pauline soteriology, as she lets Luke speak in his terms and on his own agenda. Mainville sees that the key for interpreting Lukan pneumatology is the Ascension-Exaltation of Jesus and the subsequent gift of the Spirit in the life and mission of the church. I will be recommending this new version of Mainville's work to my colleagues and students. Bien fait!

—*James B. Shelton, PhD, Professor of New Testament,*
Oral Roberts University
Author of Mighty in Word and Deed: The Role of the Holy Spirit in Luke-Acts

THE SPIRIT IN LUKE-ACTS

By

ODETTE MAINVILLE

Translated by
Suzanne Spolarich

THE FOUNDATION FOR
PENTECOSTAL SCHOLARSHIP

2016

Original edition: *L'Esprit dans l'œuvre de Luc*
La Corporation des Éditions Fides, 1991

English translation: Copyright © The Foundation for Pentecostal Scholarship, Inc., 2016. All rights reserved.

The Foundation for Pentecostal Scholarship, Inc.
1030 Atherton Lane
Woodstock, GA 30189
USA

www.tffps.org

The Scripture quotations contained herein are from the New Revised Standard Version Bible, copyright © 1989 by the Division of Christian Education of the National Council of the Churches of Christ in the U.S.A. Used by permission. All rights reserved.

All rights reserved. No part of this publication may be reproduced, stored in a retrieval system, or transmitted, in any form or by any means, electronic, mechanical, photocopying, recording or otherwise, without the prior permission in writing from the Foundation (admin@tffps.org), except for short excerpts in reviews and academic discussions.

Library of Congress Control Number: 2016943783

ISBN-13: 978-0-9960445-1-6
ISBN-10: 0-9960445-1-5

Having been exalted at the right hand of God and having received from the Father the promise of the Holy Spirit, He has poured forth this which you both see and hear.

Acts 2:33

To my mother and father

Table of Contents

Foreword to the English Translation xi
Foreword to the French Edition xv
Acknowledgements xvii
List of Abbreviations xix

Introduction | 1
  1. Purpose *1*
  2. Approach *2*

Chapter 1 State of the Question | 5
  1. Insertion of the Theme of the Spirit in Luke-Acts *8*
  2. The Spirit in Luke-Acts According to Recent Studies *12*

Chapter 2 Acts 2:33 in Its Literary Context | 27
  1. Vocabulary Analysis *27*
  2. Translation of τῇ δεξιᾷ *30*
  3. Insertion of the Verse in the Pentecost Speech *34*

Chapter 3 Exalted at the Right Hand of God | 51
  1. "Exalted" in the Septuagint and the New Testament *51*
  2. "At the Right Hand of God" in the Old and New Testaments *60*
  3. "Exalted at the Right Hand of God" in Luke-Acts *66*

Chapter 4 Acts 2:33—The Promise of the Holy Spirit | 97
  1. The Promise of the Spirit in Luke-Acts *97*
  2. The Promise of the Spirit—Essential Condition to the Messianic Fulfillment *103*

Chapter 5 Acts 2:33A—Shedding Light on Jesus | 109
  1. The Spirit and the Birth of Jesus—Luke 1–2 *110*
  2. The Spirit and the Baptism of Jesus—Luke 3:21–22 *150*
  3. The Spirit and Jesus's Entrance into Temptation—Luke 4:1 *165*
  4. The Spirit and the Inauguration of Jesus's Ministry—Luke 4:14A, 18 *172*

Chapter 6 Acts 2:33B—Shedding Light on the Church | 177
  1. The Meaning of the Pentecost Account—Acts 2:1–4 *178*
  2. The Impact of the Pentecost Event on Church Life *205*

EXCURSUS: "Speaking in Other Tongues" *208*

Chapter 7   Conclusion | 237
  1. Lukan Pneumatology: A Pneumatology in the Tradition of the Old Testament *238*
  2. A Christianized Pneumatology *245*
  3. The Spirit—Guarantee of Continuity *247*
  4. The Spirit in Service of Church Expansion *250*

Bibliography 253
Index of Names 277
Index of Ancient Sources 283

Foreword to the English Edition

I have developed a special sense of solidarity with Odette Mainville's fine book, *L'Esprit dans l'œuvre de Luc* (Montreal: Fides, 1991). This monograph is a revised version of the doctoral dissertation that Mainville successfully defended at the University of Montreal in 1989. I commend the Foundation for Pentecostal Scholarship and the translator, Suzanne Spolarich, for making this important work accessible to a larger audience with this English translation.

Several factors contribute to the sense of connection I feel with this book. First, there is the matter of timing. I pursued my PhD studies during roughly the same period that Mainville pursued hers, the late 1980s. As I embarked on my study of the work of the Spirit in Luke-Acts, I remember wondering if my approach might be a bit too novel. I feared that I might not find precursors who shared my perspective and thus struggle to establish a foundation upon which to build. My fears quickly disappeared as I found that there were numerous scholars who had paved the way by highlighting the distinctive nature of Luke's pneumatology. As early as 1888 Hermann Gunkel outlined Luke's unique approach and others, such as Eduard Schweizer and David Hill, followed in his footsteps.[1] More recently, as I read Mainville's work, I found that here too was another kindred spirit, one who shared in a remarkably similar way my own concerns and perspective. Yet Mainville is my contemporary. The more I read, the more the realized that we struggled with many of the same issues and wrestled over many of the same texts, and we did so at roughly the same time, although on different continents and largely in different languages.

Secondly, I am drawn to this book because of Mainville's methodology. Mainville, like me, sees value in combining a literary reading of the text together with the methods of redaction criticism. We both strive to

---

[1] H. Gunkel, *Die Wirkungen des heiligen Geistes nach der populären Anschauung der apostolischen Zeit und nach der Lehre des Apostels Paulus* (Göttingen: Vandenhoeck & Ruprecht, 1888), now available as *The Influence of the Holy Spirit* (trans. R. A. Harrisville and P. A. Quanbeck II; Philadelphia: Fortress Press, 1979); Eduard Schweizer, "πνεῦμα" (1956), *TDNT* 6:389–455; David Hill, *Greek Words and Hebrew Meanings: Studies in the Semantics of Soteriological Terms* (Cambridge: Cambridge University Press, 1967).

illuminate Luke's concerns and his theological perspective, and we do so by tracing the way in which he shapes his sources and develops his narrative. I sensed as I read Mainville that she was drawn to this approach because, once again like me, she wants to understand more clearly the Spirit-inspired message of the biblical author. Mainville's work, in my opinion, is marked by a concern for the life of the church and a desire to encourage and inspire. How could I not feel an affinity for a book like this?

Finally, I identify with this book because, as I have noted, so many of Mainville's conclusions affirm my own and those of other Pentecostal scholars. Yet, Mainville clearly approaches the issues from a fresh perspective. I do not know much about Mainville's church affiliation (most French-speaking biblical scholars are Roman Catholics), but writing as she does in French, she certainly interacts more seriously with French New Testament scholarship than the vast majority of Lukan scholars, myself included. Her book is a goldmine of information for this reason alone. Nevertheless, in spite of these linguistic, geographical, and cultural differences, I was impressed with how so many of her conclusions resonate with those of other Pentecostal scholars from different contexts. For example, Mainville affirms that for Luke, "the Spirit is not the origin of faith or [the] cause of salvation. He is given to the converted...for the Christian mission" (p. 15). In a similar vein she concludes, "Contrary to what one finds in Paul, Luke does not speak of the Spirit as the cause of spiritual transformation (Rom 8:5) or as the principle of new life in Christ (Rom 8:10–11, 13ff.), but rather as a power enabling the believers to fulfill their prophetic function" (pp. 250). While Mainville describes Luke's pneumatology in relation to Paul's as being more basic or "rudimentary" (p. 238), at the same time she highlights how much Luke, because of the uniqueness of his approach, has to offer to the contemporary church. Pentecost, she declares, will make the disciples of Jesus "a community of prophets in the same way that" the Spirit at his baptism "made Jesus a prophet" (p. 177). Finally, I would point out that Mainville, like Roger Stronstad, emphasizes how significantly Old Testament concepts and language about the Holy Spirit have influenced Luke's presentation.[2] In short, Mainville echoes many of the important themes and conclusions that have marked more recent Pentecostal scholarship.

---

[2] See Mainville, *The Spirit in Luke-Acts*, pp. 238–45 and Roger Stronstad, *The Charismatic Theology of St. Luke: Trajectories from the Old Testament to Luke-Acts* (2nd ed.; Grand Rapids: Baker Academic, 2012).

Foreword

In view of these affinities, I warmly recommend this insightful reading of Luke-Acts to you. It is filled with interesting exegesis and challenging observations. It affirms a Pentecostal reading of Luke-Acts, but does so, perhaps unconsciously, from a fresh perspective that interacts with a wide range of scholarship, including works from French-speaking authors that may be largely unknown to many North American readers. I trust that you will find this book as enjoyable, enriching, and edifying as I did.

Robert Menzies
Easter 2016

Foreword to the French Edition

Luke successfully accomplished the amazing feat of saying all that he had to say on the Spirit in one verse. This discovery was the point of departure of a doctoral thesis defended at the Faculty of Theology of the University of Montreal in June 1989; the revised text of the thesis is presented in this book.

This study offers a new look at Luke's writings in proposing Acts 2:33 as the interpretative key. It shows how the important passages of Luke-Acts (annunciation, baptism, ascension, Pentecost, etc.) find their meaning from the proclamation contained in Acts 2:33. It shows that Luke had to have had this proclamation in mind at the moment he structured the plan of this double volume.

The study also contributes to the emphasis of the inseparability of the pneumatological challenges and the christological and ecclesiological ones in Luke's writings. It brings out in an incontestable manner, the great theological unity of the contents of the third Gospel and the book of Acts.

The achievement of this present work is owed in great part to Professor André Myre, director of doctoral research. I express my most profound gratitude for his knowledgeable counsel, for his encouragement, and also for his precious friendship. I would also like to acknowledge Madame Line Petroff's considerable contribution. With great skill, she undertook all of the word processing preparation of the manuscript. Finally, I thank Éditions Fides for publishing this work.

Odette Mainville

Acknowledgements

In 2011, The Foundation for Pentecostal Scholarship translated its first monograph, *Empowered Believers: The Holy Spirit in the Book of Acts* by Gonzalo Haya-Prats. It gives me great pleasure to see another important title on the Holy Spirit translated into the English language, Odette Mainville's *L'Esprit dans l'œuvre de Luc* or *The Spirit in Luke-Acts*.

Like Haya-Prats's book, Mainville's grew out of a doctoral dissertation on the Holy Spirit from Luke's perspective (University of Montreal, 1989). And like his book, Mainville's supports the idea that the Spirit *in Luke's theology* provides the impetus for global outreach through the Spirit's prophetic enablement, as she writes on the last page of the book:

> It is very significant . . . that Luke refers to the text of Joel 2:28ff. to shed light on the event of Pentecost instead of the text of Ezek 36:26–27. Ezekiel's prophecy envisions the gift of the Spirit in view of a spiritual metamorphosis, which would render the human being capable of living according to God's plans. But for Luke, it is in regard to testimony that the Spirit of Pentecost is poured out (Luke 24:49; Acts 1:8). Therefore, it is the vow formulated by Joel that finds its fulfillment. The dimension conveyed by Ezekiel's text cannot, of course, simply be ousted, for the testimony of faith in Christ presupposes conversion. But the Spirit in Acts first generates an enabling power for the prophetic function.

In making this work available to English readers, a number of individuals were responsible and should be thanked: first and foremost, the author, Odette Mainville, who is now retired and making a name for herself as a novelist; our translator, Suzanne Spolarich, missionary to France and resident of Paris; David Connor and Steffen Schumacher who provided translation improvements of many of the German quotations; and Robert Menzies, missionary-scholar, who so graciously provided the Foreword.

I, along with my fellow board members Steve Gossett and C. Scott Johnson, wish to express our sincere gratitude for the part each of you played in making this translation project possible.

Robert W. Graves, President
The Foundation for Pentecostal Scholarship

List of Abbreviations

AsSeign	: *Assemblées du Seigneur*
AThR	: *Anglican Theological Review*
BETL	: Bibliotheca Ephemeridum Theologicarum Lovaniensium
Bib	: *Biblica*
BibLeb	: *Bibel und Leben*
BT	: *The Bible Translator*
BVC	: *Bible et vie chrétienne*
BZ	: *Biblische Zeitschrift*
CBQ	: *Catholic Biblical Quarterly*
CE	: Cahiers Évangile
DBGK	: Dictionnaire biblique Gerhard Kittel
DBSup	: *Dictionnaire de la Bible: Supplément*
EKKNT	: Evangelisch-Katholischer Kommentar zum Neuen Testament
ET	: English Translation
ET	: *Église et théologie*
ETL	: *Ephemerides theologicae lovanienses*
EvT	: *Evangelische Theologie*
Exp	: *Expositor*
ExpTim	: *Expository Times*
FoiVie	: *Foi et vie*
FT	: French Translation
GL	: *Geist und Leben*
Greg	: *Gregorianum*
HeyJ	: *Heythrop Journal*
IBS	: *Irish Biblical Studies*
Int	: *Interpretation*
ITQ	: *Irish Theological Quarterly*
JBL	: *Journal of Biblical Literature*
JJC	: Jésus et Jésus-Christ
JPTh	: *Jahrbuch für protestantische Theologie*
JSNT	: *Journal for the Study of the New Testament*
JTS	: *Journal of Theological Studies*
LumV	: *Lumen Vitae*
NovT	: *Novum Testamentum*
NRTh	: *La nouvelle revue théologique*
NTS	: *New Testament Studies*
NTTS	: New Testament Tools and Studies

OiC	: One in Christ
ÖTK	: Ökumenischer Taschenbuch-Kommentar zum Neuen Testament
PTR	: Princeton Theological Review
QF	: Quatre fleuves
RB	: Revue biblique
RevScRel	: Revue des sciences religieuses
RHPR	: Revue d'histoire et de philosophie religieuses
RSPT	: Revue des sciences philosophiques et théologiques
RSR	: Recherches de science religieuse
RThom	: Revue thomiste
RTP	: Revue de théologie et de philosophie
SANT	: Studien zum Alten und Neuen Testament
ScEccl	: Sciences ecclésiastiques
ScEs	: Science et esprit
Scr	: Scripture
SJT	: Scottish Journal of Theology
SKNT	: Stuttgarter kleiner Kommentar Neues Testament
TBT	: The Bible Today
TDNT	: Theological Dictionary of the New Testament
Theol	: Theology
THKNT	: Theologischer Handkommentar zum Neuen Testament
ThTo	: Theology Today
TLZ	: Theologische Literaturzeitung
TS	: Theological Studies
TSK	: Theologische Studien und Kritiken
TynBul	: Tyndale Bulletin
VCaro	: Verbum caro
WMANT	: Wissenschaftliche Monographien zum Alten und Neuen Testament
WUNT	: Wissenschaftliche Untersuchungen zum Neuen Testament
WuW	: Wort und Wahrheit
ZKG	: Zeitschrift für Kirchengeschichte
ZKT	: Zeitschrift für katholische Theologie
ZNW	: Zeitschrift für die neutestamentliche Wissenschaft und die Kunde der älteren Kirche
ZWT	: Zeitschrift für wissenschaftliche Theologie

INTRODUCTION

1. Purpose

The church of our century has given the Holy Spirit the place of honor he deserves. Protestantism, first of all, with the revival movement; next, Catholicism in the aftermath of Vatican II. Now, all of Christendom is inhaling the Spirit's regenerative breath. This renewal of the Spirit appeared in various forms of popular expression. From spectacular manifestations at the heart of Pentecostal and Charismatic groups to serious efforts of believers who listen and discern every day via the search for relevant discourse in the academic setting, the entire Christian population was shaken by this wind of renewal blowing during our era.

This rediscovery of the Spirit and the unanimous welcome that all of Christendom had for him, however, was not blessed with the removal of all ambiguity when it came to the question of "defining" or identifying this active force in the world. Indeed, a real unease remains in discussions about the Spirit. From all evidence, this discomfort is intimately linked to the specifically Christian concept of Trinitarian monotheism. Recognizing the Spirit as an autonomous entity in this theological system presents a problem, as Yves Congar explains:

> To speak of the Father and the Son, we have fairly well-defined and easily accessible notions of paternity and procreation or parentage. These terms clearly signify the first and the second Persons by their mutual relationships. "Spirit," on the other hand, states nothing of the sort. It only tells us of the third Person in common and absolute terms: "Spirit" goes with the Father and the Son; as well as "Holy"; these are not terms that signify a person. Procession can be equally applied to

the term Logos-Son. No objective revelation exists for the Person of the Holy Spirit as for the Person of the Son-Logos in Jesus and, through him, for the Person of the Father.[1]

This aspect of the question, the ontological status of the Spirit within the Trinity, obviously concerns dogmatic theology. However, to better understand the role of the Spirit in the Christian's life and in the life of the church, it remains important to see how the biblical writers perceived this role or, more precisely, to see why and how they spoke of the Spirit. This quest is launched from the New Testament author Luke.

The major importance of the theme in the writings of this author, more particularly in the book of Acts, largely justified my choice. Luke, with Paul, is the one biblical author who wrote the most about the Spirit. It is not an exaggeration to say that, in Acts, *the Spirit is an essential actor*. He is at the same time the causal principle of the birth and the growth of the church and the principle of unity between the Jesus event and the life of the church.

The study of the Spirit in Luke's writings seems a project of the utmost importance for a better understanding of the presence of Christ in his church.

2. APPROACH

The Spirit intervenes abundantly in Acts: he speaks, inspires, decides, orders, directs, etc. He is really a personified force that carries out God's intentions or has them carried out. But doesn't this role correspond quite simply to that of the Spirit in the Old Testament? Actually, the Spirit's actions in Luke reflect those already known in the Old Testament. Nevertheless, Luke's pneumatological discourse has its originality, and this originality is clearly expressed in the wording of Acts 2:33: "Being therefore exalted at the right hand of God, and having received from the Father the promise of the Holy Spirit, he has poured out this that you both see and hear."[2]

The content of this verse undoubtedly constitutes the summit of Luke's writings. All that is said of Jesus in the third Gospel leads the read-

---

[1] *Je crois en l'Esprit Saint*, T. 1. *L'Esprit Saint dans l'"Économie": révélation et expérience de l'Esprit*, p. 78.
[2] Biblical quotations are from the New Revised Standard Bible (1989) unless otherwise noted.

er to this proclamation. Jesus's exaltation via the Father's gift of the Spirit to him is the ultimate completion of his career. On the other hand, the ecclesial community springs from this completion because the Exalted One poured out the Spirit he received. In the light of Acts 2:33, reading the book of Acts becomes clearer.

Luke affirms in Acts 2:33 that the Spirit of the Father became the Spirit of Christ and that this Spirit is active in the church. The news of this event marks and characterizes Luke's pneumatological discourse. Taking this fact into account establishes Acts 2:33 as *the key to interpreting Luke's pneumatology*. This is the hypothesis to be proved.

Acts 2:33, in fact, appears to be the most appropriate entryway to Luke's pneumatology. The content of this verse positions the reader at the junction of the two periods of the narrative movement of Luke's writings: the time of Jesus—the third Gospel—and the time of the church—Acts. Not only is Acts 2:33 the junction point of the two eras, but even more, it conditions the understanding of each, which this study will demonstrate. Accordingly, Acts 2:33 becomes the logical starting point of the study of Luke's pneumatology.

This study aims to establish that the content of Acts 2:33 (1) has an influence on the understanding of the third Gospel, the first part of the verse casting an illumination on the figure Jesus; and (2) has an influence on the understanding of Acts, the second part of the verse casting an illumination on the church, the author being mainly preoccupied by questions of a christological and ecclesiological order. His pneumatological discourse is principally meant to support his Christology and serve his ecclesiology.

The study will proceed according to the following stages:

1. First, with the presentation of an overview of the various scholars' opinions of Luke's pneumatology
2. Then the study of the key verse—Acts 2:33—in its immediate context, that is to say, the missionary speech pronounced by Peter on the day of Pentecost
3. Next, the establishment of the meaning of the proclamation of the opening of the verse "exalted at the right hand of God" by studying the value of the expressions "exalted" and "at the right hand of God" in biblical thinking in general, and then in Luke's thinking
4. Then, the evaluation in Luke's writings of the scope and the importance of the promise of the Holy Spirit for the disciples and Jesus

5. After the verse analysis, the demonstration that the content of the first part of the verse, indeed, interprets Luke's pneumato-christological discourse
6. In the same manner, the demonstration of the fundamental importance of the second part of the verse for the insight of Luke's pneumato-ecclesiological discourse
7. The final stage will consist in highlighting conclusions that flow out of this study.

Exegetical concerns conveyed by the hypothesis require that it be verified at the *redaction* level of the whole Lukan writings. Additionally, I will develop a study of the form when that proves to be useful for the understanding of a given text. And, since it is the editorial dimension of Luke's writings that must be particularly taken into account, the bulk of the exegetical literature consulted will be specifically in the wake of the *Redaktionsgeschichte*, which developed in the second half of the 20th century.

CHAPTER 1

STATE OF THE QUESTION

The theme of the Spirit is fundamental in Luke's writings. This is the consensus of Lukan scholarship. But what is the place of the Spirit in the uniformity of the twofold work, Luke-Acts? How is it integrated into the author's theology?

To speak about Luke's theology presupposes, first of all, recognizing it as such, which has not always been evident. Luke, traditionally falling into the category of historian, until recently, was denied the status of theologian.[1] It is as if, over the centuries, scholars neglected to re-evaluate "his record," perpetuating *a priori* judgments about him.

This situation would be significantly changed with the advent of the *Redaktionsgeschichte*. The first monograph to apply this method was, incidentally, on Luke's writings:[2] Conzelmann's well-known book *Die Mitte der Zeit*, which appeared in Germany in 1954.[3] One would never have

---

[1] It is a fact that scholars did not recognize Luke as having original theological thinking. Thus, Cadbury speaks of the "simplicity" of Luke's theology (p. 281); Manson considers Luke as "less intellectual and less theological" than Matthew (pp. xxiv–xxvii) and, probably, than the other authors of the NT (pp. xxiv–xxvii); Goguel believes that there is not really any theology in the third Gospel (p. 367); likewise, Haenchen thinks that Luke "does not seek to develop any unified doctrine, the product of thorough reflection" (p. 91); finally, Trocmé evokes "Luke's theological infirmity" ("Le Saint-Esprit" p. 28).

[2] According to Guillemette and Brisebois, p. 452.

[3] I use the English version, *The Theology of St. Luke* (London: Faber and Faber, 1960). It is important to note here that before Conzelmann's work appeared, Vielhauer had already pointed out the characteristic traits of Luke's theology in his article "Zum 'Paulinismus' des Apostelgeschichte," translated into English, "On the 'Paulinism' of Acts." The examination of the discordances between the features of the Paul of Acts and the Paul of the letters had actually led him to the conclusion that Luke had worked out his own theology, which is a theology of the history of redemption (pp. 48–49). But, when referring to previous studies, one finds that Luke is perceived as a historian who just repeats Pauline themes: see Plummer, (pp. xxxvi, xli, xliii) and Cadbury,

guessed how important this work would become in the study of Luke's writings. Conzelmann's study was the first to question the major theological concerns that led to the composition of Luke-Acts. It clarified what constitutes the framework of Luke's theology: the history of salvation.[4] This history emerges in three stages:[5]

1. The period of Israel[6]
2. The period of Jesus's ministry[7]
3. The period of the Church era

---

who doubts that Luke has well seized the scope of Pauline concepts that he uses: ". . . one hesitates to assume that Paul's rather unique theology is shared understandingly by his biographer [Luke]. Possibly the latter had no special 'penchant' for such things; certainly he has no occasion in this work [Acts] to elaborate such matters" (p. 28). On the other hand, credit must be given to Dibelius, who, in a series of articles published between 1923 and 1949 (grouped in the posthumous collection, *Studies in the Acts of the Apostles* (ET: London: SCM Press, 1956, [German: 1951]), had already highlighted the theological character of Luke's writings. Indeed, as one of the first to apply the *Formgeschichte* to the New Testament writings, Dibelius sought to highlight the theological dimension of Luke's writings by reading the account from the point of view of a believer (cf. pp. 122, 137).

[4] It is important to note that at the same time that Conzelmann published his work, Lohse also acknowledged Luke as a theologian of salvation history in his article with the telling title, "Lukas als Theologe der Heilsgeschichte" ["Luke as Theologian of Salvation History"]. Afterwards, also note Dömer's work *Das Heil Gottes. Studien zur Theologie des lukanischen Doppelwerkes*, specifically dedicated to the topic of salvation in Luke. Dömer writes: ". . . das "Heil Gottes" nicht nur einen zentralen Inhalt der Lukanischen theologischen Darstellung ausmacht, sondern auch schon rein äusserlich ein Begriff ist, der je einmal in jedem der beiden Teile des Doppelwerks von Lukas selbständig eingefügt worden ist (Lk 3,6; Apg 28,28)," (pp.3–4). ["The 'salvation of God' constitutes not only a central content of the Lukan theological view, but also from a purely external point is a term that has been inserted independently by Luke into each of the two parts of his double work (Lk 3:6; Acts 28:28)" (pp. 3–4).] What Dömer seeks to demonstrate throughout his work is that the Lukan conception of salvation is essentially universal (see pp. 159, 203–6). That the history of salvation is at the center of Luke's theology is also clearly recognized by Schneider, who conveys this when he entitles his book that collects a series of his articles on Luke-Acts (1971–1984) *Lukas, Theologe der Heilsgeschichte, Aufsätze zum lukanischen Doppelwerk* [*Luke, Theologian of Salvation History: Essays on Luke-Acts*].

[5] Conzelmann, *Theology of St. Luke*, p. 16.

[6] According to Conzelmann, this period would extend till the end of the Baptist's ministry. He supports this point of view based on Luke 16:16a where it is affirmed: "The Law and the Prophets *were proclaimed* until John."

[7] Conzelmann points out (p.16) that this period does not correspond to Jesus's entire life but to the time of his ministry, which is defined in texts such as Luke 4:16ff. and Acts 1:1ff.; 10:38 (*Theology of St. Luke*, p. 16).

As for the Parousia, in Conzelmann's perspective, it does not constitute a stage in salvation history, but it is the end: "It corresponds to the other extreme, the Creation."[8] Luke, for his part, would abandon the hope of an early end and adjust his perspectives; as the end is still far away, the interim adjustment for a short wait is replaced by a long-term "Christian life."[9]

Therefore, he had to present an adequate solution for the delay. The Spirit would be this solution. Luke is the first, says Conzelmann, to specifically have recourse to the phenomenon of the Spirit as a solution to the problem of the Parousia.[10] In this context of waiting, in which the Parousia is postponed indefinitely, the Spirit becomes the "substitute," explains Conzelmann;[11] He is the divine power with which the disciples are vested for testimony throughout the world.[12]

Conzelmann's contribution proved to be the springboard for a new debate on Luke's theology. Whether to support it or dispute it, scholars have since constantly used his work as a reference. Furthermore, regardless of the nature of the discrepancies recorded by the scholars, in general, following the example of Conzelmann, all recognize the blueprint of salvation history as a vast background scene of Luke's theology. On this backdrop, the problem of the Parousia is the anchor for the theme of the Spirit. In light of this fact, research can be done in two stages:

---

[8] Conzelmann, *Theology of St. Luke*, p. 17.

[9] Ibid., p. 132. In the same vein, Käsemann, in "The Problem of the Historical Jesus," writes: "You do not write the history of the Church, if you are expecting the end of the world to come any day" (p. 28).

[10] Conzelmann, *Theology of St. Luke*, p. 136.

[11] Due to the response of the risen Lord, in Acts 1:8, to the question of the disciples about the time of the restoration of the kingdom, Conzelmann comes to conceive the Spirit as a "substitute": "It is not for you to know the times or periods . . . [v. 7]. But you will receive power when the Holy Spirit has come upon you; and you will be my witnesses in Jerusalem, in all Judea and Samaria, and to the ends of the earth [v. 8]." Haya-Prats challenged Conzelmann's vision (*L'Esprit force de l'Eglise. Sa nature et son activité d'après les Actes des Apôtres*, pp. 67ff. ET: *Empowered by the Spirit: The Holy Spirit in the Book of Acts*, pp. 62–71). He considers that the key text is not Acts 1:8 but rather the quotation of Joel in Acts 2:17ff. (as well as the baptism in the Spirit). And in this case, the gift of the Spirit wouldn't be "a provisional substitute for the kingdom, but rather a foretaste" (p. 66; FT: 68). Haya-Prats's point of view seems correct. If Luke resorts to Joel's text, it is because he wants to show its fulfillment, and, thereby, express his conviction that the eschatological era is inaugurated. The content of Acts 1:8 simply helps explain the manner of this fulfillment.

[12] Conzelmann, *Theology of St. Luke*, p. 136.

1. It is a question, in a wider perspective, of verifying with the scholars who were interested in the theological dimension of the writings, this general agreement around the Parousia as the place of incorporation of the theme of the Spirit in all the Lukan literature;

2. It is then a question, in a more limited perspective, of observing with the scholars who have specifically concentrated on the theme of the Spirit in Luke the angle of approach of each one. This last exercise will contribute to bringing out the originality of my own approach.

The research of the scholars will, of course, respect the chronological order within the historical limits imposed by the *Redaktionsgeschichte*.

1. INSERTION OF THE THEME OF THE SPIRIT IN LUKE-ACTS

The theology of Luke's writings as a new field of research, since Conzelmann, has attracted a number of scholars, including H. Flender, I. H. Marshall, C. H. Talbert, E. Franklin, M. Dömer, and E. Maddox.[13] We now turn to see how they understood Luke's motivations in giving the Spirit priority in his literary work.

Flender, in his work, *St. Luke: Theologian of Redemptive History*,[14] does not hold to the three-part division of history proposed by Conzelmann. Based on Luke 16:16, he believes rather that Luke considers only two phases: the old age and the new age.[15] Neither does Flender approach the eschatological question in the same way as Conzelmann. For him, it is not the delay of the Parousia which preoccupies Luke, but the tension between the eschatology already carried out by the exaltation of Christ and the world that continues. But, strangely, Flender thinks that we must correct the wrong impression that Christ is present in the community through the Spirit. He believes rather that the function of the resurrected Lord and

---

[13] These scholars are apparently the only ones who made a specific study of Luke's theology. Bovon, for his part, published two works whose titles refer to Lukan theology: the first is a state of the research, *Luc le théologien*; the second is a collection of articles on Luke's works, *L'oeuvre de Luc. Etudes d'exégèse et de théologie*. Note also the collection of articles of Schneider (already mentioned in note 4), *Lukas, Theologe der Heilsgeschichte, Aufsätze zum lukanischen Doppelwerk*.

[14] Flender's work was first presented in German, in 1964, as a doctoral dissertation at the School of Theology of Friedrich Alexander University.

[15] Flender, p. 124. Paradoxically, Conzelmann used the same text, Luke 16:16, to justify his three-part division of history in Luke.

that of the Spirit are parallel while being complementary.[16] In fact, the exalted Christ would represent God's new world in heaven (i.e., realized eschatology), while the Spirit would be the sign on the earth. Also, it would be the Spirit who would lead the church to this new world.

Marshall, who esteems Luke to be as much a theologian as a historian, as the title of his book indicates, *Luke: Historian and Theologian*,[17] deems that Luke's preoccupation is not so much salvation history as salvation itself.[18] This salvation—which, according to Marshall[19] is the key concept in Lukan theology—is realized by Jesus's exaltation linked to forgiveness. For, he explains, as forgiveness in the Old Testament was Yahweh Lord's prerogative, it is now the prerogative of Jesus made Lord. "Jesus's exaltation is the supreme saving act in Luke's eyes."[20]

As for the topic of eschatology, Luke's perspective would not mark originality in comparison to that of Paul's; it would as well be the combination of hope in the future already fulfilled in the present.[21] But, meanwhile, salvation must be carried throughout the world by the preaching of the word. It is at this stage that the Spirit enters the picture: it is under the Spirit's movement that testimony is given. Through the Spirit, the power and the presence of Christ are expressed in the church.[22]

Talbert, who wrote a book on the structure of Luke's two works, *Literary Patterns, Theological Themes and the Genre of Luke-Acts*,[23] also noted the fundamental importance of the theme of salvation history in Luke. He is of the opinion that "the architectural model" that presided over the drafting of Luke-Acts aimed to highlight this great belief within early Christianity, namely the history of Jesus and the church could not be one without the other. This model would appear in a series of remarkable complements—both literary and pastoral[24]—in respect to the content, the sequence of events, and the characters—and this, not only between the two books but also within the same book.

---

[16] Ibid., p. 135: "For Luke the present Lord and the gift of the Spirit are parallel, but independent and complementary in operation."

[17] Grand Rapids, Zondervan, 1976 (1970).

[18] Marshall, *Luke: Historian and Theologian*, p. 19.

[19] Ibid., p. 9.

[20] Ibid., p. 169.

[21] Ibid., p. 178.

[22] Ibid., p. 182.

[23] Missoula: Scholar Press, 1974.

[24] Talbert, *Literary Patterns*, p. 89.

Talbert's presentation differs only slightly from Conzelmann's. For him, the course of salvation history emerges with the righteous persons of the Jewish people, symbolized by John and his entourage to Jesus; from Jesus to the twelve (the Apostolic church); and from the twelve to the post-Apostolic church, symbolized by the church of the Gentiles.[25] For Talbert, it is important to see the great continuity that links the stages together, rather than to make separate stages like Conzelmann. In fact, these stages are joined together by a principle of subordination: John is dependent on Jesus; the apostolic church is subordinate to Jesus; the post-apostolic age is finally subordinate to the Apostolic age.[26]

Luke's motivation, therefore, would have been to mark continuity between the man of Galilee and the Exalted One who acts in the church.[27] It is surprising to notice, however, that Talbert has completely neglected to situate the role of the Spirit in this literary and theological entity of Luke-Acts.

Franklin, in his book *Christ the Lord: A Study in the Purpose and Theology of Luke-Acts*,[28] believes like Conzelmann that the "non-occurrence" of the Parousia is a central concern for Luke. But, unlike Conzelmann, he refuses to locate eschatology beyond history:

> The end, although delayed, is not ruled out; history does not exist without being affected by eschatology, and the Kingdom, although transcendent, is already exerting its influence on history.[29]

Franklin believes that the gift of the Spirit should not be seen as a substitute for eschatological expectation, but as its guarantee.[30] Because for him, it is the ascension that confirms Jesus as the Messiah, rather than the Parousia, which is an eschatological event. In this perspective, the gift of the Spirit (and the testimony which he enables) guarantees Christ's lordship.

As for Dömer, he is of the opinion that the gift of the Spirit at Pentecost must be seen as the fulfillment of the Old Testament promises and not in a strictly eschatological sense. Because, according to him, the Lukan expression in Acts 2:17 (Peter's speech)—ἐν ταῖς ἐσχάταις ἡμέραις ("in

---

[25] Ibid., pp. 106–7.
[26] Ibid.
[27] Ibid., p. 120.
[28] Philadelphia: Westminster Press, 1975.
[29] Franklin, p. 11.
[30] Ibid., p. 41.

the last days")—does not indicate the end, but rather "the times of accomplishment."[31] It is in this accomplishment of the times, he explains, that the gift of the Spirit[32] is situated for the universal mission of the salvation of all.[33]

Finally, Maddox, in *The Purpose of Luke-Acts*,[34] considers, for his part, that the gift of the Spirit is an integral part of the eschatological fulfillment and not its substitute, as Conzelmann proposed.[35] Like Dömer, Maddox considers that the coming of the Spirit fulfilled Israel's expectations as evidenced by the quotation of Joel. Dömer believes that Luke includes the "last days" as the age of the Holy Spirit and salvation.[36] He considers that the time of the church is a period "charged with eschatology," when the exalted Jesus communicates with the disciples through the mediation of the Spirit.

More important, Maddox maintains that the eschatology is already accomplished in Jesus's ministry. He explains that, following the range granted to the coming of the Spirit in Jewish theology, Jesus's proclamation in Luke 4:18—"the Spirit of the Lord is upon me"—is equivalent to saying: the kingdom of God is here. So he concludes: the coming of the Spirit corresponds to Jesus's coming, thus the eschatological fulfillment.[37]

* * *

This overview shows the close relationship between the topic of the Spirit and the question of eschatology in Luke's writings, as perceived by the scholars who are interested in the theological dimension of this work. Studies strictly focused on Lukan pneumatology will still corroborate this correlation between the themes, but they will especially highlight the particularities of the Spirit's role and action in Luke-Acts.

---

[31] Dömer, *Lukas, Theologe der Heilsgeschichte, Aufsätze zum lukanischen Doppelwerkes*, p. 152.
[32] Ibid.
[33] Ibid., p. 159.
[34] Edinburgh: Clark, 1982.
[35] Conzelmann, *Theology of St. Luke*, p. 100.
[36] Dömer, p. 138.
[37] Maddox, p. 141.

2. THE SPIRIT IN LUKE-ACTS ACCORDING TO RECENT STUDIES

The scholars in this section are those who, in the line of the *Redaktionsgeschichte*, have produced a book or an article specifically about the Spirit in Luke's writings, namely: G. W. H. Lampe, E. Schweizer, J. H. E. Hull, E. Trocmé, J. Borremans, G. Haya-Prats, A. George, M.-A. Chevallier, and J. Guillet. However, while the interests of this work lead us to focus on studies in the literary context of the *Redaktionsgeschichte*, we cannot ignore the significant contribution of the work of Heinrich von Baer.[38] Moreover, von Baer, an early critic of Luke's works, brought to light the value of Spirit as an essential issue in Luke's theological plan.

Establishing first the theme of salvation history as the basis of the Lukan redactions,[39] von Baer presents the Spirit as its axis of unity.[40] It is the Spirit, he explains, who makes it possible to distinguish the large stages of this history: (1) his promise in the Old Testament; (2) his acting in Jesus during his earthly life; (3) his pouring out on the church.[41] Underlining clearly the relationship between the proclamation of Acts 2:33 and the Pentecostal outpouring, von Baer shows the multiple "tangible and visible" effects of this effusion. Nevertheless, he thinks that it is from his sources that Luke draws the diversity of the Spirit's interventions.[42] But he definitely acknowledges that all his interventions are in the service of the church's mission: the Spirit is the cause of missionary activity; evangelization is the effect.[43]

Von Baer insists on the importance of Pentecost. He perceives it first as a moment of revelation: it is then that the community would have understood the reality of the universal lordship of the exalted Christ. He also

---

[38] *Der Heilige Geist in den Lukasschriften* (Stuttgart: W. Kohlhammer, 1926).

[39] H. von Baer writes: "Als Leitmotiv der lukanischen Komposition haben wir den Gedanken der Heilsgeschichte festgestellt" (p. 108). ["We found the idea of salvation history to be a *leitmotif* of the Lukan composition," (p. 108).]

[40] Ibid., pp. 43–112.

[41] Ibid., pp. 111–12.

[42] This opinion is very debatable because if Luke works with sources (which is likely), his use of the theme of the Spirit remains very original: it is a literary technique that *characterizes* the author's redaction (more on this later).

[43] He writes: "Als Ursache und Folge gehören πνεῦμα ἅγιον und εὐαγγελίζεσθαι zu den Elementen der lukanischen Theologie und bilden das Leitmotiv für das Doppelwerk" (p. 2). ["As cause and effect, πνεῦμα ἅγιον / *the Holy Spirit* and εὐαγγελίζεσθαι / *evangelizing* belong to the elements inherent to Lukan theology and form the *leitmotif* for the double work" (p. 2).]

perceives it as an event explaining the propagation of the word. Lastly, von Baer wondered about the ethical role of the Lukan Spirit. Although he admits that the role is not explicitly expressed, he believes, nevertheless, that the Spirit is the source of the communion that gathers the community.[44]

Lampe, in his article "The Holy Spirit in the Writings of St. Luke,"[45] recognizes, likewise, from the start, the priority role of the Spirit in Luke's writings. Indeed, he considers that "The connecting thread which runs through both parts of Luke's work is the theme of the operation of the Spirit of God."[46] But, he explains, the Spirit doesn't merely join the two parts of Luke's writings; he is, from Luke's viewpoint, the axis of unity of the whole work of salvation begun in the Old Testament, fulfilled in Jesus, and carried on in the church.[47] He insists on the similarity of the role of the Spirit in the mission of Jesus and of the church. Referring to the intervention of the Spirit at the birth of Jesus, he wrote elsewhere:

> The birth of Jesus is brought about by the arrival of the Holy Spirit; or power of God; just like the beginning of the mission of the church was to be the effect of the overflowing of a power on the disciples through the arrival of the Spirit.[48]

Although fully present in Jesus since his conception, the Spirit descends on him at his baptism to mark the messianic anointing. This anointing confers upon him a divine power for his mission: this power being, in the words of Lampe, "the same energy of the Spirit which his followers were to receive at Pentecost for the missionary task to which they had been appointed."[49] Lampe points out that Luke, however, says very little about the intervention of the Spirit "in Jesus and through him during his ministry."[50] He thinks, justifiably, that the great age of the Spirit will rise only after the death and the exaltation of Jesus.

It is as a prophet "powerful in words and in actions" that Jesus will distinguish himself, summing up in his person the figures of Moses,

---

[44] H. von Baer, pp. 183ff.

[45] Lampe's article appeared in *Studies in the Gospels. Essays in Memory of R. H. Lightfoot*, D. E. Nineham, ed., pp. 159–200.

[46] Lampe, "The Holy Spirit," p. 159.

[47] Ibid., p. 167.

[48] Lampe, "Luke," *Peake's Commentary on the Bible*, p. 824.

[49] Lampe, "The Holy Spirit," p. 168.

[50] Ibid, p. 171.

Elijah, the Servant, and all the prophets. In the same way, explains Lampe, the activity of the Spirit in Jesus will be reproduced on a broader scale in the apostles and the converts. The Spirit of prophecy announced by Joel will carry the gospel to the heart of the pagan nations.[51] But what makes possible the parallel between the mission of Jesus and that of the church is that the same Spirit animates Jesus and the church, the Spirit of God poured out by Jesus himself on the church. Lastly, despite the broad emphasis on the Spirit in his writings, Luke, according to Lampe, would have very little to say on the nature of the Spirit which is not already contained in the Old Testament.[52]

Schweizer, in his article on the Spirit in the New Testament in the *Theological Dictionary of the New Testament*,[53] defends a rather particular point of view in respect to Jesus's relationship to the Spirit. He opposes the idea that Jesus gradually grew in the Spirit, and he believes that Jesus definitively received "the Spirit at his exaltation (Acts 2:33)."[54] For Schweizer, Luke's Jesus, during his earthly existence, is not a pneumatic as in Mark and Matthew; "he is Lord of the πνεῦμα [Spirit],"[55] by virtue of Luke 1:35—where Schweizer sees the procreation of Jesus by the Spirit:

> As One who is born of the Spirit . . . is from the very first a possessor of the Spirit and not just the Spirit's object, like the pneumatic. . . . As He who from the very first possessed the Spirit in fullness, Jesus is after the resurrection the One who dispenses the Spirit to the community, Lk. 24:49; Ac. 2:33.[56]

---

[51] Ibid., p. 193.

[52] Ibid., pp. 160ff.

[53] Schweizer, "πνεῦμα," *TDNT* 6:389–455.

[54] Ibid., 6:405.

[55] Ibid.; Dunn, "Spirit, Holy Spirit," *Dictionary of New Testament Theology*, p. 698, disputes Schweizer's point of view: ". . . only with his ascension does Jesus enter upon the fullness of sonship and messianic office (Acts 2:36; 13:33), and only then does he become Lord of the Spirit." Dunn's point of view is altogether just, as this study will demonstrate more specifically in chapter 5.

[56] Schweizer, *TDNT* 6:405. In note 471, of 6:405, Schweizer recalls the position of Conzelmann, which argues that before his exaltation, Christ is the only carrier of the Spirit (*Theology of St. Luke*, pp. 179ff.). But Conzelmann's opinion is more nuanced than Schweizer's, who seems to say that the historical Jesus would have already been able to transmit the Spirit; Conzelmann believes, in fact, that Jesus is not entitled to spread the Spirit during his earthly life. Bovon considers that Schweizer "exaggerates the power of the historical Jesus over the Spirit and minimizes the Lordship of the Risen Christ over the πνεῦμα" ("Le Saint-Esprit," *Luc le théologien*, p. 226).

Because of this particular status of the historical Jesus, Schweizer thinks "the endowment of Jesus with the Spirit lay on a different plane from that of the community."[57] He adds that Jesus's baptism and Pentecost are never compared one to the other. Consequently, the symmetry, noted by several,[58] of the respective roles of Jesus under the action of the Spirit in the third Gospel and also of the disciples under the action of the Spirit in Acts would not be supported from Schweizer's perspective. He specifies:

> The fact that the baptism in the Jordan and the story of Pentecost were in no way assimilated to one another is a possible indication that for Luke the endowment of Jesus with the Spirit lay on a different plane from that of the community.[59]

From another point of view, Schweizer supports that, in Luke, a double concept of the Spirit is found: (1) an "animist" concept, in that the Spirit is an autonomous force and external to the human being (one recognizes here the Jewish influence); (2) a "dynamist" concept in that he is a fluid that fills human beings (it would be here a Hellenistic influence[60]). Schweizer emphasizes the material presentation of the manifestations of the Spirit in Luke. He considers that as a Hellenist, the latter "can portray power only in the form of substance."[61] But it remains that the Spirit is essentially one of prophecy[62] and that all the members of the community are prophets.[63] Schweizer argues, rightly, that the Spirit is not the origin of faith or cause of salvation. He is given to the converted (Acts 2:38; 5:32; etc.) for the Christian mission. Schweizer still notes that this Lukan concept differs from that of the Old Testament by the fact that the Spirit-power at work is no longer only on a one-time basis, but permanently on the entire community.

---

[57] Schweizer, *TDNT* 6:405.

[58] On this subject, see chapter 6 below.

[59] Schweizer, *TDNT* 6:405.

[60] Ibid., 6:406–7.

[61] Ibid., 6:407. Van Imschoot will dispute this point of view (see the conclusion of this study), because, for him, language materializing the Spirit remains under the threshold of metaphor. On this point, van Imschoot is certainly right.

[62] Schweizer, *TDNT* 6:412.

[63] Ibid.

Hull, who devotes a book to the Spirit in Acts,[64] describes the theology of the Spirit of this book as "an underdeveloped theology."[65] This is, he said, because the book of Acts is first and foremost a reliable historical document; accordingly, one should not expect to find a developed theology.[66] This perception of the scholar determines, to some extent, how he envisions the theme of the Spirit in Luke.

In the first chapter of his book, Hull reports how rarely Jesus mentions the Spirit in the Gospels. How does one explain that Jesus, indwelt by the Spirit, had not informed the disciples privately? Hull suggests a double explanation: (1) the inability of the disciples to receive such a teaching at this time;[67] and (2) the humility of Jesus as one come into this world as a servant. During his lifetime, Jesus would be limited to promising a helper to the disciples without being explicit. Between the resurrection and ascension, he reveals to them he will continue to be with them through the Spirit.

Despite this very "historicizing" approach, Hull knows, nevertheless, how to highlight the important features of the role of the Spirit in Acts. First of all, the Spirit "produces the community of the new era."[68] God's choice of the day of Pentecost to pour out the Spirit on the community reveals the new meaning of the feast: it is the gift of the Spirit and no longer the giving of the law that it celebrates.[69] The role of the Spirit in this community will basically be for the growth of the kingdom.[70] Like Conzelmann, Hull sees the Spirit not as an eschatological gift but as a substitute until the ultimate possession of salvation.[71]

The "filled-with-the-Spirit" disciples, as individuals and a community, are by this fact invested with the power to perpetuate the work of Christ. They become his effective witnesses.[72] Hull points out, in quite a

---

[64] J. H. E. Hull, *The Holy Spirit in the Acts of the Apostles* (Cleveland, Ohio: The World Publishing Co., 1967).

[65] Ibid., p. 172.

[66] Ibid.

[67] Hull explains that if Jesus had revealed to the disciples that he was actually inhabited by the Spirit, they would have interpreted this indwelling in terms of being the Messiah; this would have meant the end of the secret of the son of God.

[68] Hull, p. 45.

[69] Ibid., pp. 53, 77ff. On the reinterpretation of the Jewish Pentecost as a Feast of the Covenant, see the discussion in chapter 6.

[70] Ibid., p. 42.

[71] Ibid., p. 46.

[72] Ibid., pp. 74–75.

fortuitous way, however, that the overflowing of the Spirit on the community is made possible by the initial gift of the Father to the Exalted Christ (Acts 2:33).[73] He very explicitly affirms, moreover, that it is through this gift of the Spirit that continuity is insured:

> For if Jesus himself was only able to exercise His ministry as Messiah through the power of the Spirit, His Church can only continue His ministry if it is itself endued with that same power. Furthermore, Christ can only continue His ministry through the Church by arming it with the power with which He Himself had been armed (cf. Acts 1:8 with Luke 4:14).[74]

According to Hull, what makes the Spirit specifically Christian is the fact that he confers to the believers "the power or the life of God the way in which God was expressed in Christ."[75] Hull allots also an ethical function to the Spirit[76] (which, however, is never really evoked in Acts). He will say finally that Luke probably perceived the Spirit as "being at the same time Power and Person: a Power at work *in* men and a Person acting *on* men."[77]

Trocmé, in one of his articles,[78] has a rather negative perception of Luke's pneumatology. He considers that, because of the many mentions of the Spirit in Acts, one would rightly expect "that this book makes a considerable contribution to the theme [of the Spirit and the church]."[79] But such is not the case, for the following reasons, explains Trocmé: (1) Luke's theological genius is not at the height of his literary talent; (2) "[he] is interested much less in the Church than with the progress of the mission"; (3) he is dependent on his sources when he speaks about the Spirit.[80] Trocmé affirms, consequently, that Luke often has a naive way of

---

[73] Ibid., p. 127.

[74] Ibid., p. 129.

[75] Hull, p. 168. Hull cites here J. Denny, "Holy Spirit," *A Dictionary of Christ and the Gospels*, vol. 1, p. 738. It is undoubtedly necessary to make this correction to the thought of Hull, namely that Christian specificity of the Spirit stems from the fact that God's Spirit becomes Christ's Spirit (Acts 2:33).

[76] Hull, pp. 143ff., 170.

[77] Ibid., p. 156; also, pp. 173ff.

[78] Trocmé, "Le Saint-Esprit et l'Eglise d'après le livre des Actes," pp. 19–44.

[79] Ibid., p. 19.

[80] Ibid., pp. 19-21.

speaking about the Spirit and "that he did not have a very elaborate and contemplated pneumatology."[81]

For Trocmé, the gift of the Spirit causes primarily inspired testimony; he distinguishes three categories of testimonies: that of the prophets of the old and the new covenants, that of the martyrs, and that of glossolalia.[82] Trocmé insists on the importance of the Spirit for the mission: "It is not extreme to say that, for Luke, the missionary function of the divine Spirit is the central idea of the pneumatology, as rudimentary as it may be."[83]

According to Trocmé, the Spirit is the force that allows those with various ministries to achieve their task, without being at the origin of the ministries.[84] But, curiously, he does not see "in Luke's thinking a particular relationship between the gift of the Holy Spirit and the unity of the community"[85] or "the constitution of the community."[86] Trocmé explains:

> What interests [Luke] is the way in which the Spirit pushes ahead the missionary testimony in all its forms, much more than the way in which he creates or develops or gives fullness to the life connected with the church.[87]

He insists: "What interests Luke is the movement; it is not the community as such."[88] According to Trocmé, the "personalizing language" in Acts reflects a common way of expressing oneself at the time. Accordingly, it is not really indicative of a personal conception of the Spirit in Luke.

Finally, Trocmé explains that the idea of the presence of the Spirit in the community would arise from this deep conviction among the Christians that Christ was always present in their midst. Little by little, this idea of Christ's presence, "extension of the presence of the historical Jesus," evolved into that of the presence of the Holy Spirit.[89]

Borremans deals with the pneumatological question in Luke in an original way in his article "L'Esprit dans la catéchèse évangélique de

---

[81] Trocmé, "Le Saint-Esprit," p. 21.
[82] Ibid., p. 23.
[83] Ibid., p. 24.
[84] Ibid., p. 27.
[85] Ibid., p. 31.
[86] Ibid., p. 33.
[87] Ibid., p. 36.
[88] Ibid., p. 39.
[89] Ibid., pp. 40–41.

Luc."⁹⁰ His purpose is to show how Luke, in his "regressive approach . . . from the experience of the Spirit to the history of Jesus," can make the catechumens grab hold of the idea that this history is "still the actual origin of their present experience."⁹¹

Borremans poses as a basic premise that the third Gospel and Acts are the two volumes of a single work "for which the Spirit constitutes the unity and the key to understanding."⁹² According to Borremans, the Spirit would be to non-Jews what the Scriptural evidence is to the Jews. Thus, one verifies through the Spirit "the strength of the received teachings." The Gentiles, not being able to appeal to the historical experience as evidenced by the Scriptures, must rely on their current experience, i.e., a "concretely perceptible spirit, the Spirit even of God acting with power in the community, the Holy Spirit whose perceptibility is measured, in the experience of the early Christians, by the reality of their community."⁹³ The facts on which this experience rests are manifest in the fraternal community of sharing, but also, and especially, in the reality of the universality to which the community finds itself driven back.

Luke's method, according to Borremans, is to make it clear to the community that the Spirit currently so perceptible in their midst is the Spirit which acted in the beginning in Jesus. Jesus's teachings, authenticated by the Spirit, are thus assuredly solid and valid. It is the Spirit who ensures the solidity and the validity of the received teachings. He is the mediator essential "to the understanding of the history of Jesus as an act of God."⁹⁴

Borremans will then show the parallel between the experience of Jesus and that of the church:

A. It is the Spirit who intervenes at the decisive turns of history and makes the range of these moments understood, for example, the inspiration of the characters surrounding the birth of Jesus and the intervention of the Spirit in Cornelius;

B. It is the Spirit who descends on Jesus at his baptism who will also descend on the disciples at Pentecost.

---

⁹⁰ *LumV* 25 (1970), pp. 103–22.
⁹¹ Borremans, p. 104.
⁹² Ibid., p. 105.
⁹³ Ibid., p. 107.
⁹⁴ Ibid., p. 110.

But what Luke particularly wanted to highlight, according to Borremans, is that "the appeal to Jesus of Nazareth no longer appears as a superfluous detour; Jesus is becoming instead the necessary mediator of the Spirit of God, who is now inseparably the Spirit of Jesus Christ."[95]

Haya-Prats, in his book *Empowered Believers: The Holy Spirit in the Book of Acts*, notes the influence of the Old Testament on Luke's pneumatological discourse; Luke drew his themes and formulas from it. But, explains Haya-Prats, this legacy will only have been used as a cultural means for his own conception of the Holy Spirit, which he feels the need to clarify.[96]

The choice of Joel 2:28–32 (3:1–5 in Catholic versions) as an interpretative text of the manifestations of the Pentecostal Spirit places the Lukan concept of the Spirit in the charismatic line (while Paul sees the action of the Spirit as the fulfillment of Eze 36:24–28 and Jer 31:31–34, therefore at the origin of the "moral restoration").

Haya-Prats attaches certain significance to the determination of the πνεῦμα ἅγιον / *Holy Spirit* by the article. In general, he says, the article refers to the Spirit of Pentecost. But it would be only one standard of orientation because it happens that the absence of the article also indicates the Spirit of Pentecost.

Haya-Prats rejects the Spirit/power equivalence.[97] In his view, the terms "are associated with two distinct effects of interventions by God"[98]: the power—a type of superhuman energy—is responsible in Luke's gospel for the healings and exorcisms;[99] in Acts, the healings and exorcisms are attributed to the power and to the name of Jesus; the Spirit is responsible

---

[95] Borremans, p. 120.

[96] Pp. 22–24 (ET: pp. 4–6). Haya-Prats's work was first presented in Spanish, in 1967, as a doctoral thesis at the Pontifical Gregorian University, Rome, and subsequently translated into French by Romero and Faes (*L'Esprit Force de l'Eglise. Sa nature et son activité d'après les Actes des Apôtres* [Paris: Cerf, 1975]); in 2011 it was translated into English by Scott A. Ellington, with editorial comments and updating by Paul Elbert (Eugene, Oreg.: Wipf and Stock Publishers).

[97] For the discussion on the subject, see chapter 4.

[98] Haya-Prats, p. 41 (ET: p. 35).

[99] Haya-Prats believes that Luke is responsible for the introduction "by the finger of God" in the Q logion (Matt 12:28 ‖ Luke 11:20), which would have originally contained, "by the Holy Spirit." His position is in line with that of George, "Note sur quelques traits lucaniens de l'expression 'par le doigt de Dieu,'" pp. 461–66; also Yates, "Luke's Pneumatology and Luke 11:20," pp. 295–99; Guillet, "Saint Esprit—Luc-Actes," col. 179.

for the testimony. The theological distinction that Haya-Prats makes between these two forces is the following:

> Perhaps Luke had witnessed in the power the submission brought by Christ that began to blot out the marks of sin, such as demonic possession and sickness.... On the other hand, Luke had seen in the Spirit the anticipation of the gift of the last days, which consisted of exultant participation in the knowledge of God, translated in prophetic songs and the gift of tongues.[100]

Against Conzelmann, Haya-Prats considers that the communication of the Spirit to the community "is not . . . a total substitute for Christ, but rather the transfer of his prophetic mission. . . . Christ transmits to his apostles the presence of the Spirit that he received at the Jordan . . . ."[101] This gift of the Spirit is, from Haya-Prats's perspective, a highly eschatological gift. It would not necessarily mean the expectation of an imminent Parousia, but the beginning of an entirely different era. In this, the gift of the Spirit is also dynamic and temporal.

Regarding the personalization of the Spirit, Haya-Prats is of the opinion that Acts contains many indications in this direction:

> Luke goes beyond a mere anthropomorphic personification of the Spirit . . ., it is with this same concept that Luke represents the Spirit as a particular, precise, and constant manner of God's acting, but in a certain sense without God acting for himself . . .[102]

Haya-Prats considers the role of the Spirit "a constant attribution of a well-determined series of important interventions in the history of salvation . . . ," actually a subject "distinct in a certain manner from Yahweh."[103]

George, in one of his numerous articles on Luke's writings, states that one of the major roles of the Spirit in Luke's writings is to ensure unity and continuity ("L'Esprit Saint dans l'œuvre de Luc").[104] First of all, unity and continuity are between the major stages of salvation history (old covenant, Jesus, church), which Luke highlights through the "promise-fulfillment" design (e.g., the beginning of Jesus's ministry: Isa 61:1–2,

---

[100] Haya-Prats, p. 44 (ET: p. 38).
[101] Ibid., p. 52 (ET: p. 47).
[102] Ibid., p. 88 (ET: p. 92).
[103] Ibid., p. 90 (ET: p. 93).
[104] *RB* 85 (1979), pp. 500–542.

Luke 4:18–19; birth of the church: Joel 2:28–32; Acts 2:16–21). This schema is, of course, common to all the authors of the NT, specifies George, "but Luke gives more of a part to the Spirit in the promise than do the other authors."[105] In addition, unity and continuity are within the missionary work of the early church (e.g., the gift of the Spirit to the church of Jerusalem: Acts 4:24–31; to the baptized of Samaria: 8:15–18; to Cornelius: 10:44–45; 11:15; etc.).

George does not share Schweizer's opinion in respect to the characteristics of Jesus to the Spirit. He considers that, for Luke, it is very important to show that "in the time of Jesus . . . the Spirit acts on Jesus, [while] in the time of the Church . . . the risen Lord has the Spirit [i.e., Jesus is lord and giver of the Spirit as only God was in the OT]."[106] He says, in effect, that the divine action of the Holy Spirit upon Jesus is permanent, and that Jesus is "a man fully possessed [by the Spirit]."[107] But, he writes that "one of the characteristic features of Luke's thinking is that he made the gift of the Spirit to the disciples an act of Jesus the Lord, exalted in his Paschal glory."[108]

George specifies: "In Acts 2:33, Peter's words at Pentecost are the most explicit and complete formulation of the gift of the Spirit by the Risen Jesus."[109] He then shows the implications of this gift in the life of the church: the Spirit becomes "the inspirer of the word," "the animator of the life of the Church," and "the guide of the mission." He wants to know if it is possible to identify a Lukan concept of the Holy Spirit. His question, at the beginning, is general; however, he reduces the investigation to a particular aspect: "the personality of the Holy Spirit."

To check if Luke has, or has not, personalized the Spirit, George insists on bringing out "the most consistent traits and characteristics of [the Lukan] presentation of the Holy Spirit."[110] The review focuses on three different themes: (1) the various names that Luke applies to the Spirit; (2) the manner in which he describes the anointing of the Spirit; (3) the type of relations that the Spirit has with "various people who are involved in the history of Salvation: men, Jesus, God."[111]

---

[105] George, "L'Esprit Saint dans l'œuvre de Luc," p. 505.
[106] Ibid., pp. 515–16.
[107] Ibid., p. 518.
[108] Ibid.
[109] Ibid., p. 520.
[110] Ibid., p. 527.
[111] Ibid., p. 528.

George's conclusions can be summarized as follows: (1) the particularly frequent use in Luke of the title "Holy Spirit" might suggest that the name "Holy Spirit" has a personal resonance; (2) the vocabulary describing the action of the Spirit presents it as a personal action; (3) Luke seems to place the Spirit with various people as a person. But despite all these clues, George is, nevertheless, of the opinion that "no text in Luke allows judging with certainty if it exceeded the old design of the metaphorical personification of the Spirit."[112]

He points out that

> The early believers do not raise the question at first about the personality of the Holy Spirit, not any more than the prophets of the O.T. did. They simply interpret their experience from the Jewish biblical concept of the Holy Spirit, God's action among his own.[113]

Chevallier, in his article, "Luc et l'Esprit Saint,"[114] examines the role of the Spirit in Luke's writings from four points: (1) the Holy Spirit and Jesus; (2) the Holy Spirit, the church, and the mission; (3) the Holy Spirit and baptism; (4) the effects of the Holy Spirit:

1. The Holy Spirit and Jesus. Chevallier explains the imbalance between the importance of the role of the Spirit in the initial episodes and the few mentions in the rest of the Gospel by the existence of two scriptural traditions:

A. The one, from Isaiah 11:2; 42:1; 61:1, the basis of the belief that the Messiah would have the Spirit, hence the importance of the role of the Spirit in the initiatory episodes;

B. The other, in line with Num 11:29; Isa 32:15, 44:3; Eze 39:29; Joel 2:28ff, announcing the general outpouring of the Spirit on all people; the fact that this promise is realized only after the resurrection would explain the silence from the rest of the Gospel on the Spirit. Chevallier is of the opinion that "Luke systematizes somehow this representation,"[115] the extension of his story in the book of Acts enabling him to do so.

---

[112] Ibid., p. 532.
[113] Ibid., p. 532.
[114] *RSR* 56 (1982), pp. 1–16.
[115] Chevallier, "Luc et l'Esprit Saint," p. 3.

Pentecost opens up a new era. Acts 2:32–33 ("God raised Jesus . . . Exalted at the right hand of God . . .") explains the outpouring of Pentecost. Chevallier concludes: "Luke forged a strong connection between Christology and pneumatology."[116]

2. The Holy Spirit, the Church, and the Universal Mission. According to Chevallier, "the articulation between the church and the mission under the effect of the Spirit" is typical of Luke's contribution.[117] He notes the symmetry between the baptism of Jesus and Pentecost. The ecclesiological community is, by definition and by vocation, missionary, and its mission has a universal dimension (Acts 1:8). It is the Spirit that animates and directs the missionary testimony. The Spirit always ratifies the addition of new groups. Chevallier concludes: "Because of the Spirit who inhabits it, the Church can exist only for a universal mission."[118]

3. The Holy Spirit and Water Baptism. According to the announcement of the Baptist, water baptism would normally have to give way to the baptism of the Spirit. But the "autonomous" notion of Spirit baptism does not exist, states Chevallier. Water baptism remains; it is practiced on behalf of Jesus, always for forgiveness of sins (Acts 2:38). And the gift of the Spirit is attached to it—even if the order of baptism/gift of the Spirit is sometimes reversed (see Acts 8:15–18).

4. The Effects of the Holy Spirit. Chevallier points out that, in Luke, the main role of the Spirit consists in promoting prophecy and testimony. It is this presentation of the Spirit as promoter of the word that distinguishes Luke, from Paul and John, in his discourse on the Spirit.

The Old Testament rooting of Luke's discourse on the Spirit constitutes a key to his pneumatology, concludes Chevallier.[119] This attachment to the Old Testament would have enabled him to better show, through the Spirit, the continuity between Israel and the Gentile-Christian church.

Guillet, in his article "Saint Esprit—Luc—Actes des Apôtres,"[120] subscribed to the thesis of I. de la Potterie that the anointing of baptism, evoked in Luke 4:18 and Acts 10:38, is the prophetic function of Jesus

---

[116] Chevallier, "Luc et l'Esprit Saint," p. 4.
[117] Ibid., p. 5.
[118] Ibid., p. 6.
[119] Ibid., p. 12.
[120] *DBSup* 60 (1986), cols. 180–91.

rather than his messianic function.[121] Like Haya-Prats, he considers that the Spirit, in the third Gospel, doesn't have to do with the miracles that concern power; he is set apart for the word.

All of Jesus's life will be under the effect of the Spirit: "As the Spirit was at the origin of Jesus's being, he is now the source of all his acts."[122] But Guillet specifies that "never does the Spirit act apart from Jesus [and] never does Jesus act without the Spirit."[123]

The role of the Spirit becomes very apparent in the Acts of the Apostles. Guillet says that the Spirit "is the essential agent of history told in Acts."[124] This role, established at the beginning of the book (it is well highlighted in Acts 2), gives meaning to the content of the book in the manner in which the episode of Nazareth gave its meaning to the mission of Jesus. Peter, witness of the resurrection (Acts 2:33), defines the relationship between Jesus and the Spirit: Jesus promised the Spirit (Luke 24:49) and he gives him (Acts 2:33). The testimony follows.

In the wake of the story of Pentecost, Acts will present three other visible interventions of the Spirit: one in the community of Jerusalem (4:31); one in Caesarea (10:44–47); a last one at Ephesus (19:6). Each of these "pentecosts" inaugurated a new period: the launch of the mission in Jerusalem; the entry of the Gentiles into the church; and the beginning of Paul's mission at Ephesus.

Luke makes a point of placing under the responsibility of the Spirit the points of departure and the great stages of the Christian mission, explains Guillet. The Spirit is the "principle of unity."[125] He is the principle of unity between the communities, but he is this initially between the church and Jesus, because it is "the Spirit that the resurrected Jesus receives from the Father to spread out on the believers."[126] Guillet points out:

> Luke makes the gift of the Spirit by God (*Ac* 2:17 = *Joel* 3:1 [2:28]) and the gift of the Spirit by the Lord Jesus (2:33) coincide. . . . No greater than Jesus being an instrument of God, is the Spirit a repre-

---

[121] La Potterie, "L'Onction du Christ," pp. 225–52. Contra Lampe (see pp. 7–8), who sees the messianic anointing.
[122] Guillet, "Saint Esprit," p. 180.
[123] Ibid., p. 181.
[124] Ibid., p. 184.
[125] Ibid., p. 187.
[126] Ibid., p. 190.

sentative or substitute of Christ. Everywhere the Spirit intervenes, it is Jesus who acts.[127]

CONCLUSION

This research of the scholars demonstrates at the outset recognition of the fundamental importance of the Spirit in Luke's writings. Those who approached the writings from a theological perspective insisted on the essential links between Luke's eschatological concerns and the role he attributes to the Spirit. Those, on the other hand, who addressed the writings from a specifically pneumatological perspective, were able to highlight the major features of the Lukan Spirit.

The Spirit is unanimously acknowledged as the force behind the origin of the church and for its expansion. Some mentioned first his role as the principle of unity between Luke and Acts (Lampe, George), but also as the principle of unity of all of salvation history (Lampe, von Baer). They stressed the fact that it is through the Spirit that the works of Jesus are perpetuated in the church (Hull, Borremans, George, Chevallier). Also noted is the Old Testament nature of the descriptive representations of the Spirit used by Luke (Lampe, George, Chevallier).

However, very little emphasis has been placed on the importance of the content of Acts 2:33 for the overall understanding of Luke's pneumatology. Many recognize the wording of this verse as being the most explicit of the gift of the Spirit by Jesus to believers (von Baer, George, Hull, Guillet). But it is never referred to as marking the *specificity* of Lukan pneumatology, or as the key to understanding all Lukan discourse on the Spirit in relation to Jesus as well as to the church. No one saw in it the entryway par excellence to Luke's pneumatology, any more than they saw in it the synthesis of this pneumatology. Hence, this is the importance of this study as a contribution to a better understanding of a major theme in the work of Luke—the Spirit.

---

[127] Ibid.

CHAPTER 2

ACTS 2:33 IN ITS LITERARY CONTEXT

Acts 2:33[1]
τῇ δεξιᾷ οὖν τοῦ θεοῦ ὑψωθείς, τήν τε ἐπαγγελίαν τοῦ πνεύματος τοῦ ἁγίου λαβὼν παρὰ τοῦ πατρός, ἐξέχεεν τοῦτο ὃ ὑμεῖς βλέπετε καὶ ἀκούετε. / *Therefore having been exalted at the right hand of God,*[2] *and having received from the Father the promise of the Holy Spirit, He has poured forth this which you both see and hear.*

This chapter presents Acts 2:33 as the key verse of this study. After analyzing the vocabulary and making the clarifications needed for the translation of τῇ δεξιᾷ / *at the right [hand]*, an examination is made of this verse's insertion into Peter's speech at Pentecost—Acts 2:14–36; 38–39. However, this last step will be preceded by a study of the role of the speech in Acts. This exercise seems important given the author's extensive use of this literary technique, especially given his choice to make it the means of the ultimate proclamation of the lordship of Christ.

1. VOCABULARY ANALYSIS

The expression τῇ δεξιᾷ / *at the right [hand]*, referring to Christ's reign, is not particularly Lukan. It occurs eight times in Pauline literature (Rom 8:34; Eph 1:20; Col 3:1; Heb 1:3, 13; 8:1; 10:12; 12:2) and once in 1 Pet

---

[1] The adopted text is that of *Novum Testamentum Graece*, Nestle-Aland, 26th ed. (Stuttgart: Deutsche Bibelgesellschaft, 1985). This text presents no significant textual criticism problem for this study.
[2] The expression τῇ δεξιᾷ poses a translation problem. I will justify the choice "at the right hand" further on.

3:22. Absent from the Johannine tradition, it appears only twice in the synoptic tradition (Matt 22:44 ‖ Mark 12:36 ‖ Luke 20:42; Matt 26:64 ‖ Mark 14:62 ‖ Luke 22:69). In Acts, however, it is used six times (2:25; 2:33, 34; 5:31; 7:55, 56). Note that the use of "the right hand" from the perspective of the exaltation is of particular importance in the Pauline writings, in Hebrews especially, and in Acts.[3]

The verb ὑψοῦν is especially used by Luke and John. Absent from Paul's writings (with the exception of 2 Cor 11:7, which has nothing to do with Christ being elevated) and also absent from Mark's writings, it occurs three times in Matthew (11:23 ‖ Luke 10:15; 23:12 ‖ Luke 14:11 and ‖ 18:14), but not in the language of exaltation. The only occurrences in reference to the exaltation of Christ belong to John (3:14 [2x]; 8:28; 12:32, 34) and to Acts (2:33 and 5:31).[4] In Acts, the two statements are part of similar literary frameworks, that is, in a kerygmatic proclamation, at the heart of a Petrine speech: first comes the affirmation of the resurrection of Christ by God (2:32 and 5:30); then, his elevation to the right hand of God (2:33 and 5:31); and finally, the gift of the Spirit (2:33 and 5:32). Thus, the verb ὑψοῦν[5] / *exalted* would be a descriptive term in Acts (as in John) of the exaltation of Christ.

The term ἐπαγγελία / *promise* only appears, for all practical purposes, in the Pauline and Lukan writings: of fifty-five occurrences, forty come from Pauline letters and nine are from Luke-Acts (1x Luke/8x Acts).[6] Except for a few rare exceptions, the term always refers to God's promise to his people. However, it is in Luke-Acts only (with the exception of Eph 1:13 and Gal 3:14) that the object of this promise is identified with the gift

---

[3] It is usually in reference—explicit or implicit—to Ps 110:1 that the sitting of Christ at the right hand of God is expressed. However, a few occurrences (Matt 26:64 and parallels; Acts 7:55, 56) prove it to be a fusion of Dan 7:13 and Ps 110:1. In these cases, the Son of Man is identified with the exalted Christ. Regarding the identification of the Son of Man and Christ exalted by the combination of Dan 7:13 and Ps 110:1, refer to, among others, Perkin, "Mark XIV.62: The End Product of Christian Pesher Tradition?" pp. 150–55; Fuller, *The Foundations of New Testament Christology*, pp. 109–11; Hahn, *The Titles of Jesus in Christology: Their History in Early Christianity*, pp 148–61; Weeden, *Mark—Traditions in Conflict*, p. 135; Callan, "Psalm 110:1 and the Origin of the Expectation That Jesus Will Come Again," pp. 622–36.

[4] Note, however, another instance in Acts 13:17 related to the Hebrew people that God 'elevated' (*made grow*) in Egypt; also in Luke 1:52, in the *Magnificat*, which speaks of the humble 'elevated' by God.

[5] In Phil 2:9, the superlative ὑπερύψωσεν / *highly exalted* is used.

[6] The three other cases are found in 1 John 2:25; 1 Pet 3:4, 9.

of the Spirit: Luke 24:49 (implicitly); Acts 1:4–5; 2:33, 39. This specificity (which is discussed in chapter 4) would, therefore, seem to be a feature of the Lukan use of the term.

The theme of the Spirit is especially Lukan. Not only is it amply used in Luke-Acts (seventeen times in the third Gospel and fifty-seven times in Acts), but it is, in the present context, an essential element of a specifically Lukan demonstration: the gift of the Spirit to the resurrected Christ (Acts 2:33) explains the cause of the realization of the Father's promise (Luke 24:49; Acts 1:4–5) at Pentecost (Acts 2:1–4). The entire study will demonstrate the fundamental importance of the Spirit in all of Luke's writings.

The verb λαμβάνειν / *to receive*, used widely throughout the entire New Testament, is not particularly Lukan. Similarly, the noun πατήρ, except that the association of the promise to the Father is unique to Luke. On three occasions, always in the context of the framework of the demonstration mentioned above, in Luke 24:49; Acts 1:4; 2:33 (cf. also Acts 1:8), the same formula occurs: τὴν ἐπαγγελίαν τοῦ πατρός / *the promise of the Father*.

The verb ἐκχεῖν / *to pour out* is only used twice in the Gospels: in Matt 9:17 (wine poured out) and in John 2:5 (tables overturned). In the Pauline literature, it appears twice: in Rom 3:15, in the quotation of Ps 6:18 (blood poured out) and in Titus 3:6 (where, in this case, it is a matter of the Spirit being poured out). In Revelation, it is repeated nine times in the middle of chapter 16, but always to restate the same idea, that is, pouring out the cup of God's wrath (with the exception of verse 6 where it is blood that is poured out). In contrast, the book of Acts has three occurrences and all three are in relation to the outpouring of the Spirit: 2:17, 18, in the quotation of Joel 2:28, where it is a question of the promise of the Father to pour out his Spirit in the end times, and in 2:33, which states the accomplishment of this promise. In the last case, the author probably uses the same word in order to better highlight the promise/fulfillment connection.

The very common verbs βλέπειν / *to see* and ακούειν / *to hear*, used extensively throughout the New Testament, certainly cannot be cited as characterizing the Lukan style. However, the combined use of the two, found four times in Luke-Acts, is likely integrated into the consistency of a demonstration that Luke spread throughout his two books. First, it occurs in Luke 8:10, in a partial quotation of Isa 6:10—reproduced as well in Matt 13:14 and in Mark 4:12—about the unintelligibility of parables for those who are not disciples. Then, it occurs again in another traditional text (this time a double tradition) in Luke 10:24, recalling that many prophets would have wanted *to see* and *to hear* what 'you see' and what 'you hear,' but that was not given to them. Finally, in Acts 28:26–27, Luke again cites the quotation of Isaiah, but this time the complete text (Isa 6:9–10), including the words of punishment that he had omitted in the scene of the parables—Luke 8:10 (contrasted to Mark and Matthew). It is, therefore, possible that in Acts 2:33, the combination βλέπετε/ακούετε (*see/hear*) is intentionally constructed to highlight the privileged situation of the believers at Pentecost. The insistence is also well marked by the presence of the personal pronoun ὑμεῖς. They would be told somehow:

> What *you* see and hear [Acts 2:33] is what the prophets *would have wanted* to see and hear [Luke 10:24], but that Israel *refused* to see and hear. [Luke 8:10; Acts 28:26–27].

By associating these verbs in Acts 2:33, which elsewhere have a negative connotation, Luke highlights the unique destiny of those who have part in the fulfillment of the promise compared to those who have been deprived.

Thus, the study of the vocabulary, though not absolutely conclusive, strongly encourages the belief that the composition of this verse is by Luke's hand. The most significant evidence to this effect results from Luke's specific use of certain terms, such as *at the right hand, pour out, promise*, and *see/hear*.

Nevertheless, the compelling argument for a Lukan construction will be based much more solidly on theological foundations rather than on linguistic ones. Since, in fact, this verse is of capital importance to the overall understanding of Luke's pneumatology, it seems undeniable that Luke is responsible for the content and place of insertion. It is, of course, the complete study that will demonstrate this argument. But, as will be shown (pp. 34–39), an overall observation of the missionary speeches of Acts contributes to bringing to light the importance of Luke's editorial activity with regard to the speeches in general.

2. Translation of τῇ δεξιᾷ

A translation problem arises from the opening of verse 33 concerning τῇ δεξιᾷ. It is important to clarify this point because the option for one or the other of the translation possibilities will affect the christological light that this verse should normally provide in future developments.

This dative form τῇ δεξιᾷ can equally be translated as "by the right hand"—thus recognizing an instrumental meaning of the expression—rather than "at the right hand"—acknowledging then a locative meaning. The option for either of the possibilities is not self-evident. Scholars clearly demonstrate equal support for either one.[7] Grammarians and lexicologists themselves sometimes show indecision. Zerwick-Grosvenor emphasize simply that both interpretations are possible.[8] Bauer, who first appears to favor the instrumental interpretation, nevertheless, adds: "it can also be dative of place 'at' the right hand."[9] Blass-Debrunner consider, on the other hand, that here one has to see a location rather than an instrumental meaning. It is noted that the dative of place is extremely rare in the classical period and absent from the NT, with the exception of stereotypical expressions κύκλῳ / *around* and χαμαί / *on the ground* and in cases with content identical to Acts 2:33 and 5:31.[10]

---

[7] If we simply consult translations available in different reviews, monographs, or articles, we find, in each camp the following scholars, among others **(1) "by the right hand"**: O. Bauernfeind, *Kommentar und Studien zur Apostelgeschichte*, p. 43; F. F. Bruce, *The Acts of the Apostles*, p. 95; J. Cantinat, *Les Actes des Apôtres*, p. 38; F. Mussner, *Apostelgeschichte*, p. 24; G. Voss, *Die Christologie des lukanischen Schriften in Grundzügen*, p. 133; J. W. Packer, *The Acts of the Apostles*, p. 29; C. S. C. Williams, *The Acts of the Apostles*, p. 66; J. Dupont, "'Seated at the Right Hand of God.' The Interpretation of Ps 110:1 in the New Testament," *New Studies on the Acts of the Apostles*, p. 210, note 1; E. Delebecque, *The Two Acts of the Apostles*, p. 25; F. Lavallée, *The Holy Spirit and the Church: An Analysis of the Acts of the Apostles for Today*, p. 70; **(2) "at the right hand"**: W. de Boor, *Die Apostelgeschichte*, p. 57; E. Haenchen, *The Acts of the Apostles*, p. 176; R. C. P. Hanson, *The Acts*, p. 69; R. Pesch, *Die Apostelgeschichte, Apg 1–12*, p. 115; J. Roloff, *Die Apostelgeschichte*, p. 48; G. Schille, *Die Apostelgeschichte des Lukas*, p. 102; G. Schneider, *Die Apostelgeschichte, Teil 1, 1:1–8:40*, p. 263; A. Weiser, *Die Apostelgeschichte, Kapitel 1–12*, p. 89; H. Conzelmann, *Acts of the Apostles*, p. 21; J. A. Fitzmyer, "The Ascension of Christ and Pentecost," p. 426; W. Schmithals, *Die Apostelgeschichte des Lukas*, p. 33; R. F. O'Toole, "Acts 2:30 and the Davidic Covenant of Pentecost," p. 256; C. Schedl, *Als sich der Pfingsttag erfüllte. Erklärung der Pfingstperikope Apg 2, 1–47*, p. 90.

[8] Zerwick and Grosvenor, *A Grammatical Analysis of the Greek New Testament, Vol. 1, Gospels and Acts*, p. 355.

[9] Bauer, *A Greek-English Lexicon of the New Testament and Other Early Christian Literature*, p. 174, δεξιός, 2.a. Moreover, in the study of the verb ὑψοῦν, Bauer uses the expression from Acts 2:33 that he translates from the Greek as "exalted by the power of God."

[10] Blass and Debrunner, *A Greek Grammar of the New Testament and Other Early Literature*, p. 107, #199: "τῇ δεξιᾷ [Acts] 2:33 . . . is also local rather than instrumental."

In fact, if the expression should be translated as "by the right hand," it would indicate the value of the power that exalted Jesus—that is, the hand of God—and would no doubt refer to Ps 118:16, "The right hand of the Lord exalted me." If, on the contrary, it should be translated as "at the right hand," it would indicate the new condition of the exalted Christ as sitting on the heavenly throne. It would then refer back to Ps 110:1 "The Lord says to my Lord: "Sit at My right hand."

Dupont firmly stated his point of view in favor of the translation "by the right hand."[11] He lines up the following arguments:[12]

- In the New Testament, the dative of place is normally constructed with the preposition (except for some rare stereotypical expressions named above).

- The immediate context does not allow for a decisive choice for one interpretation or the other.

- Psalms 110 and 118, one as well as the other, can support the christological argument.

- The verb ὑψοῦν / *exalted* would favor seeing a borrowing from Ps 118.

- The parallel constructions of Acts 7:35 and 13:17, where it is said that God "exalted" the people from Egypt and delivered them by "his uplifted arm," can shed light on Acts 2:33 (and 5:31).

Contrary to Dupont, Gourgues believes that it is the other reading that should be preferred, i.e., shedding light on τῇ δεξιᾷ through Ps 110:1.[13] He shows that the citation of the same psalm in verse 34 estab-

---

[11] Dupont, *Études sur les Actes des Apôtres*, pp. 302–4. Of the same opinion as Dupont, Voss, *Die Christologie der lukanischen Schriften in Grundzügen*, p. 133.

[12] For a good critical review of arguments in favor of the translation "by the right hand," see Gourgues's article, "'Exalté à la droite de Dieu' (Ac 2:33; 5:31)," pp. 311ff. In this article, Gourgues clearly and convincingly refutes the most often cited arguments (including those of Dupont) against the interpretation "at the right hand."

[13] Gourgues, *À la droite de Dieu. Résurrection de Jésus et actualisation du Psaume 110:1 dans le Nouveau Testament*, pp. 164–69. (Gourgues had previously defended this position even more elaborately in an article cited in note 12, pp. 303–27). Of the same opinion as Gourgues: Wilckens, *Die Missionsreden der Apostelgeschichte. Form-und Traditionsgeschichtliche Untersuchungen*, pp. 150–52; Loader, "Christ at the Right Hand-Ps CX.1 in the New Testament," p. 200; Conzelmann, *Acts of the Apostles*, p. 21; Bertram, ὑψόω, *TDNT* 8:609, note 34.

lishes an identification "ascended into heaven" and "sitting at the right hand of God." Then, he writes: "the dialectical link between verses 33 and 34 seems to apply as well to an identification 'exalted' = 'ascended into heaven'" (the citation of v. 34 supports the assertion of v. 33). He concludes that if "exalted" is equivalent to "ascended into heaven," then it must also be equivalent to "sitting at the right hand of God."

In the internal coherence of v. 33, it must be admitted that one or the other of the readings is acceptable. That the Risen Lord has been exalted "by the right hand" or "at the right hand," does not affect his entitlement to transmit the Spirit, this empowerment resulting from the fact that, in any case, he has received it from the Father. However, for the sake of the consistency of this part of the speech devoted to the kerygma, according to Gourgues, the reading "at the right hand" should be retained. This reading is called for by the scriptural argument substantiated in verse 34,[14] as Gourgues correctly explains. Recall the wording of this verse: "David, who is certainly not ascended to heaven, yet said: 'The Lord said to my Lord: sit at my right hand.'"

Luke's decision to apply this prophetic word to Jesus is explicit when he says, "David . . . is certainly not ascended into heaven." The One who is designated by "My Lord" cannot, therefore, be David, but Jesus. However, the "sit at my right hand" (v. 34) aims to support the fact that the one referred to as "my Lord" is indeed ascended to heaven. If Luke uses this quotation, whose key element is "sit at my right hand" to shed light on v. 33, it appears logical that he intends to give to τῇ δεξιᾷ of the first verse the meaning of this interpretive element and that the sitting at the right hand of God is perceived as the immediate manifestation, or the result of

---

[14] Due to the parallel with v. 34, Schneider, *Die Apostelgeschichte, Teil 1, 1:1–8:40*, p. 275, also opts for the locative meaning rather than the instrumental meaning: "Jedoch ist der letztere Dativ eher im Sinne einer Ortsangabe als instrumental zu verstehen (vgl. V 34): Als 'zur Rechten Gottes' Erhöhter und im Himmel inthronisierter Kyrios (V 34) hat Jesus vom Vater den verheißenen heiligen Geist empfangen und 'ausgegossen.'" Additionally, Pesch, *Die Apostelgeschichte, Apg 1–12*, p. 124: "Im Blick auf 34 (Ps 110:1) ist τῇ δεξιᾷ τοῦ θεοῦ eher lokal als instrumental zu verstehen"; ["However, the latter case of the dative is to be understood in the locative sense rather than the instrumental (cf. v. 34): as the exalted one 'at the right hand of God' and as the Lord enthroned in heaven (v. 34), Jesus has received from the Father the promised Holy Spirit and has 'poured [it] out.'"] Additionally, Pesch, *Die Apostelgeschichte, Apg 1–12*, p. 124: "In the view of v. 34 (Ps 110:1), τῇ δεξιᾷ τοῦ θεοῦ is to be understood as locative rather than instrumental"]; also, Schille, *Die Apostelgeschichte des Lukas*, p. 113; Voss, *Die Christologie der lukanischen Schriften in Grundzügen*, p. 139.

exaltation. We would not see, as Gourgues[15] reminds us, how v. 34, which deals only with the location, could be introduced to support v. 33, if in this latter verse τῇ δεξιᾷ had an instrumental meaning.

It is clear, moreover, that this interpretation is already prepared by the preceding verses: "God had sworn to have one of his offspring sit on his throne" (v. 30). This is why "he has not abandoned him [Jesus] to the residence of the dead," (v. 31), but he has, on the contrary, resurrected him (v. 32). He is now exalted "at the right hand of God," i.e., he occupies the promised throne (v. 33).[16]

Finally, considered in the broader context of Lukan Christology, the sitting at the right hand of God, as inherent to the exaltation, realizes the promise of the angel at the annunciation (Luke 1:32–33) regarding the future of the child who would be born (which is discussed in detail in chapter 5). Τῇ δεξιᾷ would be descriptive of the new situation of Jesus exalted in relation to God and not of the driving force at the origin of his exaltation. In short, by his exaltation, Jesus is empowered to reign, to sit *at the right hand* of God.

3. INSERTION OF THE VERSE IN THE PENTECOST SPEECH

The christological proclamation of Acts 2:33 occurs in the context of Peter's speech on the day of Pentecost. Thus, in order to assess the significance Luke intends to give the proclamation of Acts 2:33, it seems important to know the value and the role of the literary genre which conveys it. Accordingly, the speech in general as a widely used literary technique used by the author of Acts should be examined. Therefore, verse 33 will be viewed specifically in the context of the entire Pentecost speech to evaluate the strategic value of its insertion point.

The Speeches in the Acts of the Apostles

Nearly a third of the overall content of Acts is speeches. This fact in itself demonstrates the importance the author wants to give them as the means of communicating the message he wants to deliver. Their prominence has also attracted the attention of many researchers. Of these researchers, three

---

[15] Gourgues, "'Exalté à la droite de Dieu,'" p. 326.
[16] Conzelmann, *Acts of the Apostles*, p. 21, also believes that vv. 30ff. call for this interpretation.

great names are particularly distinguished: C. H. Dodd,[17] M. Dibelius,[18] and U. Wilckens.[19]

According to Dodd, the missionary speeches are written by Luke but from memories of what the apostles could have said. The author would most likely have used sources.[20] In comparing the kerygmatic elements of the speeches to those of the Pauline letters, he concludes that these speeches reflect the kerygma of Jerusalem at its inception, without, however, literally reproducing what Peter could have said on any given occasion.[21]

Meanwhile, Dibelius strives to submit Acts to the grid of Greek historiography to verify what role can be attributed to the speeches of Acts as compared to different types of speeches reported by historians.[22] Although the results he finds are sometimes negative for the various reasons he gives,[23] the paralleling of the speeches, nevertheless, highlights some very enlightening points; Dibelius shows, in fact, that the speeches of Acts like

---

[17] Dodd, *The Apostolic Preaching and Its Developments* (1936; London: Hodder and Stoughton, 1963).

[18] Dibelius, "The Speeches in Acts and Ancient Historiography," *Studies in the Acts of the Apostles*, pp.138–85 (presented at a conference in 1944, with the title "Die Reden der Apostelgeschichte und die antike Geschichtsschreibung").

[19] Wilckens, *Die Missionsreden der Apostelgeschichte. Form-und Traditionsgeschichtliche Untersuchungen*. Other important works on the speeches must also be cited: Schweizer, "Concerning the Speeches in Acts," *Studies in Luke-Acts*, pp. 208–16; Dupont, *Nouvelles études sur les Actes des Apôtres*, pp. 58–111; Weiser, "Die Pfingstpredigt des Lukas," pp. 1–12; J. Schmitt, "La prédication apostolique. Les formes, le contenu," pp. 107–33; Zehnle, *Peter's Pentecost Discourse. Tradition and Lukan Reinterpretation in Peter's Speeches of Acts 2 and 3*; Dumais, *Le langage de l'évangélisation. L'annonce missionnaire en milieu juif (Actes 13:16–41)*, pp. 11–44; Bruce, *The Speeches in the Acts of the Apostles*; P. Schubert, "The Final Cycle in the Speeches in the Book of Acts"; Townsend, "The Speeches in Acts," pp. 150–59; Evan, "Speeches in Acts"; Lohfink, *La Conversion de saint Paul*, pp. 60–77.

[20] Dodd, *The Apostolic Preaching and Its Developments*, pp. 18–19.

[21] Ibid., p. 20. At the end of his work, Dodd presents a chart comparing "the kerygma according to the Acts of the Apostles" and "the kerygma according to Paul."

[22] Dibelius, *Studies in the Acts of the Apostles*, p. 145.

[23] Among the objections Dibelius raised against the value of the historiographic tradition shedding light on the speeches of Acts, I retain these: (1) ancient historiography developed the speech as a literary form in itself, which is foreign to the New Testament writings as a whole (p. 145; cf. also pp. 181–82); (2) speeches are much shorter in Acts than in Greek writings (p. 181); (3) the author of Acts often repeats the same themes with a didactic purpose (same pattern, same contents); (4) he also uses the direct style while the Greek historians generally prefer the indirect style to preserve the unity of their writings.

those of ancient historiography are used as an interpretative tool. The historian makes use of this literary process without necessarily being concerned about knowing whether the remarks he reports were really uttered by the person to whom they are attributed.[24] The speech, in reality, has just to identify and explain the meaning of the event to which it relates.[25] Thus, Luke would also make similar use of the speeches and, this he would do at crucial turning points for the evolution of his book. Dibelius, however, wishes to recall the important point that the speeches serve the book as a whole—the book of Acts has a theme, he states, and speeches contribute to expand it.[26] He believes, finally, that Luke can draw on sources, but that the speeches as such are products of his writing and reflect his theology. He differs slightly from Dodd on this last point. He grants, however, that these speeches placed on the lips of Peter and Paul have, nevertheless, ancient roots and that they derive from the apostolic preaching kept as memories.[27] They are, as it were, exemplary sermons.[28]

---

[24] This is the confession even of the ancient historian Thucydides (*Hist.*, 1.22,1): "I add that concerning the speeches made by some and by others, either immediately before or during the war, it was very difficult to produce the same content with accuracy, as much for myself, when I had personally heard, as for anyone who reported them to me of any particular source; I expressed the best, in my opinion, what they could have said relative to the situation, keeping in my mind, for the general thought, as closely as possible to the words actually spoken" (from J. de Romilly's translation, in the collection of "Universities of France," Paris, 1953, p. 14, according to Dupont, *Nouvelles études sur les Actes des Apôtres*, p. 88). More still, a historian could assign a speaker a speech of his own drafting, although knowing the exact content of the speech actually delivered. This would probably be the case of a speech that Tacitus attributed to Emperor Claudius (*Annals*, 11.24; on this subject see Lohfink, *La Conversion de saint Paul*, p. 61).

[25] Lohfink, *La Conversion de saint Paul*, p. 63, explains that, for the ancient author, the speech is a technique that "constitutes a handy means to give light to or to interpret [an important] figure, a given situation or a historical sequence." He adds: "[This] *means of literary expression* also applies to speeches from the book of Acts."

[26] Dibelius, *Studies in the Acts of the Apostles*, pp. 174–75. In the same vein, Cadbury, *The Making of Luke-Acts*, pp. 185–86, writes: "It is evident that the ancient writers and their readers considered the speeches more as editorial and dramatic comment than as historical tradition. Neither the form of direct quotation nor the appropriateness of the words to the speaker and his occasion proves that the writer had any actual knowledge of what was said, or indeed that a speech was delivered at all."

[27] Dibelius, *Studies in the Acts of the Apostles*, p. 184; also, pp. 154–55; 164–65. Cadbury, before Dibelius, had put forth opinions in this vein ("The Speeches in Acts," *The Beginnings of Christianity*, vol. 5, pp. 426–27).

Wilckens's position falls in line with Dibelius's, but makes Dibelius's position more soundly. Wilckens, in fact, is of the opinion that the speeches have very little traditional basis and that they are entirely Luke's composition, reflecting a later theology.[29] Wilckens's opinions seem rather excessive. Between Bruce, who holds that the speeches reproduce the sources holding to what the apostles[30] could have said almost literally, and Wilckens, who denies them any traditional basis, more nuanced positions may be proposed (those of Dibelius, for example) as, moreover, a large number of scholars do.

But it seems clear that the speeches as such are Luke's writing and that they ultimately serve the overall objectives of the book of Acts. Presenting the common elements of the missionary speeches[31] in a simple table is in itself convincing.

---

[28] Conzelmann, *Acts of the Apostles*, pp. xliii–xliv, who subscribes to Dibelius's underlying thesis, contests, nevertheless, this vision of the speeches as "exemplary sermons."

[29] Wilckens, *Die Missionsreden der Apostelgeschichte. Form-und Traditionsgeschichtliche Untersuchungen*, who supports his point of view especially in the development entitled "Die traditionsgeschichtliche Frage," pp. 72–91.

[30] Bruce, *The Acts of the Apostles*, pp. 18–21. Trocmé, *The "Book of Acts" and History*, pp. 207, 208, 217, also strongly insisted on the apostolic rooting of the speeches of Acts. A little less radical than Bruce, Marshall, *The Acts of the Apostles*, pp. 40–42, and Neil, *The Acts of the Apostles*, pp. 44–45, also firmly believe that the speeches are not Luke's pure invention but that they are based on ancient sources. Marshall writes: "In the speeches, Luke has done his best to report what was said by preachers in the early church," (p. 42). Pesch, *Die Apostelgeschichte, Apg 1–12*, p. 44, believes, as far as he is concerned, that the speeches must be studied in relation to their original contexts, holding that they reflect real situations that produced them. He stands opposed to Roloff who (p. 49) proposes that: "die Reden der Apg sind nicht in erster Linie, wie die synoptischen Jesusreden, Gefässe für die Bewahrung von Traditionen, sondern erzählerische Werkzeuge zur Veranschaulichung von Situationen. Lukas verwendet sie vorzugsweise dazu, um den "Richtungssinn des Geschehens" (M. Dibelius) herauszustellen." ["The speeches of Acts are not primarily, like the synoptic speeches of Jesus, vessels for the preservation of traditions, but narrative tools for illustrating situations. Luke uses them primarily to highlight the 'direction of events' (M. Dibelius)."]

[31] The category "missionary speeches" regroups the six following speeches: five of Peter (2:14–36, 38–39, at Pentecost; 3:12–26, to the crowd gathered in front of the temple; 4:8–12, 19–20 and 5:19–32, in front of the Sanhedrin; 10:34–43, at Cornelius's house) and one of Paul (13:16–41, at the synagogue in Antioch).

MISSIONARY SPEECHES[32]

Speaker/ Speech	Situation of Astonishing Questioning	Accompanying Explanation	Kerygma	Christian Implication
Peter				
2:14–36, 38–39	14–15	16–21	22–36	38–39
3:12–26	12	18, 21–26	13–16	17, 19–20
4:8–12, 19–20	9		10–12	19–20
5:19–32			30–31	29–32
10:34–43	34–35	43	36–41	39, 42
Paul				
13:16–41		27, 32b–36	27–31, 37	38–39

The literary unity of these speeches speaks clearly in favor of one and the same author for all of them.[33] Dupont's arguments[34] support this view:

- The speeches "are too short to be literal reproductions of what could have been said."

- Peter's speeches, which must have been delivered in Aramaic, do not show any noticeable linguistic differences compared to Paul's speech in Greek at Antioch. In addition, the Septuagint inspires the

---

[32] The chart proposed by Dupont, *Nouvelles études sur les Actes des Apôtres*, p. 62, for Peter's speeches is in six parts: "1—an introduction of circumstance; 2—a reminder of Jesus's ministry; 3—the conditions in which he died; 4—a solemn affirmation of his resurrection; 5—explanations which clarify by the Scripture the meaning of this resurrection; 6—it ends by announcing that the forgiveness of sins is offered to those who welcome the message." Dupont's chart corresponds for the most part with Schweizer's in *Studies in Luke-Acts*, p. 208. See also Wilckens's chart, *Die Missionsreden der Apostelgeschichte*, p. 54, and Dodd's, *The Apostolic Preaching and Its Developments*, pp. 21–24.

[33] I fully subscribe to Schweizer's opinion, *Studies in Luke-Acts*, p. 214, "What is clear, first of all, is the *uniformity* of the speeches, above all in their structure, but also in a considerable number of details. It seems clear that one and the same author has composed them, taking up traditional material only in particulars." This is what Lohfink proves as well (*La Conversion de saint Paul*, pp. 60–77).

[34] Dupont, *Nouvelles études sur les Actes des Apôtres*, pp. 83–89.

scriptural argumentation. A traditional Palestinian source would certainly not appeal to a Greek text to prove its argumentation.

- The same basic outline is found at the heart of each speech, be it Peter's or Paul's. Additionally, not only is the outline the same, but certain argumentation elements appear in the nearly similar wording. For example, Acts 13:34a, 35b (Paul) clearly echoes 2:24, 27 (Peter):[35]

  - That God raised him from the dead, without the possibility of his body decomposing, is what he had said: "You will not let your Holy one see decay" (13:34a, 35b).

  - But God resurrected him, delivering him from the pains of death, for it was not possible that he be held back from his power. . . . "You will not let your Holy one see decay" (2:24, 27).

And also Acts 13:36 in relation to 2:29:

  - For David . . . died, was buried with his ancestors and experienced decay (13:36).

  - . . . the patriarch David died, was buried, his tomb is with us to this day (2:29).

The speeches, therefore, would contribute to highlighting the decisive points of church growth:[36] at Pentecost, in front of the Sanhedrin, at Cornelius's house, etc. Luke thus makes the speech a persuasive technique at strategic moments taking advantage of the notoriety of the characters (Peter and Paul). And he seeks to legitimize faith in the resurrected Christ as the fulfillment of the Old Testament. It is indeed the kerygma that is at the center of the speeches.

Verse 33 within the Pentecost Speech

Acts 2:14–36, 38, 39
[14] But Peter, standing with the eleven, raised his voice and addressed them, "Men of Judea and all who live in Jerusalem, let this be known to you, and listen to what I say.

---

[35] Cf. Pesch, *Die Apostelgeschichte (Apg 13–28)*, p. 38.
[36] Cf. Mussner, *Apostelgeschichte*, p. 7.

¹⁵ Indeed, these are not drunk, as you suppose, for it is only nine o'clock in the morning.

¹⁶ No, this is what was spoken through the prophet Joel:

¹⁷ 'In the last days it will be, God declares, that I will pour out my Spirit upon all flesh, and your sons and your daughters shall prophesy, and your young men shall see visions, and your old men shall dream dreams.

¹⁸ Even upon my slaves, both men and women, in those days I will pour out my Spirit; and they shall prophesy.

¹⁹ And I will show portents in the heaven above and signs on the earth below, blood, and fire, and smoky mist.

²⁰ The sun shall be turned to darkness and the moon to blood, before the coming of the Lord's great and glorious day.

²¹ Then everyone who calls on the name of the Lord shall be saved.'

²² "You that are Israelites, listen to what I have to say: Jesus of Nazareth, a man attested to you by God with deeds of power, wonders, and signs that God did through him among you, as you yourselves know—

²³ this man, handed over to you according to the definite plan and foreknowledge of God, you crucified and killed by the hands of those outside the law.

²⁴ But God raised him up, having freed him from death, because it was impossible for him to be held in its power.

²⁵ For David says concerning him, 'I saw the Lord always before me, for he is at my right hand so that I will not be shaken;

²⁶ therefore my heart was glad, and my tongue rejoiced; moreover my flesh will live in hope.

²⁷ For you will not abandon my soul to Hades, or let your Holy One experience corruption.

²⁸ You have made known to me the ways of life; you will make me full of gladness with your presence.'

²⁹ "Fellow Israelites, I may say to you confidently of our ancestor David that he both died and was buried, and his tomb is with us to this day.

³⁰ Since he was a prophet, he knew that God had sworn with an oath to him that he would put one of his descendants on his throne.

³¹ Foreseeing this, David spoke of the resurrection of the Messiah, saying, 'He was not abandoned to Hades, nor did his flesh experience corruption.'

³² This Jesus God raised up, and of that all of us are witnesses.

³³ **Being therefore exalted at the right hand of God, and having received from the Father the promise of the Holy Spirit, he has poured out this that you both see and hear.**

³⁴ For David did not ascend into the heavens, but he himself says, 'The Lord said to my Lord, "Sit at my right hand,
³⁵ until I make your enemies your footstool."'
³⁶ Therefore let the entire house of Israel know with certainty that God has made him both Lord and Messiah, this Jesus whom you crucified."
³⁷ Now when they heard this, they were cut to the heart and said to Peter and to the other apostles, "Brothers, what should we do?"
³⁸ᵇ . . . "Repent, and be baptized every one of you in the name of Jesus Christ so that your sins may be forgiven; and you will receive the gift of the Holy Spirit.
³⁹ For the promise is for you, for your children, and for all who are far away, everyone whom the Lord our God calls to him."

Peter's speech occurs immediately after the outpouring of the Spirit on the day of Pentecost (Acts 2:1–4).[37] With firmness, boldness, and conviction, the radically transformed apostles speak to the crowd of Jews who had come from everywhere. And, to each one, it was given to hear his own language.

While the event provokes the wonder of some, it causes the sarcasm of others. The latter laugh, saying: "They are full of sweet wine." This charge then becomes the pretext to the explanation that Peter is going to provide: No, these people are not drunk, but what is happening is this . . . And then Peter initiates this long speech which interprets, in terms of eschatological fulfillment, the consecutive effervescent events at the outpouring of the Spirit.

This speech includes three main stages:[38] 1. The eschatological fulfillment (vv. 14–21); 2. Jesus's place and role in this fulfillment (kerygma) (vv. 22–36); and 3. An exhortation to conversion (vv. 38–39).

---

[37] The exegesis of Acts 2:1–4 will be done in chapter 6.

[38] For a detailed presentation of the elements comprising the speech of Acts 2:14–36, 38–39 (put in parallel with the one of Acts 3), see Zehnle, pp. 26–37. Zehnle also proposes a three-part division of the speech, but he divides it otherwise; it is "the formal address" signified by the word ἄνδρες / *men* which would mark the beginning of each part: ἄνδρες Ἰουδαῖοι / *men of Judea* (2:14); ἄνδρες Ἰσραηλῖται / *men of Israel* (2:22); ἄνδρες ἀδελφοί / *men brothers* (2:29). My subdivision corresponds, however, to the one proposed by Kremer, *Pfingstbericht und Pfingstgeschehen*, p. 167. This division better corresponds to the stages of salvation history according to the Lukan perception, namely: (1) The preparatory period; (2) The Christ event; (3) The church period. Note again the outline Gourgues retains, "Exalté to the right hand . . . ," pp. 305–6. Thus, Gourgues presents the steps of the speech's development: (1) "The Spirit truly causes the phenomenon of the diversity of languages [2:15–21]"; (2) "Christ is resur-

The Eschatological Fulfillment

Vv. 14b–15. Peter's entry follows the scoffers' charge. It aims to correct a false impression. But it is designed especially to direct attention to the explanation that will be given: "Understand what is happening." It is clear that the rest of the speech serves to shed light on the experience that provoked "what is happening," that is, the outpouring of the Spirit. This will become explicit at verse 33: "Having received from the Father the promise of the Holy Spirit, he poured out what you see and hear."[39]

Vv. 16–21. The author explains the event by scriptural evidence, citing Joel 2:28–32.[40] He presents the quotation as the anticipated announcement of what is now being realized, that is, first of all, the outpouring of the Spirit, and then the events which come from it: "It is a matter here of what had been said by the prophet Joel" (v. 16). The given explanation answers the question asked in v. 12: "What does this mean?" The comparison de Boor makes here with the Gospel episode of Luke 4:16–21 seems entirely pertinent: "Just as Jesus first expressed himself in Nazareth with Isaiah's words, Peter, here, from the prophet Joel, proclaims: 'Today these words are fulfilled in your midst.'"[41]

The two quotations (Isaiah's and Joel's) seem then to answer each other: one was marking the inauguration of Jesus's prophetic mission; the other marks the inauguration of the church's prophetic mission.

The announcement contained in Joel's text applies to eschatological times. The editorial precision added to the text, "in the last days,"[42] again

---

rected [2:22–32]"; (3) "The resurrected Christ is the one from whom the Spirit comes [2:33–35]"; (4) "Final proclamation [2:36]."

[39] This is what prompts a remark from Marshall: "The assembled crowd provided Peter with his opportunity to explain the significance of what was happening. His speech or sermon begins with an allusion to the pouring out of the Spirit as the fulfilment of prophecy and concludes with a further reference to the same event (2:33). But in between these references Peter explores more deeply the significance of the event" (*Acts of the Apostles*, p. 71).

[40] The quotation is taken from the Septuagint and not from the Hebrew text.

[41] W. de Boor, p. 59. It is important to note that Luke 4:18–21, that is, the insertion of Isaiah's text and Jesus's judgment of this quotation, is Lukan redaction. J. Schmitt also establishes a connection with the synagogue pericope, but it is with the christological section (Acts 2:22–36) that he makes the parallel. He writes: "It [the Pentecost speech] is . . . to the book of Acts what the pericope on the preaching in the Nazareth synagogue is to the third Gospel" ("*La prédication apostolique. Les formes, le contenu*," p. 117).

[42] Haenchen, p. 179, claims that the original text of v. 17 would correspond to that of codex Vaticanus (B) and also of 072, conforming to the Septuagint, and that one must read μετὰ ταῦτα ("after these things") instead of ἐν ταῖς ἐσχάταις ἡμέραις ("in the last

accentuates the author's intent to present the events as truly the day of fulfillment. But is this reading of the events by the author explained?

To understand this prophecy, it must be re-situated in the evolutionary curve of a new hope which takes shape at the time of the exile. Experience having shown the people of Israel's incapacity to live according to God's precepts, Ezekiel came to prophesy in these terms: "And I will put my Spirit in you and move you to follow my decrees and be careful to keep my laws" (Ezek 36:27). Then, in the same line of thought in 39:29: "I will no longer hide my face from them, for I will pour out my Spirit on the people of Israel." It is clear, from the prophet's perspective, that only the Spirit of God could lead and keep Israel in righteousness. At the return from the exile, prolonging this hope, Joel[43] recaptures this prophecy and confers on it a new dimension:

> And afterward, I will pour out my Spirit on all people. Your sons and daughters will prophesy, your old men will dream dreams, your young men will see visions. Even on my servants, both men and women, I will pour out my Spirit in those days. (Joel 2:28–29)

Note that if the object of the promise is the same, that is, the gift of the Spirit, the perspectives are expanded. The purpose of the gift is no

---

days"). He argues in this way: "In Lukan theology, the last days do not begin as soon as the Spirit is poured out." To this, Conzelmann, *Acts of the Apostles*, p. 19, answers that the expression ἐν ταῖς ἐσχάταις ἡμέραις / *in the last days* became stereotyped (cf. 1 Tim 4:1–2 and 2 Tim 3:1) and that it does not mean an immediate expectation of the end. As Schille (*Die Apostelgeschichte des Lukas*, p. 107) expresses it: "Die Gegenwart ist nicht die End-, sondern die Erfüllungszeit." ["The present is not the end time, but rather the time of fulfillment."] In the same perspective: Roloff, p. 53; de Boor, p. 59; Weiser, *Die Apostelgeschichte*, p. 29; Kerrigan, "The 'Sensus Plenior' of Joel, III, 1–5 in Acts II, 14–36," p. 300. Zehnle, p. 29, is probably correct when he explains the reading of B and 072 as "an attempt to correct the text of Acts in order to harmonize with Joel." As a matter of fact, Haenchen's position was not widely followed.

[43] According to Cazelles, ed., *Introduction à la Bible*, p. 461, there would be a clearer consensus of the scholars to date the book of Joel at around 400. Among the scholars named: Weiser, Trinquet, Delcor, Gelin, Sellin, Fohrer, Rinaldi, Welchbillig, Stephenson, Wolff. Lys considers from his point of view that "what this book [Joel] says concerning [the Spirit] very well takes place after the exile, whereas before the exile this perspective of a nearly universal outpouring of [the Spirit] was less precise and was linked to other forms of the presence of the spirit [on one or another]" (*"Rûach": le Souffle dans l'Ancien Testament*, p. 247, note 1). I subscribe to Lys's opinion.

longer limited to ensure the ethical conduct of the people, but this gift must become the source and the cause of prophecy.[44]

In fact, the gift of the Spirit could not be more explicitly linked to the prophecy. The last part of v. 18, which is a Lukan addition to the quotation, exposes the finality of this gift. Luke recaptures the verb already found in v. 17c (which belongs to Joel) προφητεύσουσιν / *they will prophesy* and reproduces it in v. 18b (which is not found again in Joel) exactly in the same form. The insistence is, therefore, very significant: the function of the recipients of the Spirit will be essentially prophetic (a point to be discussed at length in chapter 6, on church life). In fact, this addition divides the quotation in two, distinguishing well the contents of each part: the first concerns the new condition of the Spirit-filled; the second lists the wonders that accompany these new times.

It appears, therefore, that by shedding light on the events of Pentecost in view of Joel's text, Luke simply means to convey that the events were the exact fulfillment of what this text announced. The first part of the speech would aim to situate the advent of this day in the chronology of the history of salvation.[45]

Jesus's Place and Role in the Eschatological Fulfillment

After having completed the necessary updates, the author begins the long kerygmatic development explaining how the Pentecost event was made possible: what is happening in the community stems from what happened to Jesus. Besides, the interpretation of the Joel quotation on the promise of salvation to "everyone who calls on the name of the Lord" (v. 21) shows well the cause and effect relationship that Luke wants to establish.

In fact, the "name of the Lord" in Joel 2:32, refers, of course, to God and the salvation linked to calling on this name consists of the gathering of the exile survivors on Mount Zion (Joel 2:32b). In interrupting the

---

[44] In opposition to Buis who writes: "The perspectives opened by Ezekiel clearly go beyond—it is evident—those of Joel who does not envisage, according to him, neither lasting presence nor moral transformation" ("Joël annonce l'effusion de l'Esprit," p. 149). On the contrary, the proclamation of the word of God presupposes, first of all, a personal integration of this word. Moral conduct conformed to God's will should normally be a prerequisite to a testimony worthy of the word.

[45] Maddox, concerning the question of what Luke meant by "the last days," also believes that the accent is more on the fulfillment than on the imminence of the Parousia. He writes: "This is evident from his description of the coming of the Spirit and its effect on the apostles and those who hear them." He adds: "He [Luke] understands the 'last days' as the age of the Holy Spirit and of salvation" (*The Purpose of Luke-Acts*, pp. 137–38).

quotation (for Joel 2:32b does not appear in the Acts text), Luke engages in a new hermeneutic of the text: he applies it to the eschatological salvation henceforth linked to calling on the name of Jesus. The cutting off of the second part of the verse allows him thus to attribute to Jesus the title of Lord.[46] It is no coincidence that he immediately continues by naming Jesus (v. 22).

V. 22. The speech recalls Jesus's career on the earth. His career is characterized in terms of "miracles, wonders and signs." One may believe that, in reproducing the second part of Joel's quotation, which features the wondrous events (Acts 2:19–21), Luke not only had in mind the Pentecost events, but also Jesus's works.[47] For one must clearly see that in v. 19, Luke has again modified the Septuagint text in the following manner (the words in parentheses are some of Luke's editorial additions):

καὶ δώσω τέρατα ἐν τῷ οὐρανῷ (ἄνω) / and I will show wonders in the heaven (above)
καὶ (σημεῖα) ἐπὶ τῆς γῆς (κάτω) / and (signs) on the earth (below)

The reshaping results in a parallelism making τέρατα/σημεῖα and ἄνω/κάτω correspond with one another. One can, therefore, understand that the works of God on high and those of Jesus down below meet and merge because, rightly so, in Jesus, the Day of the Lord arrives.

Vv. 23–24. These verses present the kerygmatic nucleus in its primitive form. The plan and the foreknowledge of God (v. 23) are mentioned and, furthermore, are theological indicators that betray a Lukan wording. In fact, it is typical of Luke to present salvation history as one entity perfectly unified and "planned." Note simply of the transitional role he gives to chapters 1–2 of his Gospel: these two chapters, to use Chevallier's terms, show how the Old Testament begets the New Testament. Note also the last words of the Resurrected One at the end of the Gospel, which is

---

[46] It's the general opinion of exegetes that the title "Lord" applies to Jesus in v. 21: Pesch, *Die Apostelgeschichte, Apg 1–12*, p. 125; de Boor, pp. 60–61; Schneider, *Lukas, Theologe der Heilsgeschichte*, pp. 219–20; Kerrigan, p. 296; Bauernfeind, p. 45; Conzelmann, *Acts of the Apostles*, p. 20 (the latter points out that the interpretation of κύριος as being Jesus is only possible from the Septuagint on and not from the Hebrew text where one finds the tetragram instead), but see more particularly Roloff, "Die Bezeichnung Jesu als 'Herr' (Kyrios)," pp. 54–55. Luke avoids the confusion that could occur in the use of the title of *Lord* and, when there is a good reason, names *God*.

[47] This is the conception of Weiser, *Die Apostelgeschichte*, p. 92.

the promise of the Father. Thus, the book of Acts opens with the fulfillment of this promise. It is also very Lukan to refer to the scandal of the cross as being an integral part of the plan of salvation according to the foreknowledge of God:

1. The Son of Man will go as it has been decreed. But woe to that man who betrays him! (Luke 22:22)
2. Did not the Messiah have to suffer these things and then enter his glory? (24:26)
3. He told them, "This is what is written: The Messiah will suffer and rise from the dead on the third day . . . (24:46)
4. But this is how God fulfilled what he had foretold through all the prophets, saying that his Messiah would suffer . . . (Acts 3:18)
5. They did what your power and will had decided beforehand should happen. (4:28)
6. . . . in condemning him they fulfilled the words of the prophets that are read every Sabbath. (13:27)
7. The prophets and Moses said what would happen. (26:22b)

Nothing escapes God's will; everything is fulfillment.

For the author, however, the death of Jesus does not have in itself, a positive value. It is the means ("it was necessary that," Luke 24:26), the way of access to his resurrection (Acts 2:24)—by the fact itself, to his glory (vv. 30–31). It is, in itself, so despicable that God resurrected Jesus "for it was not possible that death keep its hold on him" (v. 24).

Vv. 25–28. Once again, the author returns to the scriptural argument to show how impossible is the hold of death. He announces: "David, in fact, said of him"; then he follows, in vv. 25–28, with the quotation, according to the Septuagint, from Ps 16:8–11.

The modifications brought about by the Greek translation favor the application of the Psalm to Jesus, which the author wants to do. Thus, in v. 26, one finds "my flesh will live in hope"; in v. 27, the translation is "your Holy One" instead of "your faithful one"; and, especially, "corruption" has been substituted for "grave." This last modification facilitates the link with the proclamation of the resurrection.

Vv. 29. The convincing argument follows right after the quotation of the Psalm, in v. 29: the Psalm could not apply to David,[48] since "the patriarch died, he was buried [and] his tomb is here to this day." David, therefore, experienced decay. This last explanation was so much more necessary that David seems in fact to speak of himself in this Psalm, points out Conzelmann.[49]

Vv. 30–31. After having demonstrated the reality of Christ's resurrection from a negative point of view, the author begins to progressively mention its positive effects. He is careful, here again, to present this fact as the fulfillment of the same messianic hope. He recalls first the promise by quoting Ps 132:11 (a promise already in 2 Sam 7:12–13): But he was a prophet and he knew that God "*had sworn with an oath to him that he would put one of his descendants on his throne.*"

Luke draws an interesting conclusion from this prophetic word, thus in advance he saw Christ's resurrection (v. 31). This conclusion is extremely enlightening as to the Lukan conception of the Messiah—because David was a prophet,[50] he knew that God had sworn in advance to have someone on his throne (v. 30); thus, in advance he saw Christ's resurrection (v. 31a).

The conjunction "thus" clearly establishes an equal link between the fact of sitting on the throne of David and Christ's resurrection. In other

---

[48] It is very clear from the start, Ps 16:8–11 was applied to David, but as explained by Schedl (p. 145): "Der geschichtliche Entstehungsort der einzelnen Psalmen ist für Lukas wenig interessant; denn die Kraft der Aussage liegt nicht beim menschlichen Wort, also auch nicht bei David, sondern beim einhauchenden und zusprechenden Geist." ["The historical origin of the individual psalms is of little interest to Luke, because the force of the statement lies not with the human word, not even with David, but with the inspiring and comforting Spirit."] Such a reinterpretation of the Psalm corresponds to the rabbinic and New Testament manner of commenting on the Scriptures and of conferring a new meaning on a traditional text, once more explains Schedl (ibid.).

[49] Conzelmann, *Acts*, p. 21.

[50] Attributing the status of prophet to David creates a problem, given there is no known biblical antecedent to justify it. Fitzmyer looked into the question ("David 'being therefore a Prophet . . .' [Acts 2:30]," pp. 232–39). He shows thus that, in extra-biblical Judaism, the idea would be present. He quotes two explicit testimonies: (1) in Qumran in the book of Psalms (published by J. A. Sanders, *The Psalms Scroll of Qumrân Cave 11 (11 Q Ps^a)*: on the subject of the Psalms of David, "All these he (David) spoke through prophecy which was given him from before the Most High" (quoted by Fitzmyer, p. 336); (2) from Josephus, *Ant.* 6.8, 2 #166: "the Deity abandoned Saul and passed over to David, who, when the divine Spirit had removed to him, began to prophesy" (quoted by Fitzmyer, p. 338).

words, to accede to David's throne, that is to become Messiah, Jesus had to enter into the resurrection.[51] And since it is as such, it goes without saying, Luke tells us, that "it is concerning him [Jesus] that he [David] said: *'He was not abandoned to the realm of the dead and his body did not experience decay'*" (paraphrasing Ps 16).

Luke ends his demonstration with this vigorous affirmation, indeed peremptory: "This Jesus, God resurrected him, we are all witnesses of it" (v. 32). And now comes v. 33 as the result of the demonstration: "Exalted at the right hand of God and having received of the Father the promise of the Holy Spirit, he poured out what you see and hear."

In vv. 34–35, Luke backs up the authenticity of the sitting "at the right hand" by referring back, once again to the scriptural proof; he does it by quoting Ps 110:1, which can not apply to David, for the latter "did not go up to heaven" (v. 34): he is still in his tomb (v. 29). Then, he draws the solemn conclusion: "Let all the house of Israel know beyond a doubt: God has made this Jesus whom you crucified both Lord and Messiah" (v. 36).

Thus, if we resume the progression of the speech, we come to the following:

- An observable, concrete situation: people prophesy in every language about the wonders of God (vv. 4–13).

- On what does this depend? The times are fulfilled and the promise of the gift of the Spirit is realized (vv. 15–22).

- How was this made possible? God accredited a man, Jesus the Nazarene, to the people, by acting through him (v. 22). Therefore, God is the principal actor. The people put this man to death (v. 23), but everything is fulfilled according to the foreknowledge of God, the plan of God. And, according to what had been announced (vv. 25–28), God resurrected him (v. 24), for God had sworn to have him sit on David's throne (v. 30).

Up to now it is God, therefore, who fully controls the situation, taking all the necessary measures so that his plans are fulfilled. He prepares Jesus for what he is destined: that is, taking over for God in governing the world. Thus, the final stage in Jesus's training, or accreditation to reign, on God's part, consists in imparting to him the essential power for the fulfillment of this function, that is, his Spirit.

---

[51] This is not without impact on the understanding of the baptism episode in Luke 3:22 (as will be seen in chapter 5).

Verse 33 becomes then the speech's point of convergence: Jesus's preparation is in anticipation of his exaltation. But this verse is also a turning point, for from this moment on it is Jesus who takes up his role, who, in a way, "takes control,"[52] because God imparted to him the power by which he himself reigned, up to then: the Spirit. It is this Spirit that the exalted Jesus poured out at the moment of Pentecost (2:2–3);[53] this is what explains the actions of the recipients (vv. 4–13). The gift of the Spirit is the fulfillment of the promise; it is also the specific mark of the new era of the church: it is under the domain of Christ's Spirit. Everything converges toward Acts 2:33, but also everything ensues from it. This is what the remainder of this research will demonstrate.

Exhortation to Conversion

Vv. 38–39. Luke calls attention to the existential implication linked to the Pentecostal reality: one must repent; be baptized in the name of Jesus Christ, because he is now Lord; in order to receive the Spirit that he can now bestow; in order to pursue the work that he himself inaugurated.

CONCLUSION

This first contact with the central verse of this study—Acts 2:33—already enables the noting of its essential role in the Lukan presentation of the Pentecostal experience. It gives meaning to the story of Pentecost: the outpouring of the Spirit on the community was made possible because Jesus first received the Spirit. Moreover, Luke's intention to make Acts 2:33 the key to reading the event of Pentecost appears clearly when, in the second part of the verse, he refers without equivocation to the event: "he received from the Father the promise of the Holy Spirit and he poured out

---

[52] In this vein Schedl, p. 147 writes: "Bisher waren alle Aussagen über Jesus sozusagen passiv. Gott war der eigentlich aktiv Handelnde . . . durch ihn Wunder wirkte, ihn auferweckte und erhöhte. Nun aber geschieht das erste activum Christologicum: der Erhöhte selbst wird wirksam, indem er 'ausgiesst.'" ["Up to now all statements about Jesus were essentially passive, so to speak; God was the actual actor . . . working miracles through him, raising him from the dead, and exalting him. But now the first *activum Christologicum* occurs: the raised one himself becomes active as he 'pours out [the Spirit].'"]

[53] Kremer, *Pfingstbericht und Pfingstgeschehen*, p. 167, writes: "Das zentrale Thema der Predigt bildet aber die Auferstehung Jesu, dies wird vor allem vv. 22–36 behandelt. Die Verbindung mit dem Pfingstereignis ist v. 33 aufgezeigt." ["However, the central theme of the sermon is the resurrection of Jesus; this is especially addressed in vv. 22–36. The connection with the Pentecost event is shown in v. 33."]

what you see and hear." Luke methodically developed the scene which called forth the explanation found in Acts 2:33:

1. The Spirit is poured out

2. The events which follow create questions for the people gathered

3. The speech explains that it is the fulfillment of the Father's promise through the life, the death, the resurrection, and the exaltation of Jesus

However, in addition to the light it brings to the immediate context in which it is integrated, the text of Acts 2:33 will have a certain impact on the global intelligence of the christological and ecclesiological orientations of all of Luke's writings. Chapters 5 and 6 will, more specifically, demonstrate this.

Chapter 3

Exalted at the Right Hand of God

The previous chapter helped situate the key verse—Acts 2:33—in its immediate context and evaluate its importance in understanding the Pentecost events. Now, it is important to study the theological impact of its terminology. This chapter will focus on the wording of the first part: *exalted at the right hand of God*. To appreciate the particular use the author makes of this phrase, it will be appropriate to verify the conceptual content of each of the expressions *exalted* and *at the right hand of God* in the Old Testament literature as well as in the other New Testament writings. Considerable attention will be given to the study of the two ascension narratives—Luke 24:50–53 and Acts 1:9–11. These two narratives, being exclusively Lukan, will prove very enlightening for the author's concept of the lordship of the Christ.

1. "Exalted" in the Septuagint and the New Testament

The verb form behind the English translation "exalted" is ὑψωθείς, the passive aorist participle of ὑψοῦν. The literal meaning of this verb is "raise." The English translation particularly shows this meaning: "to lift up," "to raise on high someone or something."[1] This meaning corresponds to the dimensional and concrete significance of the noun τὸ ὕψος, "height." However, this noun can designate, figuratively, a rank or a

---

[1] Bauer, p. 850.

disposition of pride.² In this vein, i.e., figurative meaning, the derived verb ὑψοῦν designates a raising up in honor, position, reputation, fortune, power.³ The translation of ὑψοῦν by "to exalt" can therefore be, in certain cases, more suitable than "to lift up" (even though "to lift up" is equally appropriate). The expression in Acts 2:33 corresponds to this figurative meaning.

Ὑψοῦν in the Septuagint: Its Use in Relation to the Divine

The verb ὑψοῦν⁴ occurs more than 170 times in the Septuagint (not counting its derived forms with the prefixes ὑπερ and ἀν). The use of the term that is of particular interest is its use in relation to God and with man in relationship to God. This use, which corresponds to a figurative or abstract meaning of the term, can be connected to different *Sitzen im Leben*.

Thus, the term can refer to the greatness of God in his dominion over all the earth (Ps 45:11), in his powerful interventions against his enemies (Mic 5:8), and in his final victory on the Day of Judgment (Isa 5:16). The use of the term can also show the desire of the just to see God manifest his greatness (Ps 7:7). In worship and liturgy, it serves to sing praise to God (Ps 98:5). It also describes God's sanctuary (Jer 17:12).

When it is a matter of human praise, this can only be the result of God's intervention in his favor, for God alone is exalted (Ps 148:13–14) and he alone can exalt a being (Ps 17:49). This exaltation can apply to the king (1 Sam 2:10), but it is especially the reward of the just (Ps 36:34). In fact, as Bertram tells us, the exaltation (of a human being) means drawing near to God.⁵ This is especially true of the Servant in Isa 52:13, he points

---

² Bauer, p. 850.

³ Nevertheless, note that the term is also used in a pejorative sense to describe a prideful attitude; e.g., Isa. 3:16: ". . . because the daughters of Zion are prideful (ὑψώθησαν) and they are stiff-necked . . . "; also Deut. 8:14; Ezek. 28:2; Prov. 18:12, etc.

⁴ The Greek verb ὑψοῦν translates the original Hebrew רום, נשא and גבה (see G. Bertram, "ὑψόω," *TDNT* 8:606). However, the meaning of each of these verbs is substantially the same as that rendered by ὑψοῦν, according to F. Brown, et al., *A Hebrew and English Lexicon of the Old Testament*; the translations given are the following: גבה, *to be lifted up, exalted*; נשא, *to raise, to carry, to take, to remove*; רום, *to be lifted up, exalted*.

⁵ *TDNT* 8:607.

out: "See, my Servant shall prosper; he shall be exalted [ὑψωθήσεται] and lifted up, and shall be very high [δοξασθήσεται.]"⁶ (Isa 52:13).

This sampling shows, first, that God alone is great and worthy of all praise. But it also shows that God can lift up a human being. The examples that interest this study most particularly are those concerning the king and the Servant. As for the king, however, it is about an already accomplished elevation which corresponds to the dignity of his office, thus a historic and temporarily limited elevation. But in the case of the Servant, it is presented as the reward that will have been worth his humbling and submission to the will of God.⁷ This last model is certainly the one which most inspired the christological language, as the New Testament texts examined later attest (most particularly Phil 2:6–11).

'Υψοῦν in the New Testament

The vocabulary analysis of Acts 2:33 showed that John and Luke are the only New Testament authors to use the verb ὑψοῦν in relation to the exaltation of the Christ. However, in Paul (Phil 2:6–11), it is nonetheless the verb ὑπερύψουν (v. 9) that is used. Before studying these Johannine and Lukan uses, as well as the Pauline text, it is important to consider the other instances of an ethical nature, in relation to a human being. They will reveal that a person's voluntary abasement constitutes the way to a person's elevation. Moreover, the unanimous choice of the authors (with only one exception) of the antithetical parallelism *lower/elevate*, ταπεινοῦν/ὑψοῦν, in itself, is conclusive.

Of the two examples coming from the double tradition, one of them, Matt 11:23 ‖ Luke 10:15, constitutes the announced exception. In this passage, it is a matter of the degradation that will strike Capernaum, which is expressed in the terms of Isa 14:13, 15, describing the end reserved for the king of Babylon: "And you, Capernaum, *will you be exalted* [ὑψωθήσῃ] to heaven? No, *you will be brought down* [καταβήσῃ] to Hades" (Matt 11:23a).

---

⁶ Concerning Isa 52:13, Bertram remarks: "Here ὑψωθήσεται occurs with δοξασθήσεται for the overcoming of all earthly abasement and it is thus strengthened and underlined." Bertram adds this important clarification: "To turn abasement into exaltation and lowliness into loftiness is the affair of God alone and it will be a sign of salvation" (ibid.).

⁷ The exaltation of the humble by God is a very well known notion in the Old Testament. See 1 Sam 2:7; Job 5:11; Ezek 17:24; Ps 149:4; Sir 2:1–18; Prov 3:34; 29:23.

The parallelism—although adopting the inverse movement and modifying the terminology—nevertheless, remains implicit:

- Capernaum who, having been exposed to the signs of the kingdom, should have been receptive—thus humble before God—was, on the contrary, closed to the message of the gospel.[8]

- As a consequence, Capernaum will not benefit from the elevation that would have been worth its humbling; on the contrary, it will be abased for having been proud.

The second text of the double tradition, Matt 23:12 ‖ Luke 14:11; 18:14, this time with the help of the antithetical formula, explicitly gives a lesson on true greatness, which consists of a humble attitude: "All who exalt [ὑψώσει] themselves will be humbled [ταπεινωθήσεται], and all who humble [ταπεινώσει] themselves will be exalted [ὑψωθήσεται]" (Matt 23:12).

The other examples, Luke 1:52; Jas 4:10; 1 Pet 5:6, convey exactly the same idea: God humbles the proud and elevates the humble:

1. He has brought down the powerful from their thrones, and lifted up [ὕψωσεν] the lowly [ταπεινούς]. (Luke 1:52)

2. Humble [ταπεινώθητε] yourselves before the Lord, and he will exalt [ὑψώσει][9] you. (Jas 4:10)

3. And all of you must clothe yourselves with humility [ταπεινοφροσύνην] in your dealings with one another, for "God opposes the proud, but gives grace to the humble [ταπεινοῖς]." Humble [ταπεινώθητε] yourselves therefore under the mighty hand of God, so that he may exalt [ὑψώσῃ] you in due time.[10] (1 Pet 5:5–6)

---

[8] Concerning this subject, see Bonnard, *L'Évangile selon saint Matthieu*, p. 166.

[9] The author of the letter takes up here the idea already expressed in verse 6, which recalls Mic 6:8: "He has told you, O mortal, what is good; and what does the Lord require of you but to do justice, and to love kindness and to walk humbly with your God?" On the nature of this humility required regarding God, which James addresses, see Mitton, p. 163. Vouga writes, "The exhortation (towards humility) is at the same time a promise," (p. 119); he points out: "The Lord will fill the life of those who will know how to relinquish theirs and thus escape the hold of seductions and powers."

[10] Brox, p. 236, points to the use of the root ταπει—(ταπεινοφροσύνην, ταπεινοῖς, ταπεινώθητε) as the key of the parallelism and the medium of the essential idea: "(der) Lohn Gottes am Ende, der dieser demütigen, unprätentiösen selbstlosen Grundhaltung

In this last text (1 Pet 5:5–6) the mention of "in due time" gives this passage an obvious eschatological significance. Even if this aspect is not evoked expressly in the other examples, it is, nevertheless, underlying.

The only Pauline example, 2 Cor 11:7, however, presents a particular nature; in fact, each verb of the parallelism concerns a distinct subject: Paul humbles himself to elevate the Corinthians: "Did I commit a sin by humbling myself [ἐμαυτὸν ταπεινῶν] that you might be exalted [ὑμεῖς ὑψωθῆτε], because I proclaimed God's good news to you free of charge?" (2 Cor 11:7).

The humbling of an individual reflects upon the community; therefore, it has a wider impact. The evangelical model (*humbling/elevation*), nevertheless, remains well-illustrated, as C. K. Barrett explains: Paul's attitude of self-deprivation, as much as his preaching, proclaims the gospel of God and the Corinthians find themselves spiritually enriched by it.[11] The observation of these verses provides the following constants:

- The elevation of a human being is only possible and only exists in contact with the divine, that is with his word (2 Cor 11:7) or with his action (Matt 11:23ff.).

- God alone can elevate a human being (Matt 23:12 ‖ Luke 14:11 ‖ 18:14); in the present example, God's intervention is implicitly contained in the divine passive (Luke 1:52; Jas 4:10; 1 Pet 5:5–6).

- The elevation of a human being is essentially conditioned by this person's attitude of humility.[12]

- This elevation finds its accomplishment in eschatology.

These conclusions fit well into the Old Testament perspectives of the relations of a human being to God. The prototype of the Servant (Isa

---

des Christen mit Sicherheit zuteil wird als "Erhöhung" aus der Selbsterniedrigung." ["(The) reward of God at the end, which grants confidence to this humble, unassuming, selfless attitude of the Christian, becomes "elevation" from self-abasement."] And this elevation is equal to salvation, explains Spicq, pp. 171–73.

[11] Barrett, *The Second Epistle to the Corinthians*, p. 282. In the same vein, Hughes writes: "The purpose of his self-abasement was their exaltation: through his preaching of the Gospel they were raised from the death of sin and from the degradation of their former ways and caused to sit in heavenly places in Christ Jesus," p. 384.

[12] See Adamson, p. 175; also, Cantinat, p. 411.

42:1ff.), in whom and by whom God would be able to act in virtue of his total submission, constitutes the perfect example of this abasement. How then does Jesus correspond to this model? John and Luke expressed themselves on this subject.

The four Johannine occurrences are unified in terms of meaning and vocabulary:

1. And just as Moses lifted up the serpent in the wilderness, so must [δεῖ] the Son of Man [τὸν υἱὸν τοῦ ἀνθρώπου], be lifted up [ὑψωθῆναι], that whoever believes in him may have eternal life (3:14–15).

2. "When you have lifted up [ὑψώσητε] the Son of Man [τὸν υἱὸν τοῦ ἀνθρώπου], then you will realize that I am he, and that I do nothing on my own, but I speak these things as the Father instructed me" (8:28).

3. "And I, when I am lifted up [ὑψωθῶ] from the earth, will draw all people to myself" (12:32).

4. The crowd answered him, "We have heard from the law that the Messiah remains forever. How can you say that the Son of Man [τὸν υἱὸν τοῦ ἀνθρώπου] must be lifted up [ὑψωθῆναι]? Who is this Son of Man?" (12:34).

In each example, it is a matter of the lifting up from earth—referring to the cross[13]—as his identification with the Son of Man.[14] This elevation

---

[13] Contrary to what one finds in the other New Testament writings, Schnackenburg tells us in *The Gospel according to St. John*, vol. I, p. 396, that the crucifixion is not perceived, in John, as the lowest point of humiliation: "John sees the Cross itself as 'exaltation,' as the beginning of the salvific Lordship of Christ (cf. the two-fold νῦν in 12:31 and κέκριται of 16:11), as the glorification by the Father, which is manifested in Christ's power to give life to all who belong to him." Along this same line, Barrett, *The Gospel according to St. John*, p. 178: "This verse (14) emphasizes the unique manner of his exaltation, which is not to be in clouds of glory but upon the cross." Also Brown, *The Gospel according to John (i-xii)*, pp. 145–46. Brown emphasizes, nevertheless, (p. 146) the double meaning of the Hebrew verb nasâh: "to take" and "to lift up." This verb, moreover, is the object of a play on words in Gen 40:13, 19, in Joseph's interpretation of pharaoh's officers' dreams: pharaoh will lift up the head of the cupbearer by delivering him from his captivity (v. 13); he will lift up the head of the baker in hanging it from a pole (v. 19). Thus, John would have used this term to mean the crucifixion and the glorification of Jesus at the same time (which, by the way, would verify once again this very characteristic tendency of the Johannine style to use words with a double meaning). According to Brown, to be lifted up would here

consists of a return to the "place" of origin, heaven: "No one has ascended into heaven except the one who descended from heaven, the Son of Man"[15] (3:13). But with increased power: ". . . that everyone who believes in him may have eternal life" (3:15); "And I, when I am lifted up from the earth, will draw all people to myself" (12:32).

Therefore, Jesus must be lifted up so that human beings enter into Life.[16] But equally, he must be lifted up so that the people's knowledge of Jesus be possible (John 8:28a). Finally, it is clear that Jesus's submission to God merits his elevation[17] (John 8:28b–29). John's Jesus corresponds fully to God's expectations; therefore, there is no hindrance to his elevation.

The important elements for understanding the New Testament perception of the concept of exaltation are provided from the observation of these passages of the fourth gospel. First of all, the texts clearly state the reality of the exaltation of the Christ in a spatial perspective. For example, right before the affirmation, in John 3:14–15, on the necessity that the Son of Man be lifted up, John writes, "No one has ascended into heaven except the one who descended from heaven . . ." (v. 13). This perspective is equally very clear in John 12:32, 34. It corresponds well, besides, to the cosmological vision of the Bible according to which the divinity lives in the high places (see further on).

It is clear, moreover, that this elevation is the effect of an act of God; the use of the divine passive in each one of these four texts is in this regard without question. The eschatological consequences of this elevation are equally well-accentuated: it allows the Christ to draw human beings to himself, that is to say, to have them enter into eternal life. This reading becomes particularly evident in John 3:14–15; these verses are inscribed in the instruction given to Nicodemus on the need to be born again:

---

refer then to a continuous action of ascension: "Jesus begins his return to the Father as he approaches death (xiii, 1) and completes it only with his ascension (xx, 17)."

[14] The Son of Man proves to be, in John, the link between the heavenly and earthly realities (on this subject see Barrett, *The Gospel according to St. John*, pp. 60 ff.; 177ff.).

[15] The affirmation in John 3:13, that immediately precedes the first affirmation on the elevation of the Christ, is explicit as to the preexistence of the character Son of Man in the Johannine concept. On his preexistence in John, see the study of Dunn, *Christology in the Making*, pp. 89–90.

[16] The δεῖ (3:14; 12:34) clearly emphasizes this need of death. The elevation of the Christ was necessary so that believers could have eternal life, notes Schnackenburg, *St. John*, p. 395.

[17] The prototype of the Servant is recognized (Isa 52–53).

1. "You must be born from above," (v. 7) born "of the Spirit" (v. 8), said Jesus.

2. "How can these things be?" (v. 9), Nicodemus responds.

3. "The Son of Man must be lifted up" (v. 14) "that whoever believes in him may have eternal life" (v. 15).[18]

Thus, in exalting Jesus, God conferred on him a new power, that of attracting to himself those who will believe (John 3:15ff.; 12:32). The elevation on the cross thus becomes the source of Life.[19]

The only Pauline text, using a derivative of the verb ὑψοῦν, i.e., ὑπερύψουν,[20] is Phil 2:9: "Therefore God also highly exalted [ὑπερύψωσεν] him and gave him the name that is above every name." It is the kenosis, Jesus's emptying of himself and perfect obedience that lead to his exaltation.[21] The cause and effect relationship in this regard is clearly established:

- verses 6–8 describe his abasement (ἐταπείνωσεν, v. 8);

- verse 9 moves on with the result which flows out of it: "Therefore God also highly exalted him and gave him the name that is above every name."

The Name designates the effective power over the entire cosmos, ". . . so that at the name of Jesus every knee should bend . . . and every tongue

---

[18] On this subject, Dodd writes: "The verses 13–15 . . . are directly relevant to the theme of rebirth into eternal life. The possibility of such rebirth is conditioned by the descent of the Son of Man and His ascent, or 'elevation'" (*The Interpretation of the Fourth Gospel*, p. 307). In the same sense, Brown, *John*, p. 145: "In verses 14–15 Jesus proceeds to the actual answer to Nicodemus' question, 'How can things like this happen?' Begetting through the Spirit can come about only as a result of Jesus' crucifixion, resurrection, and ascension."

[19] See van den Bussche, p. 170.

[20] Phil 2:9 contains the only use of the verb ὑπερύψουν in the New Testament. In the Septuagint, it is used once in relation to God in Ps 97:9 (God is said to be "Very High"); in Dan 4:34, Nebuchadnezzar exalts the King of heaven; in Dan 11:12, the heart of the king of the south is exalted; and in Ps 37:35, it is the ungodly who is exalted and elevated.

[21] In this regard, Murphy-O'Connor writes: "the pattern of humiliation and exaltation also appears in the Servant Song . . . . Despite his degradation, the Servant 'shall be exalted and lifted up, and shall be very high'" (Isa 11:13)," pp. 45–46.

should confess that Jesus Christ is Lord"[22] (vv. 10–11). Therefore, this power was essentially God's prerogative in the Old Testament as the prophet Isaiah testifies: ". . . to me every knee shall bow, every tongue shall swear"[23] (Isa 45:23).

The characteristics provided from the observation of the Johannine texts appear equally as a subject of this text of Philippians: the lordship of Jesus as the result of his voluntary abasement is explicitly affirmed; it is the fruit of an act of God; a universal power is attached to it; the spatial nature of this elevation is also clearly marked.

The two Lukan occurrences (Acts 2:33 and 5:31) have their specificity in relation to those of John and to that of Philippians; this specificity resides in the addition of τῇ δεξιᾷ to the verb ὑψοῦν as a local circumstantial precision:

1. τῇ δεξιᾷ οὖν τοῦ θεοῦ ὑψωθείς / "Being therefore exalted at the right hand of God" (2:33)
2. ὕψωσεν τῇ δεξιᾷ αὐτοῦ / "[God] exalted him at his right hand" (5:31)

Luke is effectively the only one to put together in one proclamation the two expressions "exalted" and "at the right hand." In order to grasp the scope of this particularity of the author, first, it is useful to retrace the biblical genesis of the expression "at the right hand." At the end of this exercise, it will be a matter of seeing how the Jesus of Luke accedes to the dignity of this seating at the right hand of God and what the impact of this seating is. Thus, the rest of this chapter will shed light on the use that Luke makes of the verb ὑψοῦν. However, note that the study of the meaning and of the scope of the exaltation of the Christ was already detailed in the preceding chapter in the framework of the presentation of the verse and that it will be continued in the coming chapters. Chapter 5 will expose the christological impact and chapter 6, the ecclesiological impact.

---

[22] Bonnard, *Philippians*, p. 46, explains: "It is because Jesus is the *Kyrios* that only the name of Jesus is so powerful . . . . God elevated Jesus Christ in order that he becomes what he is now, the Lord of the universe."

[23] Bonnard, ibid., states: "The quotation of Isa 45:23 emphasizes the universal scope of this expression," i.e., the "name of Jesus."

2. "AT THE RIGHT HAND OF GOD" IN THE OLD AND NEW TESTAMENTS

Old Testament

In the Old Testament, the metaphorical use of "the right hand" in relation to God refers at the same time to two distinct and related semantic spheres: the activity of the right hand of God and the place at the right hand of God.[24]

> A. *The right hand of God*—an expression often shortened to "the right hand"—symbolizes, in the Old Covenant, divine power in all its forms. The supporting examples are multiple and varied. Thus, it is by his right hand that God created everything (Isa 48:13a), that he gave himself a people (Ps 80:16a), that he liberates this people from Egyptian oppression (Exod 15:6), but that he also corrects them (Ps 74:11), and that he promises to them future protection (Isa 62:8). By his right hand, he procures the victory to his messiah (Ps 20:7) and destroys the enemy (Ps 21:9–10). In the same way, he will protect the refugees (Ps 17:7) just as he will compensate for human destitution (Ps 63:9). The use of this image, the right hand of God, evokes so powerfully the omnipotence of God who controls the universe and against whom no power resists.
>
> B. The right hand is also considered as the favorable place: it is there that the Lord remains to defend the poor (Ps 109:31); likewise, one's presence at the right hand protects the individual from all evil (Pss 16:7–8; 121:5). It is also perceived as the place of honor. Thus, when Bathsheba is going to plead Adonijah's cause before King Solomon, he has her sit at his right hand (1Kgs 2:19; cf. Ps 45:10). But especially, the right hand for the king is the guarantee of salvation when the Lord invites one to sit there: "The Lord says to my lord, 'Sit at my right hand until I make your enemies your footstool'" (Ps 110:1). Thus, in making the king sit at his right hand, God authorizes him to reign.[25] This last Psalm will become the standard Psalm for the interpretation of the kingship of the Christ in the New Testament.

Two important ideas emerge from the present examination: (1) The right hand of God symbolizes, on the one hand, his omnipotence; (2) It is,

---

[24] See Grundmann, "δεξιός," *TDNT* 2:37ff.
[25] See Dahood, pp. 112 ff.; Osty and Trinquet, pp. 300–301.

on the other hand, the place of honor, the guarantee of power for His messiah.

New Testament

The General Uses of the Term

The term "δεξιός" is found 54 times in the New Testament. More than half of the occurrences directly concern the exalted Christ. These will most obviously hold our attention. However, notably in the other uses, the term continues to denote priority, importance, favor. Thus, so it is when it is a question of determining or qualifying a part of the human body, e.g., right eye (Matt 5:29), right cheek (Matt 5:39), right hand (Matt 6:3), etc. It is also from the right side of the small boat that the disciples will be invited to throw out the net (John 21:6). The right hand designates again a place of dignity—the Angel of the Lord in the Holy of holies (Luke 1:11), the angel at the tomb (Mark 16:5)—and of particular favor since at the last judgment, the good will be placed at the right hand, Matthew writes (25:33).

The epithet δεξιός manifestly confers a merited value on the object that it qualifies. However, here, it is not a matter of a typical New Testament use of the term; on the contrary, it plays identical roles in Judaism, Rabbinic use, Hellenism, etc.[26] However, there is a new use when it serves to describe the post-resurrection position of Jesus.

First, recall that the seating at the right hand of God as a descriptive concept of the Resurrected One's status seems to be, very early on, a universal acknowledgment at the heart of the primitive church, as diverse testimonies attest.[27]

---

[26] On the symbolism of the right hand in ancient times, see Gourgues, *À la droite de Dieu*, pp. 38ff.

[27] Note the view defended at the beginning of the twentieth century by J. Weiss, *Das Urchristentum* [*Early Christianity*], p. 19ff. and 56ff., and by Bertram, "Die Himmelfahrt Jesu von Kreuze aus und der Blaube an seine Auferstehung," *Festgabe für A. Deissmann*, pp. 187–207 (according to Dupont, *Nouvelles études sur les Actes des Apôtres*, pp. 211ff.). According to them, the belief in the glorification would have preceded that of the resurrection. This would be the conviction that Jesus had entered into his glory, which would have led to the formulation of the belief in the resurrection. Hahn, pp. 129–35, is justly opposed to this vision of things, holding to the contrary that the belief in the resurrection was the immediate fruit of the disciples' experience. However, he probably was wrong to claim that the belief in the lordship of the Christ has been formulated, in the light of Psalm 110:1, in order to explain the delay of Parousia. I rather suggest that it was the pouring out of the Spirit that was proposed as the answer to this problem and that the belief in the lordship of Christ is associated

At this stage, we will consider, in a general manner at first, the various occurrences throughout the New Testament literature—with the exception of the Lukan occurrences. This first exercise will allow us to note simply the solid anchor of the primitive faith in the lordship of the Christ. Then we will study, in a deeper way, the facts of Luke-Acts in the light of the texts explaining the ascension, thus revealing the Lukan lines of understanding of the exaltation.

The Right Hand in Relation to Exaltation in Non-Lukan New Testament Authors

Romans 8:34 is the only case in the undisputed Pauline epistles where the exaltation of the Christ is found expressed in terms of being "at the right hand of God." Even if the theme is not particularly Pauline, the affirmation in Romans is, nevertheless, firm and unequivocal: "Who is to condemn? It is Christ Jesus, who died, yes, who was raised, who is at the right hand of God [ὃς καί ἐστιν ἐν δεξιᾷ τοῦ θεοῦ], who indeed intercedes for us" (Rom 8:34).[28]

---

with the belief in the resurrection; for the experience of the lordship, rightly so, goes back certainly to the beginning of the community. Loader believes that even if Ps 110:1 was applied early on to the Resurrected One, this seating, from the beginning, should be considered from an eschatological perspective only (p. 205). According to him, the fusion of Ps 110:1 and Dan 7:13, as it appears in certain cases (Luke 22:69; Acts 7:55–56), should support this hypothesis, the role of the son of Man being associated with the judgment. This point is much more plausible, he says, "when one considers that sitting upon a throne, ruling, and being an instrument of judgment are closely associated in apocalyptic as indeed also in the kingship ideology generally." The role of Jesus, before having been perceived as Lord, first, would have been that of intercessor only, as the following verses would let it be understood: Rom 8:34 and Heb 2:18; 4:14–16; 7:25, and probably Acts 2:33; 5:31, and 7:55ff., states Loader (pp. 205ff.). I do not share this point of view but believe, rather, that it is precisely the experience of the lordship of the Christ with its effects that had to sustain the new faith. The enlightenment of this christological fact, with the help of Ps 110:1, would come second, as a support of the proclamation already made of the exaltation of the Christ. This point of view was defended, against Hahn, by Vielhauer, "Zur Frage der christologische Hoheitstiteln," col., 576–79; Conzelmann, *Théologie du Nouveau Testament*, p. 81; Thüsing (according to Dupont, *Nouvelles études sur les Actes des Apôtres*, p. 215). As for Dupont, ibid., p. 294, he is of the opinion "that at the beginning, the image of the seating at the right hand of God was applied to the Pascal event itself," for he says, it defines an essential dimension, "the Easter event [not being] simply the resurrection, in the sense of the leaving of a tomb: it is at the same time, and also very fundamentally, the entrance of the Christ into his glory."

[28] The translation of this verse is difficult. As Leenhardt, p. 135, explains it, many believe it is necessary to translate, following v. 33, by the interrogative form each one

This passage, grouping into a single proclamation the death, resurrection, sitting at the right hand of God and interceding for us,[29] attests to the unique situation of the Christ in his relationship to God. The relative pronoun ὅς that punctuates the sentence—ὅς καί ἐστιν ἐν δεξιᾷ τοῦ θεοῦ, ὅς καὶ ἐντυγχάνει ὑπὲρ ἡμῶν / *who is at the right hand of God, who indeed intercedes for us*—accentuates the force of the christological assertions that it introduces. But this relation must be seen in a "functional" perspective as it is turned toward human beings.[30] The context (vv. 31–39) rightly aims to make the believers conscious of the security that they enjoy, since they have the Christ as defender-intercessor. Paul evokes the power with which the Christ is endowed in order to establish his argument. They get their security from the fact that the Christ occupies the divine throne.[31]

In the New Testament texts other than Paul's, the theme returns more often, especially in Hebrews. However, note the example of Eph 1:20 where the "seating at the right hand" is also explicitly affirmed as sequential to the resurrection, and stated in the same terms of Psalm 110:1: "... according to the working of his great power. God put this power to work in Christ when he raised him from the dead and seated him at his right hand in the heavenly places" (Eph 1:19a–20). In the following verses (21–23), the author describes with great clarity and precision the infinite scope of this seating of the Christ at the right hand of God:[32]

---

of the members of v. 34 (it is thus found in the Jerusalem Bible). The meaning, nevertheless, remains the same and the theme that interests us is not affected.

[29] Here, Paul would lean on the christological formula, as Barrett suggests, *Romans*, p. 173. He explains: "This is suggested by the parallel participles (died – was raised) and by the balanced relative clauses." See also Käsemann, *Romans*, p. 248; Dunn, "Jesus, Flesh and Spirit: An Exposition of Romans I. 3–4," p. 40.

[30] See Gourgues, *À la droite de Dieu*, p. 49.

[31] This is how the commentators interpret it, among whom are Murray, p. 329: "The apostle's appeal to the exalted glory, authority and dominion is related directly to the assurance of the security belonging to the elect of God"; also Wilckens, *Der Brief an die Römer*, p. 175: "Der erhöhte Christus dagegen hält den Seinen als den Auserwählten Gottes ihren Platz in der zukünftigen Wirklichkeit des vollendeten Heils gegen alle Infragestellung frei und garantiert so als Auferstandener die endzeitliche Wahrheit und Geltung ihrer Befreiung von der Macht von Sünde, Gesetz und Tod die er durch seinen Tod, für sie erwirkt hat." ["The exalted Christ, in contrast, reserves a place for those who belong to him as the chosen ones of God in the future reality of the accomplished salvation, against any questioning. Thus, he, as the Risen One, guarantees the eschatological truth and the validity of their redemption from the power of sin, law, and death, which he obtained for them through his death."]

[32] See Phil 2:10–11. On the subject of Eph 1:20, Schnackenburg remarks that no mention of the cross is found. He points out: "Es geht dem Verf. vor allem um die Ein-

- He is "far above all rule and authority and power and dominion, and every name that is named, not only in this age but also in the age to come" (v. 21)

- God "has put all things under his feet" (v. 22a rendering of Ps 8:7)

- He has made him the head over all things for the church (v. 22b)

First Peter 3:22 describes the superiority of Christ in this sense as well, but less elaborately: "[Jesus Christ] who has gone into heaven and is at the right hand of God with angels, authorities, and powers made subject to him." In the same way, Colossians 3:1, exhorting Christians resurrected with the Christ to seek those things above, points out that it is clearly "above" that the Christ is found "seated at the right hand of God."

The proclamation of the kingship of the Christ is also explicit in Hebrews. First, in verse 1:3, in evoking Ps 110:1, the author affirms that the Son, "when he had made purification for sins, sat down at the right hand of the Majesty on high."[33] Then, he defines the scope of that elevation: "Having become as much superior to angels as the name he has inherited is more excellent than theirs" (v. 4). Verses 5 and following develop with strong arguments the scope of this superiority of the Son over the angels, using every in-depth scriptural proof. The author enriches his proof with a series of antithetical comparisons between the Christ and the angels.[34] These comparisons are presented in inclusion between verses 5 and 13, verses which ask the same question: "To which of the angels did God ever say . . . ?"

The question, posed the first time (Heb 1:5), is followed by quotations designed to support the antithetical relationship between the angels

---

setzung Christi "zur Rechten Gottes," die für ihn mit dem ganzen Urchristentum die Herrscherstellung und bleibende Herrschaft Christi begründet, eben aus der Macht Gottes, der durch seinen Christus herrscht" (*Der Brief an die Epheser*, p. 75). ["The author is primarily concerned about the installation of Christ 'at the right hand of God,' which, together with all of primitive Christianity, explains the ruler position and permanent sovereignty of Christ, which comes from the power of God, who rules through his Christ."]

[33] In Hebrews, the priestly dimension is obviously highlighted; the Christ is the high priest who accomplished all purification. But the kingly dimension is also very accentuated. In fact, the kingly priesthood of the Christ is proclaimed in this epistle.

[34] On this subject, see Vanhoye, pp. 69–74.

and the Christ: Ps 2:7 (Heb 1:5a); 2 Sam 7:14 (1:5b); Deut 32:43 (1:6b); Ps 104:4 (1:7); Ps 45:7–8 (1:8–9); Isa 34:4 (1:10–12a); Ps 102:26–28 (1:12b). Finally, this tight argument finishes at v. 13b with the quotation of Ps 110:1, which constitutes the height. This height is particularly well-marked by the repetition of the opening question: "But to which of the angels has he ever said . . . ?" (v. 13a). Then, the quotation of Ps 110:1 follows: "Sit at my right hand until I make your enemies a footstool for your feet" (v. 13b).

In Hebrews 8:1, the author reiterates the affirmation of the kingly priesthood of the Christ with the support of the development which follows (always in reference to Ps 110:1): "Now the main point in what we are saying is this: we have such a high priest, one who is seated at the right hand of the throne of the Majesty in the heavens."

In 10:12–13[35] and 12:2, the themes contained in 1:3, 13 are repeated, namely the themes of the sacrifice of the Christ for sins and his seating at the right hand of God. It is the kenosis, Jesus's attitude of emptying himself, which merits his exaltation.[36]

These examples taken from the epistles bring out the power and the authority linked to the seating of the Christ at the right hand of God, but they also emphasize the location of this seating.

The gospels do not offer affirmations on the exaltation of the Christ as explicit as those in the epistles. That can be explained by the fact that the gospels tend to present Jesus in his earthly activity. But the concept, nevertheless, comes to light in certain passages. Thus, in Matthew 19:28, without the right hand being mentioned, we read: "At the renewal of all things when the Son of Man is seated on the throne of his glory . . . ."

However, in Matthew 22:43–44 (and parallels), we find the announcement of the lordship of the Messiah, and once again, supported by the quotation of Ps 110:1: "He said to them, 'How is it then that David by the Spirit calls him Lord, saying "The Lord said to my Lord, 'Sit at my right hand . . . .'"' In Matthew 26:64 (and parallels),[37] in the context of the

---

[35] Bruce, *Hebrews*, pp. 23ff., offers a good commentary on this verse. It shows the unique character of the sacrifice of the Christ in contrast with those of the Old Testament, the value of this sacrifice being reinforced by the repetition of the language of Ps 110:1. The Christ can sit on the throne, for he has, once for all, completed the sacrifice hitherto being left unaccomplished.

[36] See Phil 2:8.

[37] The parallel verses in Luke (22:69–70) include important nuances (in relation to Mark especially) to which we will return. Note that in Mark 14:62 the announced reign is eschatological, whereas in all the other cases mentioned in the NT, the seating

passion, Jesus answers the high priest who questions him about being the Messiah: "From now on you will see the Son of Man seated at the right hand of Power and coming on the clouds of heaven."[38]

In light of this overview, it is apparent that, very early on, Christian hermeneutics applied Ps 110:1[39] to the Resurrected One. The presumption can be made that this application had to be, at the same time, the expression and the argument to support the conviction, birthed from the experience of the presence and the action of the Christ at the heart of the church, that this one was the Chosen One of God and that he fulfilled (in an unexpected manner, albeit) the Jewish hope of seeing a son of David sit at the right hand of God. Also acknowledged was the cosmic scope of this reign, the domination of the Christ over all the earthly and heavenly powers being affirmed with insistence (Eph 1:21–23; 1 Pet 3:22; Phil 2:10–11; also 1 Cor 15:24–28). However, what it is also very important to note is the spatial dimension that the New Testament language conceals about the exaltation (a dimension very present in the Old Testament language). This manner of perceiving and expressing the exaltation of the Christ to lordship corresponds to what Luke is going to visualize in his accounts of the ascension.

3. "EXALTED AT THE RIGHT HAND OF GOD" IN LUKE-ACTS

A correct understanding of the originality of the Lukan affirmations (Luke 22:69; Acts 2:33; 5:31; 7:55–56) on the exaltation of the Christ to the right hand of God necessitates that these be placed in the light of the ascension accounts (Luke 24:50–53 and Acts 1:9–11). The remainder of this chapter

---

at the right hand of God is associated with Jesus's temporary lordship activity. See Loader, p. 205.

[38] Here is a fusion of Ps 110:1 and Dan 7:13.

[39] According to Loader, p. 199, there is no firm evidence that Ps 110 had been applied to the Messiah in Judaism before having been used in Christianity. He explains that the proofs of such a usage date to the second half of the third century after Jesus. But he believes, nevertheless, following the example of Hay, pp. 19ff., that in spite of the lack of evidence, the psalm would have actually been used in Judaism in reference to the Messiah and that the Christian application to Jesus would have been inspired by this usage. On the subject of the use of Psalm 110:1 in Christianity, see also Daniélou, *Études d'exégèse judéo-chrétienne*; Gourgues, *À la droite de Dieu*; Dupont, *Nouvelles études sur les Actes des Apôtres*; Callan, "Psalm 110:1 and the Origin of the Expectation that Jesus Will Come Again," pp. 622–36.

will emphasize the interpretative value of these accounts in relation to the Lukan texts on the exaltation, more particularly the text of Acts 2:33.

The Ascension: Luke 24:50–53 and Acts 1:9–11

The assertions related to the seating on the heavenly throne presuppose the return of the Christ to God. This is a reality that the New Testament authors do not miss affirming: John 20:17 (ἀναβέβηκα / *has ascended*); 1 Tim 3:16 (ἀνελήμφθη / *taken up*); Eph 4:10 (ἀναβάς / *ascended*); etc.[40] But Luke is the only one to describe this return as an event: Luke 24:50–53 and Acts 1:9–11. Thus, it is important to look for the underlying intention generally attributed to Lukan writing in the creation of these accounts. It is this last point that must first be verified.

The first step of verification of the writing style of the two ascension accounts is based upon the analysis of the style and the vocabulary of each of the accounts.

Luke 24:50–53

⁵⁰ Ἐξήγαγεν δὲ αὐτοὺς (ἔξω) ἕως πρὸς Βηθανίαν, καὶ ἐπάρας τὰς χεῖρας αὐτοῦ εὐλόγησεν αὐτούς /
Then he led them out as far as Bethany, and, lifting up his hands, he blessed them.

⁵¹ καὶ ἐγένετο ἐν τῷ εὐλογεῖν αὐτὸν αὐτοὺς διέστη ἀπ' αὐτῶν καὶ ἀνεφέρετο εἰς τὸν οὐρανόν. /
While he was blessing them, he withdrew from them and was carried up into heaven.

⁵² Καὶ αὐτοὶ προσκυνήσαντες αὐτὸν ὑπέστρεψαν εἰς Ἰερουσαλὴμ μετὰ χαρᾶς μεγάλης /
And they worshiped him, and returned to Jerusalem with great joy

⁵³ καὶ ἦσαν διὰ παντὸς ἐν τῷ ἱερῷ εὐλογοῦντες τὸν θεόν. /
and they were continually in the temple blessing God.

Textual Criticism
This text has a textual criticism problem in the main part of the account, referring to the affirmation καὶ ἀνεφέρετο εἰς τὸν οὐρανόν / *and he was carried up into heaven* (v. 51). This key element of the account is absent

---

[40] For the list of New Testament passages evoking the glorification or the ascension of the Christ and for the terminology used to this end, see Metzger, "The Ascension of Jesus Christ," *Historical and Literary Studies*, p. 80.

from Sinaiticus 01* and from the Western text (05, it[d,a,b,e,ff2,j,l*], geo[1], Aug[1/3]). On the other hand, it is attested by p[75], 01[c], 02, 03, 017, 019, 032, 033, 037, 038, 041, 044, 063, f[1], f[13], 28, 33, 565, 700, 892, 1009, 1010, 1071, 1079, 1195, 1216, 1230, 1241, 1242, 1253, 1344, 1365, 1546, 1646, 2148, 2174, Byz Lect 1[185m], it[aur,c,f,q1], vg, syr[p,h,pal], cop[sa,bo,arm,geo2], Diates, Aug[2/3], Cyril.

I believe along with the great majority of the exegetes that the reading makes up an integral part of the original text. The most currently evoked argument to explain its omission from the above-mentioned witnesses is the desire to harmonize the supposed conflicting dates of Luke 24:49, 51 and Acts 1:3, 9–11.[41] Consequently, its omission is more easily explained than its insertion, which speaks in favor of the authenticity of the reading.[42] The article of E. J. Epp, "The Ascension in Textual Tradition of Luke-Acts,"[43] shows, moreover, that the Western text has the tendency to reduce the objectifying elements of the passages on the ascension: (1) it omits Luke 24:51; (2) it eliminates the verb ἀνελήμφθη ("was taken away") of Acts 1:2, but adds καὶ ἐκέλευσε κηρύσσειν τὸ εὐαγγέλιον, in such a way that one must read this verse as follows: "up to the day when [omitted: "he was taken away"], after having given through the Holy Spirit his instructions to the apostles that he had chosen and to whom he had commanded to go and preach the gospel"; (3) it modifies Acts 1:9 to a point such that without verse 11, one could not deduce Jesus's ascension; it omits βλεπόντων αὐτῶν ("as they were looking up at the sky") and it replaces the verb ἐπαίρειν ("carried away on high," "lifted up") by

---

[41] This is the explanation given by Marshall, *The Gospel of Luke*, p. 909; Sabourin, p. 385; van Stempvoort, p. 36; R. H. Smith, p. 129; Fitzmyer, *The Gospel according to Luke (x–xxiv)*, p. 1590. In his article, "The Ascension of Christ and Pentecost," pp. 416–17, Fitzmyer explains the origin of the controversy on the subject of the authenticity of 51b. It would go back to the publication of the criticism of the New Testament by Wescott and Hort, *The New Testament in the Original Greek*, in which reservations were expressed as to the authenticity of the reading, because of its absence from Sinaiticus and from the Western text. Westcott and Hort had qualified this passage of "Western non-interpolation" (i.e., an "Alexandrian interpolation," explains Metzger, *Historical and Literary Studies*, p. 77). It is in these terms, "Western non-interpolation," that it is referred to ever since. But, with the discovery of the papyrus of Bodmer XIV (P[75]), since 1961, Fitzmyer, the Nestle-Aland and the United Bible Societies Greek New Testament no longer express any reservation on their option for the long reading (although before, it would always be inserted between brackets in the text).

[42] See Fuller, *The Formation of the Resurrection Narratives*, p. 122; also van Stempvoort, p. 36.

[43] Epp, pp. 134ff.

ἀπαίρειν ("taken away," "removed"). This rearrangement yields a nuance as to the role of the cloud, which can in this case only steal Jesus from the disciples' sight. Thus, only in verse 11 would the ascension be explicit. Once more, it must be pointed out that, even in this verse, the second εἰς τὸν οὐρανόν / *into heaven* is omitted.

Finally, explains Fitzmyer,[44] the affirmation in Acts 1:2, "up to the day when he was taken away," an affirmation which precedes, of course, the ascension account of Acts 1:9–11, commands a prior assertion of Jesus's ascension to heaven.[45]

Add to the arguments in favor of the long reading others also enumerated by Metzger in a list which appears in *A Textual Commentary on the Greek New Testament*:[46] (1) the rhythm of the account requires the presence of this clause;[47] (2) if the short reading is original, how then to account for the presence of καὶ ἀνεφέρετο . . . / *and he was carried* . . . in a wide range of so many diversified witnesses, beginning with P^{75}? (3) if the clause is an addition, it should have been expected that the scribe had used the same verb as in Acts 1:2, that is ἀναλαμβάνειν / *to take up* instead of ἀναφέρειν / *to take*; (4) the omission can be the fact of a homoeoarcton (KAIA . . . KAIA . . .) or of a voluntary excision in order to stop the apparent contradiction with Acts 1:3–11 on the subject of the 40 days.

---

[44] Fitzmyer, *The Gospel according to Luke*, p. 1590.

[45] Fitzmyer's opinion is contested by Parsons, "The Text of Acts 1:2 Reconsidered," p. 59. Parsons believes, on the contrary, that "the evidence of Acts 1:2, properly understood, supports, rather than mitigates against, reading the shorter text at Luke 24:51." Parsons is, in effect, of the opinion that ἀνελήμφθη [*he was taken up*] of Acts 1:2, just as ἀνάλημψις [*ascension*] in Luke 9:51, does not refer to Jesus's ascension "but to Jesus' entire journey back to God (burial, resurrection, departure). Exaltation in the context of the Third Gospel does not refer to the ascension" (p. 70). As for Metzger, who favors the long reading, he writes: ". . . in the present passage, it should be noted that even if one prefers the shorter form of text, which makes no explicit mention of the ascension, the description of the joyful return to Jerusalem on the part of the disciples after Jesus left them seems to suggest a parting of more than ordinary significance" (*Historical and Literary Studies* p. 78). A. D. Martin, "The Ascension of Christ," p. 326, expressed a similar opinion.

[46] Metzger, *A Textual Commentary*, pp. 190–91.

[47] On this subject, Guillaume explains: "On strictly the literary plan, the suppression of καὶ ἀνεφέρετο εἰς τὸν οὐρανόν [*and he was carried up into heaven*] would imbalance the text: the section Luke 24:50–53 would be reduced to a simple apparition scene where the actions and gestures of Jesus and the disciples, the distancing towards Bethany, the blessing, the adoration, the return to the temple, would no longer be understood" (p. 226).

Thus, it seems that all of these arguments, added to the weight of the external criticism, does not leave any doubt as to the authenticity of the reading retained by Nestle-Aland. The fact of the ascension is thus attested in Luke 24:50–53.

Finally, in verse 52, the absence of προσκυνήσαντες αὐτόν / *they worshipped him* in certain manuscripts: 05, it, sy⁵: the omission is most likely deliberate in view of a better concordance with the short reading of v. 51.[48]

Literary Analysis

Do the style and the vocabulary of Luke 24:50–53 reflect Lukan literary art? The verb which opens the account, ἐξάγειν (ἐξήγαγεν / *he led*), is almost exclusively used by Luke in the New Testament: once in Mark 15:20; once in John 10:3; once in Heb 8:9; nine times in Luke-Acts (Luke 24:50; Acts 5:19; 7:36, 40; 12:17; 13:17; 16:37, 39; 21:38). It is the same verb that the Septuagint uses to signify the intervention of God in the matter of taking the people out of Egypt (Exod 32:1); an episode that Luke evokes, in fact, three times (Acts 7:36, 40; 13:17). Luke also uses the verb with the meaning of "take out."

The term ἕως / *as far as* is used a lot by the synoptics in general (comparatively little in the Johannine and epistolary literature). However, Luke is the only one to use it with a proposition of place:[49] ἕως πρός (Luke 24:50), ἕως ἐπί (Acts 17:14), ἕως ἔξω (21:5), ἕως εἰς (26:11). It is probably a matter of a use inspired by the Septuagint:[50] ἕως πρός (Gen 38:1 and Ezek 48:1).

The verb ἐπαίρειν / *to lift* is also greatly used by Luke: six times in Luke, five times in Acts, as opposed to once in Matthew; four times in John; twice in 1 Corinthians; once in 1 Timothy; thus, eleven out of nineteen times in the New Testament. In addition, the other Lukan uses, with the exception of the present, have as an objective complement, either the eyes (Luke 6:20; 16:23; 18:13), the voice (Luke 11:27; Acts 2:14; 14:11; 22:22), or the head (Luke 21:28). Raising the hand in a gesture of blessing does not have a parallel in the NT (in 1 Tim 2:8, hands are raised, but it is for prayer). The gesture corresponds to a priestly rite found in Lev 9:22 and Sir 50:20. In this regard, Menoud objects that the priestly character of

---

[48] See Metzger, *A Textual Commentary*, p. 190.

[49] See Marshall, *The Gospel of Luke*, p. 909; Fitzmyer, *The Gospel according to Luke*, p. 1589; Jeremias, *Die Sprache des Lukas–evangeliums*, p. 323.

[50] See Fitzmyer, *The Gospel according to Luke*, p. 1589.

the Christ is not a Lukan theme and that v. 50b would be written in the liturgical style of the second century.[51] Nevertheless, most scholars believe that Luke deliberately conferred a particular nature to this gesture, visualizing it especially on the literary basis of Sir 50.[52]

This scene of Sirach presents the high priest blessing the nation: he raises his hands and blesses the people gathered who prostrate themselves: "and they bowed down in worship a second time, to receive the blessing from the Most High" (Sir 50:21).

P. A. van Stempvoort is of the opinion that the blessing of the priest in view of a "heart filled with joy" (Sir 50:23, εὐφροσύνην καρδίας) finds its counterpart in Luke 24:52, in the χαρὰ μεγάλη / *great joy* of the disciples.[53] But he believes that there is another important reason why Luke would have wanted to end his gospel with a priestly blessing. This final blessing would take up the one unfinished by Zacharias at the exit of the holy of holies at the beginning of the gospel, when he was struck with muteness.[54] The liturgical nature of the passage is much more emphasized by the mention of the temple in v. 53: ". . . and they were continually in the temple blessing God."

Note the fact that the verb εὐλογεῖν / *to bless* is also very Lukan. Of all the NT authors, Luke is the one who uses it the most (16 times; in second place, Hebrews, seven times; Matthew and Mark, each five times). As

---

[51] Menoud, p. 80.

[52] Van Stempvoort, pp. 34–35, describes this perspective particularly well. Lohfink, *Die Himmelfahrt Jesu,* pp. 167–69, also adopts and develops this point of view. In the same vein, Parsons, *The Departure of Jesus in Luke-Acts,* pp. 54–55. Also: Schlier, pp. 92–93; Grundmann, *Das Evangelium nach Lukas*; Fitzmyer, *The Gospel according to Luke,* p. 1590; Sabourin, p. 386; Ernst, pp. 672–73; Dillon, pp. 220ff. Dillon, however, not only establishes relationships in terms of the form of the texts, but also in terms of the function. He writes (p. 180): "The scenes have the same function of a solemn, impressive conclusion in each instance; and not just a literary conclusion at that, since each brings *sacred history's course to a climax* affecting the author and his readers in the present." Parsons, *The Departure of Jesus in Luke-Acts,* p. 55, contests this point, believing, as do van Stempvoort and Lohfink, that the parallel must be limited to the form only.

[53] Van Stempvoort, "Interpretation of the Ascension," p. 35, writes: "The conclusion of Luke's Gospel is one of the most beautiful 'Septuagintalisms.'"

[54] Equally of this opinion is R. H. Smith, p. 129. On the other hand, Dillon, p. 222, following Ernst, p. 612, rejects this hypothesis. He considers that nothing in the twenty-two other chapters of the gospel, any more than in Acts, establishes this opinion. He considers rather that, in Luke 24, the theme of prophecy is central, whereas the priesthood is only implicit.

to the periphrasis ἐγένετο / *it happened*, it is also Lukan.⁵⁵ The verb διίστημι / *part, leave* is only used by Luke (Luke 22:59; 24:51; Acts 27:28). He marks, here, the separation of Jesus from the disciples.⁵⁶

The verb ἀναφέρειν has a concrete connotation ("to bring" or "to take"⁵⁷), which harmonizes very well with the Lukan style.⁵⁸ It would unlikely be from the hand of a transcriber since, on the one hand, its use is very rare (10 times in the entire NT) and on the other hand, it is the verb ἀναλαμβάνειν / *to take up* that became the descriptive term of the ascension⁵⁹ to which testify Mark 16:19; 1 Tim 3:16; also Acts 1:2, 11, 22. Finally, the singular form in εἰς τὸν οὐρανόν / *into heaven* is also Lukan;⁶⁰ in two works, Luke uses the plural form only six times as opposed to 53 times for the singular form.

The verb προσκυνεῖν / *to worship*, which is not part of Lukan language (it is frequent in Johannine literature), nevertheless, has its pertinence in the present context where it serves to mark the unique nature of the scene. And the fact that the scene can effectively be enlightened by Sirach 50:20ff. constitutes in itself a support in the choice of this verb. The great joy of the disciples becomes then very legitimate,⁶¹ owing to the fact that they recognized Jesus (bowing down before him).

Finally, the presence of the disciples in the temple ends the gospel as it began: in the temple. The entire text thus undeniably carries the Lukan style. Jeremias does not hesitate to qualify it as entirely editorial.⁶² The

---

⁵⁵ See Jeremias, *Die Sprache des Lukas*, p. 323.

⁵⁶ On this subject, Jeremias, ibid., writes: ". . . ist es kennzeichnend für Lukas, daß er das Entschwinden des Erscheinenden vermerkt→1,38 . . . ." [". . . it is characteristic of Luke that he makes reference to the ascension details . . . ."]

⁵⁷ Bauer, *Greek-English Lexicon*, ἀναφέρω 1.

⁵⁸ See van Stempvoort, "Interpretation of the Ascension," p. 36.

⁵⁹ See Marshall, *The Gospel of Luke*, p. 909.

⁶⁰ See Jeremias, *Die Sprache des Lukas*, p. 323.

⁶¹ Contrary to what Menoud says, "Remarques sur les texts de l'ascension dans Luc–Actes," p. 80: "In verse 52, the χαρὰ μεγάλη [*great joy*] which animates the disciples is not motivated by anything; Jesus has just been taken away. The ascension as such would rather have been a sad motive."

⁶² Jeremias, *Die Sprache des Lukas*, p. 323: "Im V. 50–3 liessen sich keine Spuren der Tradition erkennen; dieser abschliessende Himmelfahrtsbericht wird daher lukanische Composition sein." ["In vv. 50–53 no traces of tradition are apparent; therefore, this final ascension report can be considered as Lukan composition."] Fitzmyer, *The Gospel according to Luke*, p. 1587, for his part, emphasizes well the importance of this text when he writes: "This episode not only forms the end of the Lukan Gospel, but it is the climax of the whole latter part of it, from the crucial chapter 9 on." See also

demonstration is clear: this text is Luke's and it constitutes the end of the gospel.⁶³

Acts 1:9–11

⁹Καὶ ταῦτα εἰπὼν βλεπόντων αὐτῶν ἐπήρθη καὶ νεφέλη ὑπέλαβεν αὐτὸν ἀπὸ τῶν ὀφθαλμῶν αὐτῶν. /
When he had said this, as they were watching, he was lifted up, and a cloud took him out of their sight.

¹⁰καὶ ὡς ἀτενίζοντες ἦσαν εἰς τὸν οὐρανὸν πορευομένου αὐτοῦ, καὶ ἰδοὺ ἄνδρες δύο παρειστήκεισαν αὐτοῖς ἐν ἐσθήσεσι λευκαῖς, /
While he was going and they were gazing up toward heaven, suddenly two men in white robes stood by them.

¹¹οἳ καὶ εἶπαν· ἄνδρες Γαλιλαῖοι, τί ἑστήκατε [ἐμ]βλέποντες εἰς τὸν οὐρανόν; οὗτος ὁ Ἰησοῦς ὁ ἀναλημφθεὶς ἀφ' ὑμῶν εἰς τὸν οὐρανὸν οὕτως ἐλεύσεται ὃν τρόπον ἐθεάσασθε αὐτὸν πορευόμενον εἰς τὸν οὐρανόν.⁶⁴ /

Marshall, *The Gospel of Luke*, p. 907; Lake, *The Beginnings of Christianity*, vol. 5, pp. 3–4, affirmed: "There is nothing un-Lukan in the language of Luke 24:50–3" (quoted by Menoud, "Remarques sur les texts de l'ascension dans Luc-Actes" p. 80).

⁶³ Menoud, "Remarques sur les texts de l'ascension dans Luc-Actes," pp. 76ff., had held that the third Gospel and the book of Acts formed one and the same work and that Acts 1:6 was directly related to Luke 24:49. The work would have been split into two at the moment of the formation of the canon. Luke 24:50–53 would have then been added as the introduction to Acts. Menoud would align then his position to that of Lake, *The Beginnings*, pp. 1–4, and Sahlin, pp. 11–18. Trocmé, *Le "livre des Actes" et l'histoire*, pp. 30–34, also took up this hypothesis as his own. Menoud, however, changed his mind and in an article that he wrote eight years later, "During Forty Days (Acts 1:3)" (reprinted in *Jésus-Christ et la foi*, pp. 110–17), he refutes the idea that Luke-Acts had been, at the origin, one and the same work. This thesis finds fewer and fewer followers.

⁶⁴ This account does not have any major problems of textual criticism. Nevertheless, there are some divergences between the Alexandrian text and the Western text. In v. 9, for example, the Western version (05, it^d, cop^sa, aug.) contains: εἰπόντος αὐτοῦ νεφέλη ὑπέλαβεν αὐτὸν καὶ ἀπήρθη. The other version (the one reproduced above) has the support of all the other manuscripts (with an inversion of the terms in the Vaticanus: εἰπὼν αὐτῶν βλεπόντων). Recall also that the second occurrence of εἰς τὸν οὐρανόν (v. 11) is absent from the Western text (05) and from others of the same family (242, 326, 2495, 1⁶⁰, it^{d, gig}, cop^{bo, mss}, aug.). All the other witnesses otherwise very well attest it. One can suppose that it would belong to the original text, Luke wanting, no doubt, to mark the insistence by this quadruple repetition of the expression. For a detailed discussion of the changes appearing in codex Bezae, see Delebecque, "Ascension et Pentecôte dans les Actes des Apôtres selon le codex Bezae," pp. 79–82.

They said, "Men of Galilee, why do you stand looking up toward heaven? This Jesus, who has been taken up from you into heaven, will come in the same way as you saw him go into heaven."

Literary Analysis[65]

The account of the ascension of Acts 1:9–11 is commonly accepted as Luke's writing.[66] One can hardly refer to the vocabulary to support this point of view for, in general, the terms used are also very current in the NT, with the exception of a few verbs. Ἀτενίζειν / *to gaze* is one of these verbs, for, of the 14 occurrences in the NT, 12 of them belong to Luke-Acts. Likewise ἀναλαμβάνειν / *to take up*, which Luke uses eight times in 13 and of which three of the uses designate precisely the ascension of Jesus:

Acts 1:2
ἄχρι ἧς ἡμέρας ... ἀνελήμφθη. /
until the day ... He was taken up.

Acts 1:11
οὗτος ὁ Ἰησοῦς ὁ ἀναλημφθεὶς ἀφ' ὑμῶν εἰς τὸν οὐρανόν /
This Jesus who has been taken up from you into heaven

Acts 1:22
ἀρξάμενος ἀπὸ τοῦ βαπτίσματος Ἰωάννου ἕως τῆς ἡμέρας ἧς ἀνελήμφθη ἀφ' ἡμῶν /
beginning with the baptism of John, until the day that He was taken up from us

In the last example (1:22), note a similar formulation to that of v. 11, ἀνελήμφθη ... ἀφ' ἡμῶν / *taken up ... from us*.[67] Again note the presence of the verb ὑπολαμβάνειν / *to take up* (v. 9) which is repeated four times in Luke-Acts as opposed to one other time in the rest of the NT (in 3 John 8).

But these are the typical literary devices that must be especially considered. For example, here the tendency of the author to make the faith experience concrete is very pronounced. The visibility of the event is, in

---

[65] For a detailed study of the style and vocabulary of Acts 1:6–14, see Guillaume, pp. 239–48.

[66] See further on, footnote 72.

[67] Ἀνελήμφθη is also the descriptive term of Elijah's ascension in the Septuagint (2 Kgs 2:11).

fact, marked by a series of verbs—βλεπόντων / *to see* (v. 9), ἀτενίζοντες / *to gaze* (v. 10), [ἐμ]βλέποντες / *to look at* and ἐθεάσασθε / *to behold* (v. 11)—and by the periphrasis ἀπὸ τῶν ὀφθαλμῶν αὐτῶν / *out of their sight* (v. 9).[68] Furthermore, the choice of the verb ἐπαίρω (ἐπήρθη) / *to be lifted up*, a very realistic connotation, accentuates the concrete aspect of the scene.

One can, no doubt, detect another Lukan trait in the presentation of the heavenly beings. These two men in white clothing who come to interpret the event recall the scene at the tomb (Luke 24:4) where, again, these two men appear and explain to the women the meaning of the empty tomb (while in Matt 28:2, there is only mention of an angel and in Mark 16:5, of a young man). It is also typical of Luke to define his characters by a description of their clothing:

- Jesus is wearing an elegant robe [ἐσθῆτα λαμπράν] (Luke 23:11)
- Two men in dazzling clothes [ἐσθῆτι ἀστραπτούσῃ] (Luke 24:4)
- Two men in white robes [ἐσθήσεσι λευκαῖς] (Acts 1:10)
- A man [angel] in dazzling clothes [ἐσθῆτι λαμπρᾷ] (Acts 10:30)
- Herod put on his royal robes [ἐσθῆτα βασιλικήν] (Acts 12:21).

Besides, there are only three other mentions of the term ἐσθής / *clothes* in the rest of the NT (Jas 2:2[2x], 3).

Finally, other Lukan expressions can be found: καὶ ἰδού / *and behold*—in the style of the Septuagint—(24 times in Luke-Acts)[69] as well as the temporal ὡς meaning "like," "when"—equally as frequent in the Septuagint.[70] All of these indicators enable the recognition of the Lukan style in this account of the ascension, but it is the rest of the study that will confirm it with more precision.

Origin and Form of the Ascension Accounts

The exaltation as an experience of the lordship of the Christ finds its expression very early in the framework of the kerygmatic proclamations: Rom 1:3–4; 8:34; 14:9; Eph 1:19–20; 2:5–6; 4:8–10; Phil 2:9; Col 3:1; 1 Tim 3:16; Heb 1:3; 1 Pet 3:22; etc. But these proclamations do not require

---

[68] See Pesch, *Die Apostelgeschichte, Apg 1–12*, p. 72.
[69] See Wilson, "The Ascension: A Critique and an Interpretation," p. 269; Conzelmann, *Acts of the Apostles*, p. 7.
[70] See Haenchen, *The Acts of the Apostles*, p. 149, note 7; Conzelmann, *Acts*, p. 7.

at all the recognition of the existence of a tradition on the ascension of the Christ.[71]

On the contrary, no tradition, neither oral nor written, preceded the Lukan accounts.[72] Also there is no basis to Fuller's hypothesis that the central announcement of Luke 24:51—"and was carried up into heaven"—was the object of a primitive kerygmatic formula.[73] Such a

---

[71] This is the point of view that Lohfink defended, *Die Himmelfahrt Jesu: Untersuchungen*, pp. 81–97. He concluded (p. 95): "Nirgendwo finden sich auch nur die kleinsten Indizien einer sichtbaren Himmelfahrt beziehungsweise einer Entrückung, wie wir sie von Lukas her kennen." In another work, *Die Himmelfahrt Jesu: Erfindung oder Erfahrung*, p. 19, Lohfink explained: "Offensichtlich hat Lukas, und nicht schon die Tradition vor ihm, zum ersten mal von einer Entrückung Jesu vor den Augen der Jünger erzählt. Jedenfalls haben die ersten österlichen Zeugen noch nicht von einer Entrückung Jesu am Ende der Erscheinungen gesprochen; hätten sie es getan, sähen die ausserlukanischen Himmelfahrtstexte des Neuen Testamentes anders aus." ["Nowhere can be found even the smallest evidence of a visible Ascension or a rapture, as we know them from Luke." In another work, *Die Himmelfahrt Jesu: Erfindung oder Erfahrung*, p. 19, Lohfink explained: "Apparently it was Luke—and not the tradition before him—who first tells of a rapture of Jesus before the eyes of the disciples. In any case, the first witnesses of the resurrection did not yet speak of a rapture of Jesus at the end of his appearances to them; had they done so, the non-Lukan Ascension texts of the New Testament would look different."]

[72] Among the scholars who reject the idea of a pre-Lukan tradition, other than Lohfink, are Wilson, "The Ascension: A Critique and an Interpretation," p. 269; Fitzmyer, "The Ascension of Christ," pp. 420–21; van Stempvoort, "Interpretation of the Ascension," p. 39; Talbert, *Literary Patterns, Theological Themes and the Genre of Luke-Acts*, pp. 59–60, 112ff. A good number of scholars believe, however, that even if the actual form of the text comes from Luke, nevertheless, it would have been inspired by an already existing tradition. Among these scholars are Schneider, *Die Apostelgeschichte, Teil 1, 1:1–8:40*, pp. 208–11; Marshall, *The Gospel of Luke*, p. 908; Conzelmann, *Acts of the Apostles*, p. 7; Schille, "Die Himmelfahrt," p. 193, and *Die Apostelgeschichte des Lukas*, p. 73; Parsons, *The Departure of Jesus in Luke-Acts*, pp. 62–144; Bultmann, *History of the Synoptic Tradition*, p. 286; Dillon, p. 220; he considers that the evidence is too slight to support the existence of a tradition. If such a tradition could have existed, it is not Luke 24:50–53 that must be investigated, but Acts 1:8–11; see Fuller, p. 123, 128; according to Haenchen, the empty tomb, especially Luke 24:4, could have served as a model (p. 151); cf. also Roloff, p. 25, note 35; as for Sabourin, he believes that Luke "could have elaborated his account on an ancient tradition which related a significant and apparently final goodbye of the resurrected Christ to the gathered disciples" (p. 385). Finally, note the position of Metzger, *Historical and Literary Studies*, p. 86, who sees facts behind the account: the Christ would have really been lifted up before the disciples' eyes.

[73] Fuller, p. 123, explains his point of view as such: ". . . we think that Luke has deliberately composed this closing scene. But the central statement ("and was carried up into heaven") may well be based on a primitive keygmatic formula, belonging to the Palestinian Aramaic Christological stratum. According to this Christology the resur-

perspective is entirely a conjecture since it cannot be supported by any New Testament exposition. Not only does the New Testament provide no evidence to support Fuller's hypothesis, but, to the contrary, it presents many passages on the resurrection-exaltation. Further, as Fuller proposes, if the primitive community had conceptualized or schematized an event like the one of the assumption of the Christ, it would have resulted in an analogous and simultaneous narrative to the one relating to the apparitions.[74] The materialization of the assumption would surely have followed a similar course as that of the apparitions with which it would have been linked as a conclusion, and Luke, furthermore, would not be the only sacred writer to speak of it. Yet, such is not the case. We must then hold to the New Testament facts.

Neither is it to be believed that the accounts of the ascension were inspired by a worship tradition as, for example, Schille proposes.[75] These accounts are strictly Lukan and come to light perfectly in the theological framework of Luke-Acts, as will be shown. Nevertheless, for their construction, it appears uncontested that Luke was inspired by models of people being taken away to heaven already known in Jewish and Hellenistic biblical literature, as believe numerous scholars such as Schneider,[76] Pesch,[77] Weiser[78] and Roloff.[79] The most frequently cited examples are those of Enoch (Gen 5:24), Elijah (2 Kgs 2:11–12), Esdras (2 Esd 12:10–50), and Baruch (*2 Bar.* 76).[80]

---

rection of Jesus was at the same time his assumption (rather than his exaltation) into heaven." Fuller's vision could follow on the heels of Haenchen shown in note 72.

[74] This is how Dillon responds, p. 173: "The bipartite schema (of recognition and commissioning) is clearly well established in tradition, quite independently of Luke. On the other hand, in none of the (other) accounts . . . is the disappearance or departure of the Lord recorded."

[75] Schille, "Die Himmelfahrt," p. 193: "Die Himmelfahrtserzählung wäre eine Kultätiologie für eine Versammlung der Jerusalemer Gemeinde auf dem Ölberg am 40. Tag nach dem Passa gewesen, bei welcher man der Himmelfahrt gedachte." ["The Ascension story would have been a cult etiology for a meeting of the Jerusalem church on the Mount of Olives on the fortieth day after the Passover, on which the Ascension was commemorated."] Wilson overthrew Schille's hypothesis in his article already cited.

[76] Schneider, *Die Apostelgeschichte, Teil 1, 1:1–8:40*, pp. 208–9.

[77] Pesch, *Die Apostelgeschichte, Apg 1–12*, p. 72.

[78] Weiser, *Die Apostelgeschichte. Kapitel 1-12*, p. 62. Weiser believes that the most important sources of inspiration for Luke would be 2 Kgs 12:11–12 and Sir 48:9.

[79] Roloff, *Die Apostelgeschichte*, p. 25.

[80] See the list of numerous accounts of being taken away furnished by Schneider, *Die Apostelgeschichte, Teil 1, 1:1–8:40*, p. 208.

The study led by Guillaume[81] on the accounts of the ascension (a study based substantially on Lohfink's[82] research) brings out the similarities with these models as to the form. He quotes, for example, the end of *2 Enoch* 67, relating to Enoch's[83] being taken away to heaven:

> As Enoch had promised his people, the Lord sent darkness over the Earth and total darkness occurred and covered all the men who stood with Enoch. The angels came quickly, took Enoch and led him into the highest heaven. The Lord took him and placed him in his presence for eternity. The total darkness was removed from the Earth and there was light. And all the people saw and did not understand how Enoch had been taken away. And all those who had seen these things prayed to God and returned home.

The similar aspects with Acts 1:9–11 are the following: darkness (Enoch)/cloud (Acts 1:9), to hide his being taken away from the spectators (or to serve as a vehicle); praises to God; return. In the two cases, the character is taken away from among his own. Nevertheless, the role of the angels is different.

There are even more similarities with Elijah being taken away (2 Kgs 2:9–11)[84]:

> ⁹ . . . Elijah said to Elisha, "Tell me what I may do for you, before I am taken from you." Elisha said, "Please let me inherit a double share of your spirit."
> ¹⁰ He responded, "You have asked a hard thing; yet, if you see me as I am being taken from you, it will be granted you; if not, it will not."
> ¹¹ As they continued walking and talking, a chariot of fire and horses of fire separated the two of them, and Elijah ascended in a whirlwind into heaven.

The same verb used to indicate being taken away is ἀναλαμβάνειν, in 2 Kgs 2:9–11 (according to the Septuagint) and in Acts 1:2. In both cases, it is a question of the gift of the Spirit (2 Kgs 2:9–10, 15; Acts 1:8; 2:1–

---

[81] Guillaume, pp. 248–62.

[82] Lohfink, *Die Himmelfahrt Jesu:Untersuchungen*, pp. 51–74.

[83] Guillaume, p. 252.

[84] Elijah being taken away will be mentioned again in Sir 48:9 (ὁ ἀναλημφθείς) and 1 Macc 2:58 (ἀνελήμφθη εἰς τὸν οὐρανόν); in the Jewish literature: *1 Enoch* 93:8; *Ap. Esd.* 7:6; Josephus, *Ant.* 9.2, 2; in the church fathers: Irenaeus, *Haer.*5.1; Tertullian, *An.*, 50.

36). The account of 2 Kgs 2 "aims to legitimize Elisha as the heir of his master. Likewise in Acts, the apostles are made Jesus's witnesses."[85]

Concerning Esdras and Baruch being taken away, here is the entire parallel given below by Guillaume:[86]

2 Esd 12:10–50	*2 Bar 76*
A. Revelations (12:10–26)	A. Revelations
The end of the world is approaching; Esdras must be taken away; during his remaining days, he must teach the people about the afterworld and commit to writing the received revelations.	Baruch must teach the people for forty days; at the end of this period of time, an angel tells him about his "being taken away"; other revelations are planned on top of the mountain.
B. Forty-day Period (12:36–48)	B. Forty-day Period
The time during which Esdras writes the received revelations (helped by five men).	Designated for teaching the people.
C. The Taking Away (12:49–50)	C. The Taking Away
(missing in the Latin version)	Is not related, but which, according to E. Schürer should have otherwise concluded the account (*Geschichte des jüdischen Volkes im Zeitalter Jesu Christi*, p. 309).

These two cases of being taken away contain similar important points with the context of Acts 1:9–11:

- The eschatological dimension evoked in Esdras is also in the background of Acts 1:9–11 (see Acts 2:17ff.)
- The need to teach for forty days
- The angel's presence and the mention of the mountain in Baruch
- And, finally, a person being taken away

Also noteworthy, is the taking away of Moses as told by Josephus, *Ant.* 4.8.48, where we find the motifs of the mountain and the cloud, a final meeting with intimate friends, and the taking away.[87]

---

[85] Guillaume, p. 253.
[86] Ibid., note 4.
[87] Ibid., p. 254.

These examples lead to this conclusion, following the example of Guillaume: "the Lukan accounts follow the literary form of a person being taken away."[88] Nevertheless, Lohfink[89] is probably right when he says that the Lukan account of the ascension does not rely upon a particular account of a person being taken away, but on the form "of being taken away" in general.[90] A fundamental element, nevertheless, distinguishes Luke's account from all the other accounts, as Guillaume explains it:

> . . . the Lukan elements are not in total agreement with those that we encounter in the other accounts. They differ in particular on an essential point: only Luke's character is a being who has already come out of death by resurrection; his appearances like his "being taken away" are found in a larger perspective than for the other characters.[91]

Thus, I believe that Luke is entirely responsible for the literary creation of his two accounts of the ascension. If a tradition circulated in the primitive community, there is no trace at all; the kerygmatic formulas of exaltation do not presuppose such a tradition. On the other hand, Luke would have been inspired by a known category, that of *a person being taken away*.

Meaning and Function of the Accounts

The fact that Luke is responsible for the two accounts of being taken away raises the thorny issue of the divergences between them, more particularly the one relating to the date. The scene at the end of the gospel (Luke 24:51–53) would have taken place the night of the Passover; the one at the beginning of Acts (1:3, 9–11) would take place forty days later.

In response to this last problem, Benoit[92] took up the hypothesis already proposed at the end of the last century by A. Plummer,[93] according

---

[88] Ibid., p. 261.

[89] Lohfink, *Die Himmelfahrt Jesu: Untersuchungen*, p. 78.

[90] Against Benoit, "L'Ascension," pp. 405–6, who categorically rejects the hypothesis of a Lukan borrowing of mythology or biblical tradition, even. Contrary to the other characters, who are simply lifted into the divine world, Jesus "is the Son of God by nature and . . . returns to his domain," explains Benoit.

[91] Guillaume, "Biblical and Extra-Biblical Parallels—Literary Genres," p. 261.

[92] Benoit, "L'Ascension," p. 399.

[93] Plummer, *A Critical and Exegetical Commentary on the Gospel according to S. Luke*, p. 564.

to whom the detail of the fortieth day would correspond to complementary information received by Luke in the interval separating the writing of his two books.[94] But this hypothesis is already discounted from the opening of the book of Acts since at verse 2, when Luke speaks of Jesus being taken away, he makes it very evident that he is referring to the scene at the end of the Gospel (Luke 24:50–53).[95] Far from wanting, therefore, to correct what is found, the author seems, on the contrary, to reiterate it. It must be mentioned that Plummer showed a certain skepticism as to the day traditionally held—that of the Passover—for the ascension in the gospel. He writes:

> . . . it is unthinkable that he [Luke] wishes to say that, late at night (vv. 29, 33), Jesus had led [the disciples] to Bethany and that he was lifted up into the darkness. . . . It is probable that δέ, here as in verse 44, introduces a different occasion.[96]

Here is the kind of problem which results in too literal of an approach to the text and which does not sufficiently take into account the theological intentions of the author. These attitudes, which reflect modern preoccupations, consequently risk asking false questions of the text. Should we not, on the contrary, seek clarity in even the coherence of Luke's narrative arrangements and in the theological unity of each of the two books, Luke and Acts? For even if these two works are in perfect continuity, they constitute no fewer than two autonomous literary units. Consequently, each account must be considered in its respective context.

Luke 24:50–53
Jesus is the central character of the third Gospel; therein lies the difference. While the book of Acts is expressly consecrated to the church, the third Gospel aims essentially to *present the person of Jesus Christ*. It is in function of this last objective that we must picture the account of the ascension of Luke 24:50–53. However, what does such an account have to say about Jesus? This account appears written in such a way to illustrate concretely what already constitutes a certainty to the whole primitive community, namely that the Christ is exalted. (See the previous listing of the diverse New Testament passages which attest to it.)

---

[94] Also of this opinion is Moule, "The Ascension—Acts i.9," p. 207.
[95] See Fitzmyer, *The Gospel according to Luke*, p. 1588. Contra Parsons (see note 45).
[96] Plummer, *A Critical and Exegetical Commentary*, p. 564.

The fact remains that in biblical cosmogony, the entry into the sky, the habitation of the divinity,[97] implied a rising up.[98] The ascension of the Christ thus became an essential presupposition to his lordship, that is to say, to his being seated in heaven at the right hand of God. The New Testament authors, except for John[99] and Luke, nevertheless, make reference to this being seated as an accomplished fact—an inseparable fact of the resurrection. Luke is the only one to make it the object of an account. This account, however, is harmoniously integrated into Lukan coherence. It proves to be the perfect conclusion of the gospel since it confirms the fulfillment of the solemn announcement at the beginning: "The Lord God will give to him the throne of his ancestor David. He will reign over the house of Jacob forever, and of his kingdom there will be no end" (Luke 1:32b–33).

In elevating Jesus, God thus fulfills the promise that he had formulated by the intermediary of the angel Gabriel. But Jesus, in order to enter into this function, had to "rise up" to the sky. What is said of Jesus at the beginning of the gospel (1:32–33) thus calls for what is said at the end (24:50–53). The two texts respond to and complete each other. Luke 24:50–53 is, as Marshall[100] points out, the "climax" of the gospel.

It is necessary also to see that this end constitutes the high point of a perceptible gradual progression of the last chapter.[101] It is presented as follows:

I. Vv. 1–12: Observations of the empty tomb.

II. Vv. 13–35: First recognition of the Resurrected One by the disciples of Emmaus. Episode that allows Luke to show how the Jesus event fits into God's plan of salvation, and to especially show that the cross is an essential prerequisite to his glory.[102]

---

[97] See Pss 104:2ff.; 115:16; Deut 33:26; etc.

[98] See Gen 5:24; 11:4; Judg 13:20; 2 Kgs 2:11; Isa 14:13ff.; Dan 4:10; Mark 16:19; Eph 4:9–10; Acts 2:34; John 3:13; 6:33, 38, 42; 1 Pet 3:22.

[99] John, of course, explicitly evoked the ascension of the Christ—"But go to my brothers and say to them, 'I am ascending to my Father'" (John 20:17b)—but without making it an event description.

[100] Marshall, *The Gospel of Luke*, p. 907.

[101] Parsons, *The Departure of Jesus*, p. 195, considers the scene of the ascension (Luke 24:50–53) as an effort to educate the readers on the relationship between the crucifixion and the exaltation.

[102] On the subject of this Lukan perception of the cross of the Christ as being part of God's saving plans, see the preceding chapter.

III. Appearance to the Twelve:[103]
  A. Vv. 36–43: Second recognition of the Resurrected One by the disciples.[104]
  B. Vv. 44–49: Instruction to the disciples—the content of which in respect to the scriptural evidence, vv. 44–46, corresponds to what has been said to the disciples of Emmaus; added, however, for the disciples, the announcement of the mission and the promise of help, vv. 47–49.
  C. Vv. 50–53: Departure.

This departure closes Jesus's earthly activities. A cycle is thus ended. It is typical of Luke to remove the characters at the end of a scene.[105] Here, it is an entire era that has been completed. All that was to be said on the historical role of Jesus was said. Jesus fulfilled the work that had been assigned to him in the world. He blesses the gathered disciples, thus uniting them to God and to his own destiny. Then, he finally enters into the functions which are delegated to him.

This episode, therefore, fits into a whole, contributing to highlight what Jesus was and what he will be in the future.[106] His ascension is his entry into his glory mentioned in v. 26. Everything in this episode is thus centered on the person of Jesus Christ.[107]

---

[103] I adopt, for this section, the subdivisions presented by Lohfink, *Die Himmelfahrt Jesu: Untersuchungen*, p. 148:
  A. Erkennungsscene [Recognition scene]—vv. 36–43
  B. Jüngerbelehrung [Disciples' instructions]—vv. 44–49
  C. Abschied [Departure]—vv. 50–53

[104] There was also the appearance to Peter, evoked in v. 34.

[105] See Luke 1:38, 56; 2:15, 20, 39; 3:20; Acts 10:7; 12:10. Cf. Lohfink, *Die Himmelfahrt Jesu. Untersuchungen*, pp. 170ff.

[106] See Franklin, *Christ the Lord*, pp. 36–37. He writes: "For it is not just a departure but a recognition of who Jesus really is" (p. 36). For Talbert, *Literary Patterns*, 112ff., the objective of the ascension account is to guarantee the "corporeality" of the one who is elevated and the continuity between the one who is elevated and the one who is dead. Luke's intention would be to combat the docetic tendency. Luke would prevent the separation between the spirit and the flesh of the Savior and ensure his real humanity. Therefore, it would be a matter of an anti-docetic apologetic. Talbert's perception creates a problem since it does not find support in the Gospel or in Acts.

[107] Parsons, *The Departure of Jesus*, p. 195, writes, concerning this closing scene: "If the narrator is attempting in the closing scene to educate his readers concerning the relationship between the crucifixion and exaltation, then a close-up scenic ending is the most appropriate to use. It forces the reader, through close and retrospective

Recall, however, that the whole section concerning the appearance to the Twelve remains transitional. While fixing the attention on Jesus, it still points very clearly to expanded horizons, to the ecclesial tasks which will be assumed by the disciples:[108]

1. ... and that repentance and forgiveness of sins is to be proclaimed in his name to all nations, beginning from Jerusalem (v. 47)

2. You are witnesses of these things (v. 48)

3. And see, I am sending upon you what my Father promised (v. 49a)

Luke proceeded at the end of his gospel as he had done at the beginning. He had, in fact, clearly structured the first two chapters in such a way as to place the advent of Jesus into the continuity of the salvation process inaugurated by the Old Covenant. Now, he structures this last chapter in a perspective of the beginning of the church.

Acts 1:9–11

Luke's concern to mark the continuity between the two eras—Jesus's era and the Church's era—is shown again at the beginning of the book of Acts. The five verses of the prologue clearly and explicitly assure this junction: the recall of Jesus's career (v. 1); the choice and the training of the disciples (v. 2); the appearances (v. 3); the meal that had immediately preceded his being taken away (v. 4a); and the promise that had been made to the disciples (vv. 4b–5).

But now one senses that the attention is turned in another direction. The disciples become the focal point. What should be recalled about Jesus has been condensed into a summary (vv. 1–5). From now on, everything is expressed in terms of the disciples and of the mission they have to accomplish.[109] Therefore, it is in this light that we must now consider the second

---

reading, to either share the understanding of Jesus' exaltation to include death—resurrection—ascension ... or to reject such a view."

[108] I believe, consequently, that Parsons's position should be qualified when he writes: "An overview ending which gave the after-history of Jesus or the disciples would not only radically change the content of the Third Gospel as it now stands; more importantly, it would also destroy the effect of the ending of Luke" (*The Departure of Jesus*, p. 195).

[109] See Barrett, *Luke the Historian in Recent Study*: "On the one hand, the ascension is the end of the story of Jesus. ... On the other hand, the ascension is the beginning of the story of the Church. It is from this view point that we see it in Acts. ... There, the ascension closes an epoch; here, it opens another, which will last until it ends with the

account of the ascension. For this second account will effectively have more to say about the disciples and the life of the church than about Jesus.

In the middle of his summary, Luke presents the appearances as a time of training for the disciples: after his suffering he presented himself alive to them by many convincing proofs, appearing to them during forty days and speaking about the kingdom of God (v. 3).

Three important elements come from this verse:

1. The insistence on the fact that "he presented himself alive to them" after his passion. Due to this fact, the apostles become credible witnesses. Besides, again and again, Luke will link authority with the testimony to the fact that the apostles were precisely witnesses of the resurrection: Acts 1:22; 2:32; 4:33; 10:31; 13:31; 22:15.

2. The use of the symbolic number of *forty days*. Menoud is entirely correct when he affirms that one must give "an essentially theological interpretation to this chronological note."[110] Very frequently used in the Bible,[111] this number designates a period of training or of divine revelation. Thus, the people spend forty years in the desert, Moses forty days on Sinai, Jesus forty days in the desert, etc. The use, here, by Luke is without ambiguity; even more so that he specifies:

3. ". . . *during forty days, . . . and speaking about the kingdom of God.*" Here is the third important element. The disciples receive the message that they must announce from the Resurrected One himself; thus they will be able to transmit it in utter faithfulness.[112]

Moreover, after the summary (Acts 1:1–5), the disciples ask Jesus about the moment of the reestablishment of the kingdom (v. 6). This question allows the author to correct certain views distorted by too down-to-earth expectations. It is not for them to know the time (v. 7), but the

---

return of Christ from heaven, where in the meantime He sits at God's right hand (Acts 2:33ff.; 5:31; 7:55ff.) as the Lord who through His Spirit directs the work of His Church on earth" (pp. 56–57).

[110] Menoud, pp. 111–15. Menoud bases his point of view on three criteria: (1) the Resurrected One speaks only to the Twelve, making of these "first-hand witnesses the authentic agents of the Resurrected One's thinking"; (2) the number forty has a symbolic significance; (3) "the fortieth day is not a Christian date for Luke or for the Church of the first three centuries."

[111] For a list of the uses of the number 40 in the Old Testament, see among others Enslin, pp. 64–66, and Larranaga, pp. 174–207.

[112] See Menoud, "Pendant quarante jours (Actes 1:3)," p. 114.

Resurrected One repeats one more time the sort of role that they will have to fulfill when they will have been clothed with power from the Spirit (v. 8): "But you will receive power when the Holy Spirit has come upon you; and you will be my witnesses in Jerusalem, in all Judea and Samaria, and to the ends of the earth." Having completed these instructions, the Christ rises up toward heaven disappearing behind a cloud: "When he had said this, as they were watching, he was lifted up, and a cloud took him out of their sight" (v. 9).

The intervention of the angels (vv. 10–11) happens in such a way as to confirm that the account essentially aims to edify the apostles. At first, this detail from v. 10, which shows them gazing up toward heaven, suggests a certain slowness on their part to get mobilized and committed to the process of universal evangelism; this slowness is likely linked to a somewhat paralyzing hope of an early second coming.[113] The questioning of the angels is tinted with reproach: "Men of Galilee, why do you stand looking up toward heaven? This Jesus, who has been taken up from you into heaven, will come in the same way as you saw him go into heaven" (v. 11).

Luke actually addresses the issue of the second coming in the same way that he does in v. 7: it will happen, but the timing is not revealed. The impatience caused by the delay obviously comes across from these two verses (7 and 11a). In the two cases, however, Luke remains vague. Everything seems to indicate that he still believes in this return, but he definitely notes that it is impossible to speculate about the date. What he absolutely insists on saying, however, is that this delay must not freeze missionary activity. The texts which follow and the book of Acts on the whole are based upon, in effect, this interpretation: the disciples regroup; Pentecost occurs and the momentum is given, a momentum that will lead to the fulfillment of Acts 1:8, which commanded them to take the message from Jerusalem to the ends of the earth.

Therefore, verses 7–8 and 10–11 somewhat correspond: in vv. 7–8, it is the Resurrected One who speaks in his own name; in vv. 10–11, it is God who corroborates the Resurrected One's comments by the word of his messengers. And between these two pairs of verses, Jesus's elevation to heaven is inserted, v. 9, an event which clearly indicated to the disciples that they should no longer hope for any other personal contacts with Jesus; that he would no longer appear to them, but that it is by another mode of relationship that he would show himself to them: *by his Spirit*. This is

---

[113] See Marshall, *The Acts of the Apostles*, p. 61.

what Luke is very careful to state precisely in v. 8a: "But you will receive power when the Holy Spirit has come upon you," a promise whose fulfillment will not be delayed (Acts 2:1–4).

Therefore, it is clear that the entire literary construction in which v. 9 is inscribed is done on the basis of the disciples, in an ecclesiological perspective.[114]

As for the number forty . . .
There is a tendency to link the number *forty* too much to the account of the ascension (Acts 1:9–11) or to give it more expansion than Luke himself wanted to give it. Scholars consider this number more and more as the fruit of a literary technique aiming to limit in time the duration of the appearances, during which the disciples received a particular training.[115] But, in general, we continue, nevertheless, to believe that the formulation of the text situates the ascension on this fortieth day. Yet, it is not evident.

If we attentively observe its place of insertion in the text (v. 3), we note the following:

- Just before mentioning the number, the author writes:

    In the first book . . . until the day when . . . he was taken up to heaven. (Acts 1:1–2)

    It is clear that the author recalls the episode of Luke 24:50–53, the episode that he situates quite obviously on Easter evening. Immediately after, he writes: "He presented himself alive to them . . . during forty days . . ." (Acts 1:3). However, if the author wants to indicate that the ascension precedes the fortieth day, there is an incoherence not only between the account of the gospel and that of Acts, but also between two consecutive verses in the middle of a unified account. It seems correct rather, in v. 3, that the author expressly wants to mark the time

---

[114] See van Stempvoort, "Interpretation of the Ascension," p. 39. Moreover, Parsons considerably reduces the functional scope of the account when he seeks to show that this account is first of all directed to the reader simply aiming to incite the reader to read the book of Acts (*The Departure of Jesus*, pp. 151ff.). He writes: "The crucial importance of a narrative beginning in engaging the reader in the reading act cannot be overemphasized" (p. 186). Parsons believes, therefore, that: "The narrator who worked so diligently to enable the reader to emerge from the narrative world of Luke is equally persistent in coaxing him or her to enter again . . . the story world (now Acts)" (pp. 174 and 180). To consider this account as a strategy to attract the interest of the reader is to ignore the ecclesial purposes this text essentially implies.

[115] Among others: Parsons, *Departure of Jesus*, p. 195; Talbert, *Acts*, p. 6; Schille, "Die Himmelfahrt," p. 184.

- of the disciples' training, using to this end a stereotypical number, *forty*.

- Verses 4–5 tell of the events of the meal of Luke 24:36ff. and of the promise formulated at that moment.

- In verse 6, the author continues: "So when they had come together, they asked him . . ." What follows, up to verse 8, are the thoughts on the kingdom and on the disciples' mission. However, there is no temporal precision and nothing indicates that this exchange must be linked to verse 3, that is, to situate it on the fortieth day.

- Moreover, in verse 9, as soon as the words end, the Resurrected One rises to heaven. As Menoud explains: "In the pericope Acts 1:1–12, the forty-day notice is not joined to the same account of the ascension, where one would expect to find it, if it had a chronological scope; it could have been in v. 12 next to the geographical indication."[116]

Menoud adds again that the two precise chronological facts furnished by Luke are those of the resurrection on the third day (Luke 24:7, 21, 46) and that of the gift of the Spirit on the fiftieth, "both of them are linked by their common dependence on the Jewish Pascal cycle."[117]

Moreover, during the first three centuries, if we trust the testimonies of the church fathers, the fortieth day was not retained on the liturgical calendar as the date commemorating the ascension. Benoit, even if he believes that Luke "formally mentions an interval of forty days" between the resurrection and the ascension,[118] must admit, that after examining the texts of the church fathers, that they generally do not assign any date to the ascension and if they do, it is to "present it as immediately following the Resurrection."[119]

Is it necessary to maintain that the ascension in Acts 1:9 had been thought as happening the fortieth day after the Resurrection? I am not convinced of this, but what appears certain is that the number forty is meant first and foremost to be a symbolic attestation of training given to the disciples, making them authorized witnesses.

---

[116] Menoud, "Pendant quarante jours (Actes 1: 3)," p. 114.

[117] Ibid. According to Wilson, "The Ascension: A Critique and an Interpretation," p. 272: "Thus it is not the 40 days which forces Luke to date the coming of the Spirit at Pentecost, but the date of Pentecost which forces him to use the 40 days."

[118] Menoud, p. 114. On the testimonies of the Fathers, see also Benoit, "L'Ascension," pp. 492–589.

[119] Benoit, "L'Ascension," p. 376.

Lukan Texts of Exaltation in Light of Accounts of the Ascension

The Lukan tests of exaltation fit perfectly into the author's theological and literary coherence. Consider first of all the text of Luke 22:69.[120] The synoptic presentation shows well the particular character of the Lukan version:

| ... From now on you will see the Son of Man seated at the right hand of Power and coming on the clouds of heaven. (Matt 26:64) | ... You will see the Son of Man seated at the right hand of the Power, and coming with the clouds of heaven. (Mark 14:62) | ... But from now on the Son of Man will be seated at the right hand of the power of God. (Luke 22:69) |

In the cases of Matthew and Mark, the emphasis is on the imminence of the second coming and on the role of the Son of Man as executor of God's judgment. The ἀπ' ἄρτι of Matthew, that is rendered with "from now on," marks the immediacy (*from now*, in the present)[121] in such a way that it is more so the role of the Daniel-like character in the fulfillment of his function, in a coming time, than the lordship of the Christ over the universe, which is the focus here. Moreover, Matthew 25:31, which fits correctly into the pericope of the Matthew tradition on the final judgment, supports this interpretation:[122] "When the Son of Man comes in his glory, and all the angels with him, then he will sit on the throne of his glory" (25:31).

The collusion between these two verses (Matt 25:31 and 26:64), as much on a thematic as on a terminological level, is undeniable. Moreover, in Matthew 25:31, there is a clear chronological coincidence of the seating of the Son of Man and of his coming in glory. It seems, then, that in Matthew 26:64 (as in Mark 14:62) the idea of an eschatology in the process of being fulfilled predominates.

---

[120] This verse poses no critical textual problem.

[121] See Bauer, *A Greek-English Lexicon*, p. 110.

[122] In this regard, Schweizer, *The Good News according to Matthew*, p. 499, writes: "Matthew's overall meaning is that 'from this time on' they will see the triumphant Son of Man, to whom all power in heaven and earth is given (28:18) and who will return to judge the world (25:31)." See also Grundmann, *Das Evangelium nach Matthäus*, p. 546.

In Luke, it is the expression ἀπὸ τοῦ νῦν that "from now on" translates. Luke's choice carries a semantic nuance in relation to Matthew's. The expression means, in effect, "from now." In addition to the *present* dimension, it thus conceals also the *continuity*[123] dimension. The Lukan omissions of "you will see" and of "coming on (with) the clouds of heaven" are also very significant. They evacuate from the passage the idea of eschatological imminence.

Additionally, it is clear that Luke establishes an identity relationship between Son of Man – Messiah – Son of God.[124] In verse 22:67a, the members of the Sanhedrin tell him:

- "If you are the Messiah, tell us . . ."

- Jesus answers them: "If I tell you, you will not believe; and if I question you, you will not answer" (vv. 67b–68).

- Then, he continues: "But from now on *the Son of Man will be seated at the right hand* of the power of God" (v. 69).

- The Sanhedrin's conclusion is thus the following: "Are you, then, the Son of God?" (v. 70).

This last question is absent in Matthew and Mark.

Therefore, it is clear that the Lukan modifications move the lines of orientation of the pericope. It is not the eschatological judgment (as in Matthew and Mark) that preoccupies Luke, but the immediate coming of the Messianic Reign,[125] such as the Christian community recognized, as is evidenced in Acts 2:36: "Therefore let the entire house of Israel know with certainty that God has made him both Lord and Messiah, this Jesus whom you crucified."

---

[123] See Conzelmann, *Acts of the Apostles*, p. 84, note 3, on the value of the respective choices of Matthew (ἀπ' ἄρτι) and of Luke (ἀπὸ τοῦ νῦν).

[124] For Conzelmann, ibid., there is actually, in this Lukan context, christological unity of the titles. Ernst, p. 620, is of the same opinion. On the contrary, Fitzmyer, *The Gospel according to Luke X–XXIV*, pp. 1467–68, in line with J. M. Creed, *The Gospel according to St. Luke*, p. 278, contests this opinion. He considers that the Old Testament bases of *Messiah* and *Son of God* are distinct and that the connotations of each title must be respected.

[125] Marshall, *The Acts of the Apostles*, p. 850, is correct when he says that the Lukan form of v. 69 aims, on the one hand, to avoid the unfulfilled prophecy concerning the Son of man and, on the other hand, to insist on the present exaltation of the Son of man. Marshall also notes that it is the exalted Son of man that Stephen sees in Acts 7:56.

It is interesting that the absence in Luke of the "you will see" of Matthew and Mark integrates itself well into the perspective of the whole developed by Luke. The abstraction of the speakers by the omission of the "you will see" tends effectively to fix the attention on Jesus himself and on his destiny being played out. What Luke has to say expressly concerns Jesus. Now he will be seated in glory at the right hand of God. The account of the ascension (Luke 24:50–53) confirms the fulfillment of this prophecy. But Luke does not miss showing that Jesus satisfied the requirements; his exaltation will come as the fruit of his abasement: "Was it not necessary that the Messiah should suffer these things and then enter into his glory?" (Luke 24:26).

A great theological unity comes out, therefore, from the picture Luke paints:

- 22:69 Announces the seating at the right hand of God;
- 24:26 Outlines the conditions;
- 24:51 Shows the fulfillment.

This is a great theological unity which fundamentally aims to present the Easter mystery in all of its dimensions to introduce it to the believer. Together with the account of the ascension, Luke shows in a picturesque way—in his way—that everything that had to happen to Jesus truly did occur. Having meticulously finished the picture of Jesus, he can turn toward the life of the church, which also depends, on the fulfillment of these christological events.

The texts of the book of Acts (2:33; 5:31; 7:55–56) come back to the established fact of the exaltation by presenting what it brings with it as consequences for the community. The scope of these consequences are thoroughly evaluated in chapter 6, but I mention here their characteristics.

Acts 2:33 is inserted at the center of a demonstration (Acts 2:25–36) which presupposes the fact of the ascension. Recall first of all that, even by its formulation, the verse proclaims the exaltation of the Christ: "Being therefore exalted at the right hand of God, and having received from the Father the promise of the Holy Spirit" (Acts 2:33a). Luke establishes this proclamation at verse 34b with the help of Ps 110:1: "The Lord said to my lord, "Sit at my right hand." However, just before quoting the Psalm, he brings a precision (v. 34a) which prevents any misunderstandings of the underlying intention for using this Psalm: "For David *did not ascend into the heavens*, but he himself says . . . ."

The proposition—"David did not ascend into the heavens"—clearly recalls the event of the ascension. What Luke says, in reality, is this: "What follows cannot be applied to David since he did not ascend into the heavens; his tomb is with us to this day [v. 29]. But Jesus, he ascended into the heavens; the ascension is the proof." The ascension as a reference allows Luke, therefore, to substantiate his proof. Jesus, in fact, fulfills the necessary condition to be seated at the right hand of God: he ascended into the heavens. One cannot, however, say as much of David. Consequently, it is Jesus and not David to whom Psalm 110:1 applies. It is, of course, by his obedience to God (vv. 22–24) that Jesus merited being exalted.

Finally, the second part of verse 33 refers to the fulfillment of the promise of the gift of the Spirit to the community: ". . . he has poured out this that you both see and hear" (v. 33b). Moreover, in Luke 24:49, Luke announced this outpouring as coming "from on high":[126] ". . . until you have been clothed with power from on high." Jesus's ascension into the heavens thus permitted the fulfillment of the promise.

In Acts 5:31, the exaltation of the Christ is proclaimed by Peter when he appears before the Sanhedrin. In verses 29ff., Peter says to the members of the Sanhedrin that "we must obey God rather than any human authority" (v. 29a). Furthermore, obedience to God, in this case, means "teaching the name [of Jesus]" (v. 28). And this obedience to God is commanded by the fact that "God . . . resurrected Jesus" (v. 30) and that he "exalted him to his right hand" (v. 31). Peter affirms with conviction: "We are witnesses of these things" (v. 32) that is, the events of the resurrection and the ascension. Peter can witness to the resurrection because it had been confirmed by the experience of the appearances; he can witness to the exaltation because it had been confirmed by the experience of the ascension.

As to the functional nature of this exaltation, here, it is well-defined: Luke uses the terms ἀρχηγόν and σωτῆρα (v. 31), i.e., *lord* and *savior*.[127] The exaltation of the Christ consists then in a role of governing and saving. Luke evidently perceives this role in the continuity of that of

---

[126] In Luke 24:49, the Spirit as the contents of the promise is not explicitly named. But in the next chapter, we will clearly see that it is indeed of the Spirit that Luke speaks when he writes "power from on high."

[127] The translation of ἀρχηγόν and σωτῆρα is in the *TOB*: *Prince* and *Savior*; *BJ* and *OSTY*: *Lord* and *Savior* [i.e., French translations of the Bible]. It is for this second translation that I opt because it better expresses Jesus's role at the heart of the community. Moreover, the *Greek-English Lexicon* of Bauer translates ἀρχηγόν as *"leader, ruler, prince."*

Moses.[128] In Stephen's speech, in fact, he presents Moses as ἄρχοντα, *lord*, δικαστήν, *judge*, and λυτρωτήν, *liberator* (Acts 7:35). Like Jesus, Moses had to wipe away the rejection of his own: "This Moses whom they rejected . . ." (v. 35a). Furthermore, note an increased importance in Jesus's role as compared to Moses's: while Moses is called "liberator," Jesus is called "savior." Moreover, this last title was reserved for God in the Old Covenant[129] (Isa 41:14; 44:6; 49:7, 26; 59:20; 63:16; Jer 50:34; Hos 13:4; Ps 19:15).

The lordship of the Christ is thus presented, in Acts 5:31, at the same time, as ruling over the world and as saving humanity. It is through the witness of the believers (v. 32) that it reaches the people, leading them to conversion and obtaining pardon of their sins as well as the gift of the Spirit:[130]

> God exalted him at his right hand as Lord and Savior that he might give repentance to Israel and forgiveness of sins. And we are witnesses to these things, and so is the Holy Spirit whom God has given to those who obey him. (Acts 5:31–32)

Conversion, baptism, and the gift of the Spirit are effectively fruits of the exaltation and the fulfillment of the promise. Thus, Peter concludes his speech on the day of the Pentecost:

> Repent, and be baptized every one of you in the name of Jesus Christ so that your sins may be forgiven; and you will receive the gift of the Holy Spirit. For the promise is for you, for your children, and for all who are far away, everyone whom the Lord our God calls to him. (Acts 2:38–39)

Peter can thus exhort the people because God resurrected Jesus, because this one ascended into heaven and received the Spirit, and because he poured him out:

---

[128] Williams, p. 92, speaks of the parallel in the roles of Jesus and Moses. According to him, the titles ἀρχηγόν and σωτῆρα of Acts 5:31 must be translated as *pioneer* and *savior*. The first title, he says, is also descriptive of Moses's role when he guided the people of God towards the promised land.

[129] See de Boor, p. 123. De Boor sees in this attribution to Jesus of the title of "savior," up to this point reserved for God, a recognition of Jesus's divinity by the primitive community. This appears somewhat overstated.

[130] See Schneider, *Die Apostlgeschichte, Teil 1, 1:1–8:40*, pp. 395–96.

> This Jesus God raised up, and of that all of us are witnesses. Being therefore exalted at the right hand of God, and having received from the Father the promise of the Holy Spirit, he has poured out this that you both see and hear. (Acts 2:32–33)

The effects of the exaltation of the Christ are visible and audible.

The last passage of Acts explicitly mentioning the exaltation of the Christ constitutes the conclusion of Stephen's speech: "But filled with the Holy Spirit, he gazed into heaven and saw the glory of God and Jesus standing at the right hand of God. 'Look,' he said, 'I see the heavens opened and the Son of Man standing at the right hand of God!'" (Acts 7:55–56). This passage confirms, unequivocally, the fulfillment of the prophecy of Luke 22:69: "But from now on the Son of Man will be seated at the right hand of the power of God." As in Luke 22:69, Jesus exalted is identified as the Son of Man: He lives ". . . Jesus . . . at the right hand of God . . . . I see . . . the Son of Man at the right hand of God!" The location dimension is also well-highlighted: "I see the heavens opened . . . standing at the right hand of God."

As already mentioned, the cosmogonic plans of the Bible situate heaven in the high places (see pp. 81–84). But now Luke is able to affirm Jesus's presence in heaven following his account of the ascension (Acts 1:9–11). Jesus is elevated before the eyes of the disciples: "While he was going and they were gazing up toward heaven . . ." (v. 10); ". . .This Jesus, who has been taken up from you into heaven . . . (v. 11).

The theological implication of Stephen's words is great, as Haenchen explains:

> The speech . . . depicted Israel's disobedience to God. . . . But now something totally different occurs: The Holy Spirit opens the eyes of Stephen . . . to the heavenly Reality so infinitely raised above all earthly polemics. It is, however, precisely what can there be seen that the Sanhedrin cannot bear to hear related. For if Jesus stands on the right hand of God, this must show that the Christians are right in the sight of God and that the High Council is virtually God's enemy.[131]

Stephen's vision ratifies the Christian mission, and even more, for the word of the martyr is approved by the Holy Spirit, as Stephen is, in effect, filled with the Spirit because the exalted Christ poured the Spirit out (Acts 2:33).

---

[131] Haenchen, *Acts*, p. 295.

The Lukan approach to the theme of the exaltation has its own particular distinction as the study of the texts of Luke-Acts demonstrates. While the other New Testament authors refer to the exaltation of the Christ as an accomplished fact, Luke, to the contrary, informs on its *manner* of being fulfilled.

Luke is, in effect, the only one to have made of the exaltation the description of an event in his accounts of the ascension. These accounts not only serve to pave the way to the proclamations that he plans to make, but they are supposed to insist on the importance of this reality—an insistence to mark the radical newness of the Christ's resurrected status (Luke 24:50–53), an insistence to mark the impact of this status on the Christian community (Acts 1:9–11).

No other New Testament author, as much as Luke, brings out the consequences of the exaltation (which will be highlighted in chapter 6). Certainly, in the Pauline writings the constant effects of the exaltation of the Christ is apparent, but Paul did not establish in such an explicit way the relation of cause and effect as Luke does at the beginning of Acts:

- Ascension (1:9–11)
- Pentecost (2:1–13)
- Explanatory speech (2:16–36)

Luke uses concrete language to prepare the account of the concrete experience which will be experienced at the heart of the community and which the remainder of the book of Acts will validate. An experience which is seen and heard—that of the Spirit of the Christ at work in his church.

CONCLUSION

This study on the theme of the exaltation—a fundamental theme in the New Testament—has, first of all, helped situate the New Testament facts in the stream of the Old Testament designs and terminology. In the Old Testament texts, God alone is elevated; he alone can elevate a human being, and the essential condition to the elevation of a human being is his submission to God. The attitude of abasement of the Servant of Deutero-Isaiah, who receives the approbation of God, fulfilled this condition and became the model to imitate.

The New Testament writings show that Jesus fully corresponded to the divine expectations. His service without fault, consequently, merited for him supreme recognition: *God seated him at his right hand.* This dignity is clearly known in the entire New Testament, and very early on as the ancient vestiges of traditions attest.

I have noted as well the special treatment accorded by Luke to the theme of the exaltation. Considering his intentions of bringing into the light the ecclesial impact of this reality, Luke's insistence is easily understood. However, what is important to point out is that by a very meticulous editorial work at the heart of his gospel, he had already prepared his great assertions on the exaltation of the Christ. By his modifications of the synoptic traditions (baptism, sending into the desert, inauguration of the ministry in Galilee) or by the integration of particular traditions (annunciation) he had, in effect, opened the way to the proclamation of the exaltation.

The elevation of the Christ to the right hand of God is brought to light and explained by Jesus's earthly course. It is the fruit of his unique behavior. The great christological moments of the Third Gospel point to, as well as draw light from, the ultimate proclamation of Acts 2:33. This is what chapter 5 will demonstrate. However, before then, it is fitting to see the value of "the promise of the Holy Spirit" in Acts 2:33, the topic of the next chapter.

CHAPTER 4

ACTS 2:33—THE PROMISE OF THE HOLY SPIRIT

"And having received from the Father the promise of the Holy Spirit . . ."

Does the assertion concerning the promise of the Holy Spirit draw its light strictly from the Lukan texts? Or does it fit into the vaster perspective of the messianic tradition? What is the promise of the Holy Spirit mentioned in Acts 2:33? The immediate literary context, that is Peter's speech, already furnishes the important elements of the answer to this questioning: the assertion would be, on the one hand, the destination of a long Lukan demonstration, but on the other hand, it would be the reference to the essential prerequisite to the messianic fulfillment, that is, *the gift of the Spirit* (Acts 2:30ff.).

1. THE PROMISE OF THE SPIRIT IN LUKE-ACTS

The three references to the promise of the Holy Spirit in Luke-Acts are:

Luke 24:49
καὶ [ἰδοὺ] ἐγὼ ἀποστέλλω τὴν ἐπαγγελίαν τοῦ πατρός μου ἐφ' ὑμᾶς· ὑμεῖς δὲ καθίσατε ἐν τῇ πόλει ἕως οὗ ἐνδύσησθε ἐξ ὕψους δύναμιν. /
And see, I am sending upon you what my Father promised; so stay here in the city until you have been clothed with power from on high.

Acts 1:4–5

καὶ συναλιζόμενος παρήγγειλεν αὐτοῖς ἀπὸ Ἱεροσολύμων μὴ χωρίζεσθαι, ἀλλὰ περιμένειν τὴν ἐπαγγελίαν τοῦ πατρὸς ἣν ἠκούσατέ μου, ὅτι Ἰωάννης μὲν ἐβάπτισεν ὕδατι, ὑμεῖς δὲ ἐν πνεύματι βαπτισθήσεσθε ἁγίῳ οὐ μετὰ πολλὰς ταύτας ἡμέρας. /
While staying with them,[1] he ordered them not to leave Jerusalem, but to wait there for the promise of the Father. "This," he said, "is what you have heard from me; for John baptized with water, but you will be baptized with the Holy Spirit not many days from now."

Acts 2:33

τῇ δεξιᾷ οὖν τοῦ θεοῦ ὑψωθείς, τήν τε ἐπαγγελίαν τοῦ πνεύματος τοῦ ἁγίου λαβὼν παρὰ τοῦ πατρὸς ἐξέχεεν τοῦτο ὃ ὑμεῖς [καὶ] βλέπετε καὶ ἀκούετε. /
Being therefore exalted at the right hand of God, and having received from the Father the promise of the Holy Spirit, he has poured out this that you both see and hear.

In Luke 24:49, it is clear, even if it is not mentioned, that the Spirit is the object of the promise. Acts 1:4–5 confirm[2] it, and so does 1:8a:[3] "But you will receive power when the Holy Spirit has come upon you." Luke 24:49 and Acts 1:4–5 tie the book of Acts and the gospel together, as Acts 1:4–5 explicitly recalls Luke 24:49. In the three texts, it is specified that this promise comes from the Father. The first two concern the disciples; the third concerns Jesus at first and the disciples by Jesus as the intermediary. Thus, it seems that there are two different though correlative perspectives.

The Promise and the Disciples

A detailed study of the manner of the fulfillment of this promise and its effects ensues in chapter 6. Here, specifying its nature is helpful.

---

[1] The translation is difficult. According to Bauer, *A Greek-English Lexicon* . . . , pp. 783–84, συναλίζω can be rendered as "eat with" or as "assemble," "gather." The *TOB* and *BJ* [French translations of the Bible] opt for the meaning "eat together," whereas the French translation *OSTY* opts for the meaning "be together." It is clear, however, that the scene that Acts 1:4–5 recalls is the meal of Luke 24:41ff., which immediately preceded the ascension (vv. 50–53). Cf. Dillon and Fitzmyer, "Acts of the Apostles," *The Jerome Biblical Commentary*, pp. 168–69.

[2] See Sieber, "The Spirit as the 'Promise of My Father' in Luke 24:49," p. 274.

[3] See Dillon, *From Eye-Witnesses to Ministers of the Word: Tradition and Composition in Luke 24*, p. 218.

There is no need to hesitate with respect to the nature of this promise: it corresponds to the announcement made by Joel, namely that God would pour out his Spirit on all flesh in the eschatological times.[4] Luke leads his reader to this conclusion through a very well structured literary progression:

- In Luke 24:49, the author mentions the promise without explicitly referring to the Spirit. But the description he makes is not misleading: it is about "a power from on high." Moreover, it is in terms of power that Luke usually speaks of the Spirit[5] and he often uses the terms synonymously.[6]
    - The Holy Spirit will come upon you, and the power of the Most High will overshadow you. (Lk 1:35)
    - Then Jesus, filled with the power of the Spirit, returned to Galilee . . . (4:14)
    - But you will receive power when the Holy Spirit has come upon you. (Acts 1:8)
    - . . . and they were all filled with the Holy Spirit . . . (4:31)
    - With great power the apostles gave their testimony to the resurrection of the Lord Jesus. (4:33)
    - How God anointed Jesus of Nazareth with the Holy Spirit and with power. (10:38)
- From the beginning of Acts (1:4–5) Luke recalls this promise that he defines this time, in terms of the baptism in the Holy Spirit. A baptism for which he specifies the objective—testimony—in 1:8b.

---

[4] Most scholars support identifying the promise with Joel's announcement in Joel 2:28–32; here are some of them: McPolin, "Holy Spirit in Luke and John," p. 118; Dunn, *Jesus and the Spirit*, p. 140; Turner, "Jesus and the Spirit in Lucan Perspective," p. 37; Sieber, p. 274; Ernst, *Das Evangelium nach Lukas*, p. 671; Guillet, "Saint Esprit: Luc-Actes," col. 185.

[5] See Pfitzner, "'Pneumatic' Apostleship? Apostle and Spirit in the Acts of the Apostles," *Wort in der Zeit*, pp. 211ff.; Smith, *Easter Gospels*, p. 136; Bruce, "The Holy Spirit in the Acts of the Apostles," pp. 169–70; Stravinskas, "The Role of the Spirit in Acts 1 and 2," p. 264; Lampe, "The Holy Spirit in the Writings of St. Luke," p. 165; Oliver, "The Lucan Birth Stories and the Purpose of Luke-Acts," p. 224; Tatum, "The Epoch of Israel: Luke I–II and the Theological Plan of Luke-Acts," p. 187.

[6] Gillièron, *Le Saint-Esprit. Actualité du Christ*, p. 48, does not share this point of view: ET: ". . . Luke never mistakes the Spirit and the power of God," but associates them in a complementary way, he explains. Haya-Prats, *L'Esprit force de l'Église*, p. 38 [ET: pp. 30–32], likewise rejects the idea that "Spirit" and "power" are equivalent. He only acknowledges this equivalence in Luke 24:49 (which he explains in endnote 2, p. 245 [ET: pp. 30–31]).

- Immediately after this, recall, Jesus goes away definitively (vv. 9–11).
- Pentecost occurs (Acts 2:1–4)—the fulfillment of the promise, which Luke is quick to explain in referring to the quotation of Joel 2:28–29;[7] a quotation that he inserts at the beginning of Peter's speech which immediately follows the Pentecostal outpouring.

This promise, therefore, consists in a commitment on the part of God to pour out his Spirit on the believers in order to render them able to testify, a reality that will be detailed and demonstrated in the rest of the book of Acts (see chapter 6). The editorial addition "says God" in Joel's text (Acts 2:17a) shows Luke's intention to identify very well the author of the promise[8] and to make it understood that what is happening in the community is nothing other than the fulfillment of this promise.

The link between the author of the promise and the promise itself is thus clearly marked, and the scope of this promise is explicitly expressed. The "suspense" skillfully established in Luke 24:49 is removed.[9] To do so, the author used a coherent and well-articulated demonstration. The assertion concerning the promise of the Spirit thus finds its explanation at the heart of the Lukan texts.

The Promise and Jesus

The demonstration is, nonetheless, incomplete, for the role of Jesus in this eschatological event has not yet been clarified. First of all, it is important to remember that the Spirit poured out at Pentecost is the Spirit of God: "*In the last days* it will be, *God declares*, that I will pour out *my Spirit* upon all flesh" (Acts 2:17a [Joel 2:28]). Furthermore, in Acts 2:33 we read:

---

[7] Joel's text is evidently the text at the basis of the argumentation. But it is not the only one carrying the hope or the promise of the Spirit. Several texts, in fact, can be mentioned: Isa 32:15 (". . . until a spirit from on high is poured out on us"); 44:3b ("I will pour my spirit upon your descendants, and my blessing on your offspring"); Ezek 36:27a ("I will put my spirit within you"); 39:29 ("I will never again hide my face from them, when I pour out my spirit upon the house of Israel"); Zech 12:10 ("And I will pour out a spirit of compassion and supplication on the house of David and the habitants of Jerusalem"). Several scholars consider that it is on this vast foundation of Old Testament scenes that the Lukan promise must be located, e.g., Marshall, *Gospel of Luke*, p. 907; Plummer, *The Gospel according to S. Luke*, p. 563; Fitzmyer, *The Gospel according to Luke (X–XXIV)*, p. 1585.

[8] See Guillet, "Saint Esprit: Luc–Actes," col. 185.

[9] On this subject, see the excellent article by O'Toole, "Acts 2:30 and the Davidic Covenant of Pentecost," pp. 245–58.

"Being therefore exalted at the right hand of God, and *having received from the Father the promise of the Holy Spirit*, he has poured out this that you both see and hear."

In this last text, Luke furnishes the complementary information that enables the relationship between Jesus and the Spirit to be brought to light.[10] Jesus receives the Spirit from the Father and then he makes him available. Christological antecedents pave the way to this proclamation. First, Luke 24:49: "And see, I am sending upon you what my Father promised." Immediately before this announcement, Jesus had "opened their [the disciples'] minds to understand the scriptures" (v. 45). He actually explained to them the scope of the Scriptures, namely:

> ". . . Thus it is written, that the Messiah is to suffer and to rise from the dead on the third day, and that repentance and forgiveness of sins is to be proclaimed in his name to all nations, beginning from Jerusalem . . ." (vv. 46–47)

The disciples are witnesses (v. 48) of all this. Then comes the announcement of the promise (v. 49) followed immediately by the account of the ascension (vv. 50–53).

What comes out of this schema are the following:

- The Scriptures are fulfilled in the life-death-resurrection of Jesus;
- The eschatological times have thus come;
- Consequently, the promise of the Father is going to be actualized;
- Jesus announces this imminent actualization in terms of the promise of the Father without clarifying the contents;
- But it is he, himself, who will send this promise;
- Then he is elevated to heaven.

One can presume from this moment forward that the promise can only be actualized in the absence of Jesus.[11]

At the beginning of Acts, the author recapitulates Jesus's history (1:1–3); then recalls the promise made in Luke 24:49 (v. 4), but this time he gives the contents of the promise (v. 5). The Resurrected One reaffirms the promise in v. 8a: "But you will receive power when the Holy Spirit has come upon you," and once again, he reminds the disciples of their role as

---

[10] See Fitzmyer, *The Gospel according to Luke (I–IX)*, p. 230.
[11] See John 16:7; 15:26.

witnesses: "and you will be my witnesses in Jerusalem . . ." (v. 8b). Then he is elevated before their eyes (vv. 9–11).

What emerges now are the following:

- The historic unity is clearly established by the transition between the gospel and the book of Acts that the summary contained in verses 1–3 constitutes;
- Jesus recalls the promise, this time revealing the contents: the Spirit (vv. 4–5, 8);
- Immediately after, he is taken up to heaven (vv. 9–11).

The progression of this second scenario, as compared to the first, consists in the revealing of the object of the promise. But it becomes clear that, in order for the Spirit to be poured out, Jesus must leave. For according to Acts 2:33 (and Luke 24:49 as well), it is Jesus who will send the promise of the Father. Thus becomes apparent all the pertinence of the accounts of the ascension and the judicious choice of their places of insertion.

It is Jesus who will send the promise, said the author, and, indeed, this happens in Acts 2:1–4 on the day of Pentecost. Thus, what remained for him to explain was how this would be made possible, and he does not neglect to do it—Acts 2:33 is this explanation: "Being therefore exalted at the right hand of God, and having received from the Father the promise of the Holy Spirit . . . ."[12]

But before coming to this ultimate proclamation, Luke, in order to insure the reader's understanding, as it were, produces a synthesis of his demonstration in the framework of Peter's speech:

- The eschatological times have come (Acts 2:16–17)
- The proof? The Spirit is poured out (vv. 17ff.)
- How was that possible? The Jesus event is the fulfillment of God's salvation (vv. 22–32)
- God has, consequently, exalted this Jesus (v. 33a)
- By him, the community is the beneficiary of the promise (v. 33b)

And the final conclusion Luke leads to is summarized as follows:

---

[12] Dillon, p. 219, on this subject, writes: "So far as the content of the circumlocutions for the Spirit is concerned, it can be dealt with quickly. 'The promise of the Father' is, nevertheless, 'sent' by Jesus, a combination which is explained in Acts 2:33 in the recurrent Lukan perspective of the Father's action through Jesus's mediation."

- The promised Spirit is the Spirit of the Father (Acts 2:17)
- The Father gives him to Jesus who pours him out to the community (Acts 2:33)
- The Spirit who lives in the community is the Spirit of the Christ received from the Father—or the Spirit of the Father and of the Christ

The importance of Acts 2:33 as the point of arrival of the demonstration cannot be overly emphasized. Without the proclamation that this verse contains, it would have been difficult to see Jesus's mediation role in the fulfillment of the promise which is identified as the gift of the Spirit.

2. THE PROMISE OF THE SPIRIT—ESSENTIAL CONDITION TO THE MESSIANIC FULFILLMENT

As previously noted, the idea of the "promise of the Holy Spirit" finds an explanation in the coherence of the Lukan texts. However, it is first written into the stream of the messianic tradition. Furthermore, Luke brings out this perspective very well in the speech where the key verse is inserted, verse 33. Verse 30 is, in this respect, very explicit:

> Since he [David] was a prophet, he knew that God had sworn with an oath to him that he would put one of his descendants on his throne. (Acts 2:30)

This oath recalls expressly the oracle of the prophet Nathan:[13]

> When your days are fulfilled and you lie down with your ancestors, I will raise up your offspring after you, who shall come forth from your body, and I will establish his kingdom. He shall build a house for my name, and I will establish the throne of his kingdom forever. (2 Sam 7:12–13)

It is in this oracle that the messianic hope is actually rooted. A hope which would be, thereafter, constantly evoked (see Pss 132:12; 89:3–4; 1 Chr 17:11–14; Ezek 34:23ff.), and David's characteristics would be clarified little by little. He will be servant of God (Jer 33:21); shepherd of Israel and prince in the midst of the people (Ezek 34:24); king established by

---

[13] On the subject, see O'Toole, "Acts 2:30 and the Davidic Covenant of Pentecost," pp. 245–58.

God (Jer 30:9); adopted son of God (Ps 2:7; see 25:7, 14); beneficiary of God's protection (Pss 18:51; 20:7; 28:8). But especially, the Spirit of God would rest on him:

> A shoot shall come out from the stump of Jesse, and a branch shall grow out of his roots. The Spirit of the Lord shall rest on him, the spirit of wisdom and understanding, the spirit of counsel and might, the spirit of knowledge and the fear of the Lord. (Isa 11:1–2) [14]

The gift of the Spirit will become therefore, in the Jewish context, a sign of the identification of the Messiah, the constitutive element of messianism.[15] Moreover, if Luke places the ultimate gift of the Spirit to Jesus at the moment of his resurrection, it is that in his point of view, rightly so, Jesus is made Messiah at his resurrection.[16] The relationship that he establishes between verses 30 and 31 shows this well.

---

[14] It is noteworthy that Isa 11:2 is the only text explicitly associating messianism with the gift of the Spirit. Other texts, such as Isa 42:1 and 61:1–3, are dressed rather with a prophetic character (even though they are often mentioned as messianic; see Chevallier, "Luc et L'Esprit Saint. À la mémoire du P. Augustin George [1915–1977]," p. 2).

[15] There are several witnesses relating to this criterion of the identification of the Messiah of which the following are examples: *Pss. Sol.* 17:37: "God will make him powerful in the Holy Spirit," (see also 18:7–8); *1 En.* 62:2: "The Spirit of justice was poured out on him"; *T. Levi* 18:7: "The glory of Highest will be pronounced on him and the Spirit of intelligence and of sanctification will rest on him"; *T. Jud.* 24:2: "The heavens will open on him to pour out the Spirit, the blessing of the Father." We must, nevertheless, be careful of the Christian modifications of the Testaments of the Fathers, such as mentioned in "heavens that opened"; on this subject, see Chevallier, *L'Esprit et le Messie dans le bas-judaïsme et le Nouveau Testament*, pp. 1–45; Sjöberg, "RouaH dans le judaïsme palestinien," p. 104.

[16] Luke, on this point, agrees with Paul (see Rom 1:4), but not with Mark and Matthew, who place the messianic investiture at the baptism. That Jesus was made Messiah at the resurrection is the opinion of numerous scholars: Weiss, *Earliest Christianity*, vol. 1, pp. 118ff.; Bultmann, *Theology of the New Testament*, vol. 1, pp. 43ff.; Dunn, "Spirit, Holy Spirit," *Dictionary of the New Testament Theology*, p. 698; more particularly, Hayes, "The Resurrection as Enthronement and the Earliest Church Christology," pp. 337–45, who writes (p. 337): "The fullest and clearest expressions of an enthronement Christology within the New Testament are found in Acts 2:22–36; 13:33 and Romans 1:3ff." But according to Hayes, the idea of a messianic enthronement at the resurrection depends on a primitive exegesis of the Old Testament texts reflecting royal theology, namely: Pss 110:1; 2:7; 2 Sam 7; it would not, however, be Lukan, he says, for according to Luke, Jesus is Christ since his birth (Luke 2:11). He believes, following Lindars, *New Testament Apologetic*, pp. 36–59, that the "resurrection speech" (Acts 2:22–36) must be separated from the "Pentecost speech" (Acts

Thus, after having recalled the messianic oracle (v. 30): "Since he [David] was a prophet, he knew that God had sworn with an oath to him that he would put one of his descendants on his throne," he continues with (v. 31a): "Foreseeing this, David spoke of the resurrection of the Messiah." What the author affirms here is that David's descendant being seated on the throne is directly linked to Christ's resurrection: in order that there would be a descendant on the throne of David, Jesus had to undergo the resurrection.[17] In brief, the messianic investiture of Jesus coincides with his resurrection. Moreover, it is what the author reaffirms without equivocation in Acts 13:33[18]: "And we bring you the good news that what God promised to our ancestors he has fulfilled for us, their children, by raising Jesus; as also it is written in the second psalm, 'You are my Son; today I have begotten you.'"

The quotation of Ps 2:7 necessarily brings out the messianic enthronement of Jesus. Furthermore, the moment of this enthronement is explicitly fixed in time: when God resurrected Jesus.

The remainder of the argumentation in Peter's speech supports the facts of verses 30–31:

- V. 32: vigorous reassertion of the reality of the resurrection: "This Jesus God raised up, and of that all of us are witnesses";

- V. 33: presentation of the particular status of Jesus linked to his resurrection: "Exalted at the right hand . . .";

2:14–21). Richard, "Conçu de Saint-Esprit, né de la Vierge Marie," pp. 300ff., believes as well that the texts of Acts 2:32–36 and 13:32–33 show that it is in the resurrection of the Christ that the promise concerning the sonship of the Messiah is fulfilled. But, he points out, nevertheless, (p. 303) "that in his earthly existence, Jesus was already the person that his resurrection fully disclosed."

[17] The contesting of this point of view by Marshall, *Luke: Historian and Theologian*, p. 162, is not very convincing; he writes: "The argument is not from the resurrection of Jesus to His subsequent status as Messiah, but rather from His Messiahship to the fact that as Messiah He must rise from the dead." This point of view does not have support in Peter's speech.

[18] Acts 13:33, as an affirmation, fits well into Paul's speech at Antioch. However, it was demonstrated in chapter 2 that the missionary speeches—of which Paul's at Antioch is one—are of Luke's editing. It would seem then that in Paul's speech, Luke is looking to support a fundamental idea already announced in Peter's speech (Acts 2:30–31). Dunn, *Christology in the Making*, p. 36, writes: "Here clearly the resurrection of Jesus is spoken of as a fulfillment of the divine promise to Israel, a promise expressed in Ps 2:7. The significant feature of this verse is that it uses the language of 'begetting' and specifies a particular birth-day, a day on which someone (the King, the Messiah) becomes God's son."

- Vv. 34–35: proof of his exaltation (1) by the mention of the ascension: "David did not ascend into the heavens," but Jesus did; (2) with the quotation of the normative Psalm of the exaltation, Ps 110:1;

- V. 36: final proclamation brought out by all that precedes: "Therefore let the entire house of Israel know with certainty that God has made him both Lord and Messiah, this Jesus whom you crucified."

The present development allows us to conclude that the assertion concerning the promise of the Spirit in v. 33,—"and having received from the Father the promise of the Holy Spirit"—being the point of arrival of an internal Lukan demonstration, is also the end result of the messianic hope.[19] Luke demonstrated, in effect, that this hope finds its fulfillment in the resurrection of the Christ. It is normal, consequently, to associate the gift of the Spirit with the resurrection since the resurrection is essential to being the Messiah.

CONCLUSION

The unity of the history of salvation is a fundamental preoccupation for Luke. He constantly looks to bring out the continuity in the development of its stages. He demonstrates that the Jesus event is the end of this history. By his life, his death, and his resurrection, God actualizes in him the promise of pouring out his Spirit on the people. The contents of Acts 2:33 thus show this Jesus event as the place of the actualization of the promise and as the meeting point between the Old and the New Covenants. It, indeed, affirms, in this verse, the continuity between the two eras: God promised to the people of the Old Covenant to pour out the Spirit at the end times; in bringing Jesus back to life (Acts 2:32), he gives him the gift of the promised Spirit (Acts 2:33a), and Jesus glorified pours him out on the people in the new times (Acts 2:33b). The entire explanation on the links of unity and of continuity between the two eras is thus found in the summary in Acts 2:33.

If Luke presents the fulfillment of the promise of the Spirit as the historical transition point between the Old and the New Covenants, he also makes it the literary transition point between his two works, the third Gospel and the book of Acts; these two works, however, attest to two times of

---

[19] See Voss, *Die Christologie der Lukanischen Schriften in Grundzügen*, p. 146.

the fulfillment of the promise: the time of the man Jesus and the time of the church.

It is now necessary to see the meaning of this fulfillment in respect to each of these two times. The step which follows in chapter 5 aims to demonstrate the understanding that it brings to the Jesus of the Gospel of Luke. This conclusion concerning the messianic investiture to the resurrection necessitates, in effect, a study of the christological scope of the pneumatological facts of certain texts of the gospel, such as those of the annunciation (1:31–35), the baptism (3:21–22), the testing (4:1ff.), and the inauguration of the ministry in Galilee (4:14ff.). Chapter 6 will then bring out the ecclesiological impact of the gift of the Spirit on the believers.

CHAPTER 5

ACTS 2:33A—SHEDDING LIGHT ON JESUS

"Being therefore exalted at the right hand of God and having received from the Father the promise of the Holy Spirit . . ."

The proclamation of Acts 2:33 is the culmination of a detailed demonstration previously established (chapter 2). Luke synthesized this demonstration in Peter's speech (Acts 2:14–36, 38–39), into which this proclamation is integrated. The speech is actually a synthesis of all that precedes from the annunciation up to the ascension: Jesus of Nazareth, who worked signs and wonders, is truly God's sent One (v. 22); the eschatological times are inaugurated in him and by him; what happens in the believers shows well, in effect, that the promises of God are fulfilled (vv. 17–21); but he was rejected and put to death (v. 23); God decides, nevertheless, to deliver him from death (v. 24); and in resurrecting him, he gave him David's throne (vv. 30–31); he made him Christ and Lord (v. 36); in doing so, he gave him his own Spirit, the essential factor for his reign (v. 33).

Luke seems, therefore, to say in Acts 2:33: Here it is! Everything that precedes had, then, the one objective of bringing to light this fundamental reality: *Jesus was made Christ by the Spirit of God at the resurrection.*

If everything effectively converges toward this proclamation, it is logical to think that this same proclamation must shed light on what precedes it; that it must guide its understanding; that it must be the standard of interpretation. Briefly, if Jesus is made Christ and Lord by the Spirit of God which he receives in fullness at his resurrection, (1) how then must we understand the presentation that Luke makes of him at his birth and baptism? (2) how must we understand his relationship to the Spirit during his life on earth? (3) and how must we define the nature of his historic mission?

This chapter will try to shed light on these questions. From this perspective, we turn to the texts on the Spirit which are directly related to the themes announced by these questions, namely: (1) Luke 1:31–35: Jesus's conception; (2) Luke 3:21–22: his baptism; (3) Luke 4:1: his relationship with the Spirit; and (4) Luke 4:14, 18: his historic mission. Also to be examined are the texts related to the people around Jesus's beginnings, since their interventions are explicitly introduced as support of the christological discourse.

On the other hand, the passage in Luke 3:16, dealing with the baptism of John and the baptism to come, will not be studied until the next chapter, keeping in mind the relationship of this passage to the events of Pentecost. Such will be the case as well for the texts in relationship with the future times: Luke 12:10 (blasphemy against the Spirit) and Luke 12:12 (inspiration in times of persecution).

PRELIMINARY REMARKS

The texts enumerated above, in addition to Luke 10:21—where, at the disciples return from the mission, Jesus rejoices in the Spirit—cover all the passages where the Spirit is mentioned in the third Gospel. The distribution of the texts is divided into two groups: the *first*, at the beginning of the gospel, is related to Jesus's entry into the world and to his entrance into public life; the *second*, at the beginning of the ascent to Jerusalem, coincides with the teaching to the disciples on the manner in which they should witness about Jesus.

It is, therefore, noteworthy that Luke initiates each one of the two large sections of his gospel by having the Spirit intervene. Thus, he places Jesus's mission under the aegis of the Spirit and, by anticipation, the mission of the disciples. However, it is also noteworthy that outside of these marked times, he does not mention the Spirit in the rest of the Gospel, a point to be discussed later.

1. THE SPIRIT AND THE BIRTH OF JESUS—LUKE 1–2

Luke elaborates a great production to mark the coming of Jesus into the world. He refers to numerous people whose respective contributions consist in revealing a dimension of the mystery of this coming. He is very careful, however, to note the seal of the Spirit on each stage of the development. The people speak and act under the direction of the Spirit; the central event, Jesus's conception, is also placed under the sign of the Spirit.

The study at the heart of this section will deal with the nature of (1) the role of the Spirit in the angel's message; (2) the role of the Spirit in his interventions with secondary characters; and (3) Jesus's relationship with the Spirit from his conception to his baptism.

The Spirit and the Announcement to Mary: Luke 1:31–35

Verses 31–35 of the first chapter of Luke constitute the heart of the account of the annunciation (vv. 26–38). The exegetical study of these verses is fundamental to the understanding of the messianism of Jesus in the Lukan perspective. Their contents, for all practical purposes, establish the basis of the development of Acts 2:30–36 and, principally, of the proclamation of Acts 2:33 (this is the case, of course, if placed from the point of view of the chronology of the texts, but if placed from the point of view of the Lukan christological development, the opposite is true).

The following analysis, at certain times, could give the impression that it is veering away from Luke's pneumatology, the central theme of the research. Nevertheless, we must keep in mind that the author's pneumatology is serving his Christology. Also apparent from this study is that the fulfillment of the messianic mission proclaimed in the angel's message (vv. 31–35) essentially leans on the intervention of the Spirit. Consequently, it is appropriate to carefully bring to light the christological scope of the annunciation to bring out the importance of the role of the Spirit in the fulfillment of this messianic mission.

Luke 1–2[1]*—The Literary Context of Luke 1:31–35*

---

[1] The principal works to consult on the first two chapters of the Gospel of Luke are the following: Brown, *The Birth of the Messiah*, pp. 235–499; Daniélou, *Les Évangiles de l'Enfance*; Feuillet, *Jésus et sa mère d'après les récits lucaniens de l'Enfance et d'après saint Jean*; Fitzmyer, *The Gospel according to Luke I–IX*, pp. 303–448; George, *Études sur l'oeuvre de Luc*, pp. 43–65; Laurentin, *Structure et théologie de Luc 1–11*; idem, *Les évangiles de l'enfance du Christ*; Minear, "Luke's Use of the Birth Stories"; Perrot, *Les récits de l'enfance de Jésus. Matthieu 1–2—Luc 1–2*, pp. 35–70 and "Les récits de l'enfance dans la Haggada antérieure au 2ᵉ siècle de notre ère." For a very detailed bibliography (up to 1981) on the infancy accounts, see Legrand, *L'Annonce à Marie*, pp. 364–78; also Brown, "Gospel Infancy Narrative Research from 1976 to 1986: Part I (Matthew)"; "Part II (Luke)," presents an exhaus-

One cannot ask the question of the origins of Luke 1:31–35—or of the account of the announcement to Mary of which these verses are a part—without taking into consideration the entire first two chapters of the gospel. The technique of parallelism, which constitutes the literary framework of these chapters, in effect, links the different elements into a direct interdependence. The resulting configuration springs from an editorial activity which, evidently, goes well beyond a simple organization of various traditions. The first question is, thus, to know if Luke is responsible for the construction of these two chapters; if yes, to what extent?

"The problem of the authenticity of Luke 1–2 is not new," writes Legrand, "it goes back to Marcion."[2] He made the gospel begin at 4:31.[3] The tendencies of modern criticism, of which Legrand presents a survey,[4] seem, nevertheless, to converge toward the conclusion that this is Luke's editing. The studies of the style and the vocabulary brought out important linguistic similarities between these chapters and the remainder of the Gospel and Acts.[5]

However, these resemblances are not limited to the linguistic aspect; they show themselves as well in the theological orientations. Thus, R. E. Brown firmly believes that these two chapters are the real introduction of the Gospel and that no analysis of the Lukan theology must neglect them.[6]

---

tive bibliography on the studies concerning the infancy accounts, which cover the period of 1976–1986 (pp. 468–73 of the first part of his article).

[2] Legrand, *L'Annonce à Marie*, p. 25.

[3] Marcion's attitude is generally attributed to his docetist tendencies.

[4] Pp. 25–29.

[5] The agreement on the authenticity of Luke 1–2 is rather unanimous since the beginning of the century, as proves the list of the following scholars who recognize it as such: Brown, *The Birth of the Messiah*, p. 241; Ernst, *Das Evangelium nach Lukas*, p. 27; Fitzmyer, *The Gospel according to Luke I–IX*, pp. 309ff.; George, *Études sur l'oeuvre de Luc*, p. 65; Harnack, *Luke the Physician*, pp. 96–105; 199–218; Laurentin, *Structure et théologie de Luc 1–2*, p. 14; Leany, *A Commentary on the Gospel according to St. Luke*, p. 20; Legrand, *L'Annonce à Marie*, p. 29; Machen, "The Hymns of the First Chapter of Luke," p. 38, and "The Origin of the first Two Chapters of Luke," pp. 212–17; Marshall, *The Gospel of Luke*, p. 46; Oliver, "The Lucan Birth Stories and the Purpose of Luke-Acts"; Perrot, "Le récit de l'enfance selon saint Luc," p. 36; Schmithals, *Das Evangelium nach Lukas*, p. 20; Schneider, *Das Evangelium nach Lukas: Kapitel 1–10*, pp. 29–30; Zimmermann, "Evangelium des Lukas 1–2." Some scholars, nevertheless, took a position against the authenticity of Luke 1–2, among them were Hilgenfeld, "Die Geburt–und Kindheitgeschichte Jesu," pp. 177ff.; Conzelmann, *The Theology of St. Luke*, pp. 20, 118, 172.

[6] *The Birth of the Messiah*, p. 242; of the same opinion: Fitzmyer, *The Gospel according to Luke (I–IX)*, pp. 310ff.; Minear, "The Interpreter and the Nativity Stories," pp.

These first two chapters would fulfill an analogous function to Acts 1–2: Luke 1–2 as a transition between the Old Covenant and the New Covenant in Jesus;[7] Acts 1–2 as a transition between the times of Jesus and the times of the church. The prophetic movement, very marked in Luke 1–2, can also appear as a prelude to the great prophetic movement of Acts. The theme of the Spirit, very conspicuous in Luke 1–2, is also a fundamental theme of Acts. However, especially the Christology of Luke 1:31–35 (as we will see) calls for the Christology of Acts (Acts 2:33, 36; 13:33). Finally, other particularly Lukan themes appear in these first two chapters, such as the importance accorded to Jerusalem, to the poor, to prayer, etc.[8]

The attribution to Luke of chapters 1–2 of the Gospel seems then incontestable.[9] It is possible, however, that these chapters were introduced into the Gospel only after its composition and perhaps even after the composition of Acts.[10]

Now, what about the question of the sources? Again, on this point, the scholars are almost unanimous: Luke very certainly used sources to write his first two chapters. Where there is a divergence of opinion, however, is on the origin and exact content of these sources. Some believe that they detect Hebrew antecedents and suggest that Luke translated certain material from a Hebrew source.[11] Others speak of an Aramaic source[12] (today a practically abandoned hypothesis); still others speak of a Greek

---

358ff.; Oliver, "*The Lucan Birth Stories and the Purpose of Luke-Acts*," p. 233, also shares this opinion, but, nevertheless, reckons that "the nativity stories preview the theology of Acts more than of Luke."

[7] See Chevallier, *Souffle de Dieu. Le Saint-Esprit dans le Nouveau Testament, Vol. I*, p. 163; he writes: "One of the characteristic aspects of chapters 1 and 2 of Luke is the adoption of the style and the perspective of the Old Testament. Luke showed, so to speak, how the Old Testament begot the New Testament."

[8] See Laurentin, *Structure et théologie of Luke I–II*, pp. 25ff.

[9] See on this subject Minear, "Luke's Use of the Birth Stories," pp. 112–18. Minear reports on the numerous evidences gathered by different scholars (Bultmann, Cadbury, Morgenthaler, Dodd, Plummer), whose evidences prove the harmony between the infancy narratives and the whole of Luke's two works.

[10] This is the opinion of Brown, *The Birth of the Messiah*, pp. 242–43, and of Fitzmyer, *The Gospel according to Luke (I–IX)*, p. 311.

[11] Among others, Sahlin, *Der Messias und das Gottesvolk*, p. 265; Laurentin, *Structure et théologie de Luc 1–2*, pp. 12ff.; he especially elaborated his position in his article, "Traces of d'allusions étymologiques en Luc 1–2." He gives as well, in this article, a good overview of the other positions held by different scholars.

[12] Dibelius, "Jungfrauensohn und Krippenkind, pp. 1–78; Plummer, *The Gospel according to S. Luke*, p. xxvi; B. Weiss, *Die Quellen des Lukasevangeliums*, p. 195.

source.¹³ Then, there are those who think that Luke himself composed these two chapters with the help of "oral traditions, biblical models"¹⁴ and Judeo-Christian songs.

Perhaps the preference must be accorded to this last hypothesis. I believe that Luke is responsible for the composition and structure of the first two chapters, but, nevertheless, I do not eliminate the possibility of the use of written sources. What appears without a doubt, however, is that the constitutive material of these chapters perfectly introduces the theological orientations that the Gospel of Luke will take (and Acts to a great extent). The people, the themes, the production, the literary techniques, everything is orchestrated in view of the presentation of the central person, Jesus. The foundations of Luke's Christo-pneumatology are laid here. The rest of this chapter will demonstrate it.

*Literary Analysis: Luke 1:31–35*¹⁵

1:31
καὶ ἰδοὺ συλλήμψῃ ἐν γαστρὶ καὶ τέξῃ υἱὸν καὶ καλέσεις τὸ ὄνομα αὐτοῦ Ἰησοῦν. /
And now, you will conceive in your womb and bear a son, and you will name¹⁶ him Jesus.

1:32
οὗτος ἔσται μέγας καὶ υἱὸς ὑψίστου κληθήσεται καὶ δώσει αὐτῷ κύριος ὁ θεὸς τὸν θρόνον Δαυὶδ τοῦ πατρὸς αὐτοῦ, /
He will be great, and will be called the Son of the Most High, and the Lord God will give to him the throne of his ancestor David.

1:33
καὶ βασιλεύσει ἐπὶ τὸν οἶκον Ἰακὼβ εἰς τοὺς αἰῶνας καὶ τῆς βασιλείας αὐτοῦ οὐκ ἔσται τέλος. /

---

¹³ See Gaechter, *Maria im Erdenleben*, pp. 30–36.
¹⁴ Benoit, "L'Annonciation," p. 196; of the same opinion, Brown, *The Birth of the Messiah*, p. 247; Harnack, *Luke the Physician*, pp. 96–100; Cadbury, *The Making of Luke-Acts*, pp. 62ff.; N. Turner, "The Relation of Luke I and II to Hebraic Sources and the Rest of Luke-Acts," pp. 100–109.
¹⁵ This text has no textual criticism problem.
¹⁶ According to Zerwick and Grosvenor, *A Grammatical Analysis of the Greek New Testament*, p. 169, καλέσεις, as in Luke 1:13, would convey more the idea of an imperative than a prediction.

He will reign over the house of Jacob forever, and of his kingdom there will be no end.

1:34
εἶπεν δὲ Μαριὰμ πρὸς τὸν ἄγγελον, Πῶς ἔσται τοῦτο, ἐπεὶ ἄνδρα οὐ γινώσκω; /
Mary said to the angel, "How can this be, since I am a virgin?"

1:35
καὶ ἀποκριθεὶς ὁ ἄγγελος εἶπεν αὐτῇ, Πνεῦμα ἅγιον ἐπελεύσεται ἐπὶ σὲ καὶ δύναμις ὑψίστου ἐπισκιάσει σοι· διὸ καὶ τὸ γεννώμενον ἅγιον κληθήσεται υἱὸς θεοῦ. /
The angel said to her, "The Holy Spirit will come upon you, and the power of the Most High will overshadow you; therefore the child to be born will be holy; he will be called Son of God."[17]

These verses contain the central message of the account of the annunciation to Mary (Luke 1:26–35). But first a word on the literary genre chosen as the means of this message.[18]

---

[17] The last part of the verse is difficult to translate. Zerwick and Grosvenor, *A Grammatical Analysis*, p. 172, translate the present passive participle γεννώμενον as "be born" and τὸ γεννώμενον as "the child born," clarifying that the present form is used for the future participle. Reiling and Swellengrebel, *A Translator's Handbook on the Gospel of Luke*, p. 59, translate it "that which is being begotten will be called holy (and) the son of God." A. Marshall, *The Interlinear Greek-English New Testament*, renders it, "Therefore also that holy thing which shall be born of thee shall be called the Son of God." The French translations of the Bible, *BJ*, *TOB* and *OSTY*, render respectively "the child will be holy and will be called Son of God"; "the one who is going to be born will be holy and will be called Son of God"; "the holy being who will be born will be called Son of God." Finally, the *Revised Standard Version of the Bible* opts for the following translation (for the last part of the verse): "will be called holy, the Son of God." This is the translation that I hold to, omitting the article before "Son of God," however. This is also the translation held to by Schweizer, *The Good News according to Luke*, p. 25; see Schürmann, *Das Lukasevangelium: Kommentar zu Kap. 1:1–9:50*, pp. 54–55. As to γεννώμενον, I translate it as a future, "that will be born," the context thus calling for it.

[18] The most recent monograph on the annunciation is Legrand's, *L'Annonce à Marie*. In addition to this well-researched study, note the following works: Allard, "L'Annonce à Marie et les annonces de naissances miraculeuses de l'Ancien Testament"; Audet, "L'Annonce à Marie"; Benoit, "*L'Annonciation*"; R. E. Brown, "Luke's Method in the Annunciation Narratives of Chapter One" and "The Annunciation of the Birth of Jesus," *The Birth of the Messiah*, pp. 286–330; Gaechter, "Der Verkündigungsbericht Luke 1:26–38"; Lyonnet, "L'Annonciation et la mariologie biblique: ce que l'exégèse conclut du récit lucanien de l'Annonciation" and "Le récit

The Literary Genre of the Announcement
The parallel between the announcement to Mary and the announcement accounts of the Old Testament has been established on several occasions by scholars.[19] It has thus been demonstrated that the form of these accounts corresponds to a common outline, e.g., the outline that Brown[20] presents in five steps (the outline presented here is the one of the announcement of a birth):

1. The appearance of the Angel of the Lord (or of the Lord himself)
2. Fear or prostration of the visionary confronted by the supernatural presence
3. The divine message:
    a. The visionary is called by name
    b. An expression describes the visionary
    c. The visionary is urged not to fear
    d. A woman conceives or is going to conceive a child
    e. She gives birth to a male child
    f. The name of the child is given
    g. Etymology interprets the name
    h. The future accomplishments of the child are recited
4. Objection of the visionary or request for a sign
5. Sign reassuring the visionary

The announcement to Mary clearly follows the outline of this form.[21] Nevertheless, in the Old Testament, the use of this form aims to emphasize the origin and the meaning of the vocation of the person announced to the parents.[22] It may be, however, that the announcement was addressed to

---

de l'Annonciation et la Maternité Divine de la Sainte Vierge"; Graystone, *Virgin of All Virgins: The Interpretation of Luke 1:34*.

[19] On this subject, see Allard, pp. 730–33, who establishes the parallel with the announcement to Abraham of the birth of Isaac (Gen 17:1–15); Audet, pp. 352ff., who proposes as an archetype of the genre the announcement to Gideon (Judg 6:11ff.); Laurentin, *Structure et théologie de Luc I–II*, pp. 98–99, who goes back to the birth of Samson (Judg 13) and of Samuel (1 Sam 1–2); Legrand, *L'Annonce à Marie*, p. 91, who furnishes a table of the different Old Testament models (Brown, *The Birth of the Messiah*, p. 156, does the same); see finally the study of Graystone, pp. 61–82.

[20] Brown, *The Birth of the Messiah*, p. 156.

[21] See Fitzmyer, *The Gospel according to Luke (I–IX)*, p. 335.

[22] In this case, the announcement to Abraham of the birth of Isaac and of the covenant that God will establish with him (Gen 17:15–22) and the announcement of the birth of

the person himself[23] (in this instance the form undergoes the necessary modifications). In each case, the objection invoked by the person visited shows that the objective of the announcement would be impossible to realize without the personal intervention of God. God's power is demonstrated, acting in spite of human weakness and inadequacies. God brings his salvation through human beings whose capacities, at this precise moment, are inadequate (sterility of the women, weakness of the person, etc). It is clear, on the other hand, that these divine interventions strongly impact the history of salvation. This is very evident concerning the announcement of the birth of Jesus.

It is not feasible to make an absolute archetype of any of the Old Testament models, however, for each case corresponds to a particular context and has distinctive characteristics which condition the socio-religious reading of the experience.[24] Nevertheless, in all of the cases is a double constant: (1) the event announced is an act of God; (2) the hero of the event will have a specific role to play in the history of salvation.

The Angel's Message: The Announcement of the Child
The formulation of v. 31 corresponds exactly to the stereotypical phraseology of the Old Testament birth oracle.[25] This is clearly shown by putting the verse in parallel with three examples below taken from the Septuagint:

Samson in relationship to the role that he will have to play against the Philistines (Judg 13:1–25).

[23] In this case, the announcement to Gideon, who would have to fight the Midianites (Judg 6:11–18).

[24] Legrand, *L'Annonce à Marie*, p. 101, is correct in writing: "... if the genre can and must serve as a guide in the interpretation of a text, it only does so up to a certain point. It remains too ambiguous to serve as the ultimate principle of explanation. One has to look further for the principle of the internal organization of the text."

[25] See Ernst, *Das Evangelium nach Lukas*, p. 69; Fitzmyer, *The Gospel according to Luke (I–IX)*, p. 346; Grelot, "La naissance d'Isaac et celle de Jésus," p. 462.

Luke 1:31
καὶ ἰδοὺ συλλήμ-
ψῃ ἐν γαστρὶ καὶ
τέξῃ υἱὸν καὶ κα-
λέσεις τὸ ὄνομα
αὐτοῦ Ἰησοῦν. /

"And now, you
will conceive in
your womb and
bear a son, and
you will name
him Jesus."

Gen 17:19b
ἰδοὺ Σαρρα ἡ γυνή σου τέξεταί σοι υἱὸν καὶ καλέσεις
τὸ ὄνομα αὐτοῦ Ἰσαάκ. / "your wife Sarah shall bear
you a son, and you shall name him Isaac."

Judg 13:5a
ὅτι ἰδοὺ σὺ ἐν γαστρὶ ἔχεις καὶ τέξῃ υἱόν. /
"for you shall conceive and bear a son."

Isa 7:14b
ἰδοὺ ἡ παρθένος ἐν γαστρὶ ἕξει καὶ τέξεται υἱόν,
καὶ καλέσεις τὸ ὄνομα αὐτοῦ Ἐμμανουήλ. /
"Look, the young woman is with child and shall
bear a son, and shall name him Immanuel."

In these oracles, there is common terminology: the use of the same verbs (τικτεῖν, καλεῖν), the same nouns (γαστρί, ὄνομα, υἱόν) and the giving of the name to the infant (Ἰσαάκ, Ἐμμανουήλ, Ἰησοῦν). The closest model to Luke 1:31 is, nevertheless, Isa 7:14b. This is hardly surprising considering, on the one hand, the messianic character of the oracle of the prophet (contrary to the oracles of Gen 17:19b and Judg 13:5a), and, on the other hand, Luke's desire to confer on this text a precisely messianic impact.

Another important detail to note on the subject of v. 31 is the fact that the name is attributed by divine authority; this indicates that God saved the child for the accomplishing of His works[26] and that his destiny is determined by God.[27] Unlike Matt 1:21, the meaning of the name is, however, not given.[28] But, it was not, first of all, the meaning of the name which interested the author, Schürmann points out, "but rather the fact that the name was given by God."[29]

The Angel's Message: The Identity of the Child

After the oracle of v. 31, the movement of the text presents two distinct times: (1) vv. 32–33; (2) vv. 34–35. Although the messianic orientation is

---

[26] See Schürmann, *Das Lukasevangelium: Kommentar zu Kap. 1:1–9:50*, p. 46.
[27] See Danker, *Jesus and the New Age according to St. Luke*, p. 11.
[28] In the message to the shepherds, Jesus is, however, announced as Savior (Luke 2:11).
[29] Schürmann, *Das Lukasevangelium: Kommentar zu Kap. 1:1–9:50*, p. 46, note 47.

evident in each one of the two times, nevertheless, two levels of messianic Christology are distinguishable, written in a progressive relationship, each one of the levels corresponding respectively to the first (vv. 32–33) and to the second time (vv. 34–35).

i. The Terminology (vv. 32–33)

Οὗτος ἔσται μέγας: "This one will be great." In the announcement to Zechariah (Luke 1:11–20), the angel said of John: "He will be great in the sight of the Lord" / ἔσται γὰρ μέγας ἐνώπιον τοῦ κυρίου. John's greatness did not only satisfy human norms; his greatness was recognized by God.[30] However, with the insertion of the demonstrative οὗτος[31] / *this one*, the author can show his intention to mark the distinction between Jesus and John.[32] This distinction is effectively accentuated by attributing to Jesus the absolute form of the qualifier μέγας / *great*, whereas John's greatness is relative.[33] Laurentin also makes note that the use of the adjective "great" without addition is reserved to God[34] (Pss 48:2; 76:2; 86:10; 96:4; 135:5; 145:3; 147:5; Jer 10:6).

Ὑψίστου: the superlative ὕψιστος—literally "the most high"—bears a strong Hellenistic mark. From a purely poetic use at first, it will be used later on in the religious domain to designate the temple of the divinity as the "highest"[35] place. But it is also applied to the divinities. Thus, a temple is built to Ζεὺς ὕψιστος.[36]

In the Septuagint, apart from a few passages where it is used topographically, ὕψιστος always designates God.[37] It translates the Hebrew

---

[30] In the same manner, Luke had preserved the moral integrity of John's parents saying of them: "Both of them were righteous before God" (Luke 1:6a).

[31] According to Reiling and Swellengrebel, *A Translator's Handbook*, p. 55, οὗτος would only have value as a personal pronoun. It seems, however, that in inserting it in his text, Luke truly wanted to designate Jesus in a particular way and mark the distinction. It would, consequently, play the role of a demonstrative pronoun.

[32] See Laurentin, *Structure et théologie de Luc I–II*, p. 36.

[33] See Fitzmyer, *The Gospel according to Luke (I–IX)*, pp. 325, 347.

[34] Laurentin, *Structure et théologie de Luc I–II*, p. 36. Also, Schweizer, *The Good News according to Luke*, pp. 614ff.

[35] See Bertram, "ὕψιστος," *TDNT* 8:614ff.

[36] Ibid. See also ὕψιστος, 2, in Bauer, *A Greek-English Lexicon*. According to Bauer, the expression Ζευς ὕψιστος is found in Pindar, *Nem.*, 1, 60 [90]; 11, 2; Aeschylus, *Eum.* 28; etc.

[37] Bertram, "ὕψιστος," p. 617. The term appears 128 times in the Septuagint.

term עֶלְיוֹן "the Most High," "the exalted one"[38] (Gen 14:18; Dan 4:14). In the Hebraic world, this epithet made into a noun, עֶלְיוֹן, is strictly reserved for God. Therefore, it takes on an absolute character and transmits an identical connotation to the Greek term ὕψιστος. Seeing the equivalence, it is apparent that the authors of the Septuagint did not hesitate to use this well-established Hellenistic concept to qualify God, knowing that it would not leave any ambiguity as to the scope of the title attributed to God.

In pre-Christian Judaism, the title frequently appeared to designate Yahweh.[39] In the New Testament, it can be found almost exclusively in the Lukan writings:[40]

- Jesus will be called the Son of the Most High (Luke 1:32)
- The power of the Most High will overshadow Mary (1:35)
- John will be called the prophet of the Most High (1:76)
- Those who practice love will be called children of the Most High (6:35)
- A man who had demons calls Jesus Son of the Most High God (8:28)
- Stephen affirms that the Most High does not dwell in houses made with human hands (Acts 7:48)
- Paul and his companions are qualified as slaves of the Most High God (16:17)

It is clearly evident that the expression ὕψιστος is part of Lukan vocabulary and that it designates God as in Hellenism and the Septuagint. It remains to be seen if Luke wanted to establish a distinction between "Son of the Most High God" (v. 32) and "Son of God." (v. 35).

Κύριος ὁ θεός: "The Lord God." The title applied to God in this form does not necessarily reflect a Lukan manner of speaking of God. In the infancy accounts, it is found again two other times: "[John] will turn many of the people of Israel to the Lord their God" (1:16); in Zechariah's prophetic psalm: "Blessed be the Lord God of Israel" (1:68). The four other uses have synoptic parallels and are inscribed in Old Testament quotations: Luke 4:8, 12; 10:27; 20:37. This designation of God is used frequently, however, in the book of Revelation (10 times).

---

[38] Ibid. See also Fitzmyer, *The Gospel according to Luke (I–IX)*, pp. 347–48.

[39] *Jub.* 16:18; *1 En.* 9:3; 10:1; 46:7; 60:1, 22. In Qumran, it is often found in its Hebraic form: 1QS 4:22; 1QapGn 12:17; 20:12, 16; 21:2, 20; 22:15, 16, 21. On this subject, see Legrand, *L'Annonce à Marie*, p. 155.

[40] Only two other uses of ὕψιστος are found outside of Luke-Acts: Mark 5:7 and Heb 7:1.

The rest of the vocabulary—θρόνος, βασιλεύειν, Ἰακώβ, βασιλεία, εἰς τοὺς αἰῶνας—is not particularly Lukan. These terms and expressions are all found numerous times in other books of the New Testament.

ii. The Christological Impact

The messianic orientation of Luke 1:32–33 is undeniable. The points of similarity with Nathan's oracle are striking. Legrand established the following parallel, reproduced in its entirety:[41]

Luke 1:32–33	*2 Sam 7:9–16*
He will be *great* and will be called the *Son* of the Most High.	I will make for you a *great* name, like the name of the great ones of the earth. He shall be a *son* to me.
The Lord God will give to him the *throne* of his ancestor David.	I will establish the *throne* of his kingdom *forever*.
He will reign over the *house* of Jacob *forever*, and of his *kingdom* there *will be no end*.	Your *house* and your *kingdom* shall be made sure *forever* before me.

Luke's text has obviously been constructed according to the oracle, to show its fulfillment in Jesus.[42] The repetition of key terms is not a mistake: *great, son, throne, house, reign, forever* (*without end*). However, a question is posed on the subject of the title "son of the Most High." Did tradition perpetuate identifying "son of David" = "son of the Most High" (or "son of God")? Is the use of the title here truly of a messianic character?

(a) The Title Son of God *in the Old Testament and in Judaism.* First of all, it is important to verify if the title "son of God" was actually used in the

---

[41] Legrand, *L'Annonce à Marie*, p. 156. See also Laurentin, *Structure et théologie de Luc I–II*, p. 71; Brown, *The Birth of the Messiah*, p. 310.

[42] First recall that Nathan's oracle, as such, remained very much alive in the Old Testament tradition as in the Jewish tradition. It became, at the same time, the foundation and the reference point of the messianic hope (on this subject, see George, *Études sur l'oeuvre de Luc*, pp. 262ff.), thus attest the following Pss 89:4–5, 30, 37; 132:11–12 and the texts of the prophets Isa 9:6; 11:2; Jer 23:5; 33:15; Zech 6:12 (see also Isa 55:3; Ezek 34:23–24; 37:24–25; Amos 9:11). The later Old Testament tradition equally attests to this hope (1 Mac 5:27; Sir 47:11), as well as the inter-testamentary writings (as much in the Hellenistic as in the Palestinian milieu) still demonstrate the importance of this expectation (4QFlor 10–13; 1QSb 5:27–28; *Pss. Sol.* 17:21; *Sib. Or.* 3:47b–50).

Old Testament and in Judaism to designate the future Messiah. The Old Testament has different uses of the title. Applied to angels, in the plural form, it regularly designates the members of the heavenly court (Pss 29:1; 82:1, 6; Job 1:6; 2:1). In Gen 6:2, where it is a question of the sexual union of the sons of God and the daughters of men, it probably conceals a mythological connotation. On several occasions, the title designates, with a certain partiality, the people of God: "Then you shall say to Pharaoh, 'Thus says the Lord: Israel is my firstborn son'" (Exod 4:22). In this example, as in the others (Deut 14:1; Hos 11:1; Isa 1:2; Wis 18:13), the designation aims especially to accentuate the particular affective relationship that binds God to his people. "Son of God" is still used to characterize the person whose moral behavior is judged as conforming to the justice of God (Sir 4:10; Wis 2:18).

But the use of greatest interest is the one that refers to the king of Israel. There are only two attestations of this use: "I will be a father to him, and he shall be a son to me" (2 Sam 7:14a, repeated in 1 Chron 17:13; 22:10; 28:6), and "I will tell of the decree of the Lord: He said to me, 'You are my son; today I have begotten you'" (Ps 2:7). These texts make explicit reference to the earthly king. But was the title retained in the later tradition in order to designate the expected Messiah?

The Old Testament has no example with this meaning;[43] the Jewish literature does not have any either,[44] although the theme of "son of God" is very developed. The only place, in Judaism, where a similarity between this title and the Messiah could have been made, would be in the text of the pseudo Daniel (4QPsDnA^a). But Fitzmyer, who studied the document,[45] considers that the titles found there do not apply to the Messiah. Here is the reconstitution of the text that he proposes:

> [But your son] shall be great upon the earth, [O King! All (men) shall] make [peace], and all shall serve [him. He shall be called the son of] the [G]reat [God], and by his name shall he be named. He shall be

---

[43] More so Conzelmann, *An Outline of the Theology of the New Testament*, p. 76, deems that the title "son of God" is not synonymous with Messiah, even when it is used for the king of Israel.

[44] Ibid.

[45] See Fitzmyer, "The Contribution of Qumran Aramaic to the Study of the New Testament."

hailed as the Son of God and they shall call him Son of the Most High.[46]

Fitzmyer thinks that the titles could be applied to the son of some enthroned king, possibly an heir of David's throne. The context of the Hasmonean reign would then need to be explored.[47]

Nathan's oracle (2 Sam 7:11c, 12bc, 13b, 14a) is also explicitly reproduced in Qumran (4QFlor 10–13). But would that imply an identification of the son of God/Messiah?[48] Schweizer believes, rather, that in this case as elsewhere in the inter-testamentary literature the promised "son of God" is no longer understood as an individual but as "the holy remnant of Israel of the last days."[49]

The slim evidence found does not allow belief that the Hebraic tradition conserved the title "son of God" of the oracle of 2 Sam 7:14 as a figure of the identification of the Messiah.[50] But it has, nevertheless, always referred to the promise that it contains as a pledge of the hope in the

---

[46] Fitzmyer, "The Contribution of Qumran" pp. 393–94, shows the amazing parallel between the contents of this fragment and Luke 1:32, 35, as much in the formulation as in the terminology.

[47] Ibid. When Fitzmyer brings up the question again in his work *The Gospel according to Luke (I–IX)*, pp. 206–7, he separates categorically all association of "son of God"/Messiah in the Qumran document. See also the discussion of the theme by Schweizer, "The Concept of the Davidic 'Son of God' in Acts and Its Old Testament Background."

[48] This is the belief of Fuller, *The Foundations of New Testament Christology*, p. 32.

[49] Schweizer, "The Concept of the Davidic 'Son of God,'" p. 190. The *Testament of Levi* (4:2, 4) consists of this proclamation: "Nevertheless, the Lord answered your prayer to separate you from injustice and to be a son for him, a servant and a minister of his Presence. . . . A blessing will be given to you, thus to all your descendants, until the Lord visits all the nations for the mercy of his son forever." (Text quoted from Dupont-Sommer and Philonenko, eds., *La Bible. Écrits intertestamentaires, Bibliothèque de la Library Pléiade*, pp. 339–40). Nevertheless, caution must be used concerning the place of this last text when considering the numerous Christian changes made to the *Testaments of the Twelve Patriarchs*. See on this subject Dupont-Sommer and Philonenko, p. 814; also Paul, *Intertestament*, p. 64.

[50] Since the study of Dalmann, *The Words of Jesus*, pp. 268–89, the general tendency has been to deny the application of the title "son of God" to the Messiah. See among others Ladd, *A Theology of the New Testament*, p. 160; Taylor, *The Names of Jesus*, p. 53; Fitzmyer, *The Gospel according to Luke (I–IX)*, p. 206; Conzelmann, *An Outline of the Theology of the New Testament*, p. 76. Bultmann, *Theology of the New Testament, Vol. 1*, p. 50, puts forth this prudent commentary: "Whether 'Son of God' was already current as a messianic title in Judaism is uncertain and debated, it has not proved to have been so used."

coming of the messianic reign. Otherwise stated, Nathan's oracle has always proved to be the foundation text of the expression of this hope.

Considering this fact, it appears likely that at the moment when post-Easter faith recognizes in Jesus the fulfillment of the hope, it refers back to the founding oracle and it exploits the entire dimension. It is very possible then that having found the application of the title "son of God" to Jesus as the most appropriate, this faith explicitly wants to include this part of the oracle that contains it. In fact, the application could appear to Luke much more pertinent that, up to then not used, the title now accentuated the radical newness of Jesus's messianism. In any case, Luke could not be more explicit:

> He will be great, and will be called the Son of the Most High, and the Lord God will give to him the throne of his ancestor David. He will reign over the house of Jacob forever, and of his kingdom there will be no end. (Luke 1:32–33)

The designation of Jesus as "son of the Most High" is clearly linked to the accession to David's throne.

(b) The Eschatological Fulfillment of Nathan's Oracle. But when will this messianism be fulfilled? Not at the birth, but, as shown in the preceding chapter, at the resurrection. The accession to David's throne actually coincides, in Luke's perspective, with the resurrection of the Christ: "Since he [David] was a prophet, he knew that God had sworn with an oath to him that he would put one of his descendants on his throne. Foreseeing this, David spoke of the resurrection of the Messiah" (Acts 2:30–31a). The same idea is explicitly taken up again in Acts 13:33: "What God promised to our ancestors he has fulfilled for us, their children, by raising Jesus; as also it is written in the second psalm, 'You are my Son; today I have begotten you.'"

It is clear, however, that the method of fulfillment does not exactly correspond to the initial expectation expressed in the oracle. The prophet envisaged, at the outset, the perpetuity of the Davidic dynasty. The subsequent historical events changed the perspectives. The dynasty being interrupted at the time of the Exile, one would from then on have the tendency of pushing the hope of the fulfillment of the oracle[51] to the eschatological

---

[51] Some evidence of an eschatological reinterpretation of Nathan's oracle can be found in the first book of Chronicles. The following parallel of the original oracle in 2 Sam 7:14–16 with its repetition in 1 Chron 17:13–14 brings out the following variants:

times. But, although one had the opportunity to put off its fulfillment to the end times, with the completely mysterious aspect or unknown that it could convey, one had certainly not anticipated a messianism such as the one exercised by the exalted Christ.[52]

---

2 Sam 7:14–16	*1 Chron 17:13–14*
[14] I will be a father to him, and he shall be a son to me. When he commits iniquity, I will punish him with a rod such as mortals use, with blows inflicted by human beings.	[13a] I will be a father to him, and he shall be a son to me.
[15] But I will not take my steadfast love from him, as I took it from Saul, whom I put away from before you.	[13b] I will not take my steadfast love from him, as I took it from him who was before you.
[16] Your house and your kingdom shall be made sure forever before me; your throne shall be established forever.	[14] But I will confirm him in my house and in my kingdom forever, and his throne shall be established forever.

Michaeli, *Les livres des Chroniques, d'Esdras et Néhémie*, pp. 101–2, deems that the Chronicler's suppression of the phrase announcing the correction to the king in 2 Sam 7:14b was necessary, for, he says, "such disobedience would have been unworthy of the Messiah-King." Still more important are the changes made concerning the *house*, the *kingdom*, and the *throne*. Now, it is a matter of the House and the Kingdom of God. "Therefore, it is a theocracy where the Kingdom of God is more clearly highlighted than that of the Messiah" (ibid). The fact that the Davidic line was called to "last forever in [the] House and [the] Kingdom [of God]" marks the eschatological character of the text, especially since at the time of the writing of Chronicles, the Davidic dynasty had been interrupted.

On the other hand, the projection of the oracle to the end of time is very explicit in the Qumran writings. Thus, in 4QFlor 1:10–11a, the oracle is at first quoted (version of Dupont-Sommer and Philonenko, pp. 410–11), ET: "And Yahweh declares to you that he will build you a house; and I will raise up your posterity after you, and I will affirm his royal throne forever. I will be a father for him, and he will be a son for me." The interpretation which immediately follows is unequivocal: "It is David's seed who will rise up with the one seeking for the Law [and] who will be enthroned in Zion at the end of time" (vv. 11b–12). Other examples are found in *Pss. Sol.* 17:21; *Sib. Or.* 3:47b–50.

[52] If one refers to *2 Baruch* or to 2 Esdras, which date from the beginning of the Christian era (1st century or beginning of the 2nd century), one finds that in certain areas the awaited kingdom was actually perceived in earthly terms: (Dupont-Sommer and Philonenko), ET: "And its primacy will last forever until the world of corruption ends and the announced times are fulfilled" (*2 Bar.* 40:3). "After those years my son the Messiah will die, and all who draw human breath" (2 Esd 7:29).

Luke, besides, insisted on correcting all possible misunderstanding on the subject of the nature of Jesus's messianism by putting in the mouths of the disciples, in Acts 1:6, the question on the moment of the reestablishment of the kingdom: "Lord, is this the time when you will restore the kingdom to Israel?" The events following constitute Luke's response: Jesus is taken away (Acts 1:9–11) and the Spirit is poured out (Acts 2:1–4). Peter's speech interprets the meaning of these events: the kingdom of God began with Jesus's exaltation. This is the proof that Luke decides to give in Acts 2:32–36. He proclaims

1. *The resurrection of Jesus:*

   This Jesus God raised up, and of that all of us are witnesses. (v. 32)

2. *His exaltation:*

   Being therefore exalted at the right hand of God, and having received from the Father the promise of the Holy Spirit, (v. 33a)

3. *He shows the method of the fulfillment of the kingdom:*

   . . . he has poured out this that you both see and hear. (v. 33b)

4. *He illustrates the nature and the christological scope of the exaltation with the help of the quotation of Ps 110:1: (i) this exaltation consists of the seating of the Christ at the right hand of God, (ii) at this seating is linked the power to reign:*

   The Lord said to my Lord, "Sit at my right hand, until I make your enemies your footstool." (vv. 34b–35)

5. *He draws the conclusion of his demonstration:*

   Therefore let the entire house of Israel know with certainty that God has made him both Lord and Messiah, this Jesus whom you crucified. (v. 36)

But in order to be able to discover all the christological implications of the announcement of the angel, now it is necessary to see the other part of the verbal message (Luke 1:34–35).

i. The Authenticity of the Verses (vv. 34–35)

The question of the authenticity of Luke 1:34–35 was raised for the first time by Hillmann[53] at the end of the 19th century. According to him, these verses should be considered as a gloss. Harnack[54] took up this hypothesis and developed it. It was reckoned that in reality v. 36 should follow v. 33. The link would be very logical: the angel, after having delivered the message on the subject of the future of the child, would confirm this message with the sign: "And now, your relative Elizabeth . . ." (v. 36). In fact, the question of the authenticity was posed in relation to the question of the virginal conception, which would be absent from Luke without these two verses. Thus, it was suggested that the original text did not contain them; they would rather have subsequently been added by a scribe.[55]

However, these two verses—or more specifically v. 35—undoubtedly carry Luke's mark. The themes transmitted in v. 35 are characteristic of his theology.[56] For example, the reference to the Spirit as the divine participant is a typically Lukan choice. It is also characteristic of Luke to associate the noun πνεῦμα with the epithet ἅγιον. He uses the expression πνεῦμα ἅγιον thirteen times in his Gospel (as opposed to five times in Matthew and four times Mark) and forty-one times in Acts. He uses, in a common manner, the term δύναμις with the meaning of *power*[57] 10 times in his Gospel and 7 times in Acts (as opposed to two times in Matthew and two times in Mark). As for the association of the Spirit and power, as noted in the preceding chapter, this was a Lukan particularity and that often these terms had a synonymous value. In the same way, Luke was practically the only one to use the expression ὕψιστος with its absolute meaning to designate God (see discussion above). As for the verb ἐπέρχομαι, except for Eph 2:7 and Jas 5:1, all its New Testament occurrences belong to Luke-Acts (Luke 1:35; 11:22; 21:36; Acts 1:8; 8:24; 13:40; 14:19). The

---

[53] Hillman, "Die Kindheitsgeschichte nach Lukas," (according to Legrand, *L'Annonce à Marie*, p. 29).

[54] Harnack, "Zu Luke 1:34–5" (according to Legrand, p. 29).

[55] Note that Bultmann, *L'histoire de la tradition synoptique*, p. 362, considers the entirety of verses 34–37 as a later addition, but of Luke himself.

[56] See on this subject Legrand, "L'arrière-plan néo-testamentaire de Luc 1:35," pp. 162ff. Legrand shows in a convincing manner the Lukan character of v. 35 as much linguistically as theologically, following thus the work undertaken by Taylor (on the two verses, 34–35, in fact) at the beginning of the century, in his work *The Historical Evidence for the Virgin Birth*, pp. 40–87.

[57] See Grundmann, "δύναμις," *TDNT* 2:300ff.

verb ἐπισκιάζειν is also Lukan (Luke 1:35; 9:14 and Acts 5:15; the two other uses belong to Matt 17:5 and Mark 9:7).

But the most convincing argument in favor of the authenticity of vv. 34–35 probably comes from the literary form of the account. It is very clear that this account and the one of the announcement of the birth of John follow exactly the same model, as the following parallels[58] in Luke 1 demonstrate:

Birth of John (vv. 11–20)	*Birth of Jesus (vv. 26–38)*
1. The Angel of the Lord appears (v. 11)	1. The Angel Gabriel was sent to Mary and to Zechariah (vv. 26–27)
2. Zechariah is troubled (v. 12)	2. Mary is troubled (v. 29)
3. The message:	3. The message:
a. Zechariah (v. 13)	a. Rejoice, favored-one of God (v. 28)
b. Fear not (v. 13)	b. Fear not (v. 30)
c. Elizabeth will bear a son (v. 13)	c. You will conceive (v. 31)
d. You will call him John (v. 13)	d. You will call him Jesus (v. 31)
e. He will be great in the Lord's sight, etc. (vv. 15–17)	e. He will be great, etc. (vv. 32–33)
4. How will I know that this is so? (v. 18)	4. How can this be? (v. 34)
5. Angel's response (v. 19)	5. Angel's response (v. 35)
6. The sign (v. 20)	6. The sign (v. 36)

The parallel shows well the correspondence of each step of one account to the other. And it is clear here that Mary's question in v. 34, "How can this be?" corresponds to Zechariah's "How will I know that this is so?" (v. 18). It is the same for the angel's response from one account to the other as well. Moreover, taking out verses 34–35 would break the biblical "pattern" of announcement accounts as Brown clarifies: "The biblical pattern of the annunciation of birth . . . provides for a "How" question to be posed by the recipient and to be answered by a sign."[59]

It is evident, therefore, that not only vv. 34–35 are an integral part of the account of the announcement to Mary, but also that they are necessary

---

[58] The parallel of the two announcements comes from Brown, *The Birth of the Messiah*, p. 297. See also, the parallel of Graystone, *Virgin of All Virgins*, pp. 61ff.; the latter shows a general correspondence between the two accounts in terms of structure and sequence, but also "at times, an exact correspondence of words, expressions and poetic form" (note that it is a "contrast-parallel" that Graystone seeks to highlight). See also, Ellis, *The Gospel of Luke,* p. 71.

[59] Brown, *The Birth of the Messiah*, p. 302.

elements to the parallel between the two announcements (to Mary and to Zechariah).

ii. The Christological Impact

The two-part message of the angel (vv. 32–33 and 35) is interrupted by Mary's question (v. 34): "How can this be, since I do not know a man?" This verse has much written about it. Actually, the impact and the reason for Mary's question have been questioned.

It is clear that the euphemistic formulation "since I do not know a man" is a biblical expression to designate a sexual relation (see Judg 11:39; Gen 4:1, 17; 19:8; Matt 1:25). Taken literally, the question does not appear reasonable,[60] since Mary is engaged to Joseph. Different solutions were thus proposed of which the most held are the following: (1) Mary could have believed that it was a matter of an immediate conception while she was only engaged;[61] (2) the angel's announcement was going against the vow of virginity that she had made.[62]

These types of solutions betray an historicizing approach to the question and, in a certain manner, would not sufficiently take into account the theological intent. On the other hand, modern scholars, following Gewiess,[63] are more inclined to see in verse 34 a literary device seeking to pre-

---

[60] Bultmann, *L'histoire de la tradition synoptique*, p. 362, qualifies this question as absurd.

[61] Of this opinion, Ellis, *The Gospel of Luke*, p. 71; Thompson, *The Gospel according to Luke*, pp. 53ff.; Plummer, *The Gospel according to S. Luke*, p. 24.

[62] This opinion would go back as far as Gregory of Nyssa (around AD 386), according to Brown, *The Birth of the Messiah*, p. 304. It was shared by most of the church fathers. It was also held in a general manner by the Catholic tradition. It is the thesis that Graystone defended with nuances (see "Reflections and Conclusion," *Virgin of All Virgins*, pp. 147–151); also, McHugh, *The Mother of Jesus in the New Testament*, pp. 193–99; Laurentin, *Structure et théologie de Luc I–II*, pp. 176–88. Note also the hypothesis of Audet, "L'annonce à Marie," pp. 369ff., according to which Mary would have understood the prophecy of Isa 7:14 as the announcement of the birth of the Messiah to a virgin. Audet considers that ἐπεί must be translated not as "since"—causal meaning—but as "since then"—temporal meaning. Audet, therefore, formulates Mary's question as follows: "How will this be since then (this is the hypothesis: fulfillment of Isaiah's prophecy), I must not know any man?" The explanation furnished to Mary would then be found in v. 35. It would not, however, imply perpetual virginity. Ceroke, "Luke 1:34 and Mary's Virginity," subscribes to the views of Audet, but with the nuance that the virginal conception would make Mary's perpetual virginity possible in her marriage with Joseph.

[63] Gewiess, "Die Marienfrage Luke 1:34."

pare the announcement which comes in the following verse.[64]

It is actually clear that, for Luke, the essence of the account lies in the divine revelation contained in verse 35. Besides, even if Gewiess's line of thinking appears to be the most valid, there is no other choice than to note that it does not have the appeal to fully satisfy. The logical objective of verse 34 is, actually, far from evident. One understands that Luke wanted to put on Mary's lips an objection that leads to the unveiling of the powerful intervention found in v. 35 (a characteristic technique of the "announcement" genre, previously discussed). But it is difficult to understand, however, that he chose an objection which proves incongruous with what precedes, since in v. 27 Mary is given in marriage to a man of the line of David. Thus, everything is present so that eventually Mary gives birth and that this birth fulfills the essential condition of the messianism, Joseph being of Davidic descent. To furnish the explanation of the vow of virginity is a hypothesis that does not find real support in the text, and much less in the social context of the era. To say, with Vermes,[65] that the conception would take place during the very first ovulation of the young woman—παρθένος referring, he says, to pre-puberty—a period during which there must not have been sexual relations—would prove also to be pure speculation, once again, going beyond the facts of the text.

Therefore, it does not seem possible to resolve the question. It is not known whether Luke had in mind the idea of the virginal conception, for on the one hand, the angel's speech in v. 35 does not carry that idea (as we shall see); on the other hand, Mary's question in v. 34 does not necessarily presuppose it.

But, whatever the reasons motivating the formulation of v. 34, the pneumatic-christological impact of v. 35 remains the same: "The Holy Spirit will come upon [ἐπελεύσεται] you and the power of the Most High will overshadow you." Note again the equivalence of the expressions "Holy Spirit"/"power of the Most High." As Fitzmyer explains: "The parallel 'Holy Spirit' and 'power of the Most High' is thus intended in order to

---

[64] Gewiess's line of thinking is followed by Schürmann, *Das Lukasevangelium: Kommentar zu Kap. 1:1–9:50*, pp. 49ff.; Schweizer, *The Good News according to Luke*, p. 29; Fitzmyer, *The Gospel according to Luke (I–IX)*, p. 348; Marshall, *The Gospel of Luke*, p. 70; Brown, *The Birth of the Messiah*, p. 308; Schneider, *Das Evangelium nach Lukas*, p. 50; Stöger, *L'évangile selon saint Luc*, p. 50; etc. Graystone, *Virgin of All Virgins*, pp. 104–5, on the other hand, rejects this interpretation. He believes that the question is well "placed" for the young woman of Nazareth who was not yet married and not "placed" as a simple literary technique for Luke.

[65] Vermes, *Jesus the Jew. A Historian's Reading of the Gospels*, pp. 218–22.

leave these two elements to mutually explain each other." [66] Every sexual connotation is to be excluded from this formulation. This calls for, on the contrary, in the Old Testament line, the special intervention of God.

Therefore, the verb ἐπέρχομαι ἐπί / *come upon* has nothing to do with the idea of engendering. One reads, for example, in Isa 32:15, which certain people consider as the literary model of Luke 1:35, the following: ἕως ἂν ἐπέλθῃ ἐφ᾽ ὑμᾶς πνεῦμα ἀφ᾽ ὑψηλοῦ / *until the spirit from on high is poured out on us*.

Thus, in this text of Isaiah, it is a matter of the favorable intervention of God at the place of Israel on the Day of the Lord, so that finally a reign of justice and peace is established. Here are again some other examples where the text of the Septuagint uses ἐπέρχομαι ἐπί / *come upon*:

> ... a spirit of jealousy comes on him /ἐπέλθῃ αὐτῷ πνεῦμα (Num 5:14)
>
> ... a great wind came / πνεῦμα μέγα ἐπῆλθεν (Job 1:19)
>
> ... a spirit glided past my [Eliphaz's] face / πνεῦμα ἐπὶ πρόσωπόν μου ἐπῆλθεν (Job 4:15)

As for the other Lukan uses of the term ἐπέρχομαι /*come* (Luke is the only author to use it, with the exception of Eph 2:7 and Jas 5:1, as previously noted), they have absolutely nothing to do with the sexual act of engendering. Here is the idea respectively transmitted by each one of these other texts:

- The stronger one who overpowers [in the parable of the strong man who guards his castle] (Luke 11:21–22);

- Foreboding of what is coming upon the world [apocalyptic context] (21:26);

- The Spirit will come on the disciples (Acts 1:8);

---

[66] Fitzmyer, *The Gospel according to Luke*, p. 350. Also, Schneider, *Das Evangelium nach Lukas*, p. 51: "Die beiden Satze von V 35a interpretieren sich gegenseitig; [Both clauses of v. 35a interpret themselves mutually]"; Grundmann, *Das Evangelium nach Lukas*, p. 58. In other respects, Reiling and Swellengrebel, *A Translator's Handbook on the Gospel of Luke*, p. 59, see a nuance between the two expressions "power of the Most High" and "Holy Spirit": "The expression (*dunamis hupsistou*) is almost synonymous with *pneuma hagion*, the difference being that *pneuma* has in view the character of divine action and its effectiveness."

- Simon the magician fears that misfortune will come upon him (8:24);

- The words of the prophets coming on [attaining] [Paul's warning in the Antioch speech] (13:40);

- The Jews coming there from Antioch and from Iconium [to attack Paul] (14:19).

None of the preceding usages is thus of a sexual character, neither does it convey the idea of engendering.

This conclusion also applies to the second member of the sentence. The verb ἐπισκιάζειν / *overshadow* represents the manifestation of God in his role as protector. Thus it is in the well-known example of Exod 40:35:[67] "Moses was not able to enter the tent of meeting because the cloud settled upon it [ἐπεσκίαζεν ἐπ' αὐτὴν], and the glory of the LORD filled the tabernacle."

The entire context of Exodus shows well that it is a matter of the glorious presence of God that watches over the Israelite camp and protects them in their continuation of the itinerary in the desert. Other examples where the same verb, or its derivatives, appears again show the protection of God at the location of the people:

- God protecting from a cloud those escaping from Jerusalem (Isa 4:5)

- The cloud covers the Israelite camp (Num 10:34)

- God protects his chosen ones (Ps 91:4; Deut 33:12)

- The cherubim's wings cover the ark of the covenant (Exod 25:20)

As for Luke, he uses ἐπισκιάζειν / *overshadow* two other times:

---

[67] See Laurentin, *Structure et théologie de Luc I–II*, pp. 73–74; Lyonnet, "Le récit d'Annonciation et la Maternité Divine de la Sainte Vierge," pp. 44–46; Grelot, "La naissance d'Isaac et celle de Jésus," p. 574; Schweizer, "Le Nouveau Testament," p. 144. On the other hand, Legrand, "Fécondité virginale selon l'Espirit dans le Nouveau Testament," p. 787, note 5, does not believe that Exod 40:35 sheds light on Luke 1:35, for he explains, even if ἐπισκιάζειν translates the Hebrew *shâkan* associating in this way with the theme of the *shekinah* (divine habitation among humans), this typology does not integrate the role of the Spirit."

- At the moment of the transfiguration (Luke 9:34; synoptic use: Matt 17:5; Mark 9:7);

- In its literal meaning, the verb designates Peter's shadow which touches the sick when he passes by (Acts 5:15).

In light of the examples above, it is noteworthy that the verb ἐπισκιάζειν / *overshadow* is not used euphemistically to mean sexual relations. Neither is it used in this way in Luke 1:35a. Therefore, the logical consequence of this conclusion must be drawn: *the Spirit in Luke 1:35 does not play the role of parent.*[68]

What role then does he play? Chevallier writes, "To Mary's very precise question (in v. 34) that poses a problem that we today would call

---

[68] This verdict is unanimous with the scholars. But in almost a unanimous way, these uphold, nevertheless, that there is a virginal conception by the Spirit in Luke 1:35. How does one explain or justify this step backwards when drawing conclusions that flow from such an observation? It is interesting, for example, to note that Fitzmyer, in his article, "The Virginal Conception of Jesus in the New Testament," after a very detailed study of the New Testament texts, came to exactly this conclusion that only Matt 1:18 contains a clear assertion of the virginal conception. But following the critique of this conclusion made by Brown, *The Birth of the Messiah*, pp. 299–301, Fitzmyer, *The Gospel according to Luke*, p. 338, decided against it and admitted that there was, in fact, virginal conception in Luke 1:35. Brown held that, from the parallel between John and Jesus, the virginal conception should flow. This parallelism always brings out more in favor of Jesus: such is his basic postulate. More, then, must also be brought out when treating Jesus's conception. John's conception, in one sense, was miraculous, considering his mother's age, but Jesus's involved an even greater heavenly intervention. In this regard, Brown, "Luke's Description of the Virginal Conception," p. 361, wrote: "The virginal conception of Jesus would fit the pattern perfectly, for then the power of God would overcome not simply the incapacity of the two parents, but the complete absence of a human father." Thus, according to Brown, while John is filled with the Spirit in the womb of his mother, the Spirit conceives Jesus. It seems, nevertheless, that Brown's argument remains on the level of hypothesis and that it does not have, consequently, the proof value that he wanted to attribute to it. It is not because the virginal conception integrated itself well into the "pattern" that one would be justified for all that to make it a fact, real or literary. Finally, how do the scholars get themselves out of this imbroglio deriving from the fact that, on the one hand, v. 35 does not contain the idea of engendering, but on the other hand, it is used as the supporting point to affirm the virginal conception in Luke? Well, one will say, following Barrett, *The Holy Spirit and the Gospel Tradition*, p. 8, that Jesus's conception is not "an act of paternity on the part of a god, but [is due] to the supernatural and non-material action of the Holy Spirit." This opinion of Barrett is, in fact, representative of that of scholars in general on the subject. The problem remains intact, however, since this perception does not find support in Luke's text.

sexual, the angel responds in non-sexual terms by quoting the *pneuma hagion* [*Holy Spirit*]."[69] In response to this, Legrand adds: "One could also say that to a question of a biological nature, the angel gives a theological response."[70] It is in this sense, Legrand indicated, that one must seek to clarify the question of the role of the Holy Spirit. For the consequences that Luke draws from his intervention are, indeed, purely theological ("this is why the child to be born will be holy; he will be called Son of God," Lk 1:35).

However, to bring into light the particular character of the Spirit's intervention on behalf of Jesus through Mary, it is appropriate to conduct a comparative study on the nature of his interventions on behalf of other characters in the first two chapters of Luke, and more particularly on John's behalf.

The Spirit and the Secondary Characters of Luke 1–2

Elizabeth and Zechariah

By using the same model to announce the births of Jesus and John, Luke conveyed the particular relation that linked the children. This relation is defined early by the scene of Mary's visitation to Elizabeth (Luke 1:39–56). This scene, the occasion of the first contact between John and Jesus, marks the respective situation of each one:[71] John, by the intermediary of his mother, recognized Jesus's superiority and, in him, the coming of salvation.[72]

Therefore, as soon as Elizabeth hears Mary's greeting, the child leaps in her, καὶ ἐπλήσθη πνεύματος ἁγίου ἡ Ἐλισάβετ / *and Elizabeth was filled with the Holy Spirit* (v. 41); she exclaimed with a loud cry: "Blessed are you among women, and blessed is the fruit of your womb. And why has this happened to me, that the mother of my Lord comes to me?" (vv. 42–43). "Filled with the Holy Spirit," here, is a typical Lukan expression to speak of the ability to prophesy, as the five other occurrences in Luke-Acts give evidence (Luke 1:67; Acts 2:4; 4:8; 9:17; 13:9). It is under the dynamic of the Spirit that Elizabeth can, in reality, utter these revelations.

The verb ἐπλήσθη is a passive aorist (*was filled*). The punctual or temporary (aorist) character of the inspiration as well as the exterior origin

---

[69] Chevallier, *Souffle de Dieu*, p. 145.
[70] Legrand, *L'Annonce à Marie*, p. 24.
[71] See Fitzmyer, *The Gospel according to Luke*, p. 357.
[72] I will come back to this later when treating John's prophetic mission.

of the source of inspiration (passive) are emphasized. Elizabeth's experience thus takes on the traits of Old Testament experiences,[73] thus Num 11:25b, concerning the seventy elders who had to assist Moses in his functions: "When the spirit rested upon them, they prophesied."[74] Then in v. 29: "Would that all the Lord's people were prophets, and that the Lord would put his spirit on them!"

As to the episode concerning Zechariah (Luke 1:67–79), the same conclusions can be drawn. Zechariah is going to pronounce a Psalm—in an Old Testament way—which aims to bring into light the relationship of promise/fulfillment between salvation which comes and the one who is announced. The introductory verse gives to Zechariah his letter of credit: "Then his father Zechariah was filled with the Holy Spirit [ἐπλήσθη πνεύματος ἁγίου] and spoke this prophecy . . ." (v. 67). The same verb—ἐπλήσθη—is used; the same cause and effect relationship is established: *because* he "was filled with the Holy Spirit," Zechariah was able to prophesy.

Simeon (and Anna)

Simeon and Anna are both prophets. This is said explicitly of Anna, implicitly of Simeon. Simeon's presentation, actually, is that of the prophet (Luke 2:25ff.): the Spirit is on him and God reveals to him his plans;[75] καὶ πνεῦμα ἦν ἅγιον ἐπ' αὐτόν / *and the Holy Spirit was upon him* (v. 25b) must be understood as a force which inhabits him on this precise occasion. The absence of the article and the separation of the noun and the adjective by the verb lead Plummer to paraphrase in this way: "an influence that was holy was on him."[76] As to ἐπ' αὐτόν / *upon him*, the accusative form indicates a movement, that is the coming of the Spirit on Simeon, rather than a permanent possession.[77]

After this presentation of the prophet, Luke continues in designating the Spirit as the source of the revelation: "It had been revealed to him by the Holy Spirit that he would not see death before he had seen the Lord's

---

[73] See Chevallier, *Souffle de Dieu*, p. 163.

[74] See also Ezek 11:5; Isa 61:1.

[75] See Chevallier, *Souffle de Dieu*, p. 163.

[76] Plummer, p. 66. Brown, *The Birth of the Messiah*, p. 438, contests Plummer's interpretation, for, he writes: "The use with the article in the next verse shows that Luke is thinking of the Holy Spirit." The meaning meant by Plummer's paraphrase seems correct. However, it is not evident that this meaning comes from the absence of the article.

[77] See Plummer, p. 66; also, Lagrange, *Évangile selon Saint Luc*, p. 48.

Messiah" (v. 26). Finally, it is under the guidance of the Spirit that Simeon came to the temple: "Guided by the Spirit [ἐν τῷ πνεύματι], Simeon came into the temple" (v. 27). Therefore, it is with insistence that Luke affirms the divine origin of Simeon's knowledge and his guidance towards the temple. The appeal to the Holy Spirit actually aims to show the supernatural character of the dynamic that enables him to make known the events of salvation.[78]

As for Anna, Simeon's feminine counterpart, it is surprising that her intervention (Luke 2:36–38) is not specifically supported by the Holy Spirit. On the other hand, in presenting her as a prophet who announces in the child the liberation of Jerusalem, Luke implicitly affirms that she is also inspired.

John the Baptist

Luke shows an evident concern in presenting John's parents as worthy and irreproachable persons (Luke 1:5ff.). Both of them are of the priestly tribe, their belonging to the Jewish race has no ambiguity.[79] As to Zechariah's and Elizabeth's moral integrity, Luke does not allow for any doubt: "Both of them were righteous before God, living blamelessly according to all the commandments and regulations of the Lord" (1:6).

Faithfulness to the commandments and regulations of the Lord satisfied the demands of Jewish justice (since the Old Testament notion of justice was translated by obedience to the Law, see Gen 15:6). But, in order to forewarn of any risk of assimilation of this conformity to the Law to an exterior practice, Luke clarifies that they were "righteous before God." This precision, moreover, contributes to annihilating all judgment of guilt which could have been brought against the sterility of the couple.[80]

Mentioning Elizabeth's sterility is not a matter of chance. It reveals, on the contrary, Luke's evident decision to inscribe Elizabeth into the line

---

[78] Schürmann, *Das Lukasevangelium: Kommentar zu Kap. 1:1–9:50*, p. 124, writes: "Daß er ein geistbegabter Prophet war, macht recht eigentlich sein Doppelzeugnis VV. 29–32.34f wertvoll." ["The fact that he was a spirit-gifted prophet makes his double report (vv. 29–32, 34f.) quite valuable."] Also, Marshall, *The Gospel of Luke*, p. 118.

[79] Even though a priest was not required to marry a woman of priestly descent, such a union confers to the couple a special distinction. In this case, it likely served to elevate the origin of the precursor—if one adds to this that Elizabeth was of the noble line of Aaron; the name of Elizabeth, besides, is not without recall of the name of Aaron's wife in Exod 6:23.

[80] See Fitzmyer, *The Gospel according to Luke (I–IX)*, p. 323; Brown, *The Birth of the Messiah*, p. 258.

of these women whose pregnancy occurs from a miraculous initiative of God: Rebecca, Rachel, Hannah, but especially Sarah (Gen 21:2), who, was the first to conceive and give birth in her old age. The theological reason justifying the appeal to this typology is from then on very clear: noting the divine election of the child from before his birth and announcing the key role that he will have to assume in the fulfillment of God's salvation plans.

The presentation is, therefore, successful: the couple is of pure Jewish tradition and the role that is incumbent upon them fits in perfectly in the biblical line. Nothing is new, except that the event that is about to happen is at the same time the last act of an era and the first sign of another.

To present the precursor, Luke chooses the literary framework of the annunciation (Luke 1:11–20), previously mentioned. This choice confirms, on the one hand, the Old Testament roots of the entire account around John's coming; on the other hand, it is a revelation of the nature of John's mission. The scene takes place in the temple. Having already established Zechariah's priestly ascent, he is now in the fulfillment of the functions inherent in his status. No other liturgical frame could better illustrate the traditional anchoring that Luke decides to confer on the events: the temple, the physical meeting place of all the Jews on earth; the religious symbol of the same faith that gathers them; the point of convergence of the historic reality of God's people.

As to the heavenly character who is going to enter the scene (1:11), no one needs to recall the nature of his role. The Angel of the Lord, a biblical figure aiming to preserve divine transcendence, is neither more nor less than the manifestation of God himself to humanity. The appeal to this literary device here aims thus to mark the divine origin of the event. After having reassured Zechariah, the Angel shares the objective of his visit: the couple will conceive a son to whom they will give the name John. The insistence on the name must be considered more so in relation with the meaning of the fact of giving a name than with the etymological contents of the name itself. For, Brown explains, the prenatal attribution of the name in the Bible is a retrospective interpretation:[81] the career and the accomplishments being already known, one uses them to interpret the name of the subject.[82] Brown clarifies: "It is a symbolic way of saying to the reader that God foresaw and ordered the role that the subject would

---

[81] *The Birth of the Messiah*, p. 272, note 29.
[82] Etymologically, the name *John* means *the Lord grants favor*.

play."[83] What is essential for Luke, is to inform the reader that the name was imposed by God.[84]

Then, the Angel proceeds to the description of the one who is going to be born (vv. 15–17)—a moral description in fact. He will be the joy and elation of his parents and of many; here is found the first indication of the atmosphere which prevails in the Lukan infancy accounts. Contrary to Matthew's accounts where hints, tricks, and plots crisscross, where the forces of evil break loose against the all powerful will of God to make salvation come, the Lukan accounts present the coming of the Messiah as a happy and grand event rendered possible by the availability and unanimous participation of the characters. It is a matter of messianic joy.

The descriptive formulas which follow (v. 15) are essentially Old Testament, characterizing either a great biblical character or a state or a status. Applied to John, they are evidently preludes to his mission. The anticipated ascetic practice—and confirmed in Luke 7:33—concerning abstaining from wine and fermented drink corresponds to the abstention imposed on Samson by the intermediary of his mother at first (Judg 13:4, 14) and on Samson himself (Judg 13:5, 7). It corresponds equally to the Nazirite requirements described in Num 6:3–4. Finally, the Septuagint—from which Luke is inspired—adds to the prescription to abstain from shaving with regard to Samuel (1 Sam 1:11), abstention also from wine and intoxicating drink. John is thus identified to these Nazirites whose important function implied a special consecration to God. It was a consecration, in many cases, preceding even birth (Samuel and Samson; also Jeremiah, who is, however, not presented as a Nazirite, Jer 1:5, and the servant, Isa 49:1, 5).

In John's case, however, this consecration has a particular blessing: it is guaranteed by the Spirit: "Even before his birth he will be filled with the Holy Spirit [καὶ πνεύματος ἁγίου πλησθήσεται]" (Luke 1:15b). This is the first mention of the Spirit of God in Luke. How is this presence of the Spirit characterized in John? As noted earlier, the verb form used to speak of Elizabeth's and Zechariah's inspiration was an aorist passive—ἐπλήσθη / *was filled*, which indicated at the same time the exterior origin of the force acting in them and the temporary aspect of its action. This verb was not reused in relation to Simeon, but the meaning of the triple intervention of the Spirit on his behalf placed it, without equivocation, in the line of those who, under the punctual help of the Spirit, spoke and acted in God's

---

[83] *The Birth of the Messiah*, p. 272, note 29.
[84] See Gen. 16:11; 17:19; Isa 7:14; 1 Kgs 13:2.

name. Therefore, it is clear that the action of the Spirit in these three characters is brief and circumstantial. They only have a momentary instrumental role and what they become afterwards is unknown to us.

However, everything is different in John's case: "Even before his birth he will be filled with the Holy Spirit." The verb used is the same: πίμπλημι. It is equally in the passive, indicating thus the exterior character of the source of the dynamic. It is in the future, and it is understandable! But where John is set apart from the three other prophets who had to announce the coming of Jesus is in the fact that he will be inhabited by the Spirit even before his birth, therefore in permanence. And this coming of the Spirit on John intervenes, or manifests itself, for the first time during Mary's visit to Elizabeth (Luke 1:41–44). Luke is careful to clearly state, "When Elizabeth heard Mary's greeting, the child leaped in her womb" (v. 41). Already, therefore, the child "enters into his function" and prophesies through the mouth of his mother who recognizes the Lord in the child that Mary carries.

In Old Testament times, the inhabiting of the Spirit in the king also took on a permanent character (see 1 Sam 16:13), but it was limited to the time of his reign. In John's infilling, not only his entire lifetime is covered, but it even precedes his birth. It seems, then, that it is the ultimate importance of John's role that is being accentuated. It is a role without precedent that demands a preparation without precedent. John's training could not carry any error and this guarantee would only be assured under the aegis of the Spirit.

John, then, would be invested with the Spirit in permanence. How then will Jesus's spiritual infilling be distinguished from John's?

The Spirit and Jesus

As just shown, the intervention of the Spirit in the secondary characters of Luke 1–2 aimed essentially to make them prophets. Elizabeth, Zechariah, Simeon (and Anna) inspired by the Spirit, announced the divine character of the events surrounding Jesus's birth. Their role was, however, very punctual. John's role is also of a prophetic type. But the importance of his mission merits his being filled with the Spirit from his mother's womb and being thus preserved in righteousness up to his entrance on the scene as an adult. For, although Elizabeth's, Zechariah's, Simeon's, and Anna's interventions surrounded the event even of Jesus's birth, John's was linked to Jesus's public mission.

When it concerns Jesus, the nature and the objective of the Spirit's activity are no longer the same. The Spirit is no longer a source of inspiration; neither does he directly touch the beneficiary of his intervention, Jesus.

The Spirit is not, in Jesus, a source of inspiration, but a guarantee of protection.

It seems clear, in fact, that the action of the Spirit has the role of protecting the child from all evil, as the cause-effect relationship indicates, introduced by διό / *therefore*, between the parts of Luke 1:35. For it is a fact that the formulation of this verse is very clearly intended in two occurrences:

1. The announcement of a fact: "The Holy Spirit will come upon you, and the power of the Most High will overshadow you;"
2. The consequence of this fact: "therefore the child to be born will be holy; he will be called Son of God."

To be "holy" implies being exempt from all evil. However, how does one enter into this world, how is one born of Adam (see Luke 3:38; Acts 17:26) without carrying in oneself the mark of sin unavoidably attached to his descendants? How does one avoid Jesus being in any way put in contact with evil? Luke responds to this requirement by placing his conception under God's direct and immediate protection. It is the power of the Spirit of the Most High who prevents Jesus from being touched by evil.

Thus, in Jesus, God recreates, exempt from evil, fallen humanity. Jesus is, like Adam, the son of God[85] (Luke 3:38), but different from Adam[86] in that he conquers evil. It is thus that Luke presents him—as the conqueror of evil—in placing the temptation account (Luke 4:1–13) immediately after the genealogy which takes Jesus's ascent back to God going through the first man, Adam[87] (see further on, "The Spirit and Jesus's Entrance into Temptation," pp. 165ff.). Thus, it would be in a perspective of a new creation that it would be necessary to see the role of the Spirit in

---

[85] I use here the expression "son of God" in the same sense that it is used to designate Adam in the genealogy, i.e., as the first human of creation.

[86] It is true that the typology of the New Adam is, first and above all, Pauline (see 1 Cor 15:45–49; Rom 5:12–21; Eph 4:22ff.; Col 3:9ff.; also, implicitly, in Phil 2:6–11). But it appears equally in a thread in Luke; see Chevallier, *Souffle de Dieu*, pp. 149–50.

[87] See Grundmann, *Das Evangelium nach Lukas*, p. 58.

Luke 1:35,[88] a perspective that corresponds well to the Jewish thought where the Spirit is perceived as a creative power and not a parent.[89]

The idea of a creator Spirit occurs frequently in the Old Testament. One finds it in Ezek 37:14; Gen 1:2; Pss 33:6; 104:30; 147:18; Job 27:3; 33:4; etc. In rabbinical literature, though rare, one finds, nevertheless, some mention of the power of the Spirit to recreate life in the messianic days. For example, Ezek 37:14 is taken up in *Ez Rabba* 48:102d.[90] Thus, if we held absolutely to speaking of engendering in relation to 1:35, we would have to speak of the engendering of a new world in the person of Jesus.

Notably then, the intervention of the Spirit at Jesus's birth does not make him either a prophet or even a messiah. On the contrary, everything in this account is pushed towards the future. For the Spirit will effectively make him a prophet at his baptism (see further on, "The Spirit and the Baptism of Jesus," pp. 150ff.) and a messiah at his resurrection (see chapters 2 and 3).

The Spirit's intervention thus brings out the radical newness of Jesus's role in the fulfillment of salvation and the uniqueness of his relation to God, as Schweizer explains again:

> Verse 35b brings out the unique character of the person Jesus. The translation ("therefore the child to be born will be holy; he will be called Son of God") is appropriate, since "be called" means "be set apart" for God's service (Isa 4:3; see 35:8; 62:2 Exod 13:12; Lev 23:2,

---

[88] See George, *Études sur l'oeuvre de Luc*, pp. 219–20, (see note 5, p. 219); also, Legrand, "Fécondité virginale," pp. 786ff. The latter writes, p. 790: "Thus, with the coming of the Christ into this world, the eschatological times began. The Spirit is given and he began to insufflate a new life. He creates in Jesus a renovated humanity.... Jesus is the head of the line in this new existence."

[89] On this subject, Schweizer, *The Good News*, p. 29, writes: "In Judaism, genitive power is not associated with the Spirit but rather creation (Ps 33:6; Gen 1:2) and new creation (Ezek 37:14). Here, then, is where the emphasis lies. Mary experiences what took place when the Spirit caused the world to arise out of chaos and life out of dried bones. It has nothing to do with her virtue or her nature nor with the active procreative will of Joseph. The presence of God 'overshadows' Mary just as the cloud of God overshadowed the tent of meeting."

[90] *Ez Rabba* 48:102d: "God says to Israel: 'In this world, my Spirit has put wisdom in you, but in the world to come, my spirit will make you live again as it is said: "I will put my Spirit within you, and you shall live," Ezek 37:14.'" The same reference is repeated in *Gen. Rab.* 96:60d.

37 LXX). In other words, the child will be son of God as something set apart for the deity.[91]

I subscribe to Schweizer's opinion, but only in part, for concerning the aspect of his last affirmation, I do not believe that Schweizer, like most of the scholars, unveils all the meaning contained in the assertion "he will be called holy, Son of God." Further unveiling is necessary, but first, an overview of the interpretation of the title "Son of God" in Luke 1:35, which will allow a more complete interpretation.

Note first of all that the scholars agree on the messianic scope, according to the purest Hebraic tradition, as conveyed in verses 32–33. The title "Son of the Most High" would, therefore, have a royal connotation. All agree generally as well on the fact that the title "Son of God" (v. 35) receives a new aspect in relation to the preceding verses, and this is because of the Spirit's intervention.

Apart from the scholars who read without hesitation the title "Son of God" as an ontological assertion,[92] most have difficulty setting forth a clear conceptualization of the value of this new aspect. Thus, George will say that Luke is the only one to base the title "Son of God" on "the exceptional character of the divine intervention" and "on the holiness of Jesus."[93] He adds: "Jesus is united to God at a depth that goes beyond everything that the Old Testament and Judaism could conceive. By this, he is the Son of God in an absolutely new way."[94] This newness that George speaks of would come from the unique relation of intimacy of Jesus with the Father.

Marshall writes simply:

> We found possibly the idea that, as the one engendered by the Holy Spirit, the child would be holy as the bearer of the Spirit. The description culminates in the expression υἱὸς θεοῦ [*son of God*], here undoubtedly in its full meaning as the one engendered by God.[95]

---

[91] Schweizer, *The Good News according to Luke*, p. 30.

[92] Among those, Laurentin, *Structure et théologie dans Luc I–II*, pp. 72ff.; Richard, "Conçu du Saint-Espirit, né de la Vierge Marie," p. 316; Lyonnet, "Le récit de l'Annonciation," pp. 44ff.; Geldenhuys, *Commentary on the Gospel of Luke*, p. 76; Stöger, *L'évangile selon saint Luc*, p. 52.

[93] George, "Jésus Fils de Dieu," p. 220.

[94] Ibid.

[95] *The Gospel of Luke*, p. 71.

Danker writes without more explanation: ". . . the evangelist, as it is clear in vv. 36–37, uses here the expression in a unique sense. The Holy Spirit must be perceived as the Father of Jesus."[96] Chevallier suggests that the intervention of the Spirit would consist in marking the engendering of Jesus, the Messiah, as Son of God according to Ps 2:7, in parallel to the creation of Adam in Gen 2:7 where God "breathes into his nostrils the breath of life." He clarifies:

> Luke . . . could well have dreamed about this role of the breath of God communicating life and giving birth to a "son" when he was writing the message of the Angel Gabriel . . . the birth of Jesus is as it were of Adam's type of birth which outclasses Isaac's type . . . the divine breath gives birth to the Messiah, Son of God.[97]

Schneider writes:

> Because the Spirit of God created the child, he will be "holy" and will be called holy; and, in a sense, will be "son of God," in which one can almost speak of his nature ("Seinshaft"). The divine relation confessed in the faith is explained and founded in the origins of Jesus. It is not understood as "functional" or "adoptive."[98]

Fitzmyer and Brown see in the title "Son of God" an element of the primitive kerygma in the line of Rom 1:3–4. Fitzmyer says first that there is an equation between "Son of the Most High" and "Son of God,"[99] since the title constitutes very early an element of the kerygma, as Rom 1:3–4 and 1 Thess 1:10 suggest.[100] He points out, however, that, even if it does not yet bring out a metaphysical connotation or an identity of substance, it cannot be reduced to a simple adoptive meaning: "Its explicit relation of the title at Jesus's conception connotes much more."

Brown is equally resistant to an adoptive interpretation of the title; he explains: "It is not a question of the adoption of a descendant of David by his crowning as son of God or his representative; it is a question of the Son of God conceived in Mary's womb by the creative Spirit of God."[101]

---

[96] *Jesus and the New Age according to St. Luke*, p. 13.
[97] *Souffle de Dieu*, p. 149–50.
[98] *Das Evangelium nach Lukas*, p. 51.
[99] *The Gospel according to Luke*, pp. 206–8.
[100] This is also the opinion of Conzelmann, *An Outline of the Theology of the New Testament*, pp. 76–82.
[101] *The Birth of the Messiah*, p. 312.

He considers that the christological contents of v. 35 correspond to Rom 1:3–4, but that Luke situates at the conception what Paul situates at the resurrection.[102] He recognizes the messianic impact of the title, but clarifies: "The coming of the Holy Spirit in 1:35b . . . and the overshadowing by the power of the Most High in 1:35c . . . actually engender the child as son of God—there is no adoption here."[103]

Thus, these scholars stress, in general, the added dimension conferred to the title "Son of God" consecutively at the intervention of the Spirit. Of the opinions given, the interpretative line which seems the most adequate is, however, the one which points to Rom 1:3–4.

It seems clear, in fact, that the Lukan development which includes vv. 32–33 and 35, reflect the primitive confession incorporated in Rom 1:3–4:

v. 3: περὶ τοῦ υἱοῦ αὐτοῦ τοῦ γενομένου ἐκ σπέρματος Δαυὶδ κατὰ σάρκα, /
concerning his Son, who was descended from David according to the flesh,

v. 4: τοῦ ὁρισθέντος υἱοῦ θεοῦ ἐν δυνάμει κατὰ πνεῦμα ἁγιωσύνης ἐξ ἀναστάσεως νεκρῶν, Ἰησοῦ Χριστοῦ τοῦ κυρίου ἡμῶν. /
and was declared to be Son of God with power according to the spirit of holiness by resurrection from the dead, Jesus Christ our Lord.

The parallel is so direct between Rom 1:4 and Luke 1:35, explains Legrand, "that the two texts can be written synoptically, all the key terms of Luke's verse are found in the text of Romans. The two texts fit into the same themes, divine relation, Power, Holiness and Spirit."[104]

Thus here is the parallel:

Luke 1:35	Rom 1:4
"The *Holy Spirit* will come upon you, and the *power* of the Most High will overshadow you; therefore the child to be born *will be holy*; he will be called *Son of God*."	. . . and was declared to be *Son of God* with *power* according to *the spirit of holiness*.

---

[102] Ibid., p. 313; see also Hahn, *The Titles of Jesus in Christology*, pp. 297–98; Ernst, *Das Evangelium nach Lukas*, p. 73; Schürmann, *Das Lukasevangelium: Kommentar zu Kap. 1:1–9:50*, p. 55.

[103] Brown, *The Birth of the Messiah*, pp. 313–14.

[104] Legrand, "Fécondité virginale," p. 789.

The correspondence of the themes is found equally between Rom 1:3 and Luke 1:32, adds Legrand: "The similarity is again more striking if one observes that the context as well is identical since that of Romans (1:3) as that of Luke (1:32) insist on the Davidic origin of Jesus."[105]

Luke 1:32	Rom 1:3
his ancestor David	from David according to the flesh

The parallelism of the texts appears convincing: Luke reproduces, in elaborating, the gradation found in Rom 1:3–4. What Romans tells us, in reality, is that (1) Jesus correlates to the sine qua non condition of the Messiah: he is of the line of David according to (by means of) the flesh; (2) but he only accedes to this messianism at the resurrection, in the power, according to (by the intervention of[106]) the Spirit of holiness. These two levels of messianism are found in Luke 1:32–33 and 35.

The Old Testament anchoring of vv. 32–33 has already been shown. In these two verses, Luke intended to affirm without equivocation the fulfillment of the messianic hope of Israel in Jesus, this latter corresponding to the criteria of the line of David. This having been well established, he, nevertheless, wants to express a new dimension—and unsuspected in Judaism—of the messianism of Jesus, to which he accedes by his exaltation. Therefore, Christ's entry into the function of his kingship takes place by the gift of the Spirit in Acts 2:33. It is to this new honor that the title "Son of God" makes reference in v. 35; that is to say, the form of messianism that only comes in the resurrection. The cause and effect relationship, clearly marked by the διό ["therefore"], directly seeks to show that the designation "Son of God" now takes on a new character in relation to that of v. 32, "Son of the Most High." Διό introduces the consequence of the intervention of the Spirit: Jesus will be holy, Son of God because the Spirit intervened.

The presence of the Spirit on Mary ensures that the "atmosphere" where the child must take on life is under God's direct protection, in such a manner that in no way can he be put in contact with evil. He is by this

---

[105] Ibid. See also Chevallier, *Souffle de Dieu*, 150–51.

[106] Myre, *Un souffle subversif*, p. 93, note 211, considers that "the two [occurrences of] *kata* of Rom 1:3–4 are . . . to be understood instrumentally." He explains: "Jesus is born of the seed of David in the way that humans are conceived; and he was established as the Son of God, following the manner of acting of the breath of God. The activity of the flesh explains that Jesus was a descendant of David, that of the breath, that he had been established as the Son of God."

fact introduced into the sphere of holiness, i.e., into God's sphere: "it is why the child to be born will be holy." He is holy because he is protected from the womb of his mother. Then, three times, in Acts, Luke qualifies the Messiah as "holy" in an absolute sense: first in Peter's speech in 2:27b, next in Paul's speech in 13:35b, both of them quoting Ps 16:10 (from the Septuagint): ". . . you will not let your Holy One experience corruption." Then, in Acts 3:14, where the title "Holy," joined to the title "Righteous," is applied to Jesus: "You have rejected the Holy and righteous One . . . ." In the preceding verse, the author has just spoken of Jesus as glorified: "The God of Abraham, the God of Isaac, and the God of Jacob, the God of our ancestors has glorified his servant Jesus, whom you handed over . . . ." (v. 13). Then, he continues (v. 14): "but you rejected the Holy and Righteous One . . . ." What emerges here is that "Servant," "Holy," and "Righteous" become the attributes of Jesus glorified. Thus, they emerge elsewhere in Acts:

- In 4:27, 30: Jesus is qualified as "holy servant"

- In 7:52: the prophets who announced the coming of the Just One were killed

- In 22:14: Ananias says to Paul that God had destined him to see the Righteous One

Thus, the titles "Servant," "Holy," "Righteous," which are only found in Acts,[107] become applicable to Jesus only in consideration of his new situation as the glorified Messiah. The title "Holy" in Luke 1:35 would make reference to this condition of Jesus, a condition to which Jesus accedes by the power of the Spirit (Acts 2:33a: "Exalted at the right hand of God, he received from the Father the Spirit of the promise . . .").

As to the title "Son of God,"[108] it is rarely used in Lukan literature. In the third Gospel, it is pronounced by the angel in the verse under consideration, 1:35. It comes back afterwards in the mouth of Satan in 4:3, 9 and

---

[107] An exception is made for "Holy;" once in the third Gospel, Jesus is called "Holy" (in 4:34—from the triple tradition). But, the title is uttered by a demon; thus, by a supernatural power who can, by anticipation, unveil Jesus's real identity.

[108] I only mention, here, the occurrences where the expression "son of God" appears and not those where it is a question of "son" in relation to the Father, or "son" used alone. I will return to the simple use of the title "son" in studying the baptism episode.

the demons in 4:41; 8:28.[109] But it is never put on the lips of human beings. Note, for example, that in Luke 24:47, the centurion says: "really this man was righteous" instead of "Son of God" as in the parallel gospels (Mark 15:39 and Matt 27:54).[110] As for the meeting before the Sanhedrin, the question is asked of Jesus, "Are you, then, the Son of God?" (Luke 22:70a). But the response is sufficiently evasive to still let the mystery hang: ὑμεῖς λέγετε ὅτι ἐγώ εἰμι. / *you say that I am* (22:70b).

In this last case, the parallel with the account of the annunciation must be noted. The christological affirmations of Luke 1:32, 35 and 22:67, 70 correspond with one another:

- The Lord will give to him the throne of his ancestor David. (1:32)

- The child to be born will be holy; he will be called Son of God. (1:35)

- If you are the Messiah, tell us. (22:67)

- Are you, then, the Son of God? ... You say that I am. (22:70)

The same progression, or deepening of the traditional messianic title,[111] appears in the two cases. A notable difference must, however, be mentioned: in the mouth of the angel, the proclamation is unequivocal; in the mouth of the unbeliever, it remains a question and provocation. The reality of Jesus's messianism can only be welcomed by faith.

The mention of "Son of God" remains thus, in the gospel, as mysterious by design.[112] On the other hand, in Acts, the only use that is made of it truly designates Jesus as "glorified." It is the reference in 9:20 where Paul is preaching in the synagogues: "And immediately he began to proclaim Jesus in the synagogues, saying, 'He is the Son of God.'"

Therefore, the rest of the text shows that the title sheds light on the title of Messiah and characterizes exactly Jesus's messianism. First of all, in v. 21, Paul's integrity is contested; then in v. 22, Luke writes, "Saul

---

[109] See note 108; what is said on the subject of the utterance of the title "holy" by supernatural beings applies equally for the title "Son of God." See George, *Études sur l'œuvre de Luc*, p. 222.

[110] Concerning the motive of the Lukan modification of the source, see the section "The Spirit and Jesus's Entrance into Temptation: Luke 4:1," pp. 165ff.

[111] See George, *Études sur l'œuvre de Luc*, p. 227.

[112] See George, *Études sur l'œuvre de Luc*, p. 235; Sabourin, *L'Évangile de Luc*, pp. 67–68.

became increasingly more powerful and confounded the Jews who lived in Damascus by proving that Jesus was the Christ." Thus, Paul proclaims, "Jesus is the Son of God . . . proving that [he] was the Christ."

The title "Son of God," therefore, only takes on its true value in the exaltation of the Christ. More precisely, the title goes back to the new status conferred on Jesus in the gift of the Spirit by the Father at the moment of his resurrection.

In the account of the annunciation, the parallelism between Luke 1:32 and 35 is straightforward. The titles "great" and "Son of the Most High" of v. 32 correspond to the titles "Holy" and "son of God" of v. 35. But, once again, this parallelism is progressive. The Spirit is the agent of this progression. In fact, it is obvious that the introduction of the Spirit as the justifying cause (διό / *therefore*) of the two predicates of v. 35 essentially aims to mark this progression in relation to the predicates of v. 32.

The facts of v. 32 (and 33) would thus have as a goal the indicating of the fulfillment of the hope of Israel. They situate very well Jesus's messianism in the tradition of 1 Sam 7:14. On the other hand, the Christian experience showed that Jesus's messianism, as demonstrated in the community, clearly transcends all human anticipation. And it is by the power of the Spirit that the Christ attained such a level (Acts 2:33). Thus, in the second part of the account of the annunciation (v. 35), Luke already wants to announce this dimension, this new messianism that would only be realized in Jesus's resurrection. In order to do this, he places Jesus, from before his conception, under the direct protection of this same power that would enable him then to fulfill this unique function, that is, the Holy Spirit.

Thus, whereas the title "Son of the Most High" (v. 32) in Luke's point of view, went back to the Jewish hope flowing from 1 Sam 7:14, the title "Son of God" (v. 35) goes back to the newness of the messianism which could only be known through the Pascal mystery.[113] "Son of God" takes on, then, a special, unique connotation because of the uniqueness of Jesus's messianism defined in Acts 2:33. Emerging then from this parallelism (vv. 32–33 ‖ 35) are two levels of language: that of the Jewish faith and that of the Christian faith.[114]

---

[113] See Chevallier, *Souffle de Dieu*, p. 149.

[114] This is what Legrand suggests in *L'Annonce à Marie*, p. 203, when he writes: "If Luke 1:32–35 is constructed according to the same technique, this means that faith in Christ announced by the Lukan Church (v. 35) corresponds to the promises of the Old Testament (vv. 32–33): the Christ in whom we believe is the fulfillment of the messianic promises. . . . The alternation of two languages, that of the Bible and that of explicit Christian preaching, can show, in Luke, the desire to connect the new order to the old."

The uniqueness of salvation—like the unity of the succession of its steps—is, indeed, a very Lukan preoccupation (as noted in the preceding chapters and as will be seen again in the next chapter). In the text of Luke 1:32–35, the need to mark this continuity was more than ever an imperative. Israel had hoped for the Messiah for centuries; this Messiah came, but in an unexpected way. Therefore, it was necessary to demonstrate that this Messiah was the very one who accomplished God's promises. Luke shows that the historic waiting period had been satisfied in evoking Nathan's oracle (vv. 32–33). However, he had also to realize the eschatological dimension of this fulfillment; this he assures when he makes the Spirit intervene (v. 35), anticipating in this way the solemn proclamation of Acts 2:33.

When all is said and done, the passage of Luke 1:32–35 recognizes two levels of messianism: (1) the one Israel expected; (2) the one realized, not expected by Israel, but recognized by the Christian community. And what is obvious is that for Luke, the Spirit is the agent of this eschatological realization, as Acts 2:33 attests: "Being therefore exalted at the right hand of God, and having received from the Father the promise of the Holy Spirit." Since he had to affirm in Acts 2:33 that the Spirit is responsible for the messianic fulfillment, he had to mention it at the moment when he announces this future messianism, at the beginning of his gospel.

Finally, contrary to what many scholars say,[115] it is a fact that Luke does not move back to the conception the messianic moment that Paul places at the resurrection (Rom 1:3–4); because, for Luke as for Paul, Jesus's enthronement coincides with his resurrection. What Luke tells us, however, is that from the conception, the "necessary mechanisms" (if one can allow such technical and down to earth language to express the ineffable) are put in place by God to assure his plan of salvation in Jesus. The Spirit's invasion of Mary is God's guarantee that the messianism to which Jesus is called could be realized. By this invasion of the Spirit, Jesus is preserved from all the flaws of the first creation, so that in him and by him the new creation comes. To this new creation corresponds a new messianism, that of Jesus Christ exalted, which Acts 2:33, 36 establish.

---

[115] Among others, Brown, *The Birth of the Messiah*, pp. 315–16; Dunn, *Christology in the Making*, p. 151; Barrett, *The Holy Spirit and the Gospel Tradition*, p. 45; Hahn, *The Titles of Jesus in Christology*, p. 263; Schürmann, *Das Lukasevangelium: Kommentar zu Kap. 1:1–9:50*, p. 55; Bock, *Proclamation from Prophecy and Pattern: Lucan Old Testament Christology*, p. 68.

2. THE SPIRIT AND THE BAPTISM OF JESUS— LUKE 3:21–22

The messianic interpretation of the baptism of Jesus in the synoptic gospels rallies the majority of the exegetes (see further on). In Luke's case, however, it is far from certain that this understanding of the text acknowledges well the author's intentions. On the contrary, when the episode on the whole is considered as a redaction of the two works, it can be noted that it is oriented more in the sense of a prophetic reading. The Spirit given to Jesus at his baptism invests in his function of prophet. This is what will be shown in this section. But first, it is appropriate to correct an important problem of textual criticism.

Textual Criticism

v. 21 Ἐγένετο δὲ ἐν τῷ βαπτισθῆναι ἅπαντα τὸν λαὸν καὶ Ἰησοῦ βαπτισθέντος καὶ προσευχομένου ἀνεῳχθῆναι τὸν οὐρανὸν /
Now when all the people were baptized, and when Jesus also had been baptized and was praying, the heaven was opened

v. 22 καὶ καταβῆναι τὸ πνεῦμα τὸ ἅγιον σωματικῷ εἴδει ὡς περιστερὰν ἐπ' αὐτόν, καὶ φωνὴν ἐξ οὐρανοῦ γενέσθαι, σὺ εἶ ὁ υἱός μου ὁ ἀγαπητός, ἐν σοὶ εὐδόκησα. /
and the Holy Spirit descended upon him in bodily form like a dove. And a voice came from heaven, "You are my Son, the Beloved; with you I am well pleased."

The only important problem of textual criticism of Luke 3:21–22 is found in the last part of v. 22.[116] Instead of σὺ εἶ ὁ υἱός μου ὁ ἀγαπητός, ἐν σοὶ εὐδόκησα, / *You are my Son, the Beloved; with you I am well pleased*,[117] the codex Bezae (05), the old Latin (except e), as well as the Fathers (Justin, Clement of Alexandria, Origen, Method, Augustine, Hilary) read υἱός μου εἶ σύ ἐγὼ σήμερον γεγέννηκά σε / *you are my son; today*

---

[116] Nestle-Aland indicates two other minor cases: (1) in certain manuscripts (02, 038, 044, f^{1,13}) ὡσεί occurs instead of ὡς; (2) εἰς (05) instead of ἐπ'.

[117] Supporting this reading: Lagrange, *L'évangile selon saint Luc*, p. 115; Cullmann, "La signification du baptême dans le Nouveau Testament," p. 129; Geldenhuys, *Commentary on the Gospel of Luke*, p. 148; Marshall, *The Gospel of Luke*, p. 154; Fitzmyer, *The Gospel according to Luke*, p. 484; Schürmann, *Das Lukasevangelium: Kommentar zu Kap. 1:1–9:50*, p. 189; Schneider, *Das Evangelium nach Lukas: Kapitel 1–10*, p. 90; Ernst, *Das Evangelium nach Lukas*, p. 15; Schweizer, *The Good News*, p. 77; Metzger, *A Textual Commentary on the Greek New Testament*, p. 136; Juel, *Luc-Acts. La promesse de l'histoire*, p. 45.

I have begotten you.[118] The option for one or the other of the readings can have a considerable impact on the understanding of the nature of Jesus's historic mission. If the second reading should be privileged, the messianic impact of the account would then be evident from the quote of Ps 2:7. But it seems right that the first reading should be retained.

This reading, which agrees with Matt 3:17 and Mark 1:11 and which is generally believed to join Ps 2:7a ("You are my Son") and Isa 42:1b ("My chosen, in whom my soul delights"), finds solid support from excellent quality manuscripts: p⁴, 01, 02, 03, 017, 020, 032, 037, 038, 041, 044, 0124, f¹, f¹³, 28, 33, 565, 892, 1009, 1010, 1071, 1079, 1195, 1216, 1230, 1241, 1242, 1344, 1365, 1546, 1646, 2148, Byz Lect I^{69s,m}, 70^{s,m}, 185^{s,m}, it^{aur,e,q}. Thus, the weight of the external criticism is convincing. It would be risky, indeed, to speculate that all the important manuscripts of those supporting the first reading, coming from various origins, have modified the codex Bezae.

The internal criticism equally favors the option for the first reading. For example, note that at the moment of the transfiguration, the heavenly voice again presents Jesus as son and servant:

οὗτός ἐστιν ὁ υἱός μου ὁ ἐκλελεγμένος,[119] αὐτοῦ ἀκούετε. /
This is my Son, my Chosen; listen to him! (Luke 9:35)

The chosen one can, in fact, refer to Isa 42:1, or again to Isa 49:7, where the Servant is designated as God's "chosen." Therefore, there would be harmony between Jesus's presentation at his baptism and at the transfiguration. But, the most convincing factor in favor of the first reading is the following: the exact wording of the second reading is found without any problem of textual criticism in Acts 13:33 in the framework

---

[118] Supporting this second reading: *La Bible de Jerusalem: La Traduction Œcumenique de la Bible*; Leany, *A Commentary on the Gospel according to St. Luke*, pp. 110–11; Sabourin, *L'Évangile de Luc*, pp. 122–23; Benoit and Boismard, *Synopse des quatre évangiles en français*, p. 18; Legault, "Le baptême de Jésus et la doctrine du Serviteur souffrant," p. 149; Feuillet, "Le baptême de Jésus," pp. 334–35; George, *Études sur l'œuvre de Luc*, pp. 216–17; Grundmann, *Das Evangelium nach Lukas*, p. 107; Stöger, *L'évangile selon saint Luc*, p. 124; Legrand, "L'arrière-plan néotestamentaire de Luc 1:35," pp. 166–68.

[119] Certain manuscripts render ἀγαπητός / *beloved* instead of ἐκλελεγμένος / *chosen* (02, 04, 018, 024, 032, 033, 037, 041, f¹³, 28, 33, 565, 700, 1009, 1010, etc). This reading is habitually perceived as an assimilation to Mark 9:7. Assimilation is again evident, but in Matt 17:5 this time, in this other reading which adds, after ἀγαπητός, ἐν ᾧ εὐδόκησα / *beloved, in whom I am well pleased* (04, 05, 044, 1^{12m,19,31,47,48,49} etc).

of Paul's speech at Antioch, in relation to Christ's resurrection. Now, in this context, the resurrection is presented as the moment of the messianic enthronement of the Resurrected One. It seems to me that Luke had to reserve this very special formula of Ps 2:7 to signify the radical newness of the status of the Resurrected One, his universal lordship. In resurrecting him, God "engendered" him Lord of the universe, a scope that cannot be contained in Luke 3:22. Thus, it would be rather strange that Luke would have returned to the same text to designate two different stages of Jesus's vocation.[120]

Taking all these indicators into account, I must opt in favor of the first reading, and, consequently, seek to grasp the way in which Luke understood this formula that he introduced in his Gospel.

The Christological Impact of the Baptism

In Mark and Matthew, the physical scene of the baptism is well established: John baptizes in the Jordan; Jesus come from Galilee to be baptized by John; at his coming out of the water the theophany occurs. In Luke, this scene is almost completely indistinct: the Baptist is not named—the elementary logic wanted it as such since he has just been thrown into prison (v. 20); no geographic precision (one must go back to v. 3 to find it); but especially even the act of the baptism is hardly mentioned: "Now when all the people were baptized, and when Jesus also had been baptized and was praying . . . ."

Uniting his destiny to that of the people, which is only mentioned in Luke, Jesus submits himself to the same baptism as they (the gathering of the people becomes, as it were, the only background scene). But this baptism is only quickly mentioned with the help of the aorist passive infinitive βαπτισθῆναι / *to be baptized*. This fact (his baptism) already in the past, we find Jesus praying.[121] This is the first important point to which Luke wants to call attention. The entry into expeditious matters orients,

---

[120] This is Cullmann's position, "La signification du baptême dans le Nouveau Testament," p. 129. See also la Potterie, "L'Onction du Christ," p. 236.

[121] There is nothing surprising in that Jesus is presented in prayer just before the revelation that established him in his functions! All the great moments of Jesus's earthly career are always preceded by prayer in Luke: 3:21 (baptism); 6:12 (before choosing the disciples); 9:18 (before Peter's confession); 9:28–29 (before the transfiguration); 11:2 (before the teaching on prayer to the disciples); 22:41–44 (before entering into the passion); 23:46 (before his death). Luke will accord every bit as much importance to prayer in the primitive community. Note just this significant example: before the outpouring of the Spirit at Pentecost the community was gathered in prayer (Acts 1:14; 2:1).

first of all, toward this action: Jesus is praying. Once the attention is fixed on Jesus, Luke introduces the theophany (3:21b–22).

Thus, the physical aspect of the baptism diminishes to leave room for the capital event to follow, which appears as the consequence of Jesus's prayer.

The image of the sky opening (in Mark, the heavens rip open) is not without recall at the same time to Isa 63:19 and Ezek 1:1. The comparison with Ezekiel situates the reader in the perspective of the heavenly vision through which a revelation is transmitted. Thus it is for the prophet in exile when "the sky opens and [he was] a witness of divine visions." This reading is certainly not foreign to the context of the episode of Jesus's baptism, but the comparison with Isa 63:19c would better correspond to the global representation of the events as the fulfillment of a long awaited hope: "O that you would tear open the heavens and come down" (Isa 63:19c). Finally, the heavens open—or rip open—and God comes to answer, in sending Jesus, the vow expressed by the prophet Isaiah.

The interpretation most upheld by the scholars on the subject of Luke 3:22 is in the messianic line. In fact, one sees in the scene, Jesus's investiture as Messiah.[122] The position of Dunn on this subject is without equivocation: "At this moment, the eschatological hopes of the prophets of a Messiah anointed of the Spirit are fulfilled."[123]

Sabourin, for his part, deems that, already being Messiah through his conception, Jesus receives the Spirit again at baptism in view of his prophetic mission.[124] As for Fitzmyer, he is of the opinion that, in the combination of Ps 2:7 and Isa 42:1, we must not see the expression of a very precise form of messianism, but that "it is preferable to conserve it thus in its 'Lukan vagueness'—without excluding the possibility that it could lead to a greater fullness of understanding."[125] He proposes to read from it a special relation to God in terms of filiation expressed in the first part of the verse (in reference to Ps 2:7), with a connotation of obedience and of suffering conferred by the reference to the Servant (Isa 42:1) in the second part.[126] Marshall equally believes that we must see the display of Jesus as

---

[122] Geldenhuys, *Commentary on the Gospel of Luke*, p. 147, sees here, however, the confirmation of Jesus's eternal filiation.

[123] *Baptism in the Holy Spirit*, p. 27; also, Müller, *Lukas-Evangelium*, p. 29.

[124] *L'Évangile de Luc*, pp. 120–21; in the same sense, Stöger, *L'évangile selon saint Luc*, pp. 124–25 (except that Stöger speaks of a messianic work instead of a prophetic mission).

[125] *The Gospel according to Luke*, p. 486.

[126] Ibid. Fitzmyer's position, nevertheless, poses the problem that, in Isa 42, the Servant is not presented as suffering, but rather as having a prophetic role to assume.

Messiah Servant[127] in this verse, but without evoking the dimension of suffering, contrary to Fitzmyer. For Schürmann, the baptism is the occasion of the messianic anointing to which he makes reference in Acts:

> The baptism event must then also be understood as the anointing of the Spirit of the Messiah. Thus, explicitly, and implicitly in Acts 4:27 in light of Ps 2:2, Jesus became, from this fact, πλήρης πνεύματος ἁγίου [*full of the Holy Spirit*] (Luke 4:1; see 4:14), probably fulfilling the announcement of Isa 11:2b (see 11:3 LXX, ἐμπλήσει [*filled*]).[128]

Ernst believes that "the descent of the dove makes plain for all to see what had already been announced in the private setting of the annunciation scene (Luke 1:26–38)."[129] As for Lampe, he is of the opinion that the Spirit is fully present in Jesus since his conception; he explains that at his baptism

> the descent of the dove . . . indicates the messianic anointing which pours out [to Jesus] the necessary divine powers for his mission, that is to say, the same energy, that of the Spirit, that his disciples had to receive at Pentecost in view of the missionary task that would be assigned to them.[130]

The common denominator of the messianic reading made by the scholars is the identification of the contents of the first part of v. 22 to Ps 2:7. Other scholars judge, however, that we should not necessarily relate "You are my son" to Ps 2:7, but that it could very simply constitute the beginning of Isa 42:1, the verse concerning the Servant. Thus, as Gils[131] observes, the translation of the Septuagint for the word עבד by παῖς is repeated 340 times in the 807 occurrences of the MT.[132] This is the translation that is found in Isa 42:1. However, παῖς can just as well mean "son" as "Servant." Gils explains then:

> Thanks to this ambiguity, the word υἱός could have been introduced there where, however, παῖς with the meaning of "servant" would have

---

[127] *The Gospel of Luke*, pp. 156ff.

[128] *Das Lukasevangelium: Kommentar zu Kap. 1:1–9:50*, pp. 194–95.

[129] *Das Evangelium nach Lukas*, p. 153; see also, Schneider, *Das Evangelium nach Lukas: Kapitel 1–10*, p. 92.

[130] "The Holy Spirit in the Writings of St. Luke," p. 168.

[131] *Jésus prophète d'après les évangiles*, pp. 56ff.

[132] This translation is found again in Theodotion and Matt 12:18, while δοῦλος / *servant* is found in Aquila and Symmachus.

better followed the thought of the primitive Christian tradition, which is still in contact with Isaiah. The choice of υἱός explains much more easily that, in Hellenistic Christianity, the term παῖς was not familiar.[133]

Similarly, Jeremias considers that it is reasonable to believe that the ὁ υἱός μου / *my son* of the voice at the baptism represents the christological development of the ὁ παῖς μου / *my child* original.[134]

The pre-synoptic tradition on Jesus's baptism would then quote Isa 42:1 only. And in this perspective, Jesus would have been presented as a prophet[135] rather than as a messiah at his baptism. Luke would adopt this line of thought as well in 3:22: the Spirit is given to Jesus in view of his prophetic mission, his messianism only coming at the resurrection. This thesis was first defended by Gils,[136] and then upheld in a very well-articulated manner by la Potterie in his article "L'Onction du Christ."[137]

The fact that Luke interpreted the baptism as a prophetic investiture does not mean, however, that he had received a different tradition from that of Matt 3:17 and Mark 1:11, where παῖς / *child* had already become υἱός / *son*. He could still use this evolved tradition and give it a prophetic orientation. The rest of his gospel, as well as certain passages of Acts, also confirm this prophetic reading of the baptism account. The historic Jesus

---

[133] *Jésus prophète d'après les évangiles*, pp. 56–57. Jeremias, *New Testament Theology*, pp. 53–54, comes to the same conclusions as Gils; Schürmann, *Das Lukasevangelium*, p. 192, note 31, rejects this perspective.

[134] *New Testament Theology*, p. 54.

[135] Cullmann, *Christologie du Nouveau Testament*, also believes that the words at the baptism are from Isa 42:1, but he is of the opinion that these words define Jesus's mission as Servant of Yahweh, baptized in view of his suffering and death. "Jesus [acquires] the certitude that he [must] fulfill the mission of l'Ebed Yahweh" (p. 60ff.). Legault, "*Le baptême de Jésus et la doctrine du Serviteur souffrant*," pp. 147–66, defends the same position as Cullmann.

[136] *Jésus prophète d'après les évangiles*, pp. 49–73.

[137] Pp. 225–52. La Potterie believes, following Ménard, "'Pais Theou' as Messianic Title in the Book of Acts," that "if Jesus is designated as the Servant, it is in view of a prophetic mission." He supports this opinion with the verses which follow where it is said that the Servant must be "the light of the nations" (v. 6) and that "the islands are waiting for his teaching" (v. 2). Mollat, "The Role of Experience in the New Testament Teaching on Baptism and the Coming of the Holy Spirit," pp. 130ff., equally believes that at his baptism Jesus receives the prophetic investiture; also of this opinion: O'Reilly, *Word and Sign in the Acts of the Apostles*, pp. 30ff.; Haya-Prats, *L'Esprit force de l'Église*, pp. 170–75 (ET: pp. 202–8); Dumais, *L'actualization du Nouveau Testament*, pp. 122–23.

of Luke exercises the role of prophet, which the following section will show.

Jesus as Prophet

The characteristics of Jesus as Prophet are clearly brought out in the Gospel of Luke,[138] as well as in Acts, in the setting of retrospective readings. The examples below, presented in four different regroupings, are in effect without equivocation as to Luke's intentions to situate Jesus's earthly ministry in the prophetic line.

Jesus and His Own Presentation as Prophet

The key text by which Luke presents Jesus's mission as expressly prophetic is Luke 4:16–21.[139] Jesus comes to the synagogue on the Sabbath (v. 16); he is given the scroll of the prophet Isaiah (v. 17); he reads what is found there:

> The Spirit of the Lord God is upon me, because he has anointed me to bring good news to the poor. He has sent me to proclaim release to the captives and recovery of sight to the blind, to let the oppressed go free, and to proclaim the year of the Lord's favor. (vv. 18–19 / Isa 61:1)

It is to be noted that this quotation from Isaiah is only found in Luke, although the two other synoptic gospels also relate the episode of the synagogue (Matt 13:54–58; Mark 6:1–6). After this reading, Jesus declares: "Today this scripture has been fulfilled in your hearing" (v. 21). Jesus applies this prophecy of Isa 61:1 to himself. The content of this prophecy effectively summarizes his entire ministry. It is important to point out, moreover, that the announcement of Isa 61:1 is directly connected to that

---

[138] See Smith, *Easter Gospels*, pp. 136–37; also Minear, *To Heal and to Reveal*, p. 102; the latter writes: "It is significant, to a greater degree than is often recognized, that all four Gospels speak of Jesus as a prophet. Certainly in Luke this term is used without reservation to refer to Jesus' vocation." Still other scholars are interested in the important role of Jesus as prophet in the Gospel of Luke: Hastings, *Prophet and Witness in Jerusalem*; Voss, *Die Christologie der lukanischen Schriften in Grundzugen*, pp. 155–70; Carruth, "The Jesus-as-Prophet Motif in Luke-Acts"; Busse, *Die Wunder des Propheten Jesus*; George, *Études sur l'œuvre de Luc*, pp. 79–84; Vesco, *Jérusalem et son prophète*.

[139] The synagogue episode presents Jesus as "Messiah-Prophet," writes Samain ("Le discours-programme de Jésus à la synagogue de Nazareth. Luc 4:16–30," p. 32); one should rather say that this episode presents him as "prophet destined to become Messiah."

of Isa 42:7,[140] where the description of the role of the Servant is presented in 42:1; Isa 42:7 reads: "[I have destined you] to open the eyes that are blind, to bring out the prisoners from the dungeon, from the prison those who sit in darkness."

Not only does Jesus apply the words of Isa 61:1 to himself, but he also clearly presents himself as a prophet when, in 4:24 (parallel Matt 13:57; Mark 6:4), he affirms, "Truly I tell you, no prophet is accepted in the prophet's hometown." Moreover, he justifies the orientation of his mission in comparing it with Elijah's (vv. 25–26)—see further on the parallel Jesus/Elijah and Elisha (v. 27).

The anointing to which Luke 4:18 refers cannot be other than that of the baptism. In fact, Luke 4:16ff. marks the inauguration of Jesus's ministry, which immediately follows his baptism—if an exception is made of the episode of the temptations (4:1–13), where the Spirit descends on him. The anointing of the Spirit at the baptism was thus in view of enabling him to fulfill his prophetic role: "The Spirit of the Lord is upon me, because he has anointed me to bring good news . . . ." This is exactly what Luke, himself, confirms in Acts 10:38: ". . . how God anointed Jesus of Nazareth[141] with the Holy Spirit and with power; how he went about doing good and healing all who were oppressed by the devil, for God was with him."

The study of the episode at the synagogue in Nazareth thus allows for this conclusion to be drawn: Jesus receives the Spirit at baptism in view of the earthly prophetic mission that he will have to fulfill.[142]

---

[140] See la Potterie, "L'Onction du Christ," p. 237; also Samain, "Le discours-programme," p. 31.

[141] This mention "of Nazareth" in Acts 10:38 echoes back to that of Luke 4:16: "He came to Nazareth where he had been raised."

[142] This is what la Potterie, "L'Onction du Christ," demonstrates in particular, pp. 234–39. Lentzen-Deis, *Die Taufe Jesu nach den Synoptikern*, supports this point of view. Speaking of the baptism, he writes: "Hier ist Jesus, entsprechend der Schilderung im übrigen Lk–Ev, in besonderer Weise unter dem "prophetischen" Vorstellungsbild gezeichnet (Luke 4:14, 18) . . . Jesus wird öfters als der gottgesandte "Prophet" beschrieben (4:24; 7:16; 7:39; [9:19 par]; 13:33; 24:19) . . . . Die Taufe und die danach folgende Geistbegabung wird von Lk nach 4:18 im Sinne der "Salbung" von Jes 61:1 verstanden" (p. 285). ["Here, Jesus is depicted in a special way under the 'prophetic' image, in accordance with the description in the rest of Luke (Luke 4:14, 18) . . . On multiple occasions, Jesus is described as the God-sent 'prophet' (4:24; 7:16; 7:39; [9:19 par]; 13:33; 24:19) . . . . The baptism and the subsequent Spirit-endowment is understood by Luke, according to 4:18, in the sense of the 'anointing' in Isaiah 61:1."] Also, O'Reilly, *Word and Sign in the Acts of the Apostles*: "At his baptism . . . Jesus was anointed as prophet; he was called by God and entrusted with the mission of announcing the good news of eschatological salvation in word and deed

Jesus, Prophet Like Moses

The vision that Luke has of Jesus of Nazareth is reflected distinctly in the testimony of the disciples of Emmaus: "They replied: 'The things about Jesus of Nazareth, who was a prophet mighty in deed and word before God and all the people'" (Luke 24:19). Jesus was a prophet mighty in deed and word before God and all the people. Furthermore, he is the one who, like Moses, came to save the people (Isa 61:1). In retrospect of Stephen's speech, Moses is obviously presented as a liberator (Acts 7:35) and as the savior of the people (Acts 7:25). So, this one is described as "powerful in his words and deeds" (Acts 7:22b), therefore, in the same terms that Jesus is described by the disciples of Emmaus. This Moses, Stephen recalls, quoting Deut 18:15, had said: "'God will raise up a prophet for you from your own people as he raised me up'" (Acts 7:37).

This prophet announced by Moses is certainly identified as Jesus in Peter's second speech:[143] "Moses said, 'The Lord your God will raise up for you from your own people a prophet like me'" (Acts 3:22). "'And all the prophets, as many as have spoken from Samuel and those after him, also predicted these days'" (v. 24). Jesus is, thus, in Luke's perspective, the new Moses.[144] He accomplished the work of freedom in the power of the Spirit with which he was vested.

Jesus, the New Elijah

Contrary to Matthew and Mark, it is Jesus and not John that Luke wants to identify as Elijah; Jesus is the eschatological prophet par excellence.[145]

(Luke 4:18f.). To enable him to announce that salvation effectively, that is, to inaugurate the era of salvation by bringing about the salvation which his preaching announced, Jesus was equipped with the gift of the Spirit, the Spirit of prophecy" (p. 31).

[143] On the subject, see Hill, *New Testament Prophecy*, p. 51: also, Lampe, "The Holy Spirit in the Writings of St. Luke," p. 164.

[144] For the comparison between Jesus and Moses in the synoptic tradition, see Gils, *Jésus prophète d'après les évangiles*, pp. 30–47.

[145] See Hahn, *The Titles of Jesus in Christology*, pp. 372ff., more particularly pp. 376–77. Franklin, *Christ the Lord*, p. 68, deems that it is not the typology of the prophet of the end times that interests Luke, but rather the description of Jesus "as a prophetic person whose ministry and person are one with those of the prophets of old." He adds (p. 69): "Luke sets out to present Jesus as a prophetic person and his ministry as the fulfillment of the earlier prophets." Franklin's judgment of Jesus's prophetic role is correct in that it relates Jesus's ministry as the prolongation of the ministry of the Old Testament prophets. But the eschatological dimension is, nevertheless, very present, especially if we consider that eschatology, in Luke's perspective, seems more about fulfillment than the end times.

Admittedly, two passages are found where John exercises a role that Elijah should play at the end times, i.e., to prepare the Day of the Lord, for it is a question of:

> He [John] will turn many of the people of Israel to the Lord their God [see Mal 2:6]. With the spirit and power of Elijah he will go before him, [see Mal 3:1, 24], to turn the hearts of parents to their children, [Mal 3:24] and the disobedient to the wisdom of the righteous, to make ready a people prepared for the Lord. (Luke 1:16–17)

> And you, child, . . . you will go before the Lord to prepare his ways. (Luke 1:76)

What is observed in these passages is that John's role is limited to that of precursor. In eschatological times, Elijah must, in reality, play a double role: that of precursor and that of prophet. Luke keeps the function of precursor for John, but he is not the eschatological prophet. He is the last of the Old Covenant prophets. "He still belongs to the time of the promise [of the law and of the prophets,] not to the time of the fulfillment."[146] It is Jesus who will incarnate Elijah in his function of prophet. Of course, John exercises a prophetic ministry, but it is Jesus who will be "acting" as Elijah.

Notably, in a systematic way, Luke eliminates from his sources the passages where John is identified as Elijah. Thus it is of the text of Q where Jesus praises the Baptist (Matt 11:7–19 ‖ Luke 7:24–28). In the two texts, John is qualified as a prophet, even the greatest of the prophets that ever were in Israel (Matt 11:9, 11; Luke 7:26, 28). Matthew clarifies: "and if you are willing to accept it, he is Elijah who is to come" (v. 14), but Luke omits this portion of the text. In the same way that he will not retain this text of the tradition said to be of Mark (Matt 17:10–13 ‖ Mark 9:11–13) where once again Jesus explains to the listeners that John the Baptist is the awaited Elijah. Finally, John's clothing description is not found in Luke either—"clothing of camel's hair" (Matt 3:4 ‖ Mark 1:6)—that tends once again to identify him with Elijah.

On the other hand, the episode of Nain (Luke 7:11–17) evidently places Jesus's miraculous activity in the light of that of Elijah (1 Kgs 17:8–24). In fact, the parallel between the two miracles—the resurrection

---

[146] Samain, "Le discours-programme," p. 26, in line with Conzelmann, *The Theology of St. Luke*, pp. 16, 22ff. See also la Potterie, "L'Onction du Christ," p. 231; Schnider, *Jesus der Prophet*, pp. 92ff.

of the son of the widow of Nain by Jesus and the resurrection of the son of the widow of Zarephath by Elijah—is rather apparent.[147]

Luke 7:11–17[148]	*1 Kgs 17:10–24*
[11] Jesus goes to Nain; [12] meets the widow at the gate of the city;	[10] Elijah goes to Zarephath meets the widow at the gate of the city;[149]
her only son is being carried to be buried;	[17] her only son dies;
[14] Jesus gives life to the son;	[19–22] Elijah revives the child;
[15] Jesus gives the child to his mother.[150]	[23] Elijah gives the child to his mother.

The reaction of the crowd following Jesus's gesture is to recognize him as a great prophet: "A great prophet has risen among us!" (7:16a), and to also recognize God's visitation: "and God has looked favorably on his people!" (16b). In the same way, the widow of Zarephath had recognized Elijah as a bearer of God's word (17:24), thus as a prophet.[151]

---

[147] See the parallel establish by Fitzmyer, *The Gospel according to Luke*, p. 656, which I reproduce in large part.

[148] According to Jeremias, *Die Sprache des Lukasevangeliums*, pp. 156–60, Luke in vv. 13–15 keeps a tradition which is his alone, but vv. 11–12 and 16–17 are his writing. Fitzmyer, *The Gospel according to Luke*, p. 656, believes, for his part, that the editorial changes are only in v. 11 (though the placing of the episode would not be Luke's) and in vv. 16–17.

[149] Gils, *Jésus prophète d'après les évangiles*, p. 26, believes as well that "the literary formulas attest to Luke's dependence concerning the account dedicated to Elijah." He takes up, for example (note 1), the relationship at the level of the vocabulary between Luke 7:11 and 1 Kgs 17:9–10 (LXX):

Luke 7:11–12: καὶ ἐγένετο ἐν τῷ ἑξῆς ἐπορεύθη εἰς πόλιν καλουμένην Ναΐν . . . . ὡς δὲ ἤγγισεν τῇ πύλῃ τῆς πόλεως, καὶ ἰδοὺ . . . . αὐτὴ ἦν χήρα . . . . / he went to a town called Nain . . . . As he approached the gate of the town . . . . and she was a widow . . . .

1 Kgs 17:9–10: . . . πορεύου εἰς Σαρεπτα . . . . καὶ ἐπορεύθη εἰς Σαρεπτα εἰς τὸν πυλῶνα τῆς πόλεως, καὶ ἰδοὺ ἐκεῖ γυνὴ χήρα. / . . . Go now to Zarephath . . . . and went to Zarephath. When he came to the gate of the town, a widow was there.

Also, between Luke 7:15 and 1 Kgs 17:23, where the same formula is found: καὶ ἔδωκεν αὐτὸν τῇ μητρὶ αὐτοῦ. / *and he gave him to his mother*.

[150] Fitzmyer, *The Gospel according to Luke*, p. 656, sees in Jesus's gesture, when he gives the child to his mother, an allusion to Elijah's same gesture.

[151] Schnider, *Jesus der Prophet*, pp. 108ff., takes up the similarities between the two texts, but he also highlights Jesus's superiority. Elijah prays to the Lord to give life to

Other evidence coming from Luke's gospel enable the parallel Jesus/Elijah to be fleshed out even more. Note first the end of the episode at the synagogue, already noted, where Jesus recalls that the prophets are not welcome in their hometowns (4:24); he supports this word by quoting the cases of Elijah (vv. 25–26) and Elisha (vv. 27–28). Then, when he has finished speaking, the crowd, irritated by his words, wants to throw him from the cliff. The fact that they want to kill him after his own presentation as a prophet brings to mind Elijah's situation when he must flee under death threats (1 Kgs 19:3ff.).[152]

At the moment when he begins to go up to Jerusalem, Luke alone opens the sequence with this detail: "When the days drew near for him to be taken up, he set his face to go to Jerusalem" (9:51). The concept used, ἀναλαμβάνειν / *to be taken up*, is the same one that the Septuagint uses (2 Kgs 2:11) to speak of Elijah being taken away.[153] In the same way, in Luke 9:54, the disciples want to make the fire of heaven fall on the Samaritans as Elijah did on his adversaries. La Potterie points out:

> Jesus condemns this excessive zeal, but will say of himself a little further on, in pretty similar terms, that he "came to start a fire on the earth" (XII, 49), that must evidently be understood metaphorically. But the formula used recalls the activity of the great prophet during Ahab's era.[154]

Note again these two verses (Luke 9:61–62) that appear as an addition to Q (compare Matt 8:19–22 to Luke 9:57–62), where Jesus's remark strangely recalls Elijah's remark to Elisha:

> Another said: "I will follow you, Lord; but let me first say farewell to those at my home." Jesus said to him, "No one who puts a hand to the plow and looks back is fit for the kingdom of God." (Luke 9:61–62)

Certainly evoking the scene between Elijah and Elisha (1 Kgs 19:19–21), the demands posed by Jesus remain, nevertheless, more intransigent.

---

the child (1 Kgs 17:20–22); Jesus simply says: "Young man, I say to you, rise!" (Luke 7:14).

[152] Juel, "Social Dimensions of Exegesis: The Use of Psalm 16 in Acts 2," p. 51, writes: "All those familiar with biblical stories know that one or the other of these prophets had met with a hostile reception among their own people; Elijah especially, faced with death threats, was obliged to flee."

[153] See in chapter 3 the parallel established between the ascension and Elijah being taken away.

[154] "L'Onction du Christ," 226.

Finally, in Luke 22:43 (a verse only in Luke), this scene of the passion, where the angel strengthens Jesus in the garden of Gethsemane, recalls that of 1 Kgs 19:4–8 where Elijah, taken by discouragement, is also comforted by an angel.

All these indicators, though of unequal value, attest to Luke's intention to present Jesus as an eschatological prophet, as a new Elijah. Other Lukan passages are found where Jesus is said to be a prophet without any particular identification. Thus it is when Simon the Pharisee questions Jesus's attitude when faced with a woman in sin: "If this man were a prophet, he would have known who and what kind of woman this is who is touching him—that she is a sinner" (Luke 7:39).

In addition, during the ascent into Jerusalem, Jesus, envisaging his imminent death, declares: "Yet today, tomorrow, and the next day I must be on my way, because it is impossible for a prophet to be killed outside of Jerusalem" (Luke 13:33).

Finally, note the other cases conserved by Luke that are found as well in Matthew and Mark. For example, Herod is perplexed at what he hears about Jesus: ". . . it was said by some that John had been raised from the dead, by some that Elijah had appeared, and by others that one of the ancient prophets had arisen" (Luke 9:7–8). This perception of the people regarding Jesus is expressed in the same terms in 9:19. At the moment of the passion, the guards questioned Jesus under the title of prophet; even if it is only mockery, the title reflects, nevertheless, Jesus's reputation among the people: "They also blindfolded him and kept asking him, 'Prophesy! Who is it that struck you?'" (Luke 22:64).

The proof of the quoted examples—certain ones are without equivocation—leaves absolutely no doubt as to the value of the anointing that Jesus received at his baptism—he is invested with the Spirit in view of his earthly prophetic mission. Now remains the drawing of a conclusion about the meaning of the divine proclamation at the baptism: "You are my Son, the Beloved; with you I am well pleased."

Jesus "Son-Prophet"

As previously noted, the title "son of God" is hardly used by Luke, and rare uses are reserved for the designation of Jesus as Messiah. However, what about the use, here, of the title "Son"? First, let me clarify that the first use that he makes of it is at the baptism. Since the episode of the baptism has a prophetic scope and not a messianic one, what meaning then can the designation "my Son" have in the "mouth" of God toward Jesus?

The fact that Luke had put the genealogy immediately after the divine proclamation "You are my Son" is very significant.[155] It is clear, in fact, that in introducing this genealogy, Luke breaks the rhythm of the sequence—ministry of the Baptist/baptism of Jesus/temptation/beginnings in Galilee—such as found in the other synoptic gospels. He deliberately places it after God has presented Jesus as his son. It is necessary then for Luke to define this filiation and that's what he does by referring to this literary device frequently used in the Bible, the genealogy (Luke 3:23ff.).

Contrary to Matt 1:1–16 that presents a descending genealogy from Abraham, Luke presents an ascending genealogy that starts with Joseph and goes back to God.[156] The last name of the genealogy is Adam "son of God." According to Talbert, the genealogy interprets the baptism account:

> The precise relation between the account of the baptism and the genealogy seems to be the fact that both end with the designation of Jesus as Son. Consequently, the genealogy defines the Son of 3:22b as Son of Adam.[157]

However, Adam, who could not resist the forces of evil, did not know to honor the title that was linked to his rank among the creatures (Gen 1:26). Jesus, on the other hand, would know how to conquer these same forces that got the better of Adam, as the account of the temptations placed immediately after the genealogy demonstrates.[158]

We probably should not push too much, in Luke, the analogy of the new Adam, which is an especially Pauline category (Rom 5:14; 1 Cor

---

[155] See Chevallier, "Luc et l'Esprit Saint," p. 3, who writes, "Luke continues with the genealogy of Jesus, which would be an unusual place if precisely it were not introduced by the proclamation of the engendering of the son on this precise day, and if the list of the ancestors did not go back to the mention of the first origin: 'son of Adam, son of God.'" Chevalier sees, correctly, when he says that the return of the genealogy back to God gives its meaning to the title "Son" and justifies from this fact its place of insertion in the third Gospel. However, he is wrong to perceive the episode of the baptism from the messianic angle, as indicated in his use of the term "engendering."

[156] The "it was believed," which precedes the mention of Joseph as the father of Jesus, has generally been read as a confirmation by Luke of the virginal conception: Marshall, *The Gospel of Luke*, p. 162; Sabourin, *L'Évangile de Luc*, p. 124. It could, nevertheless, apply to the entire genealogy, in such a way that it could be paraphrased thus: "he was, it was believed, of this ascendance son of Joseph, son of Heli . . . ." Fitzmyer, *The Gospel according to Luke (I–IX)*, p. 499, however, contests this reading; he writes: "The cl., 'as it was thought,' added by Luke, modifies solely 'the son of Joseph,' and is not to be understood with the further list of genitives."

[157] *Literary Patterns*, pp. 117–18.

[158] This is the point of view proposed by Jeremias, "Αδαμ," *TDNT* 1:141.

15:22, 45–49). However, it is Jesus's solidarity with all of humanity[159]—by the fact of the universality of salvation[160]—and the new creation in Jesus that are especially emphasized in this genealogy.[161] This is how Feuillet understands it:

> One would only know to accord such importance because between the two accounts of the Baptism and the Temptation, Saint Luke inserted a genealogy going back all the way to Adam. Concerning the Baptism, it seems that one can deduce from there his intention of presenting Jesus as the point of departure of a new humanity, the prototype of the baptized.[162]

This is, therefore, the special relation of Jesus to God that is also meant: Jesus is worthy of the title because he was the only righteous, (see Wis 2:18 Ps 73:15; Sir 4:10), perfect servant, as God had wanted in Adam; this servant on whom God put his Spirit (Isa 42:1; 61:1).

Jesus is then the one who corresponds in every respect to God's expectations. He is the son in whom God is pleased.[163] This perfect[164] Son will know how to render a perfect testimony of God. It is thus in his quality as Son par excellence that Jesus is made prophet at his baptism—he is

---

[159] See Schweizer, *The Good News according to Luke*, p. 80. Talbert, *Literary Patterns*, p. 118, clarifies: "The one who is declared Son at his baptism is a full participant in our common lot as Sons of Adam. . . . But it is the humanity of Jesus as Son of God that Luke is at pains to emphasize in the baptism narrative and its context."

[160] See Schneider, *Das Evangelium nach Lukas: Kapitel 1–10*, p. 94; Ernst, *Das Evangelium nach Lukas*, p. 157; Grundmann, *Das Evangelium nach Lukas*, p. 111.

[161] Fitzmyer, *The Gospel according to Luke (I–IX)*, p. 498.

[162] "Le récit lucanien de la tentation (Luke 4:1–13)," p. 617.

[163] Cullmann, "La signification du baptême," pp. 129–32, sees this "son" as *l'Ebed Yahweh*: "at the time of his baptism, Jesus was charged with the role of *l'Ebed Yahweh* who takes on himself the sins of his people . . . he is baptized for the pardon of sins . . . for he is the son of whom Isaiah speaks . . . Jesus is baptized in view of the substitutive suffering" (p. 130). Feuillet, "Le baptême de Jésus," p. 239, contests this point of view under the pretext that the reference is to Isa 42:1 and not to Isa 53; the accent would not bear thus on the expiatory suffering.

[164] The fact of being a perfect human being before God makes Jesus worthy to be called *Son*. This opportunity is, in principle, offered to all human beings. It is a question of living according to God's ways. Thus Luke writes (Luke 6:35): "But love your enemies, do good, and lend, expecting nothing in return. Your reward will be great, and you will be children of the Most High." In the same way, Paul says (Rom 8:14): "For all who are led by the Spirit of God are children of God." Also: "And because you are children, God has sent the Spirit of his Son into our hearts, crying, 'Abba! Father!'" (Gal 4:6). And finally, in Gal 3:26: "For in Christ Jesus you are all children of God through faith."

the only one capable of presenting to humanity the true face of God. The perfection of the testimony that Jesus will have rendered to God as eschatological prophet during his earthly mission will make him worthy, in the resurrection, to accede to the heavenly throne and to reign over the universe (see Acts 2:33). In other words, his superiority as Son, in his human nature, makes him worthy to accede to the royal functions, by the gift of the Spirit at the resurrection.

In brief, the anointing of the Spirit at the baptism makes the Son Jesus the eschatological Prophet, while the anointing of the Spirit at the resurrection makes the Son Jesus the Messiah.

3. THE SPIRIT AND JESUS'S ENTRANCE INTO TEMPTATION—LUKE 4:1

Clearly, the mission confided to Jesus at his baptism is a prophetic mission. God is the guarantor of the success of this mission by sending his own Spirit on Jesus. However, Jesus will, nevertheless, have to undergo the test that will demonstrate his enablement to fulfill the function with which he is charged; the test that will demonstrate that he is the only righteous one in confronting evil. The epithet *Righteous*, in its absolute sense, will inevitably become the descriptor of the moral perfection of the Christ, as the following passages of Acts give evidence:

- But you rejected the Holy and Righteous One. (3:14a)

- They killed those who foretold the coming of the Righteous One. (7:52b)

- The God of our ancestors has chosen you . . . to see the Righteous One and to hear his own voice. (22:14)

Note, however, that even before presenting Jesus as the Righteous One in Acts, Luke, with his editorial touch in Luke 23:47, makes the centurion say: "Certainly this man was righteous." This is contrary to what Matt 27:54 and Mark 15:39 render: "Truly this man was God's Son!" For Luke, it was too soon to present Jesus as Son of God; it was first necessary that he be found righteous; it was the essential condition for his accession to the function of Son of God. The centurion's words, at the junction of two eras, will thus confirm what will have been shown by the account of the temptation, that is, on the one hand, that Jesus is righteous and has earned the designation of that title which will characterize the resurrected Messiah, and, on the other hand, that he is the Righteous One.

Thus, it is under the guidance of the Spirit that Jesus will experience the test of the temptation. But how does Luke exactly perceive the intervention of the Spirit in this event? A synoptic presentation of the texts related to Jesus's entrance into temptation will better bring out Luke's originality:

Matt 4:1	*Mark 1:12*	*Luke 4:1*
Τότε ὁ Ἰησοῦς ἀνήχθη εἰς τὴν ἔρημον ὑπὸ τοῦ πνεύματος πειρασθῆναι ὑπὸ τοῦ διαβόλου. / Then Jesus was led up by the Spirit into the wilderness to be tempted by the devil.	Καὶ εὐθὺς τὸ πνεῦμα αὐτὸν ἐκβάλλει εἰς τὴν ἔρημον. / And the Spirit immediately drove him out into the wilderness.	Ἰησοῦς δὲ πλήρης πνεύματος ἁγίου ὑπέστρεψεν ἀπὸ τοῦ Ἰορδάνου καὶ ἤγετο ἐν τῷ πνεύματι ἐν τῇ ἐρήμῳ / Jesus, full of the Holy Spirit, returned from the Jordan and was led by the Spirit into the wilderness.

The type of intervention of the Spirit in Matthew and Mark is, in the Old Testament manner, an exterior force acting on Jesus. In Mark, the nature of the verb chosen confers a coercive character to this force's action. The verb ἐκβάλλειν / *to drive* is actually the one used eleven times by Mark to describe exorcism (Mark 1:39; 3:23; etc). In Matthew, the instrumental role of the Spirit is also evident (by the preposition ὑπό / *by*), but the verb used—ἀνάγειν / *to lead*—is stripped of every constraint. The author obviously wanted to preserve Jesus's autonomy and freedom. The same remark applies concerning the verb in the Lukan version. But what is striking, in Luke's case, is the dominant place given to the Spirit at the moment of Jesus's departure into the desert.

Note first of all the editorial handiwork in the first verse, which contains the first mention of the Spirit πλήρης πνεύματος ἁγίου / *full of the Holy Spirit*.[165] Absent in Matthew and Mark, this part of the sentence joins the baptism and temptation accounts separated by the insertion of the genealogy. The vocabulary and the formulation are evidently specifically Lukan. Thus, of the 35 New Testament occurrences of the verb ὑποστρέφειν / *to return*, 32 are in Luke-Acts.[166] The two works count as well 10 of the 16 occurrences of the adjective πλήρης / *full*.[167] In addition, the

---

[165] See Jeremias, *Die Sprache des Lukasevangeliums*, pp. 114–15.

[166] The other New Testament uses are found in: Gal 1:17; Heb 7:1; 2 Pet 2:21.

[167] Matthew counts two occurrences: 14:20; 15:37; Mark, two: 4:28; 8:19; John, one: 1:14; and one in 2 John 8.

combination of πλήρης + genitive is characteristic of Luke: his 10 uses of the term πλήρης are in fact in such a combination—as opposed to two other times in the New Testament (Mark 8:19 and John 1:14). Finally, of the 10 uses, five have *Spirit* in the genitive (Luke 4:1; Acts 6:3, 5; 7:55; 11:24).

This first part of the verse, thus, unites two originally successive episodes according to tradition. But this joining could have simply been read as follows: Ἰησοῦς δὲ ὑπέστρεψεν ἀπὸ τοῦ Ἰορδάνου / *Jesus returned from the Jordan*. Why then this insistent mentioning of the Spirit—πλήρης πνεύματος ἁγίου / *full of the Holy Spirit*—especially if one considers that the author conserves, in the other part of the verse, the intervention of the Spirit already understood in the source? It seems correct to say that this is Jesus's new situation, baptized in the Spirit, which is here signified specifically as πλήρης πνεύματος ἁγίου. "Being full of the Spirit" is the essential condition for the prophetic announcement of the eschatological news that is coming.

In order to clearly see this specificity in Jesus (that equally proves the Christian prophet's prerogative), his situation must be compared to that of those who prophesied at his coming at the beginning of the Gospel, including John the Baptist.

These prophets, as previously seen, were "filled with the Spirit." However, the term used, the verb πίμπλημι, is always in the passive: Luke 1:41 (Elizabeth) and 1:67 (Zechariah): ἐπλήσθη; 1:15 (John): πλησθήσεται. The divine passive form is recognized, which indicates just as much the origin of the force acting in those as the act of filling that confers this force. In order to speak of the Spirit dwelling in Jesus, Luke now uses the adjective form πλήρης that is translated by "full." Jesus is full of the Spirit. Thus, here, it is a matter of the condition subsequent to the act of filling. It is, in fact, the permanent indwelling of the Spirit which is signified by the use of the adjective πλήρης.[168] John, it is true, was permanently gifted by the Spirit, but this Spirit was "poured out" on him for a very specific task and for this task only: to prepare the way for Jesus. As for Jesus, he is full of the Spirit in an absolute manner. The permanent presence of the Spirit in John is functional; in Jesus, the Spirit is part of his being.

---

[168] This is Marshall's opinion, "The Significance of Pentecost," p. 355: "The adjective *plērēs* is used to describe the state of a person who is full of the Spirit, and it describes the state of Jesus after His baptism (Luke 4:1), the seven deacons (especially Stephen, Acts 6:3, 5; 7:55), and Barnabas (Acts 11:24). Thus it refers to a permanent endowment that becomes part of a person's character.

Jesus's baptism in the Spirit marks the specificity of Jesus's relation to the Spirit.[169] Luke signifies it clearly when he clarifies that it is in coming back from the Jordan that Jesus is found "full of the Spirit"—thus coming up from his baptism.

However, as Marshall remarked, other Lukan characters are found who are equally said to be "full of the Spirit." It is a quality of the Seven (Acts 6:3), Stephen (6:5; 7:55), and Barnabas (11:24). But these characters are of the post-Pentecostal period and, thus, people who were also baptized in the Spirit to accomplish a task analogous to Jesus's earthly mission, i.e., a prophetic task.[170] Believers become then bearers of the Spirit as Jesus of Nazareth was (this point is more completely developed in the following chapter).

The baptism in the Spirit thus enabled Jesus to fulfill the function linked to the new order, which would be fully inaugurated in Jesus's death and resurrection.[171] The newness of the situation commands a radically new prophetic speech. It is the speech of the Spirit. The agents of this new speech—first of all Jesus, then the Christians—must, consequently, be filled with the Spirit to adequately utter this speech. That is to say, they must be enabled permanently by the Spirit. The Spirit becomes the intrinsic component of the believing person, the prophet of the new times (see Acts 2:17). Thus, the Christians baptized in the Spirit at Pentecost will also benefit from a prophetic status analogous to that of Jesus of Nazareth.[172]

---

[169] See Reiling and Swellengrebel, *A Translator's Handbook*, p. 186.

[170] Lagrange, *Évangile selon saint Luc*, p. 128, is correct in saying that πλήρης πνεύματι ἁγίου [*full of the Holy Spirit*] is not "an essential prerogative of the Savior." Of the same opinion, Barrett, *The Holy Spirit and the Gospel Tradition*, p. 21, and Feuillet, "Le récit lucanien de la tentation (Luke 4:1–13)," p. 617. But Feuillet is wrong to assimilate the two formulas "filled with the Spirit" and "full of the Spirit" when he writes that "something exactly similar" to πλήρης (*full*) is said in the infancy narratives. Just like Feuillet, Dupont, "Les tentations de Jésus dans le récit de Luc (Luke 4:1–13)," p. 10, does not seem to establish a distinction between the two formulations.

[171] Feuillet, "Le baptême de Jésus," p. 333, insists on the capital importance that Luke accords to the outpouring of the Spirit on Jesus at his baptism; he is of the opinion that Luke wants to mark, by this episode, "the beginning of the new order and the prelude of Pentecost."

[172] However, it must be clarified that if the adjective πλήρης / *full* is used in relation to the Christians, the passive participial form of πίμπλημι / *filled* will still be present. There are many examples of this: Acts 2:4: "They were all filled with the Holy Spirit"; here it makes references to the initial action, i.e., to the Pentecostal outpouring that makes them *pneumatikoi*. It is the same situation concerning Paul, in 9:17, where An-

It must have seemed important to Luke to present Jesus as bearer of the Spirit at the moment when he was going to be confronted by Satan, as Conzelmann explains:

> In the description of Jesus as bearer of the Spirit there is implied his relation to the powers of the world. It is not accidental that it is in the story of the Temptation that Luke emphasizes the relationship between Jesus and the Spirit. It is in the encounter with Satan that the endowment with the Spirit is made manifest, and Satan has to yield. At the same time we see what constitutes the redemptive character of that period free from Satan which is now beginning.[173]

What remains to be studied is the second mention of the Spirit in this same verse, which is also found in Matthew and Mark. Luke's text presents, nevertheless, a particular formulation that divides the specialists on its understanding. Is ἐν τῷ πνεύματι / *by/in the Spirit* an instrumental dative or a dative of manner?[174]

The question is not easily solved. In general, grammarians and linguists do not really propose normative rules, but rather indicative signs.

---

anias says to him: "Saul, my brother, the Lord sent me to you . . . so that you recover your sight and be filled with the Holy Spirit." In the other cases (4:8, 31; 9:17; 13:9), it seems to be a matter of a punctual renewing to pronounce a prophetic word (Peter—4:8; Paul—13:9); or again, to mark a special time (4:31—at the end of prayer, "they were all filled with the Holy Spirit"). See on this subject Marshall, "The Significance of Pentecost," p. 355.

[173] Conzelmann, *The Theology of St. Luke*, p. 180.

[174] Many scholars have the tendency to see in the locution ἐν τῷ πνεύματι / *in the Spirit* the state in which Jesus finds himself following his baptism. In this sense, Plummer, *Luke*, p. 107, writes "He was led in (not into) the wilderness; i.e., in His wanderings there, as in His progress thither, He was under Divine influence and guidance." As to DuPont, "Les tentations," he writes that "it is a matter of an influence exercising itself from the interior, by intimate inspiration, not as one led by a guide" (p. 11). Also of this opinion, George, "L'Esprit dans l'œuvre de Luc," pp. 516–17; Haya-Prats, *L'Esprit force*, pp. 77–78 (ET: pp. 76–77); Conzelmann, *Theology of St. Luke*, p. 28; Schweizer, "The New Testament," p. 405; Chevallier, *Souffle de Dieu*, p. 125; the latter sees in ἐν τῷ πνεύματι / *in the Spirit* a power "enveloping" Jesus. On the other hand, other scholars believe that it is the instrumental sense that must be privileged. Fitzmyer, *The Gospel according to Luke*, p. 514, believes that the passive form of the verb commands this interpretation, adding that "whether *en* be understood of agency or influence, Luke is certainly suggesting the subjection of Jesus to the Spirit." Also opting for the instrumental meaning: Grundmann, *Das Evangelium nach Lukas*, p. 114; Ernst, *Das Evangelium nach Lukas*, pp. 157–58; Marshall, *Luke*, p. 169.

As Bauer explains: "A strictly systematic treatment is impossible."[175] The study of the grammar and the style of Luke's Gospel led by Antoniadis,[176] shows the author's very strong tendency to use ἐν to express the state or the manner[177] rather than the instrumental character.[178] But as to the precise case of Luke 4:1, Antoniadis does not situate it either in one or the other of these two categories. She considers it, nevertheless, as a substitute for ὑπό, but adds (strangely!) that it "implies additionally a mystical idea that it is difficult to clarify."[179] As for N. Turner, he gives as a principle, first to always ask if the first meaning of ἐν, or if the predominant meaning "in"/"into" (in: space, time, or metaphor) is applicable. Then, only if this meaning is inapplicable, consider the context and the parallels in the biblical and secular Greek.[180] But Hutton is undoubtedly right in saying that "the justification of a given translation is often found in the immediate context."[181]

It is not certain, however, that Hutton's principle is a big help in the text that preoccupies us, Luke 4:1b, for Luke's tendency is always to use ἐν when he wants to speak of characters under the influence of the Spirit. Thus, we find:

- [John] will go before him [God] ἐν πνεύματι [*in spirit*] and power of Elijah. (It is a matter, here, of course, of the spirit of Elijah and not of the Holy Spirit). (Luke 1:17)

- [Simeon] came into the temple ἐν τῷ πνεύματι [*in the Spirit*]. (2:27)

- He will baptize you ἐν πνεύματι ἁγίῳ [*in Holy Spirit*] (3:16b; note, here, that the Matthean version uses ἐν as well).

- Then Jesus ἐν τῇ δυνάμει τοῦ πνεύματος [*in the power of the Spirit*] returned to Galilee. (4:14)

---

[175] *A Greek-English Lexicon*, p. 257.
[176] *L'évangile de Luc. Esquisse de grammaire et de sytle*, pp. 209–14.
[177] In this case, Luke 4:14; 8:43; 11:21; 16:22; 21:25; 22:44; 23:12; 23:40.
[178] In this case, Luke 14:31, 34; 16:15; 24:19.
[179] *L'évangile*, p. 211.
[180] "The Preposition *en* in the New Testament," p. 113. He writes: "The fact that there is flexibility does not mean that there is no general rule at all, or that *in* is not the commonest meaning of the preposition."
[181] "Considerations for the Translation of Greek *en*," p. 170.

Considering this Lukan practice, one can suppose that Luke himself inserted the ἐν into the text.

As to knowing whether this change has a bearing on the understanding of the text is difficult to say. It is very possible that ἐν τῷ πνεύματι / *in the Spirit* introduces here a dative of manner and that is in the same coherence as the editorial addition of the first part of the verse: "And Jesus, full of the Holy Spirit, returned from the Jordan." The ἐν τῷ πνεύματι / *in the Spirit* would reinforce the affirmation at the beginning of the verse.[182] Luke could have wanted to say that Jesus was led "in the Spirit" instead of "by the Spirit," thus better preserving his autonomy.[183] However, this remains hypothetical, and one has to admit that the meaning of the episode would hardly be altered if one translated ἐν as "by" instead of as "in." What matters, for Luke, is to say that Jesus goes to the desert under the leading, or the influence, of the Spirit.[184]

On the other hand, some see in the choice of the verb ἄγω another indicator supporting the option in favor of the dative of manner. While Matthew uses ἀνάγειν, whose literal meaning is "to lead" from a lower place to a higher place (as in Luke 4:5), Luke opts for ἄγειν. The literal meaning of ἄγειν is also "to lead," " to bring," but it can also mean "to guide" in the figurative sense.[185] Luke retains, for sure, the passive form of the verb—ἤγετο (indicative imperfect passive); however, being conjugated in the imperfect, it conveys the idea of continuity, contrary to the aorist ἀνήχθη of Matthew, which designates a punctual action. One could then say: "He was being guided in the Holy Spirit into the desert." "'In the Spirit,' that is to say, in conformity to what God wanted and for what God had enabled him," writes Gilliéron.[186] Thus, the "passive verb [would mark] God's action and 'in the Spirit' the manner of this action," as states George.[187]

But finally, what is important for Luke at the beginning of the account of the temptation is to show the origin of the force which dwells in

---

[182] See Hanna, *A Grammatical Aid to the Greek New Testament*; the latter also believes that ἐν τῷ πνεύματι / *in the Spirit* is an "anaphoric" reference to the preceding line.

[183] Feuillet, "Le récit lucanien de la tentation," p. 617, believes that Luke in fact wants Jesus to conserve the initiative of his action.

[184] In this regard, Dupont, "Les tentations," p. 11, writes: "It is a matter of an influence exercising itself from within, by an intimate inspiration, not in the way one is led by a guide."

[185] This is the meaning that Bauer recognizes in ἤγετο of Luke 4:1, *A Greek-English Lexicon*, p. 14.

[186] *Le Saint-Esprit*, p. 52.

[187] "L'Esprit Saint dans l'œuvre de Luc," p. 517.

Jesus at the moment he confronts Satan. The preponderant place accorded the Spirit is, in this regard, very significant. Jesus, presented as the Son who must play the role of eschatological prophet, has to demonstrate his aptitude for fulfilling this function. Besides, it is as the Son that he is questioned by Satan:

- "If you are the Son of God, command this stone to become a loaf of bread." (Luke 4:3)
- "If you are the Son of God, throw yourself down from here." (v. 9)

The victory over Satan will become the guarantee of the witness to God that this Son-Prophet will deliver to the world; it is the letter of guarantee for Jesus. But it is only in having the Spirit intervene that Luke will be able to furnish this guarantee.

The Lukan sequence of the episodes marking Jesus's public beginnings is, therefore, very logical:

1. The baptism account presents Jesus as the Son
2. The genealogy defines this filiation
3. The temptation guarantees Jesus's aptitude to fulfill his mission

What remains now is for Jesus to begin his ministry; it is again under the sign of the Spirit that he will do it.

4. The Spirit and the Inauguration of Jesus's Ministry—Luke 4:14a, 18

The episode of Jesus's return into Galilee for the inauguration of his ministry closes the sequence related to Jesus's entrance into public life. Jesus was gifted of the Spirit at his baptism; indwelled by this Spirit, he conquered Satan in the desert; he returned to Galilee to begin his mission, always under the influence of the Spirit.

Once again, examining the synoptic presentation of the texts will contribute to bringing out the preponderance of the role of the Spirit in the Lukan version.

Matt 4:12	Mark 1:14a	Luke 4:14a
Ἀκούσας δὲ ὅτι Ἰωάννης παρεδόθη ἀνεχώρησεν εἰς τὴν Γαλιλαίαν. /	Μετὰ τὸ παραδοθῆναι τὸν Ἰωάννην ἦλθεν ὁ Ἰησοῦς εἰς τὴν Γαλιλαίαν . . . /	Καὶ ὑπέστρεψεν ὁ Ἰησοῦς ἐν τῇ δυνάμει τοῦ πνεύματος εἰς τὴν Γαλιλαίαν . . . /
Now when Jesus heard that John had been arrested, he withdrew to Galilee.	Now after John was arrested, Jesus came to Galilee . . .	Then Jesus, filled with the power of the Spirit, returned to Galilee . . .

It is clear, according to the witnesses of Matthew and Mark, that the underlying source of this text of the triple tradition[188] evokes John's arrest, something that Luke cannot show since in 3:20, even before Jesus's baptism, he already made reference to this arrest. Therefore, consequently he modifies his source, but also, he integrates the proper elements to serve his purposes. In fact, the vocabulary of 14a is entirely Lukan: ὑπέστρεψεν, δυνάμει, πνεύματος / *returned, power, Spirit*.

An attentive look at this verse shows that the editorial activity, of which it was the object, inscribes itself into the logic and the coherence of that of 4:1a. Thus, in 4:1a, Luke had first of all clarified that Jesus was "full of the Spirit" following his baptism. Then, he had chosen the formulation ἤγετο ἐν τῷ πνεύματι / *was led in the Spirit* to speak of the force acting in him at the moment of his departure into the desert. In 4:14a,

---

[188] Schürmann, *Das Lukasevangelium: Kommentar zu Kap. 1:1–9:50*, pp. 221–24, defended the thesis according to which verses 14–15 of Luke 4 would be inspired by a source particular to Matthew and Luke (Q), which would contain some variants in respect to the Markan source. Schürmann deems that a tradition that he calls "Bericht vom Anfang" ["Account from the beginning"] had developed very early, parallel to the passion accounts, for, he submits, the importance of the ἀρχή / *beginning* of the mission had to be brought out in the same way as the passion. Schürmann's position seems difficult to support. On the one hand, the similarity of the texts of Matthew and Mark shows the dependence of Matthew relative to Mark, or to a source common to the two of them; on the other hand, the vocabulary of Luke 4:14a is essentially Lukan. Delobel, in his article, "La rédaction de Luc IV: 14–16a and the 'Bericht vom Anfang,'" pp. 203–23, severely criticized Schürmann's thesis. Delobel supports, on correct grounds, that the Lukan version comes from the editorial work of the author. Other scholars will say, on the other hand, that Luke 4:14–16 depends on a particular source: Grundmann, *Das Evangelium nach Lukas*, p. 118; Manson, *The Gospel of Luke*, pp. 39–40.

again, he adds to his source to clarify that it is once again in the same power that Jesus returns to Galilee: ἐν τῇ δυνάμει τοῦ πνεύματος / *in the power of the Spirit*.

The addition of πλήρης πνεύματος ἁγίου / *full of the Holy Spirit* in 4:1 made the connection between the episode of the temptation and that of the baptism, indicating by the fact the origin of the dynamism that would strengthen Jesus in the desert—Jesus was going to undergo the trial in the power conferred by the spiritual anointing of the baptism. In 4:14a, ἐν τῇ δυνάμει τοῦ πνεύματος / *in the power of the Spirit* likely connects the beginning in Galilee to the account of the temptation, but especially to that of the baptism,[189] signifying again that it is always in the same power that Jesus is going to, henceforth, fulfill his ministry. This is what Luke confirms explicitly in v. 18 when he places on Jesus's lips the words of Isa 61:1: "The Spirit of the Lord God is upon me because the Lord has anointed me."

The anointing of the Spirit at the baptism enabled Jesus to undergo the trial; this same consecration will enable him from then on to fulfill his mission.[190] The remainder of the gospel tells the unfolding of this mission. However, writes Guillet: "The scene of Nazareth gives its meaning to the entire story: it signifies that Jesus's every action is the work of the Spirit."[191]

CONCLUSION

With this chapter, the originality of Luke's pneumatic-christological language has emerged—language guided and controlled by the proclamation of Acts 2:33:

---

[189] See Guillet, "Le Saint-Esprit dans les évangiles synoptiques," col. 179.

[190] Ibid., col. 180. Fitzmyer's translation, *The Gospel according to Luke*, p. 523, "armed with the power of the Spirit," renders well the underlying idea of ἐν τῇ δυνάμει τοῦ πνεύματος of Luke 4:14a. In the same vein, Thompson, *The Gospel according to Luke*, p. 90, writes: "Jesus, who has received the Holy Spirit for his mission, and in that Spirit's power has been tested and found true to God, now in the same power begins his public ministry."

[191] Guillet, "Saint Esprit: Luc-Actes," col. 180. To this, add Fitzmyer's commentary, *The Gospel according to Luke*, p. 523, "In Lukan theology, the *dynamis* that Jesus possesses is not limited to the miraculous power (for healing or exorcising, as chiefly in Mark); it is closely associated with the Spirit under whose guidance he teaches and interprets Scripture." See also Grundmann, *Das Evangelium nach Lukas*, p. 118.

> Being therefore exalted at the right hand of God, and having received from the Father the promise of the Holy Spirit, he has poured out this that you both see and hear.

For it is the awareness as evidenced by this proclamation—that is, that the exalted Christ reigns over the universe—that gives birth to the questioning, from back to front, about Jesus's historic mission, to which the third Gospel wants to bring a response.

This questioning roots itself, in fact, in the community experience of the powerful and effective action of the Resurrected One. If Jesus becomes the Messiah in the resurrection, by the Spirit he receives from the Father (Acts 2:31–33), one must then understand that his entire earthly career was preparatory to this ultimate elevation. And the witness rendered to God by Jesus during his ministry was perfect. Moreover, at what moment does this testimony begin? At the baptism. Jesus is thus invested, at this very moment, with the power to witness. In reality, Luke used the baptismal tradition that he knew, and he confers on it a prophetic impact. The reference, in Luke 4:18, to the quotation of Isa 61:1 confirms it: "The Spirit of the Lord is upon me, because he has anointed me to bring good news to the poor."

The Spirit-anointing of the baptism assures the validity of Jesus's testimony. But then again the dignity of the one to carry this testimony must be shown. The episode of the temptations answers this need. Jesus, under the influence of the Spirit, conquers Satan in the desert (Luke 4:1ff.) and establishes the proof of his moral perfection. He shows that he is this perfect son that Adam did not know how to be. The excellence of his filiation, therefore, explains God's favor which makes Jesus the eschatological prophet.

But, finally, how was Jesus able to enter the world marked by sin without being in any manner tainted by it? Luke again meets this difficulty by placing his conception under the aegis of the Spirit. Jesus's perfection which makes him the Son, that is to say, the human being par excellence during his earthly life, will merit for him, in the resurrection, the position of Son of God, that is, Christ and Lord of the universe (Acts 2:36).

However, once again, Luke makes the experience of the lordship of the Christ, expressed in Acts 2:33, the believer's starting point in reading about the historical passage of Jesus in the world. It is the proclamation that he decides to make in Acts 2:33 which commands the editorial work that he makes on the received evangelical traditions. It is to avoid being in contradiction with Acts 2:33 that he must bring the editorial changes that we observe at the heart of the third Gospel.

Therefore, from this Lukan point of view, Jesus is, during his earthly life, the bearer of the Spirit. In the resurrection, he becomes Lord of the Spirit and he spreads him through the Christian community (Acts 2:33b; see Acts 2:2–4a). This community becomes, in turn, the bearer of the Spirit and can, from this fact, perpetuate the prophetic work inaugurated by Jesus.

The objective of the next chapter is to understand the new situation of the church coming from the Pentecostal outpouring and to see how this situation can be clarified from Acts 2:33.

Chapter 6

Acts 2:33b—Shedding Light on the Church

"He has poured out this that you both see and hear."

The assertion contained in Acts 2:33b unveils, at the end of a long theoretical demonstration, i.e., Peter's speech in Acts 2:17–36, the cause of the expressions witnessed by the crowd in Jerusalem for the festivities of the Jewish Pentecost. But, it is also the anticipated explanation of the events recorded in the entire book of Acts, events which will direct the birth of the church community and from which its development will spring forth.

The first part of Acts 2:33—"Being therefore exalted at the right hand of God, and having received from the Father the promise of the Holy Spirit"—proved to be the finishing point of Jesus's mission (in literary terms, the Gospel of Luke); the second part—"He has poured out this [the Holy Spirit] that you both see and hear"—will prove to be, on the other hand, the starting point of the disciples' mission (in literary terms, the Acts of the Apostles). The Spirit, received from the Father by the Christ and poured out on the community at Pentecost, becomes, therefore, the unifying principle between the two eras.

Just as the baptism was the inaugural event of Jesus's ministry, Pentecost will be the inaugural event of the disciples' ministry. It will make them a community of prophets in the same way that baptism had made Jesus a prophet. In and by the Spirit of Pentecost, the Christian community will perpetuate Jesus's missionary work and will bring his gospel to the extremities of the earth.

Considering the capital importance of the event of Pentecost for the overall understanding of the Acts of the Apostles, it seems fundamental (1) to evaluate its conceptual impact and (2) to establish its factual value. In this perspective, the present chapter will have the double objective of researching the meaning of the Pentecost account and appreciating the impact of the event[1] on church life.

1. THE MEANING OF THE PENTECOST ACCOUNT— ACTS 2:1–4

The research of the meaning of the Pentecost account of Acts 2:1–4 will take place through the following stages: (1) the analysis of the vocabulary to help clarify Luke's literary activity in this account; (2) the evaluation of the principal explanations proposed for this account and the presentation of an interpretation that finds support in the coherence of the double work Luke-Acts.

Vocabulary Analysis: Acts 2:1–4

2:1 Καὶ ἐν τῷ συμπληροῦσθαι τὴν ἡμέραν τῆς πεντηκοστῆς ἦσαν πάντες ὁμοῦ ἐπὶ τὸ αὐτό. /
When the day of Pentecost had come, they were all together in one place.

2:2 καὶ ἐγένετο ἄφνω ἐκ τοῦ οὐρανοῦ ἦχος ὥσπερ φερομένης πνοῆς βιαίας καὶ ἐπλήρωσεν ὅλον τὸν οἶκον οὗ ἦσαν καθήμενοι /
And suddenly from heaven there came a sound like the rush of a violent wind, and it filled the entire house where they were sitting.

2:3 καὶ ὤφθησαν αὐτοῖς διαμεριζόμεναι γλῶσσαι ὡσεὶ πυρὸς καὶ ἐκάθισεν ἐφ' ἕνα ἕκαστον αὐτῶν, /
Divided tongues, as of fire, appeared among them, and a tongue rested on each of them.

---

[1] I use the term *event* without, however, questioning its historical foundation. I have chosen instead a literary approach of the account. What is important, consequently, is to evaluate the place and role of this account in the entire narrative of Acts.

2:4 καὶ ἐπλήσθησαν πάντες πνεύματος ἁγίου καὶ ἤρξαντο λαλεῖν ἑτέραις γλώσσαις καθὼς τὸ πνεῦμα ἐδίδου ἀποφθέγγεσθαι αὐτοῖς.[2] /
All of them were filled with the Holy Spirit and began to speak in other languages, as the Spirit gave them ability.

2:1

ἐν τῷ / *when the*: with an infinitive (συμπληροῦσθαι, inf. pres. pass.) is almost uniquely used by Luke:[3] 32 times in Luke and seven times in Acts. It is usually used with the present infinitive, more particularly in a temporal sense (of duration).[4]

συμπληροῦσθαι / *had come* (inf. pres. pass.): Luke is the only New Testament author to use this verb. He does so three times (Luke 8:23; 9:51; Acts 2:1) and in each case, he uses it in the passive form.

πεντηκοστή / *Pentecost* is also only used three times in the New Testament. One of the occurrences belongs to Paul (1 Cor 16:8); the two others to Luke (Acts 2:1; 20:16).

2:2

ἄφνω / *suddenly* appears three times in Acts (2:2; 16:26; 28:6) and nowhere else in the New Testament. The literary context of 16:26 bears certain analogies with 2:2: Paul and Silas are in prayer, singing God's praises in the midst of other prisoners (v. 25); suddenly a violent earthquake occurs (ἄφνω δὲ σεισμός / *suddenly an earthquake*). The term is therefore linked, as in 2:2, to a cosmic phenomenon announcing a heavenly intervention.

ἦχος / *sound*: three of the four occurrences of this term belong to Luke (Luke 4:37; 21:25; Acts 2:2)—the other one is found in Heb 12:19.

---

[2] This text has no textual criticism problem that could have a major impact on its comprehension.

[3] According to Blass and Debrunner, *A Greek Grammar*, #404; see also Antoniadis, *L'evangile de Luc*, pp. 148, 213.

[4] Luke 1:8, 21; 2:6, 27, 43; 5:1, 12; 8:5, 40, 42; 9:18, 29, 33, 36, 51; 10:35, 58; 11:1, 27; 12:15; 17:11, 14; 18:35; 24:4, 15; Acts 2:1; 3:16; 4:30; 8:6; 9:3; 19:1.

πνοῆς / *wind*: the only two New Testament uses of the term πνοή belong to the book of Acts (2:2; 17:25).

βιαίας / *violent* is a hapax.

2:3

διαμεριζόμεναι / *separated* appears 11 times in the New Testament, of which six are in Luke (11:17, 18; 12:52, 53; 22:17; 23:34) and two are in Acts (2:3, 45) (elsewhere: Matt 27:35; Mark 15:24; John 19:24).

2:4

ἐπλήσθησαν . . . πνεύματος ἁγίου / *were filled with . . . Holy Spirit*: this formulation is undeniably Lukan. As shown in the preceding chapter, it was the typical formula used by Luke to speak of the spiritual infilling of certain characters associated with the announcement of salvation in Jesus; in Luke: John (1:15), Elizabeth (1:41), Zechariah (1:67), and Simeon (1:25–27); in Acts: the disciples (2:4); Peter (4:8); the community (4:31); Paul (9:17; 13:9).

λαλεῖν ἑτέραις γλώσσαις / *to speak in other languages*: in an analogous context, at the moment of the Gentile Pentecost in 10:46, λαλούντων γλώσσαις / *speaking in tongues* is found. Also, in 19:6 when the Spirit came on the Ephesians following the imposition of hands by Paul, the baptized ἐλάλουν γλώσσαις / *they spoke in tongues*. Note in 2:4 the presence of the indefinite adjective ἑτέραις / *other*, but this case will be discussed later in the chapter.

This linguistic study demonstrates in a convincing manner that the composition of Acts 2:1–4 is from Luke's hand.[5] The study of the conceptual and theological sketches of the account, moreover, will confirm this first observation. Many will maintain, nevertheless, that the account relies on pre-Lukan material.[6] But, then again, the exact vote between tradition

---

[5] Adler arrives at this conclusion, *Das erste christliche Pfingstfest. Sinn und Bedeutung des Pfingstberichtes Apg 2:1–13*, pp. 32–35. And this conclusion still finds a lot of support: Lohse, "πεντηκοστή," *TDNT* 6:51. Haenchen, *The Acts of the Apostles*, pp. 173ff.; Bauernfeind, *Kommentar und Studien zur Apostelgeschichte*, p. 36; Schneider, *Die Apostelgeschichte: Teil 1, 1:1—8:40*, p. 239; Mussner, *Apostelgeschichte*, pp. 22–23.

[6] Even if the account is obviously of Luke's hand, he could have been inspired from a tradition, be it an oral tradition. Many believe that there is in fact, at the basis of the account, a tradition founded on an experience of glossolalia that Luke would have

and redaction would prove very difficult[7] and not very significant for this study. The redaction criticism will show, however, that the account is understood very well in the coherence of Luke's double work.

Understanding The Event

Proposed Explanations
Numerous scholars throughout the twentieth century interpreted the Lukan Pentecost in the light of the events of Sinai and the giving of the Law (Exod 19:20).[8] Interesting factors encouraged the exploration of such an idea:

---

reworked. Among them, Marshall, "The Significance of Pentecost," p. 364; Davies, "Pentecost and Glossolalia," pp. 228–31; Trocmé, Le "livre des Actes" et histoire, p. 201; Lohse, "πεντηκοστή," TDNT 6:51 and "Die Bedeutung des Pfingstberichtes im Rahmen des lukanischen Gerschichtswerk," pp. 422ff.; according to Lohse, we would find here only an oral tradition of speaking in tongues—γλῶσσα—(of a collective ecstatic expression) that Luke would have transformed into the miracle of languages—διάλεκτος (v. 6). Of the same opinion, Samain, "Le récit de la Pentecôte, Ac 2, 1–13," p. 255; Sleeper, "Pentecost and Resurrection," p. 391; Grundmann, "Der Pfingstbericht der Apostelgeschichte in seinem theologischen Sinn," p. 585; Charlier, L'évangile de l'enfance de l'Eglise, pp. 130–31; Pesch, Die Apostelgeschichte, Apg 1–12, pp. 99ff. For others, the original background of the source consisted precisely in the miracle of languages: Schweizer, TDNT 6:411, note 516; Conzelmann, Acts of the Apostles, p. 15. For Roloff, Die Apostelgeschichte, p. 39, it is also a tradition of the miracle of languages that Luke would use, but this tradition would come from Antioch and would mark the missionary beginnings outside of Palestine of which Antioch is the first center. As for Haenchen, pp. 173–74, he considers that Luke could not really count on the help of sources: "there was no ancient or uniform tradition." Luke would have simply been inspired from the Old Testament model of the creation where God breathes into the man the breath of life. In the same way, the Spirit now creates the new man. Finally, Williams, A Commentary on the Acts of the Apostles, p. 62, believes that the basis of the Pentecost account would be an oral or written source (perhaps Aramean) that would have contained the account of the missionary vocation of the Twelve.

[7] On this subject, see Dibelius, Die Werdende Kirche, p. 30; Lohse, "Die Bedeutung des Pfingstberichtes," p. 426.

[8] Kretschmar, "Himmelfahrt und Pfingsten," pp. 209–53, proved to be a pioneer in this way. Many researchers followed in his footsteps: Bovon, Luc le théologien, pp. 115–16; Cabie, La Pentecôte, pp. 89–96; Charlier, L'Évangile de l'enfance de l'Église, pp. 119ff.; Delcor, "Pentecôte (La fête de la)," col. 875–76; Dunn, Baptism, pp. 48–49; Dupont, Nouvelles études sur les Actes des Apôtres, p. 208; Fitzmyer, "The Ascension of Christ and Pentecost," pp. 433ff.; Gourgues, "Lecture christologique du Psaume CX et fête de la Pentecôte," pp. 13–14; Haya-Prats, L'Esprit force de l'Eglise, p. 188; Knox, The Acts of the Apostles, p. 86; Kremer, "Was geschah Pfingsten? Zur Historizität des Apg 2:1–13 berichteten Pfingstereignisses," pp. 201–3; L'Eplattenier, Les Actes des Apôtres, p. 28; Le Deaut, "Pentecôte et tradition juive," pp. 142–44;

the presence of the same cosmic phenomena in the two theophanies: noise, wind, fire (Acts 2:2–3; Exod 19:16–19);[9] reading the Christian Pentecost as the fulfillment of the promise of the gift of the Spirit (see Joel 2:28–32; Ezek 36:26–27) and the fulfillment, from this fact, of the hope of a new covenant between God and humanity (see Jer 31:31–34); coincidence of the dates.[10] But such an interpretation was only possible in consideration of the new meaning accorded to the Jewish feast itself.[11] In fact, Pentecost is not, originally, the Covenant Feast, but the Harvest Feast (Exod 23:16). This joyous celebration which comes seven weeks after Passover—from which the title Feast of Weeks is derived (Deut 16:9–10)—is supposed to be a time of thanksgiving for the fruits of the earth (Deut 16:9–11). Leviticus is very explicit as to the date of this feast and as to the offerings which are related to it.

If one only held to the official Jewish writing, one would have to admit that in the era of the New Testament, one does not yet know of any other meaning of the feast. It would be necessary to wait until the 2nd century after Jesus to find an explicit parallel between the moment of the giving of the Law and the date of Pentecost in the Rabbinic writings. In about AD 150, Rabbi Jose ben Halafta writes in the Seder Olam (v):

> The Israelites sacrificed the Passover lamb in Egypt the 14th of Nisan and it was a Thursday . . . the third month, the sixth day of the month,

---

O'Reilly, *Word and Sign in the Acts of the Apostles*, p. 22; Pesch, *Die Apostelgeschichte, Apg 1–12*, p. 99, note 1; Potin, *La fête juive de la Pentecôte*, pp. 299ff.; A. Richardson, *An Introduction to the Theology of the New Testament*, pp. 118–19; Samain, "Le récit de la Pentecôte," pp. 241–46ff.; Stravinskas, "The Role of the Spirit in Acts 1 and 2," pp. 263–69; Weiser, *Die Apostelgeschichte: Kapitel 1–12*, p. 78.

[9] See Dupont, *Nouvelles études sur les Actes des Apôtres*, pp. 194–95; Kretschmar, "Himmelfahrt und Pfingsten," pp. 243ff.

[10] For Haenchen, pp. 172–74, the coincidence of the dates is not, in itself, an indication of the support of a theological parallel of the events of the Lukan Pentecost and Sinai. In line with Bauernfeind, *Die Apostelgeschichte*, p. 55, Haenchen believes that the dating of Pentecost depends on Luke's former adoption of the forty days for the ascension. Haenchen writes: "Luke fixed on this date because he had adopted the tradition of the forty days (Bauernfeind). The advent of the Spirit was simply dated to coincide with the next feast. Originally the tradition of the forty days had nothing to do with Pentecost" (p. 174).

[11] On the evolution of the meaning of the Jewish Pentecost, see Hruby, "La fête de la pentecôte dans la tradition juive," pp. 46–64; Le Deaut, "Pentecôte et tradition juive," pp. 127–138; Cabie, *La Pentecôte*, pp. 15–31; Kremer, *Pfingsbericht und Pfingstgeschehen*, pp. 11–27; Lohse, *TDNT* 6:45–49; Potin, *La fête juive de la Pentecôte*, pp. 117–42.

the ten commandments were given to them and it was the Sabbath day.[12]

Passover being celebrated the 14th of the first month (Nisan), the sixth day of the third month is thus the day of Pentecost. In about AD 270, Rabbi Eleazar ben Pedat expressed it this way: "Pentecost is the day when the Torah was given."[13] Moreover, the book of the Jubilees, which dates more than likely from the 2nd century before Christ,[14] of which numerous fragments have been recovered in the Qumran caves, contains a clear association of the gift of the Law on the day of Pentecost:

> In the first year of the Exodus of the children of Israel from Egypt, in the third month on the sixteenth day of that month, the LORD spoke to Moses, saying, "Come up to me on the mountain, and I shall give you two stone tablets of the Law and the commandment, which I have written, so that you may teach them."[15] (Jub 1:1)

We read again in 6:17: ". . . it is ordained and written in the heavenly tablets that they should observe the feast of Shebuot in this month, once per year by year.[16]

It is thus evident that already during the times of Jesus—at least in the Qumran circle—the promulgation of the Law was commemorated during this feast. One can probably suppose that even if no orthodox Jewish writing offers testimony in this sense, this new meaning of the feast had to have been known. It is common, even normal, that a practice be adopted before its literary echoes are traced. What is certain, in any case, is that since the first centuries of Christianity, the Jewish Pentecost underwent a change in meaning and that it has since been linked to the Sinai events. There is nothing to be surprised about, explains Hruby; this feast followed an evolution analogous to that of the Passover: "It is a question of 'making historical' the ancient feast of pre-Israelite origin, in relation to the cycle

---

[12] Quoted by Le Deaut, "Pentecôte et tradition juive," p. 134.

[13] See Cabie, p. 21.

[14] On the dating of the book of the *Jubilees*, see Stone, ed., *Jewish Writing of the Second Temple Period*, pp. 100ff.; also Caquot and Philonenko, "Introduction générale," *La Bible. Ecrits intertestamentaires*, p. LXXIV.

[15] Wintermute, "Jubilees," p. 52.

[16] Ibid, p. 67.

of the seasons, and of their insertion into the history of Israel as the story of God's teaching applied to his people."[17]

From an agricultural feast, Passover had become the memorial of the Exodus; closely linked to the Feast of the Passover, the Feast of Pentecost will acquire a meaning equally linked to the event of the Exodus, or as the commemoration of the day of the giving of the Law.[18] The Lukan Pentecost as the feast of the giving of the Spirit also closes the Passover cycle. Must the meaning be based upon this new interpretation of the Jewish feast? Many scholars refuse to do so. The principal motivation of this refusal is, in a general manner, extremely simple: the themes of the New Covenant and the giving of the Law are not found in Luke's account.[19] Added to this motivation, for some, is the concern of protecting the historicity of the fact of Pentecost.[20]

---

[17] Hruby, p. 47; also Menoud, *Jésus-Christ et la foi*, p. 121, note 2.

[18] Lohse, *TDNT* 6:48, believes that the immediate occasion of the change of meaning would be the destruction of the temple, the ancient pilgrimages no longer possible to be held for the offering of the fruits of the land at the temple. Schillebeeckx, "Ascension and Pentecost," p. 343, believes equally that it is the fall of Jerusalem that brings about the change in the meaning. The latter will mention the late date of this shift in order to deny every influence of the Jewish feast on the Lukan Pentecost. This association of the new meaning of the feast to the fall of Jerusalem is, however, hypothetical; it is a very late date, considering the testimonies that are found at Qumran.

[19] Of this opinion see: Chevallier, *Souffle de Dieu*, p. 159; Haenchen, p. 172; Hull, *The Holy Spirit in the Acts of the Apostles*, pp. 78–79; Lohse, "Die Bedeutung des Pfingstberichtes," p. 429; Marshall, "The Significance of Pentecost," p. 364ff.; Menoud, p. 121; Jaubert, *La notion d'Alliance dans le judaïsme aux abords de l'ère chrétienne*, p. 449; Sleeper, p. 390; Trocmé, *Le "livre des Actes" et histoire*, p. 203; O'Toole, "Acts 2:30 and the Davidic Covenant of Pentecost," pp. 246–50; de Vaux, *Les Institutions de l'Ancien Testament II*, p. 397.

[20] This is Marshall's case, "The Significance of Pentecost," pp. 364–65, who writes: "It is impossible to account for the story without some original event in Jerusalem to spark it off. . . . Moreover, it must have happened at Pentecost, for there is no reason why Luke should arbitrarily have chosen this date." In the same vein, Menoud, pp. 120ff., believes that a historic event is the source of the account. He insists on the fact that Pentecost is, with the Passover, the only Jewish feast to be Christianized and that it could not have been if it had not first been known to the ancient church. Finally, he deems that "the account is historical in this sense that it is very likely on the day of Pentecost that the apostles received the spiritual force and the courage to preach for the first time" (p. 122). These scholars also support the historicity of the initial event: Mann, "Pentecost in Acts," p. 127; Dunn, "Feast of Pentecost," pp. 784–85; finally, Kremer, *Pfingstbericht und Pfingstgeschehen*, pp. 261ff., believes as well that a historic event is at the origin of the account, but that the concrete form known from it (wind, tongues, fire) comes from a Lukan Midrashic development.

But it is on the basis of Luke's redaction, first and above all, that we must try to enlighten his Pentecost account.

An Interpretation in Lukan Coherence
The interpretation of the Christian Pentecost in the line of the fulfillment of the Sinai Covenant proved to be an attractive idea to explore for many scholars, as noted. And even if the follow-up to the study will show that this lead does not furnish the key to the reading of the Lukan Pentecostal account (Acts 2:1–4), nevertheless, the theme of the new Covenant—fundamental in Christianity—underlies the Christo-pneumatological contents of the entirety of Acts 1–2.[21]

It is, however, not certain that the theme of the Covenant is the principal idea to explore, for the double Lukan work furnishes its own keys of interpretation. In this case, it is in the line of the fulfillment of the words of the Baptist on the baptism (Luke 3:16) that the account of Pentecost is best understood.[22]

The Logion on the Baptism in John's Ministry
There are two versions of the logion on Spirit-baptism, that of Mark and that of Q:

---

[21] See Chevallier, *Souffle de Dieu*, pp. 175, 186–87. The latter brings out this midrashic commentary of Exod 19:16ff., taken from Philo, *Decal.* 46–47: "From the middle of the fire which poured down from heaven a voice was heard to their astonishment, for the flame became a word articulated in the language familiar to the hearers and what was said was so clear that they seemed rather to see it than hear it." Also this midrash Rabba on Deut 5 which, relating the giving of the Law at Sinai, clarifies that the voice of the Lord "came in seventy languages, so that each nation could hear the Law in his own language." The clarity of these texts commands comparisons at least on the level of their forms: that of Acts 2:1–13 and that of the Midrash on Exod 19 and Deut 5. It is even probable that Luke was inspired from the verbal contents of these Midrashes, desiring to give them a new scope. And that, in the same manner, he can use a known category, that of the taking away—more particularly, that of Elijah (2 Kgs 2:9–10)—to construct Jesus's ascension accounts (see chapter 4), for the meaning that Luke confers to Jesus's ascension has nothing to do with what was found in these different cases of being taken away in the Old Testament, Jewish or Hellenistic.

[22] See Marshall, "The Significance of Pentecost," pp. 366–67; also Schneider, *Die Apostelgeschichte: Teil 1, 1:1–8:40*, p. 247: "Die Verwendung der genannten Motive des Sturmes und des Feuers steht bei Lukas in Beziehung zu der Ansage des Täufers . . . Die Erfüllung dieser Ankündigung im Pfingstgeschehen kennzeichnen Apg 2:2f die Stichworte ἦχος ὥσπερ φερομένης πνοῆς und γλῶσσαι ὡσεὶ πυρός." ["The use of the mentioned motifs of the storm and fire stands in Luke's writing is interrelated to the announcement of John the Baptist. . . . The key words ἦχος ὥσπερ φερομένης πνοῆς [*a sound as being borne of wind*] and γλῶσσαι ὡσεὶ πυρός [*tongues as of fire*] denote the fulfillment of this announcement in the event of Pentecost in Acts 2:2f."]

Mark: "I have baptized you with water; but he will baptize you with the Holy Spirit." (1:8)

Q: John answered all of them by saying, "I baptize you with water; but one who is more powerful than I is coming; I am not worthy to untie the thong of his sandal. He will baptize you with the Holy Spirit and fire." (Matt 3:11 ‖ Luke 3:16)

Luke chose the Q version. It is in considering the entire context of John's preaching that one will be able to bring out the motives that directed this choice and, at the same time, shed light on the meaning of the key words of the retained version—πνεύματι ἁγίῳ / *Holy Spirit* and πυρί / *fire*.

After John's presentation as prophet-precursor according to the triple tradition (Mark 1:1–6/Matt 3:1–6/Luke 3:1–6), Luke continues with a tradition of Q on the imminence of the judgment:

John said to the crowds that came out to be baptized by him, "You brood of vipers! Who warned you to flee from the wrath to come? Bear fruits worthy of repentance. Do not begin to say to yourselves, 'We have Abraham as our ancestor'; for I tell you, God is able from these stones to raise up children to Abraham. Even now the ax is lying at the root of the trees; every tree therefore that does not bear good fruit is cut down and thrown into the fire." (Luke 3:7–9; cp. Matt 3:7–10)

The Baptist's menacing tone with regard to those who believe that their title alone of "sons of Abraham" merited their escaping the anger reflects a general climate of social injustice. It should be well noted that in Luke, it is the crowds—and not only the Pharisees and the Sadducees as in Matt 3:7[23]—who are admonished by John. The call to conversion is thus

---

[23] It is difficult to know who, Luke or Matthew, changed the source. Fitzmyer, *The Gospel according to Luke I–IX*, p. 467, tends to favor the Matthean version as being more faithful to the source, because of the figure used to qualify the listeners—"brood of vipers"—(see Matt 12:34; 23:33). Also in favor of Matthew's version, Ellis, *The Gospel of Luke*, p. 88, believes that "the crowds is a deliberate generalization for 'Pharisees and Sadducees' (Matt 3:7), since, for Luke, the reproach is addressed to the entire nation." Of the same opinion: Sabourin, *L'Evangile de Luc*, p. 115; Conzelmann, *Theology of St. Luke*, p. 20. On the other hand, one can suppose that Luke introduced "the crowds" to harmonize with the pericope 10–14 on the fruits of conversion which is precisely addressed to the crowds (v. 10: "The crowds asked [John] . .

addressed to all the people. And Luke marks even more so the urgency by specifying "even now [δὲ καί]²⁴ the ax is ready" (Matt 3:10 only has "now [δέ]"). As to enumerating the fruits of conversion (vv. 10–14: sharing clothing and food; fair imposition of taxes; proper military behavior), it aims most certainly to give details of the effects that conversion must produce, but it also contributes to point out the social defects for which the nation is denounced as a sinner: egotism, dishonesty, violence, etc.

Luke thus describes with great detail the moral deterioration undermining all of the people. Against such a background scene, the menace appears still more justified. It is against this same background scene that the logion on the baptism of the one who comes must be read: "He will baptize you with the Holy Spirit and fire."

Before making any comparison there might be between this preaching of the Baptist and the Pentecost event—or moving toward a symbolic reinterpretation—it is critical first to research the meaning of the prediction in the context of John's ministry or of the tradition before Q. To this end, the element of "fire," a key theme in this entire section, could well be the most pertinent point of departure.

The term reappears three times on the Baptist's lips. Given its places of insertion in Q, its occurrences are notably close together. According to the Matthean version, it appears immediately before the logion on the baptism, in the middle of the logion, and immediately after:

1. Even now the ax is lying at the root of the trees; every tree therefore that does not bear good fruit is cut down and thrown into the fire. (Matt 3:10)

."). Note once more these two supporters of the Matthean version among the scholars who were interested in the study of Q: Schulz, *Q: Die Spruchquelle der Evangelisten*, p. 366; Hoffmann, *Studien zur Theologie der Logienquelle*, p. 17. On the other hand, Marshall, *The Gospel of Luke*, pp. 138–39 and Leany, *A Commentary on the Gospel according to St. Luke*, pp. 106–7, think that Luke reproduced the original version, considering that Matthew has the tendency to make the Pharisees and Sadducees objects of denunciation (see Matt 12:34; 16:1; 23:33). Also of this opinion: Schweizer, *The Good News according to Matthew*, p. 48; Schürmann, *Das Lukasevangelium*, p. 163; Ernst, *Das Evangelium nach Lukas*, p. 141; Tinsley, *The Gospel according to Luke*, pp. 44–45. This option for the Lukan version also finds support with scholars who studied Q: Polag, "The Text of Q," in Havener and Polag, *Q, the Sayings of Jesus*, p. 123; Schenk, *Synopse zur Redenquelle der Evangelium*, p. 17.

[24] The combination of the two particles δὲ καί is a Lukan technique to mark insistence: 2:4; 3:12; 5:10, 36; 9:61; 10:32; 11:18; 12:54, 57; 15:12; 16:1, 22; 18:9; 19:19; 22:12.

2. I baptize you with water for repentance, but one who is more powerful than I is coming after me; . . . He will baptize you with the Holy Spirit and fire. (3:11)

3. His winnowing fork is in his hand, and he will clear his threshing floor and will gather his wheat into the granary; but the chaff he will burn with unquenchable fire. (3:12)

In Luke, the term is repeated in 3:9, 16, 17, but the first and the second mentions are separated by two Lukan traditions which do not belong to Q: the one on the fruits of conversion (vv. 10–14)[25] and the one on the questioning about John's identity (v. 15). We can, therefore, conclude that, in the source, the three mentions of the term are deliberately spaced and intentionally desired in the same literary pattern. The Baptist—or the author of the source—would have held with much insistence on the meaning that he wanted to give the term, a meaning which, we would not know to doubt, is the same for the three occurrences.[26] What is this meaning? Verses 9 and 17 are without equivocation:

- every tree therefore that does not bear good fruit is cut down and thrown into the fire (v. 9);

- but the chaff he will burn with unquenchable fire (v. 17)

It is a question then of a destructive fire, an eschatological instrument of the judgment;[27] an interpretation which finds support in well-known Old Testament texts, such as Mal 3:2, 19, 21.

Thus it is of the image of the straw burning in the fire on the day of the judgment evoked in Isa 5:24 and 47:14. In the same way, Amos

---

[25] Most scholars believe that this pericope (Luke 3:10–14) evidently comes from a Lukan source: Ernst, p. 143; Grundmann, *Das Evangelium nach*, p. 103; Manson, "John the Baptist," pp. 411–12. Others, on the contrary, believe that it is from Q, but would have been omitted by Matthew: Marshall, *The Gospel of Luke*, p. 142; Plummer, *The Gospel according to S. Luke*, p. 90; Schürmann, p. 169. One would conceive with difficulty that Matthew had left off this section that would have furnished for him a supplementary light on the way to bring about conversion. On the contrary, this pericope, in Luke, breaks the rhythm of the initial plan. It is from all evidence a Lukan insertion.

[26] Thus believes van Imschoot, "Baptême d'eau et baptême d'Esprit Saint," pp. 657–58.

[27] It is thus that van Imschoot understood it, ibid., p. 658: ". . . the fire which will consume the sterile trees or the straw is, according to a common figure with the prophets and in the apocalypses, the image of the divine judgment punishing the guilty.

predicts against Israel's enemies and against Israel (1:4) destruction by fire. Isaiah (66:15) takes up the same threat against Jerusalem, accentuating it with the announcement of the perpetuity of the fire (66:24).[28] However, it must be noted that, for the prophets of Israel, this fire of the judgment is not only destruction; it is at the same time a place of purification (Mal 3:3; Isa 4:4).

This double function of the fire corresponds to the role that the texts of Q give to it: the fire destroys what is bad (the tree which does not produce good fruit and the chaff); in so doing, it purifies the mass of these bad elements. "In the same way, the judgment, which condemns the guilty, amputates the community of its spoiled members and thus purifies it," writes van Imschoot.[29] This interpretation, which inscribes itself perfectly into the context of John's preaching, seems to be essential.[30] And it is in recognizing this known semantic value of the fire that the first member of the formula must now be considered: ἐν πνεύματι ἁγίῳ / *in Holy Spirit*.

Two readings of this expression are possible: (1) ἐν πνεύματι ἁγίῳ / *in Holy Spirit* in the Old Testament sense of the Holy Spirit;[31] (2) ἐν πνεύματι / *in spirit* (without ἁγίῳ / *holy*) in the sense of wind.

---

[28] The idea of punishment by fire on the day of the Lord is also present in the intertestamental literature (the following translated quotations are taken from *La Bible. Ecrits intertestamentaires*, eds. Caquot et al.): 4[2] Esd 13:10: "... he sent forth from his mouth something like a stream of fire, and from his lips a flaming breath, and from his tongue he shot forth a storm of sparks." *Pss. Sol.* 15:4–5: "The man who worships will never be burned by evil: neither the flame of the fire, nor the anger aimed at injustices will reach him, when they will come from the Lord on the sinner, to annihilate all their assurance."

[29] "Baptême d'eau et baptême d'Esprit Saint," p. 658.

[30] Different interpretations were suggested by scholars as to the role of the fire in the formula ἐν πνεύματι καὶ πυρί / *in Spirit and fire*. Some, in line with van Imschoot, will say that the righteous and the evil have to undergo the test of the fire, the first for their purification, the second for their destruction: Haya-Prats, pp. 131–32 (ET: pp. 145–46); Chevallier, *Souffle de Dieu*, pp. 90–100; Marshall, *The Gospel of Luke*, p. 146; Barrett, *The Holy Spirit and the Gospel Tradition*, p. 126; Dunn, *Baptism*, p. 12. Others only recognize a destructive role in the fire; it will serve to annihilate the impenitent: Sabourin, p. 117; Lang, "πῦρ," *TDNT* 6:943; Brown, *New Testament Essays*, p. 136; Schürmann, p. 174. Others still consider the fire as a symbol or synonym of the Spirit in which the Messiah will baptize: Plummer, p. 95; Lagrange, *Evangile selon Saint Matthieu*, p. 53; Bonnard, *L'Evangile selon Saint Matthieu*, p. 38.

[31] The Spirit is said to be "holy" only three times in the Old Testament: Isa 63:10–11; Ps 51:13.

Speaking of baptism or judgment, *in the Spirit* could actually have Old Testament roots. For example, Chevallier remarks that in the Old Testament there is a very well-known prophetic text which evokes "a judgment by the breath of the Messiah;"[32] it is a question of Isa 11:4: "But with righteousness he shall judge the poor . . . with the breath of his lips he shall kill the wicked."

It would not be a question, in this case, of the breath which is wind, but specifically the divine breath. The repetition of this text of Isaiah in the Qumran shows "that this prophecy was alive at the time of John the Baptist," Chevallier[33] adds: "'. . . by the breath of your lips you will put to death the ungodly'[34] (1QS 65:24)."

Dunn, who is of the opinion that the announcement of the baptism in the Holy Spirit and fire goes back to John,[35] accords great importance to the Qumran influence, for, he says, "John almost certainly had some contact with the sect, even if only peripheral—sufficient at least for him to adopt (and adapt) some of their ideas."[36]

Reading the first member of the logion on the baptism in Q in this perspective is possible, but the entire context of John's preaching strongly compels opting for the other component, that is, the wind.[37] Verse 17, more particularly, dictates this reading since the winnowing supposes the

---

[32] Chevallier, *Souffle de Dieu*, p. 100.

[33] Ibid.

[34] More explicitly again in 1QS 4:20ff. this idea of purification by the Holy Spirit is expressed: "He will purge for himself the building [of the body] of each man . . . in order to purify him by the Spirit of Holiness of all ungodly acts; and he will make spring up over him the Spirit of truth as lustral water."

[35] Also of this opinion, van Imschoot, "Baptême d'eau et baptême d'Esprit Saint," pp. 659ff.; Sullivan, "'Baptism in the Holy Spirit': A Catholic Interpretation of the Pentecostal Experience," p. 55; Schürmann, pp. 175ff.; Giblet, "Baptism in the Spirit in the Acts of the Apostles," p. 164. According to Giblet, Joel's prophecy being well known, the Baptist envisions, consequently, the baptism to come in the Holy Spirit and fire. Giblet explains that, on the one hand, the preaching of the Baptist was not "all negative" and that, on the other hand, the mention of the "stronger" evokes the disposition of the active power of God and the Spirit.

[36] Dunn, *Baptism*, pp. 9–10. In this line, van Imschoot also believes that the Holy Spirit and fire are actual words of the Baptist and that the Holy Spirit is certainly of the Old Testament: ". . . in the Old Testament, from which the Baptist's speech is clearly inspired, the spirit is holy, because he is divine, because he is the one from the holy God" ("Baptême d'eau et baptême d'Esprit Saint," p. 661); also Sullivan, pp. 55–56.

[37] Opting for this interpretation: Barrett, *The Holy Spirit*, p. 126; Best, "Spirit-Baptism," p. 240; Schmitt, "Le milieu baptiste de Jean le Précurseur," p. 394; Schweizer, "Le Nouveau Testament," p. 133.

intervention of the wind.[38] The connection of verses 16 and 17 becomes then clearly logical:[39]

> He will baptize you with the wind and fire; his winnowing fork is in his hand to clear his threshing floor and to gather the wheat into his granary; but the chaff, he will burn with unquenchable fire.

Moreover, this image of the winnowing is very biblical. Thus, Isa 41:16: "You will winnow and the wind will carry them away." (See also Jer 15:7; 51:2).

Therefore, John baptized in water to signify conversion; "the one who is greater," he will baptize (judge) in wind and fire, that is to say, will bring the final judgment.[40] "Baptism" would be thus understood in a figurative sense to mean the judgment. Consequently, water, wind and fire are three instruments of the same process that continues: (1) a preparatory period for judgment which consists of a conversion signified by water; (2) the actual judgment which takes place in wind and fire. This last operation will allow for the separation of the righteous (the wheat) from the evil (the chaff), the latter being destined for the fire.

It is very possible that Isa 4:4 was the Baptist's source of inspiration.[41] Found in this passage are, actually, the three elements that would have contributed to the formulation of the logion: water, breath and fire.

It seems then that an analysis, which rigorously recognizes the context of the era and the apocalyptic climate which underlies John's preaching, leads one to believe that the latter was waiting for an imminent judgment of "the one who is greater." This is where the urgency comes from to convert and to publicly profess one's conversion by the baptism that he proposes. It is the Day of Yahweh that is expected and this day is judgment day. It is, therefore, normal that John mentions it by using the traditional images that depict it.[42] It is true that the gift of the Spirit is part of

---

[38] See Best, "Spirit-Baptism," p. 240.

[39] See Barrett, *The Holy Spirit*, p. 126.

[40] See Tugwell, "Reflections on the Pentecostal Doctrine of 'Baptism in the Holy Spirit,'" p. 269. He considers that, indeed, the baptism of the Messiah announced in Matthew and Luke is a baptism of judgment: "This is a threat, not a promise."

[41] Also suggested by Beasley-Murray, *Baptism in the New Testament*, p. 37, and Chevallier, *Souffle de Dieu*, p. 100.

[42] Based on syntax, one could object to this reading of the logion of Luke 3:16, which is that the first part concerns the baptism of conversion while the second concerns the baptism of judgment. The two uses of the pronoun "you"—which designate in the two

the eschatological expectations (Joel 2:28; Ezek 36:26–27; Isa 32:15; 44:3), but it will be the reward of the righteous. Nevertheless, John's tone is much more threatening than rewarding.[43] And as Coppens expresses it,

> ... this Messiah, eschatological judge, he [John] represents him. ... as a winnower cleaning the threshing floor, gathering the wheat for the loft, but burning the straw, the chaff. In the context of such an image, one does not expect the mention of the Holy Spirit but that of the breath of the wind, which the winnower needs to sort out the grain and the chaff, symbol of separating the righteous and the evil.[44]

Therefore, the intervention of wind and fire, in all the symbolism that they bring, constitutes, in John's perspective, the successive stage in its proper intervention.[45] However, it is evident that the Q tradition, as Luke received it, in light of Christian experience, already conferred to the wind a new scope.[46] The step was easy to take; it was not even necessary to change the terminology; it was sufficient to enrich it.

---

cases, the same crowd—do not have, one would say, the same scope: the first "you" is restrictive, while the other is global. The first concerns those who accept the baptism of water ("I baptize you in water") and who, consequently, find salvation in it; while the second concerns everyone ("the one who will baptize in wind and fire"); all will receive this baptism: some for their salvation, others for their loss. One can, on the contrary, completely respecting the Baptist's thinking, detect nuances in the formulation. John obviously addresses everyone, in the two cases; except that, in the first case, one can understand the implied, "I offer to you, to everyone, a baptism in water, and in fact, I baptize those who accept it." The narrative context permits such a reading without any problem.

[43] Schweizer, "Le Nouveau Testament," p. 132, deems equally that through these images of the judgment, one would not know immediately to consider the wind as a gift of grace. Once again, the image of the ax in Jer 46:22 designates punishment (see Ps 74:5–6). Also in *1 En.* 91:8–9, the punishment of the sinner is thus described: "In that time, the expression will be cut from its roots ... the idols of the pagans will all be delivered ... to an ardent fire."

[44] Coppens, "L'imposition des mains in the Actes des Apôtres," p. 429; also, Benoit and Boismard, *Synopse des quatre évangiles en français*, p. 78A.

[45] See Schweizer, "Le Nouveau Testament," p. 133.

[46] Chevallier, *Souffle de Dieu*, p. 106, believes, for his part, that even at Q's level, the tradition rendered "he will baptize you in wind and fire" and that it is only in the course of history that the epithet "holy" was introduced into the Q tradition. Moreover, certain scholars will support that the Q source only contained *fire* as a figure of judgment, and Christians, in light of Mark, added the πνεύματι ἁγίῳ / *Holy Spirit*. Among these scholars: Schulz, *Q: Die Spruchquelle der Evangelisten*, pp. 368–69; S. Brown, "'Water-Baptism' and 'Spirit-Baptism' in Luke-Acts," pp. 136; Bultmann, *Histoire de la tradition synoptique*, pp. 301–2. The reasoning of these latter scholars

Besides, even if the Q version reflects a Christian reinterpretation, in regard to the Spirit, it conserves to the fire its instrumental value as an element of judgment.[47] For it is very plausible that, at the beginnings of Christianity, when the Parousia was still feverishly expected, one believed obviously that the impenitent would undergo the fire of the judgment. The threat would, however, be abandoned afterwards, as the Markan version testifies.[48] Although this perception of the judgment is no longer so adequate at the time of the composition of the third Gospel, it was in the Baptist's preaching that Luke (as well as Matthew) wanted to recognize it. He would have, thus, deliberately kept this significance[49] in faithfulness to the spirit of John. Thus, the choice of the logion of Q brought the double advantage of communicating the meaning transmitted by John's words (threat of the judgment by fire), without sacrificing the new tone that it would confer on the Passover event. In fact, Luke could not evoke the context of John's preaching and take away from it the threatening announcement that characterizes it. On the other hand, for the comprehension of John's prophecy in the heart of the community, he had to recognize the new Christian experience of the Spirit. As for the Spirit, he was also perceived as a "means" by which believers accede to their new status.[50] The verse could thus be understood as such in terms of Q: by the

---

leans in great part on the Syriac Sinaiticus reading which inverses the order of Spirit *holy/fire* into *fire/Spirit holy*. The inversed order would lead to believe in an interpolation. John the Baptist would have had in mind Mal 3:2, where "the refiner's fire" and "the fuller's soap" are brought in. Thus, the water/fire of Malachi would be at the origin of the parallel between the baptisms established by John. Afterwards, having experienced the gift of the Spirit, one would have replaced the two elements in the order they are found. And finally, *fire* would have been completely omitted (Markan version). However, as Beasley-Murray explains, this position is upheld with difficulty: "It is doubtful that the Old Syriac has preserved the right reading of Matt 3:11 against the otherwise universal manuscript tradition of Matthew and of Luke" (p. 36).

[47] Thus believe Schürmann, Lang, Sabourin, et al. (see note 30).

[48] The study of Kloppenborg, "The Announcement of Judgment in Q," in his work *The Formation of Q*, pp. 102–70, shows the importance of the threat of the apocalyptic judgment in the Q document, as well as the importance of the theme of the Parousia (see Luke 12:35–59; 17:23–37).

[49] Contrary to what Quesnel believes, *Baptisés dans l'Esprit*, p. 38, writing, "In using analogous terms to those Matthew used, Luke announces . . . a different reality. The fire designates for him not the fire of judgment, but the tongues of Acts 2:3." Also Chevallier, *Souffle de Dieu*, p. 103, who believes that already in Luke 3:16, Luke understood the fire as "a figure of the divine breath." Luke 3:16 would be then seen as a hendiadys.

[50] Beasley-Murray, p. 37, taking up again the complete formula of v. 16—John's baptism and baptism of "the one who is greater"—insists on this point: "This ought not to

baptism of water, the repentant person indicates his conversion; by the Spirit, he becomes a Christian; by the fire, the impenitent one perishes.

There is no doubt that Luke captured very well the meaning and the value of the logion of Q. However, he gives it, in Acts, a brand new significance. A significance, which, up to a certain point, proves to be contradictory with that contained in the words attributed to John. Why did he opt for the logion of Q? Why did he not rather choose the one of the Markan tradition which, rightly, eliminated the threatening element and seems to correspond exactly to his vision of Christian baptism as such expressed in Acts 1:5 and 11:16?

Luke made a deliberate and coherent choice, which is justified very well as the study of the texts of Pentecost will demonstrate. However, first of all, the meaning of the baptism of the Spirit and of fire in the Lukan perspective should be determined.

Baptism in Luke's Perspective

On two occasions Luke makes explicit reference to the words of John the Baptist (Matt 3:11 ‖ Luke 3:16) on baptism; it is a question of Acts 1:5 and 11:16. But the wording of these two references are so very similar to the Markan version than to the Q version when it is a matter of speaking of the announced baptism. On two occasions—in Luke 24:49 and in Acts 1:8—he evokes this same baptism but in veiled terms. Moreover, these four allusions to the baptism to come are essentially oriented toward Pentecost as the place of their fulfillment. In order to grasp the meaning that Luke wanted to give the Pentecost event, it is necessary to see in which terms and in which contexts he mentioned this event.

i. Luke 24:49

Luke ends his gospel on a promise, as observed in chapter 4: "And see, I am sending upon you what my Father promised; so stay here in the city until you have been clothed with power from on high." This word from the Resurrected One is situated in the framework of the appearing to the Twelve during a meal (Luke 24:41–42), the evening of Easter. Immediately after, Jesus is taken away to heaven. The terminology of this verse is to be noted. The wording, in itself, does not explicitly refer to any specific event. However, the terminology which composes it cannot be mistaken.

---

be interpreted as meaning, 'He will baptize by the *agency* of water, by the *gift* of the spirit and by the *agency* of fire'; the ἐν [*in*] as well as the simple dative signify in each case the instrument or means employed in the baptism. The Spirit is an agency comparable with water and fire."

The promise (ἐπαγγελία / *promise*) is the key term. Of what promise is it? The descriptive noun "power" (δύναμις) of this promise already reveals its tone. We saw, in effect, that Luke describes the Spirit as a power and, very often, uses the two terms—Spirit and power—in a synonymous way (see chapter 4). Acts 1:8 leaves, moreover, no doubt: ". . . you will receive power, when the Holy Spirit comes upon you."

But this is not the only indication. In Acts 2:38b–39a, Luke clearly identifies the promise as the Holy Spirit: ". . . you will receive the gift of the Holy Spirit. For the promise is for you . . . ." Finally, the key verse, alone, already furnishes all the light:

> Being therefore exalted at the right hand of God, and having received from the Father the promise of the Holy Spirit, he poured out this that you both see and hear. (Acts 2:33)

Acts 2:33 shows in effect how Luke 24:49 became reality:

Luke 24:49
And see, I am sending . . . what my Father promised . . . from on high.

Acts 2:33
Being therefore exalted at the right hand of God, and having received from the Father the promise of the Holy Spirit . . .

The Ascension account (Luke 24:50–53) which comes immediately after the promise (v. 49) confirms the statement on the exaltation of Acts 2:33a.

Luke 24:49
. . . upon you . . . , so stay here in the city until you have been clothed with power from on high.

Acts 2:33
. . . he has poured out this that you both see and hear.

Moreover, at what moment was the promise, announced in Luke 24:49 and presented as a fait accompli in Acts 2:33, realized? At Pentecost: "All of them were filled with the Holy Spirit" (Acts 2:4). Of course, Luke 24:49 does not yet state anything explicitly about the baptism. But the link that connects it to Acts 1:4–5 is unequivocal.

ii. Acts 1:4–5

"While staying with the disciples, Jesus ordered them not to leave Jerusalem, but to wait there for the promise of the Father. 'This,' he said, 'is what you have heard from me; for John baptized with water, but you will be baptized with the Holy Spirit not many days from now.'"

These two passages (Acts 1:4–5 and Luke 24:49) correspond:

Luke 24:49	Acts 1:4–5
Meal (Luke 24:41–42)	While eating with them
Stay here in the city	he ordered them not to leave Jerusalem
I am sending upon you what my Father promised	but wait there for the promise of the Father
Until you have been clothed with power from on high	you will be baptized in the Holy Spirit

The promise of the Father, proclaimed by Jesus, is the act of being baptized in the Spirit. And, obviously, it is Acts 2:33 that explains how Acts 1:4–5 would be rendered possible: Jesus, exalted, received from the Father the promise of the Spirit; consequently, he was in the position to pour him out.[51] When? At Pentecost (Acts 2:2–4).

---

[51] The relation between Acts 2:33 and Luke 24:49/Acts 1:4 is explained very well by Kremer ("Die Voraussagen des Pfingstgeschehens in Apg 1:4–5 und 8," p. 151): "Dieser Vers (Apg 2:33) erklärt in der Form eines Berichtes die Aussage von Lk 24:49 und Apg 1:4; denn er beschreibt einen doppelten Vorgang: 1. Der erhöhte Herr 'nimmt' die Gabe der Verheissung vom Vater in Empfang; sie stammt also nach Lukas vom Vater, ist nicht bloss vom Vater verheissen. 2. Der zur Rechten Gottes Thronende 'giesst' sie über die Jünger aus (vgl. 2:17–18; Joel 3:1–2); nicht unmittelbar der Vater gibt den Geist, sondern der Sohn." ["This verse (Acts 2:33) explains in the form of a report the statement of Lk 24:49 and Acts 1:4; since it describes a double event: 1. The exalted Lord 'receives' the gift of the promise from the Father, which, according to Luke, comes from the Father and is not merely promised by the father, and 2. The One enthroned at the right hand of God 'pours' it out upon the disciples (cf. 2:17–18; Joel 3:1–2 [2:28–29])—it is not the Father who directly gives the Spirit, but rather the Son."]

What is new in Acts 1:4–5 in relation to Luke 24:49 is the explanation of the contents of the promise: the Baptism in the Spirit. But there is more: Acts 1:4–5 refers expressly to the words of the Baptist in Luke 3:16—as already noted. First of all, in Acts 1:4–5, it is the Resurrected One who accounts for the words of the precursor and, in fact, a promise of the Father (also in Luke 24:49). He recalls the nature of the baptism conferred by John (baptism in water); then, speaks of the baptism that soon the disciples will receive (the baptism in the Holy Spirit) without pointing out who the giver would be.[52] What is surprising is that Luke only speaks of the Holy Spirit and not of fire. He seems to support (as pointed out before) the Markan version, which he could have done as well in the introduction of the logion in his Gospel. What is surprising again is that he repeats, in the account of Pentecost, the notion of fire and unites it once again to that of the Spirit. What logic would thus support what appears, initially, as an inconsistency?

iii. The Lukan Choice of the Q Logion

As mentioned earlier, Luke certainly captured well the meaning and the value of the logion in Q on the baptism *in the Holy Spirit and in fire*, where the fire would be considered as a threatening purifying element, but that he preferred this version of Q to the Markan version,[53] while Acts 1:5 clearly demonstrates that Christian baptism, according to Mark, is understood. This is not only shown in Acts 1:5, but also in Acts 11:16, where Peter mentions the outpouring of the Spirit at Cornelius's home in a similar formula to Acts 1:5: "'John baptized with water, but you will be baptized with the Holy Spirit'" (Acts 11:16).

These two examples do not leave any doubt: in the Lukan perspective, Christian baptism is baptism in the Holy Spirit, and the threat no longer has any reason for being.[54] If, therefore, Luke (3:16) kept the Q

---

[52] The passages of Acts 1:5 and 1:8 leave it to be understood that it is the Father who will impart the Spirit; on the contrary in Luke 24:49, it is Jesus. But, in Acts 2:33, it is Jesus who makes of him a gift, having first received him from the Father. See Chevallier, *Souffle de Dieu*, p. 108.

[53] See Sullivan, p. 56.

[54] Dunn, *Baptism*, pp. 42–43, considers that the disciples' vicarious sufferings of the Christ on the cross constitute the baptism in fire. Only after the cross, says Dunn, Jesus became apt to fulfill the other aspect of the prophecy of the Baptist, which is to baptize in the Spirit. To this Marshall, "The Significance of Pentecost," p. 351, retorts, "This exegesis is improbable since the motif of the fire is clearly present in the actual

version, it is that in addition to better corresponding to the climate of John's preaching, it would prepare the new interpretation that he intended to give to fire in his Pentecost account. This new interpretation is, however, not a breach: there would also be a work of purification in Christian baptism. However, the purifying agent will henceforth be the Holy Spirit (see Ezek 36:26–27). There is a dimension which is very probably implied in the metaphoric identification of the Spirit to fire (see Isa 6:6–7).[55]

But this dimension is certainly neither the only nor even the most important in the perspective of Acts 2:2ff. On the contrary, the author envisions very clearly this identification by means of the word—to which, moreover, the whole of the book of Acts attests. Fire becomes, in this perspective, the symbol of prophetic ardor with which the Spirit empowers believers. This association of fire to prophecy is already known in Jer 20:9: "If I say, 'I will not mention him, or speak any more in his name,' then within me there is something like a burning fire shut up in my bones." And in 23:29: "Is not my word like fire, says the Lord?" The choice of the image of the tongues as the means of the fire becomes, therefore, most eloquent. These *tongues of fire*, symbol of the power of the Spirit, will allow for the word to be proclaimed in *all the tongues*.

The day of Pentecost thus becomes the point of departure of the great work of the church (as seen in the second part of this chapter). For, as Peter explains just after the event (Acts 2:16–18), what happens there on that day is what God had promised by the prophet Joel (2:28–29):

> Then afterward I will pour out my spirit on all flesh; your sons and your daughters shall prophesy, your old men shall dream dreams, and your young men shall see visions. Even on the male and female slaves, in those days, I will pour out my spirit.

In a visible and audible way (Acts 2:33), the disciples are clothed with a power from on high (Luke 24:49), the power of the Holy Spirit (Acts 1:8), the promise of the Father (Luke 24:49; Acts 1:4–5); they are baptized in the Holy Spirit, as John had first announced (Luke 3:16) and as the Resurrected One had himself confirmed (Acts 1:5). And all of this

---

story of Pentecost." Marshall explains thus the omission of the fire in Acts 1:5: "Rather the term 'fire' is omitted at this point because it is metaphorical, and the saying concentrates on the reality."

[55] In this perspective, Giblet, p. 164, considers as well the activity of the Spirit, in Christian baptism, as purifying: ". . . the purifying activity of the Spirit, which transforms those who have received the baptism of conversion."

occurred because "Jesus the Nazarene, a man attested to you by God with deeds of power, wonders, and signs that God did through him [Acts 2:22] . . . this man, handed over to you according to the definite plan and foreknowledge of God, you crucified and killed by the hands of those outside the law [v. 23] . . . [this man] God raised him up [v. 24, 32] . . . and made him both Lord and Messiah" (v. 36). In so doing, God exalted him at his right hand and gave him the Holy Spirit of the promise. Having thus received the Spirit from the Father, Jesus was then in the position to pour him out;[56] which can be seen and heard (Acts 2:33b).

Thus, it becomes very clear that, in writing Acts 2:1–4, Luke wants to affirm the fulfillment of the baptism announced by the Baptist (Luke 3:16). It is in this vein that one must look for the meaning of the Pentecost account: *Pentecost is the baptism in the Holy Spirit.*[57]

From the Baptism of John to Pentecost
Luke took care to establish the necessary bridges between the announcement of the baptism and its fulfillment. The previously examined texts (Luke 24:49; Acts 1:4–5; 1:8; 11:16) furnish the complementary and explanatory narrative elements that facilitate the establishing of this connection (Luke 3:16/Acts 2:2–4) and consequently present Pentecost as the fulfillment of the baptism in the Spirit.[58] Reading these texts (see figure, p. 203) allows one to see clearly that they serve as beacons for the reader, orienting progressively toward a summit—the outpouring of the Spirit. The unity of the vocabulary, the correspondence of the concepts, and the sequence of the ideas (see figure, p. 204) clearly attest to the role that is incumbent on these texts as linking-agents between the announcing text (Luke 3:16) and the announced text (Acts 2:2–4).

---

[56] Thus Conzelmann writes, *Theology of St. Luke*, p. 174: "If the Son can baptize with the Spirit (Luke iii,16) or, to be more exact, can pour out the Spirit (Luke xxiv, 49)—after his exaltation and not before—it is only because he has received the Spirit from the Father for this very purpose (Acts ii, 33)." In the same vein, Sleeper, p. 392, writes: "Thus, for Luke, the resurrection and ascension are indispensable prerequisites to the coming of the Holy Spirit, as Acts 2:33 demonstrates." Also Schillebeeckx, p. 339: "The departure of Christ . . . , as a necessary preliminary to the bestowal of the Spirit, is strongly emphasized by St. Luke himself in Acts 2:33."

[57] See Marshall, "The Significance of Pentecost," p. 351; S. Brown, p. 141; O'Reilly, p. 43; Kremer, *Pfingstbericht und Pfingstgeschehen*, p. 187.

[58] Kremer, in his article, "Die Voraussagen des Pfingstgeschehens in Apg 1:4–5 und 8," pp. 145ff., has clearly shown the role of these texts (Luke 24:49; Acts 1:4–5, 8; 11:16) in the Lukan presentation of Pentecost as the fulfillment of the baptism announced by the Baptist.

Finally, it is clear that the terminology of these passages has a lot to say about the perception that Luke has of the baptism of the Spirit.[59] This baptism is described as "gift" which is "sent" from "on high," "suddenly appears from heaven," "comes on," "rests on," is "poured out," "received," "clothes," "fills." This baptism is thus characterized by the communication of the Spirit as heavenly grace to the ones baptized.[60] The Spirit is the object of the promise of the Father.[61] This promise is attributed to the Father, because he is the ultimate giver as Act 2:33 proves: "And having received from the Father the promise of the Holy Spirit . . . ."[62] And the promise is to those who repent and are baptized in the name of Jesus Christ:

> Repent, and be baptized every one of you in the name of Jesus Christ so that your sins may be forgiven; and you will receive the gift of the Holy Spirit. For the promise is for you, for your children . . . . (Acts 2:38–39)

The wording of Peter's exhortation presents the pattern of the Christian baptismal experience: faith (conversion), baptism, gift of the Spirit. What is surprising, initially, is that Christian baptism does not abolish John the Baptist's ritual, as Luke 3:16 implies. More still, this ritual is required even when the Spirit had already been outpoured. Such is the case with Cornelius:

> "Can anyone withhold the water for baptizing these people who have received the Holy Spirit just as we have?" So he [Peter] ordered them to be baptized in the name of Jesus Christ. (Acts 10:47–48)

What is remarkable in this last episode is that the baptism cannot be in view of the pardon of sins as in Acts 2:38, since the conversion is

---

[59] On the study of the terminology of the passages of Luke-Acts on the baptism in the Spirit, see Sullivan, pp. 56ff.

[60] On the grounds of this terminology, Sullivan is of the opinion that the term "baptize" in the expression "baptize in the Holy Spirit," must be taken in the metaphorical sense and that it is equal to "receive the gift of the Spirit" (pp. 57 and 60).

[61] Concerning the theme of the promise in Luke's writings, see chapter 4.

[62] See Bruce, "The Holy Spirit in the Acts of the Apostles," p. 170. He recalls: "The promise was given not only in John the Baptist's words about the mightier one who would baptize with the Holy Spirit (echoed by the risen Christ in Acts 1:5) but earlier still in the oracle of Joel 2:28–32. In the narrative of Pentecost, it is Joel's oracle that is quoted by Peter in partial explanation of the phenomena."

already guaranteed by the gift of the Spirit. Furthermore, the observation of the different baptismal episodes of Acts reveals a constant: the baptism of water is always in the name of Jesus Christ. Thus it is with the Samaritans: "For as yet the Spirit had not come upon any of them; they had only been baptized in the name of the Lord Jesus" (Acts 8:16). Similarly with the Ephesians: "On hearing this, they were baptized in the name of the Lord Jesus" (Acts 19:5). Then the author adds: "When Paul had laid his hands on them, the Holy Spirit came upon them" (v. 6).

What comes out of all the baptismal scenes of Acts is the new sense conferred on water baptism. Although it had been expressly ministered in view of conversion by John, it now becomes the external meaning or public manifestation of the commitment to follow Jesus Christ. However, this reinterpretation is certainly not in discontinuity, for the conversion claimed by John was preparatory to the welcoming of Jesus. This is clearly what Luke explains in his statement that he borrows from Paul: "Paul said, 'John baptized with the baptism of repentance telling the people to believe in the one who was to come after him, that is, Jesus'"[63] (Acts 19:4).

This Jesus having come, the believer must now signify his faith by a concrete gesture. And this gesture is the baptism of water. It was a gesture so much more meaningful that it is done even by Jesus in the Jordan. "Would not this be Luke's unique way to link the baptismal practice of the Church to the person of Jesus?" questions Haulotte.[64] In all the cases, however, baptism is only authentically Christian when the Spirit is poured out (see Acts 8:16; 19:5–6). There is the essential link between Pentecost and Christian baptism. There is a Christian baptism because Jesus himself received the Spirit (Acts 2:33a) and poured him out (Acts 2:33b; 2:2, 4). We understand that this baptism is in the name of Jesus Christ, since Jesus Christ is from now on Lord and giver of the Spirit.

The vocabulary analysis, again, reveals an important characteristic of the Spirit: *power*. Luke's insistence on this trait of the Spirit is not without reason; the Spirit/power is, in effect, in the author's perspective, the explicative principle of the church's birth and expansion. It is this dimension,

---

[63] On this subject, S. Brown, p. 142, writes: "Furthermore, the water-baptism performed by John was only efficacious because of the same faith in Christ which is required of the Christian neophyte." This statement carries a flagrant anachronism. There is, in fact, a clear distinction between believing "in the one who must come" and believing in the Resurrected One, for even if, in the two cases, faith has the same person as its object, its contents is altogether different.

[64] Haulotte, "L'impact du baptême de Jean sur la vie de l'Eglise primitive," pp. 58–59.

that of the church, which will occupy the second part of this chapter. However, first, it is appropriate to draw some conclusions on the study of the first part.

First of all, concerning the choice of the logion of the Q version on baptism (Luke 3:16), I propose a double motivation to Luke's choice:

1. A desire to faithfully translate—or as faithfully as possible—the apocalyptic climate inspiring John the Baptist's preaching, a choice that did not ignore, however, a part of this logion—the part bearing on the Holy Spirit—already indicates an evolution in relation to the Johannine stratum.

2. The perspective of a reuse and a reinterpretation of the elements of *Holy Spirit* and *fire* in the Pentecost context.

This choice registers perfectly with Luke's habit of anchoring the New Covenant into the Old, or of establishing bridges between the two eras; the option for the Q logion permits, in this case, a transition between two eras where each one of them is found represented by one or the other of the elements:

1. The expected baptism, in fire;
2. The proven baptism, in the Holy Spirit.

The foregoing examination shows again the great literary and theological unity of the two Lukan works. In addition, it allows for the observation of the futility of looking at Pentecost from another light than that already offered by the Lukan theological framework. Pentecost is neither more nor less than the baptism in the Spirit announced at the beginning of the third Gospel—a baptism which allows the disciples to carry out the church's mission that is incumbent upon them.

LUKE 3:16 ANNOUNCEMENT

I baptize you with water; but one who is more powerful than I is coming; I am not worthy to untie the thong of his sandals. He will baptize you with the Holy Spirit and fire.

Luke 24:49
See, I am sending upon you what my Father promised; so stay here in the city until you have been clothed with power from on high.

Acts 1:8
You will receive power when the Holy Spirit has come upon you.

Acts 1:4–5
While staying with them, he ordered them not to leave Jerusalem, but to wait there for the promise of the Father. "This," he said, "is what you have heard from me; for John baptized with water, but you will be baptized with the Holy Spirit not many days from now."

Acts 11:16
And I remembered the word of the Lord, how he had said, "John baptized with water, but you will be baptized with the Holy Spirit."

ACTS 2:2–4 FULFILLMENT

Suddenly from heaven there came a sound like the rush of a violent wind, and it filled the entire house where they were sitting. Divided tongues, as of fire, appeared among them and a tongue rested on each of them. All of them were filled with the Holy Spirit and began to speak in other languages, as the Spirit gave them ability.

TERMINOLOGY

Luke 3:16	Luke 24:29	Acts 1:4–5	Acts 1:8	Acts 11:16	Acts 2:2–4	Acts 2:33
I (John)		John		John		
baptize with water		baptize with water		baptize with water		
He, more powerful						
baptize with the Holy Spirit		baptize with the Holy Spirit	Holy Spirit	baptize with the Holy Spirit	filled with the Holy Spirit	Holy Spirit
fire					tongues of fire	
	promise of the Father	promise of the Father				promise of the Father
	power		power			
	stay in the city	do not leave Jerusalem				
	send		receive			receive
	on you		come upon you		rested on each of them	pour out
	clothed					
	from on high				came from heaven	
		heard from me (Jesus)		word of the Lord	noise– tongues	see, hear

2. THE IMPACT OF THE PENTECOST EVENT ON CHURCH LIFE

The entire book of Acts shows the effects of the baptism event of Pentecost. The Christian community essentially becomes the Spirit community. Its works are those of the Spirit. Thus, the works of the Spirit will be observable on two levels: (1) on the level of community life and (2) on the level of missionary expansion. In the following pages, we see first how the Spirit animates the prophetic testimony of the believers; then we see how he directs the missionary activity to the ends of the earth.

The Spirit and the Prophetic Mission

O' Reilly rightly evaluates the impact of Pentecost upon the church when he writes: "The event of Pentecost occupies the same place in the life of the church as Jesus's baptism in the Jordan occupied in his life."[65] Pentecost will, indeed, be to the disciples what baptism was to Jesus: as baptism was the inaugurating event of Jesus's prophetic mission, thus Pentecost will be for the disciples.[66]

As shown in the preceding chapter, Luke, with great detail, placed Jesus's entry into ministry under the move of the Spirit:

- Jesus returns from the Jordan "filled with the Holy Spirit" (Luke 4:1a, Luke's redaction);

- He is led into the desert "in the Spirit" (4:1b);

- After the testing in the desert, he comes back to Galilee "in the power of the Spirit" (4:14, "in the power of the Spirit," is redactional);

---

[65] O'Reilly, p. 30. Sharing O'Reilly's point of view: Haya-Prats, p. 185 (ET: p. 222); Dunn, *Baptism in the Holy Spirit*, pp. 23ff.; Dumais, "Ministères, charismes et Esprit dans l'œuvre de Luc," *L'Actualisation du Nouveau Testament*, pp. 125ff.; Minear, *To Heal and to Reveal*, pp. 122ff.; Hill, *New Testament Prophecy*, p. 95; Samain, pp. 232–34, 246; Borremans, "L'Esprit Saint dans la catéchèse évangélique de Luc," p. 144; Pfitzner, "'Pneumatic' Apostleship?" p. 200; Chevallier, "Luc et l'Esprit Saint," p. 5.

[66] La Potterie, "L'Onction du Christ," p. 252, writes: "This coming of the Spirit to the Jordan had an eschatological impact: it was a prelude to the gift of Pentecost, the outpouring of the Spirit on the entire Church." See also Dunn, *Baptism*, p. 40.

- At the synagogue of Nazareth, he reads the text of Isaiah 61:1 (the insertion of Isaiah 61:1 is redaction) and he applies the contents of the text to himself: "The Spirit of the Lord is upon me, because he has anointed me to bring good news to the poor . . ." (Luke 4:18).

As previously demonstrated, the anointing is that of his baptism. Therefore, this anointing makes him a prophet, as other texts confirm, describing his words at the synagogue:

- "no prophet is accepted in the prophet's hometown" (Luke 4:24);

- Jesus clarifies his missionary options from Elijah's experience at Zarephath (vv. 25–26);

- but, especially, the contents of the prophecy of Isaiah 61:1, which contribute to defining Jesus's mission, are clearly of a prophetic tone: Jesus was anointed of the Spirit to *announce the word*. And this is what he will do all throughout the Gospel.

Jesus's baptism was, therefore, a baptism in the Holy Spirit, which enabled him to fulfill his prophetic mission.[67] This will also be the effect of Pentecost on the gathered disciples:[68]

- "tongues as of fire" rested on each of them (Acts 2:3);

- they are "all filled with the Holy Spirit" (v. 4a);

- and they began "to speak in other languages," i.e., to prophesy (see Excursus below) "as the Spirit gave them ability" (v. 4b);

- "all, Jews and proselytes, Cretans and Arabs, [heard them] announcing in [their] own languages God's deeds of power" (vv. 6ff.);

- when Peter begins speaking, he applies the prophecy of Joel to the community (vv. 16ff.).[69]

---

[67] This is what Luke will say again, with insistence, in Peter's speech at Cornelius's house: "You know the message he [God] sent to the people of Israel, *preaching peace by Jesus Christ*—he is Lord of all. That message spread throughout Judea, beginning in Galilee after the baptism that John announced: *how God anointed Jesus of Nazareth with the Holy Spirit and with power*; how he went about doing good and *healing all who were oppressed by the devil, for God was with him*" (Acts 10:36–38).

[68] Thus Coppens expresses, p. 431: "[The gift of the Spirit] will appear as a gift of power qualifying for apostleship."

Through the outpouring of the Spirit, the disciples, therefore, also become announcers of the word. They are made prophets, as verified in the details throughout the book of Acts and examined below. But first, a word on the meaning of "speaking in other languages."

---

[69] See Samain, p. 244, note 35, on the parallelism between the application of Isaiah 61:1–2 to Jesus and the application of Joel 2:28–32 to the community. See also Schmitt, "La prédication apostolique. Les formes, le contenu," p. 117; *Le Saint-Esprit*, p. 122. See finally "the parallelism between the beginning of Jesus's ministry and that of the apostles'" established by Sauvagnat, "Se repentir, être baptisé; recevoir l'Esprit. Actes 2, 37ss," p. 77.

* * * EXCURSUS: "SPEAKING IN OTHER TONGUES" * * *

Does "speaking in other tongues" (Acts 2:4) evoke a phenomenon of glossolalia or of xenoglossolalia?[70] In the present context, it seems clear that Luke has xenoglossolalia in mind for the following reasons:

- First of all, the text does not say that the disciples began to speak "in tongues," but "in other languages" (ἑτέραις γλώσσαις).

- Verse 6 (as well as verse 11) specifies that people from all the nations (see verse 5) heard them speaking in their own language. The question of the hearers in verse 8 is also very clear: "How is it that we hear, each of us, in our own native language?"

The indications, nevertheless, lead us to believe that the author would have used and refashioned a tradition of glossolalia. Otherwise, how would the scoffing of certain hearers be explained (Acts 2:13, vestiges of the glossolalia tradition) if the language were clear and coherent? Moreover, on two other occasions in Acts, in the contexts of the outpouring of the Spirit as well, it is a question of "speaking in tongues"—and not "in other languages." Luke writes about the Gentile "Pentecost" at Cornelius's house: ". . . the gift of the Holy Spirit had been poured out . . . for they heard them speaking in tongues . . ." (Acts 10:45b–46). In Ephesus, as well, after Paul had laid hands on them, the Spirit came on the Ephesians and "they spoke in tongues and prophesied" (19:6b).

These examples support the belief that the phenomenon of speaking in tongues as the effect or sign of the gift of the Spirit was the object of a known tradition in the primitive community. Luke then would have made use of it. But in Acts 2:4, he must lightly modify this tradition to harmoniously link the two constitutive parts of the account of Pentecost:[71] the one related to the gift of the Spirit (vv. 2–4) and the one related to the foreign hearers gathered in Jerusalem (vv. 5–13). From glossolalia at the origin, the tradition would have been modified into xenoglossolalia.[72] And, in the

---

[70] See on this subject the development of Chevallier, *Souffle de Dieu*, pp. 185–90, to whom I largely refer here.

[71] According to Kremer's study, *Pfingstbericht and Pfingstgeschehen*, pp. 87–267, the two parts of the text (vv. 1–4 and vv. 5–13) would come from two different traditions.

[72] This is the opinion of many scholars, for example, Pesch, *Die Apostelgeschichte, Apg 1–12*, pp. 99–101; Weiser, p. 81; Haenchen, p. 175; Chevallier, *Souffle de Dieu*,

present context, the miracle of tongues can no doubt be read as the antithesis of Babel.[73] But, more precisely, as Conzelmann proposes:

> The substratum would not then have offered a symbolic portrayal of the spread of the gospel worldwide, but an account of the gospel's spread as actually accomplished by a miraculous, and eschatological act of God.[74]

It appears clear, in fact, that it is the universal character of evangelization, *already* experienced, that Luke seeks to highlight: the word is *already* heard by all the peoples:[75] "Now there were devout Jews from every nation under heaven living in Jerusalem" (in Acts 2:5, also, there occurs an enumeration of nations, vv. 9–11, in all the languages: ". . . in our own languages we hear them speaking about God's deeds of power" [v. 11b]).

Apparent also is the relationship established between the symbol and the experience: the "tongues as of fire" (v. 3), apportioned on the disciples, charges them to spread the wonders of God in all the languages of the world.[76] The power of the Spirit (symbolized by the fire) confers on the recipients the gift of prophecy. The "tongues as of fire" enable them to "speak in tongues" or in "other languages," i.e., to prophesy. It is significant that at two other places where Luke evokes speaking in tongues after

---

p. 188. For others, the xenoglossolalia is original: Conzelmann, *Acts of the Apostles*, p. 15; Schweizer, *TDNT* 6:411, note 516.

[73] For this interpretation, see Bruce, "The Holy Spirit in the Acts of the Apostles," p. 171; Davies, pp. 228–31; Neil, *The Acts of the Apostles*, p. 72; A. Richardson, p. 119; Samain, pp. 250ff.; Sleeper, p. 290; de Surgy, "Langue," *Vocabulaire de Théologie Biblique*, col. 655; Trocmé, *Le "livre des Actes" et l'histoire*, p. 203; Wilson, *The Gentiles and the Gentile Mission in Luke-Acts*, p. 126. The church fathers had already made this antithetical comparison Pentecost/Babel: Ambrose, *Serm.* 36 (P. L. 17, 675–676); Augustine, *Enarrat. Ps.* LV, 10 (*NPNF* 8:213); *Serm.* 271 (P. L. 38, 1245–1246); Gregory Nazianzus, "On Pentecost," 41, XVI (*NPNF* 7:384; P. G. 36, 449); John Chrysostom, *Hom* 2 on Pentecost (P. G. 50, 467). (This information on the Fathers, for the most part, was taken from Samain, p. 252, note 45).

[74] Conzelmann, *Acts*, p. 15. See also Schneider, *Die Apostelgeschichte: Teil 1*, p. 250.

[75] Schneider, *Die Apostelgeschichte: Teil 1*, p. 250, subscribes to this interpretation: "Lukas ordnet die "Glossolalie" der missionarischen Verkündigung zu. Sie befähigt zu jenem weltweiten Zeugnis, das den Aposteln 1,8 zugesagt und aufgetragen ist." ["Luke associates 'glossolalia' with the missionary proclamation. It empowers the global witness that is promised and applied to the disciples (1:8)."] See also, Delcor, "Pentecôte," col. 858.

[76] See O'Reilly, p. 58; Kremer, *Pfingstbericht und Pfingstgeschehen*, p. 216; Cerfaux, p. 185; Potin, p. 309; Hill, *New Testament Prophecy*, p. 96.

a gift of the Spirit, he assimilates it to prophecy: "For they heard them speaking in tongues and extolling God" (Acts 10:46); ". . . in our own languages we hear them speaking about God's deeds of power" (Act 2:11b); "They spoke in tongues and prophesied" (19:6b).

In brief, what one can deduce from these examples is that Luke knew this tradition of "speaking in tongues" and he reuses it to mean the enablement to prophesy, which is the result of the gift of the Spirit.[77] And this is the case as much for the Gentile "Pentecost" (10:46)—as we have seen—as for the Jewish Pentecost.[78]

The validity of this interpretation is explicitly confirmed by the quotation of Joel 2:28–32 from the beginning of Peter's speech, which is precisely supposed to be a clarification of the meaning of Pentecost. The testimony of the believers filled with the Spirit is heard in all the languages of the world.

* * *

---

[77] This is also the interpretation of Conzelmann, *Acts*, p. 15, and Chevallier, *Souffle de Dieu*, p. 188.

[78] See Hill, *New Testament Prophecy*, p. 96.

A Community of Prophets Filled with the Spirit

As previously stated, Pentecost will be for the disciples what baptism was for Jesus. It makes of them a community of prophets in the same way that baptism made Jesus a prophet.[79] Luke will make evident the missionary continuity and the theological unity between Jesus's ministry and the disciples' ministry, in establishing the Spirit as the principle of continuity and unity.[80]

Why is the Spirit given? To bear witness to Jesus:[81]

> But you will receive power when the Holy Spirit has come upon you; and you will be my witnesses in Jerusalem, in all Judea and Samaria, and *to the ends of the earth*. (Acts 1:8)

The missionary program is thus traced—to witness of Jesus; the field of action determined—to the ends of the earth. The Pentecost account (Acts 2:1–13) constitutes a miniature presentation—or a prefiguring—of the accomplishment of the program:

Acts 2:3–4: The Holy Spirit is poured out

Acts 2:5, 11: "Every nation under heaven" (the ends of the earth) hear "them speaking [in their own languages] about God's deeds of power" (witness).

All the receivers of the Spirit effectively become prophets; this is what the head of the apostles affirms in explaining the event with the quotation from Joel: "this is what was spoken through the prophet Joel: 'it will be . . . that I will pour out my Spirit upon all flesh, and your sons and your daughters shall prophesy'" (2:16–17). The rest of the speech shows un-

---

[79] In this vein, Marsh, "Holy Spirit in Early Christian Teaching," p. 104, writes: "It is the story of the Gospel all over again: the Spirit-directed, prophetic ministry of Jesus continues in the Spirit-directed, prophetic ministry of the Church."

[80] Borremans, p. 105, corroborates this point of view: ". . . in dealing with his work, one cannot forget that the gospel is the first volume of a unique work for which the Holy Spirit constitutes the unity and the key for understanding." In this line, see also Lampe, "The Lukan Portrait of Christ," p. 174; Pfitzner, p. 222; Smalley, p. 68.

[81] Thus Gilliéron states, p. 123: "That the apostles and preachers of the Word are and remain the witnesses of Christ before all men, such is therefore the major role that Luke recognizes in the work of the Holy Spirit." In the same vein, see Coppens, p. 430.

questionably that it is the *Spirit of Jesus Christ* that is given to the disciples:[82]

- God had accredited Jesus to the people (v. 22);
- But he was crucified (v. 23);
- God, however, resurrected him (vv. 24; 32);
- And exalted him, *giving him the Spirit* of the promise that *Jesus, in turn, poured out* on the community (v. 33).

Thus the Spirit becomes the principle of unity between the disciples' ministry and Jesus's ministry: *Jesus perpetuates his work through the disciples by his Spirit that he poured out on them.*[83] The entire apostolic ministry will thus be possible because, first of all, Jesus himself received the Spirit and then he poured him out. This is what Luke shows afterwards in associating the Spirit with the disciples' preaching.

Again and again, in effect, Luke authenticates the witness in presenting the speaker as "filled with" or "full of" the Spirit.[84] Thus, Peter is πλησθεὶς πνεύματος ἁγίου / *filled with the Holy Spirit* (Acts 4:8) when he must justify himself before the Sanhedrin after having healed a crippled person in the temple (3:1–9). It is, therefore, while "filled with the Holy Spirit" that he explains to the Sanhedrin that "by the name of Jesus Christ of Nazareth, whom you crucified, whom God raised from the dead . . . that this man is standing before you in good health" (v. 10). This circumstance becomes then the pretext of another speech where Peter explains the mystery of salvation (vv. 9–12). But there is more to this scene: there is the fulfillment of the promise of the help of the Spirit in times of persecution:

> When they bring you before the synagogues, the rulers, and the authorities, do not worry about how you are to defend yourselves or what you are to say; for the Holy Spirit will teach you at that very hour what you ought to say." (Luke 12:11–12)

---

[82] Pfitzner, p. 234, writes: "Although the Spirit is only once called the Spirit of Jesus (16:7), such an identification is presupposed throughout Acts."

[83] Understandably, Franklin writes: "The link between the exalted Jesus and the Christian is the Spirit which, however, does not bring Jesus but empowers witness to him" ("The Ascension and the Eschatology of Luke-Acts," p. 197). See also Marsh, p. 104.

[84] Hill, *New Testament Prophecy*, p. 96, clarifies: "'being filled with the Spirit' would, in Jewish usage, be tantamount to saying 'becoming prophets.'"

The Spirit is thus the guarantor of the witness given to Jesus. It is because Peter is "filled with the Holy Spirit" that he can affront his persecutors and pronounce the right words about Jesus.

In the same way, Stephen, ἄνδρα πλήρης . . . πνεύματος ἁγίου / *a man full . . . of the Holy Spirit* (Acts 6:5), has to defend himself before the Sanhedrin. But the power of the Spirit which animates him closes the mouths of his adversaries: "they could not withstand the wisdom and the Spirit with which he spoke" (v. 10). The Jews did not know how to recognize God's salvation: that is Stephen's reproach. He characterizes their attitude of resistance against the Holy Spirit (7:51).[85] Stephen's words exasperate his hearers (7:54). But, nevertheless, they are correct since, having finished speaking, he is allowed, πλήρης πνεύματος ἁγίου / *full of the Holy Spirit*, to envision "God's glory and Jesus standing at the right hand of God" (7:55). Thus, Stephen's prophetic witness is guaranteed by the Spirit.

It is also under the move of the Spirit that Paul will initiate his preaching work. Ananias informs him, in fact, that the Lord sent him to Paul so that he may recover his sight and be "filled with the Holy Spirit" (9:17). Immediately afterwards, Paul begins his ministry of evangelism: "For several days he was with the disciples in Damascus, and immediately he began to proclaim Jesus in the synagogues saying, 'He is the Son of God'" (Acts 9:19b–20). Barnabas, who is sent to Antioch by the Jerusalem community, is equally described as πλήρης πνεύματος ἁγίου / *full of the Holy Spirit* (Acts 11:24). Moreover, under the influence of his teaching (v. 26) "a great many people were brought to the Lord" (v. 24).

Finally, all the members of the community gathered in prayer were "filled with the Holy Spirit and spoke the word of God with boldness" (4:31). Always, therefore, the announcing of the word is incited and authenticated by the Spirit. (This last example shows, however, that even if the believers were permanently inhabited by the Spirit since Pentecost, Luke likes to recall, on occasion, the source of the dynamism which inspires and strengthens them. Similarly in 13:9: "Thus . . . Paul, filled with the Holy Spirit, looked intently at him and said . . . ." What Luke probably seeks to say, as Borremans proposes, is that the Spirit is never the believer's possession, but that he must always be given to him again: "The Holy

---

[85] Here is a concrete example of the sin against the Spirit that is reported by the Markan tradition (Mark 3:29|Matt 12:31) and the Q tradition (Luke 12:10 ‖ Matt 12:32).

Spirit experienced in the Church is always received and . . . no one ever possesses him for oneself."[86])

Like Jesus, therefore, who, "full of the Spirit" at his baptism, comes to announce the Good News of salvation, the disciples "filled with the Spirit" at Pentecost, spread this Good News from Jerusalem to the extremities of the earth.[87]

A Community of Accredited Prophets

When at the synagogue (Luke 4:18ff.) Jesus attributes to himself the words of Isaiah 61:1, he recognizes that the spiritual anointing of his baptism makes him a prophet "to announce the Good News to the poor." But, linked to the announcement of this Good News, is a concrete action in favor of the sick and oppressed: "He sent me to proclaim to the captives freedom and to the blind the recovery of their sight."[88]

Indeed, Jesus will inaugurate his ministry with signs of physical and mental liberation (Luke 4:31ff.). These actions will come, in such a way, to accredit his ministry. This is the perception even of Luke, expressed by the intermediary of Peter: "You that are Israelites, listen to what I have to say: Jesus of Nazareth, a man attested to you by God with deeds of power, wonders and signs that God did through him among you . . ." (Acts 2:22).

In the same way the disciples, invested with the Spirit, will see their ministry accredited by signs and wonders, as was the case for Jesus of

---

[86] Borremans, p. 120.

[87] Barrett, *The Holy Spirit*, p. 101, rightly notices: "It is important to observe that Luke describes Jesus in the same terms as the apostles, whom he portrays as inspired teachers and miracle-workers." Conzelmann, however, considers that this point of view must be nuanced: ". . . we must not overlook the qualitative distinction. For one thing, Jesus is in his time the only bearer of the Spirit. He has received the Spirit in a different way from the community. It is said only of him that he was 'anointed' (Acts 10:38; 4:27; Luke 4:18). Finally, the phrase 'in the power of the Spirit' is used only of him (Luke 4:14; 10:21)" (*Theology of St. Luke*, p. 180, note 1). It does not seem that the qualitative distinction Conzelmann intends to bring is truly present in the arguments that he puts forth. The distinctions enumerated are at the level of formulations and forms, but not on a level of effects. The true difference between Jesus's status and that of the disciples comes from the resurrection/exaltation, where Jesus becomes Lord of the Spirit.

[88] La Potterie, p. 231, also perceives the anointing as having a double effect; it confers "the strength in the proclamation of the word and the power of the miracles." Mollat sees the anointing likewise ("The Role of Experience in the New Testament Teaching on Baptism and the Coming of the Holy Spirit," p. 131).

Nazareth.[89] They accomplished works similar to those that he accomplished.[90] Thus, they will witness of Jesus, both in proclaiming his word and in accomplishing his works.[91] The effects of the gift of the Spirit will not only be *heard*, but they will be *seen*: "and having received from the Father the promise of the Holy Spirit, he has poured out this that you both see and hear" (Acts 2:33b).

The works of the apostles can be seen and heard in the same way that those of Jesus were during his public ministry: "For I tell you that many prophets and kings desired to see what you see, but did not see it, and to hear what you hear, but did not hear it" (Luke 10:24).

A few examples suffice to establish how the works of the Spirit of Christ are *seen* and *heard* through the disciples' ministry. Immediately after having shown the events of Pentecost as consequences of the exaltation of the Christ, Luke presents a summary of the activities of the community (Acts 2:42, 47). Already, in this summary, he announces (v. 43) that "many signs and wonders were being done by the apostles."[92] Then, from the following pericope, he shows Peter and John going to the temple[93] where the first healing will take place (3:1–10). It is a question of a "man lame from birth [who], daily, was being carried to the gate of the temple . . . so that he could ask for alms" (v. 2). At the name of Jesus, Peter commands him to walk (v.6). Seeing the result, "the people were utterly astonished" by what had happened to him (v. 11). Peter then begins speaking (second missionary speech) to explain that it is by the power (v. 12) of Jesus (v. 16) put to death by the Jews, but resurrected (v. 15) and glorified by God (v. 13) that the healing had been accomplished. This healing, however, will call for the two disciples, Peter and John, to appear

---

[89] In this regard, Franklin, p. 198, writes: "supplementing the witness of the Spirit are the miracles which in the gospel are associated with faith in Jesus as the instrument of God (7:16, 22–23; 13:17) and in Acts are signs of his Exaltation (Acts 4:10–12)."

[90] See Lampe, "The Lukan Portrait of Christ," p. 175.

[91] As writes Pfitzner, p. 234: "by the Spirit's power, the words and deeds of the apostles represent the continuation of Jesus himself."

[92] This affirmation of Acts 2:43 is repeated verbatim in Acts 5:12.

[93] As he is in the habit of doing (see Luke 1–2), Luke must show the Old Testament anchoring of the Christian faith: it is towards the temple, in order to be conformed to a fundamental practice of the Jewish religion—prayer at fixed hours of the day, in this case, that of the ninth hour—that Peter and John were heading when they accomplished the healing of a lame man. Thus, the work of salvation initiated by God in the Old Covenant, brought to its fullness in Jesus, is now perpetuated through the Christian community. There is no breach and this is what the first chapters of Acts demonstrate with insistence.

before the Sanhedrin (4:1ff.). In the course of this appearance, Peter "full of the Holy Spirit" begins speaking and says (third missionary speech):

> Rulers of the people and elders, if we are questioned today because of a good deed done to someone who was sick and are asked how this man has been healed, let it be known to all of you and to all the people of Israel, that this man is standing before you in good health by the name of Jesus Christ of Nazareth, whom you crucified, whom God raised from the dead. (vv. 8–10)

This first missionary activity furnishes important information on this subject. The healing administered by Peter (Acts 3:1–11) happens, in the literary chronology of Acts, immediately after Peter's speech (Acts 2:14–41), if an exception is made of the summary inserted between the two texts. It appears, as it were, to ratify the explanation furnished by Peter, in his speech, about the events of Pentecost. The word is thus accredited by the sign. One hears and one sees the works of the Spirit through the apostolic activity.

It is in the name of Jesus, by his power, that of his Spirit that he promised (Acts 1:8) and transmitted (Acts 2:2–4), that Peter accomplishes the healing. The prophetic witness, which is conveyed by word and by sign, is the fruit of the gift of the Spirit of Jesus, who has been made Christ and Lord (Acts 2:36). Besides, as already seen, it is while "full of the Holy Spirit" that Peter explains to the Sanhedrin the origin of the power that animates them, him and his brothers, and by which he proclaims the wonders of the Paschal Mystery (Acts 4:8–10).

At this stage, a significant parallel between Jesus's missionary beginnings and those of the apostles is established: on this subject see the chart on page 235.[94]

Thus, Jesus is the first one baptized in the Holy Spirit. This baptism renders him apt to assume his prophetic vocation and to proclaim the coming of the kingdom. God ratifies his mission by signs and wonders. Jesus is then the only one to be full of the Spirit in a permanent manner, without yet being Lord of the Spirit with the power to make him available. At Pentecost, the disciples are also baptized in the Holy Spirit—because Jesus has now become Lord of the Spirit by his exaltation and has poured him out on them. They become in their turn able to witness and to perpetuate

---

[94] Compare the chart on page 235 to the one produced by Dumais, p. 121. Dumais's chart seeks, however, to show that the Spirit is the element of unity between the two volumes of Luke-Acts.

the work of Christ. The miracles that they perform validate their preaching. Thus, through the Pentecost experience, the disciples are enabled to accomplish the works that Jesus, following his baptism, accomplished, i.e., announce the Good News and heal the sick.

By the healing of the lame man at the temple, Christian preaching in a Jewish place was thus marked with the divine seal. It will be the same in a pagan context. Indeed, Paul's preaching is also supported by signs. However, it is necessary to first point out that his ministry was, from the very beginning, under the aegis of the Spirit. In the first account of his vocation (Acts 9:1–19), Ananias tells him the following:

> "Brother Saul, the Lord Jesus, who appeared to you on your way here, has sent me so that you may regain your sight and be filled with the Holy Spirit." And immediately something like scales fell from his eyes, and his sight was restored. Then he got up and was baptized. (Acts 9:17–18)

Paul's mission, although oriented toward the Gentiles, is explicitly situated in the line of the apostolic mission: "But the Lord said to him [Ananias], 'Go, for he is an instrument whom I have chosen to bring my name before Gentiles and kings and before the people of Israel'" (Acts 9:15). He will have to "carry [the] Name," that is, to witness of the resurrected Christ, as the first believers had done before him (see Acts 3:16; 4:7, 18). His letters of credibility are thus well attested: he is mandated by the Resurrected One and invested in the power of the Spirit. Immediately after, Luke relates in the form of a summary, Paul begins "to proclaim in the synagogues [of Damascus] that Jesus is the son of God" (Acts 9:20). And just as soon as he comes on the scene, he undertakes his first missionary voyage (Acts 13:1ff.).

It is on this voyage that Luke relates Paul's first speech at Antioch (Acts 13:16–42); a speech that has many similarities in form, content, and argumentation to Peter's first speech given on the day of Pentecost (see "The Speeches in the Acts of the Apostles," pp. 34ff.). Immediately after this speech, according to the narrative chronology of Acts, Paul works his first miracle in Lystra (Acts 14:8–11). And, what is striking, here again, are the similarities to the one worked by Peter at the temple of Jerusalem[95]

---

[95] See the parallel established between these two miracles—Peter's, Acts 3:1–10 and Paul's, Acts 14:8–11—by Neirynck, "The Miracle Stories in the Acts of the Apostles," p. 176.

(Acts 3:1–10). It is a matter again of a paralytic since birth. He regains the use of his legs after Paul commands him to stand "upright on his feet" (14:10).

What is especially important is the parallel that can be made between these two miracles—Peter's and Paul's—and the one worked by Jesus himself (Luke 5:17–26) in the account of the paralytic who was lowered through the roof. The factors of these three miracles have so much in common that Schneider presents them in his synoptic chart, which is reproduced on page 219 (and 220, in English).[96]

This triple comparison leads Schneider to conclude, and rightly so, that Luke deliberately established the parallels, not only between Peter's and Paul's miracles, but especially with Jesus's miracles; for this reason, Luke wanted to inscribe the works of these two apostles into continuity with those of Jesus.[97]

---

[96] Schneider, *Die Apostelgeschichte: Teil 1*, pp. 307–8. (This chart is reproduced by O'Reilly, p. 132.)

[97] Schneider, *Die Apostelgeschichte: Teil 1*, p. 308: "Da der Acta-Verfasser nicht nur die beiden Hauptgestalten Petrus und Paulus hinsichtlich der Wunder einander angleicht, sondern auch den Jesus seiner Evangelienschrift in diesen Angleichungsprozeß einbezieht, geht es ihm nicht eigentlich um einen Ausgleich zwischen 'petrinischem' Christentum und 'Paulinismus' . . . Vielmehr geht es ihm um die Kontinuität der kirchlichen Lehre und der 'Sache Jesu' überhaupt, die von Jesus über Petrus und die Apostel bis zu Paulus und damit bis zur eigenen 'nachpaulinischen' Gegenwart gewährleistet ist." ["Since the author of Acts not only aligns the two main figures, Peter and Paul, in regard to the miracles but also includes the Jesus of his gospel account in this process of alignment, his purpose is actually not to strike a balance between 'Petrine' Christianity and 'Paulinism'. . . . Rather, he is concerned with the continuity of the church's teaching and the 'matter of Jesus' in general—a continuity guaranteed by Jesus through Peter and the apostles up to Paul and, thus, up to his [the author of Acts's] own 'post-Pauline' present."]

The Healing of a Lame Man

Jesus (Luke 5:17–26)	Peter (Acts 3:1–10)	Paul (Acts 14:8–11)
	2. καί τις ἀνὴρ χωλὸς ἐκ κοιλίας μητρὸς αὐτοῦ	8. Καί τις ἀνὴρ . . . χωλὸς ἐκ κοιλίας μητρὸς αὐτοῦ
18. φέροντες	2. ἐβαστάζετο	
	3. ὃς ἰδὼν	
	4. ἀτενίσας (Πέτρος) εἰς αὐτόν	9. οὗτος ἤκουσεν . . . ἀτενίσας (Παῦλος) αὐτῷ
20. ἰδὼν (ὁ Ἰησοῦς) τὴν πίστιν αὐτῶν	(cp. 3:16)	9. ἰδὼν ὅτι ἔχει πίστιν
20. εἶπεν	εἶπεν	10. εἶπεν
23. ἔγειρε καὶ περιπάτει	(7. ἤγειρεν αὐτόν) 6. περιπάτει	10. ἀνάστηθι
25. καὶ παραχρῆμα	7. παραχρῆμα δέ	
25. ἀναστάς	8. ἔστη καὶ περιεπάτει	10. περιεπάτει
25. ἀπῆλθεν εἰς	εἰσῆλθεν . . . εἰς . . . περιπατῶν καὶ ἁλλόμενος	10. ἥλατο καὶ περιεπάτει
25. δοξάζων τὸν θεόν	αἰνῶν τὸν θεόν	
26. εἴδομεν	9. εἶδεν	11. ἰδόντες
26. ἅπαντας	πᾶς ὁ λαός	11. οἵ τε ὄχλοι
26. λέγοντες		11. λέγοντες
26. ἐδόξαζον τὸν θεόν	αἰνοῦντα τὸν θεόν (cp. 4:21)	(11b–13)
	10. καθήμενος	8. ἐκάθητο
26. καὶ ἐπλήσθησαν φόβου	10. καὶ ἐπλήσθησαν θάμβους καὶ ἐκστάσεως	
26. ἔκστασις		

The Healing of a Lame Man

Jesus (Luke 5:17–26)	Peter (Acts 3:1–10)	Paul (Acts 14:8–11)
	2. and a man lame from his mother's womb	8. And a man . . . lame from his mother's womb
18. carrying	2. was being carried	
	3. who saw (Peter & John)	9. this man heard . . .
	4. (Peter) gazed at him	(Paul) gazed at him
20. (Jesus) seeing their faith	(cp. 3:16)	9. (Paul) seeing that he had faith
20. said	said	10. said
23. Stand up and walk	7. raised him up	10. stand up
	6. walk	
25. and immediately	7. and immediately	
25. he stood	8. he stood and walked	10. he walked
25. he went to	he went . . . into . . . walking and leaping praising God	10. he leaped and walked
25. glorifying God		
26. we have seen	9. saw	11. saw
26. all	all the people	11. the crowd
26. saying		11. saying
26. they glorified God	praising God (cp. 4:21)	(11b–13)
	10. he sat	8. he sat
26. and filled with awe	10. and they were filled with wonder and amazement	
26. amazement		

To this we can add that Luke also wanted to mark the ratification of their works in the same manner that Jesus's works had been marked.[98]

The interpretation of the miracles in terms of ratification of the word is, moreover, the one explicitly furnished by Luke himself when he writes on the subject of Paul and Barnabas: "speaking boldly for the Lord, who testified to the word of his grace by granting signs and wonders to be done through them"[99] (Acts 14:3). And again, before the Jerusalem assembly, Paul and Barnabas show that, in the same way, God guaranteed their evangelization of the Gentiles: "The whole assembly kept silence, and listened to Barnabas and Paul as they told of all the signs and wonders that God had done through them among the Gentiles" (Acts 15:12).

The first community, in their prayer, will ask God precisely to affirm its preaching with signs:

> Lord . . . grant to your servants to speak your word with all boldness, while you stretch out your hand to heal, and signs and wonders are performed through the name of your holy servant Jesus. (Acts 4:29b–30)

Note here that the believers are qualified as "servants" in the image of the "holy servant," Jesus. They are like Jesus: prophets (witnesses of the word), accredited by God (by signs). God confirms them unquestionably in the response that he accords to their prayer: "When they had prayed, the place in which they were gathered together was shaken; and they were all filled with the Holy Spirit and spoke the word of God with boldness"[100] (4:31).

---

[98] In this vein, O'Reilly writes: "in both Gospel and Acts the miracle has the function of authenticating the claims of the miracle-worker; it is a visible sign which confirms the words that he speaks" (p. 134). According to O'Reilly, it is as prophets like Jesus that the disciples are accredited by their miracles (p. 182). See on this subject section 4 ("Significance of Signs and Wonders in Acts," pp. 178–90) of his book. See also George, *Études sur l'œuvre de Luc*, pp. 138, 190.

[99] See Acts 2:22.

[100] Here, a promise of Jesus is accomplished: the Spirit will be given as fruit of prayer: ". . . how much more will the heavenly Father give the Holy Spirit to those who ask him!" (Luke 11:13). This promise concludes a teaching on prayer (Luke 11:9–13) coming from document Q. The Matthean version contains, however, "good things" (Matt 7:11) instead of "the Holy Spirit." From all evidence, Matthew has the most original form (see Barrett, *The Holy Spirit*, p. 127). Luke's editorial reworking has the effect of making the teaching on prayer a teaching on the quality of prayer. For him, the answer par excellence of prayer is the gift of the Holy Spirit.

This text, which clearly evokes the original event of the outpouring of the Spirit, has this to tell us: the Spirit is never lacking in the church community; he always renews them. He is its strength in its action and its light in its witness. As soon as the "servants" were "filled with the Holy Spirit, [they] announced the word of God with boldness." But this text (4:31) is also a warning against foolhardiness: the Spirit is only given if the community gives itself to God in prayer; if it lets itself be guided by God, as Acts 5:32 assumes: "And we are witnesses to these things, and so is the Holy Spirit whom God has given to those who obey him" and 15:8: "And God, who knows the human heart, testified to them by giving them the Holy Spirit, just as he did to us."

It is only in listening to the Spirit that the works of God are accomplished.

In this regard, Luke gives another example in the person of Stephen. Among the seven chosen ones, the precise remark is made that Stephen was "a man full of faith and the Holy Spirit" (Acts 6:5).[101] Because of his spiritual disposition, it is given to him to accomplish wonders and signs: "Stephen, full of grace and power, did great wonders and signs among the people" (Acts 6:8). It is noteworthy that this precision about Stephen's powers shortly precedes the long speech that he is going to address to the Sanhedrin (7:1—8:3). Stephen's prodigious acts, therefore, constitute, here again, the divine seal that ratifies his witness.

It is clear, nevertheless, that the miracles of Acts are, as a general rule, linked to the name of Jesus (3:6; 3:16; 4:10; 4:30; 5:30) rather than to the Spirit.[102] It is not of less importance that the signs and wonders evoked in 2:43 and 5:15 result from the outpouring of the Spirit that precedes them. Concerning Stephen, the acts that he accomplishes are explicitly linked to the power that inhabits him (6:8). Moreover, the question of the members of the Sanhedrin about the origin of the power that allowed the healing of the lame man in the temple put "power" and "name" in parallel, in such a way that the two terms can be read in a synonymous manner, or as mutual explanations. The question is thus formulated: "By what power or by what name did you do this?" (Acts 4:7).

Moreover, in Luke, power refers habitually to the Spirit. Thus, the miracles are accomplished in the name of Jesus by the power of his Spirit. Notably, besides that, often in Acts the Name signifies expressly Jesus

---

[101] This is how Barnabas is described in Acts 11:24: "He was a good man, full of the Holy Spirit and of faith."

[102] See O'Reilly, p. 43, note 92.

glorified.[103] Thus it is in the following texts:

> ". . . let us warn them to speak no more to anyone in this name." So they called them and ordered them not to speak or teach at all in the name of Jesus. (Acts 4:17b–18)
>
> As they left the council, they rejoiced that they were considered worthy to suffer dishonor for the sake of the name. (Acts 5:41)

The following verse shows well that *the Name* designates Jesus glorified:

> And every day in the temple and at home they did not cease to teach and proclaim *Jesus as the Messiah*. (5:42)

Thus, the miracles accomplished in this Name are done by the power of Jesus made Lord by the Spirit of God. They testify to the word of the disciples who teach this Name.

A Community of Prophets—Collaborators of the Spirit

Up to now the Spirit has been presented as a guaranteeing force of the witness and power responsible for the wonders. But for Luke, it is more than a force or hidden power. His presence is so evident and his action so felt that it becomes natural to refer to him as an "active member" of the community, or, better yet, as the head of the community.[104]

Thus, one can lie to the Holy Spirit: "Ananias, why has Satan filled your heart to lie to the Holy Spirit?" (Acts 5:3). One can put him to a test: "How is it that you have agreed together to put the Spirit of the Lord to the test?" (Acts 5:9).

Of Jesus, the Spirit witnesses, with the believers, that "God exalted him at his right hand as Leader and Savior that he might give repentance to Israel and forgiveness of sins" (Acts 5:31): "And we are witnesses to these things, and so is the Holy Spirit whom God has given to those who obey him" (5:32).

---

[103] This meaning of the Name designating Jesus glorified is, however, exclusive. The study of Ziesler, "The Name of Jesus in the Acts of the Apostles," pp. 28–41, demonstrates that one can speak of a unique concept of the Name, but that the uses are diverse.

[104] Along this line, Hill writes: "The Church is in and lives by the power of the Spirit. This does not mean only that the Church receives the help of the Holy Spirit: the implication is rather that the Spirit is the main hero of the story" ("The Spirit and the Church's Witness: Observations on Acts 1:6–8," p. 23).

Stephen, in his speech, accuses the Jews of opposing the Holy Spirit: "You stiff-necked people, uncircumcised in heart and ears, you are forever opposing the Holy Spirit" (7:51). This opposition to the Holy Spirit, in spite of his evident interventions, is it not exactly the illustration of the unpardonable sin against the Spirit:[105] "but whoever blasphemes against the Holy Spirit will not be forgiven" (Luke 12:10). This sin, resistance in front of the evidence, is bad faith of which the most striking example is found in Acts 4:16–17:

> What will we do with them [Peter and John]? For it is obvious to all who live in Jerusalem that a notable sign has been done through them; we cannot deny it. But to keep it from spreading further among the people, let us warn them to speak no more to anyone in this name.

To have deliberately refused the salvation offered is, moreover, the great reproach addressed by Paul and Barnabas to the Jews:

> Then both Paul and Barnabas spoke out boldly, saying, "It was necessary that the word of God should be spoken first to you. Since you reject it and judge yourselves to be unworthy of eternal life, we are now turning to the Gentiles." (Acts 13:46)

Furthermore, the book of Acts closes on this condemnation addressed by the Holy Spirit, through the mouth of Paul, to the noteworthy Jews of Rome:

> Paul made one further statement: "The Holy Spirit was right in saying to your ancestors through the prophet Isaiah, 'Go to this people and say, "You will indeed listen, but never understand, and you will indeed look, but never perceive." For this people's heart has grown dull, and their ears are hard of hearing, and they have shut their eyes; so that they might not look with their eyes, and listen with their ears, and understand with their heart and turn—and I would heal them.' Let it be

---

[105] Guillet, "Saint-Esprit: Luc-Actes," col. 186, refuses to see in Stephen's reproach (Acts 7:51) the equivalence of the unpardonable blasphemy (Luke 12:10), arguing that Stephen himself is going to pray that God pardons his executioners (Acts 7:60). One can answer back to Guillet that what makes the sin unpardonable is the deliberate choice of the guilty to remain in their blindness, refusing by the fact to ask for pardon. The answer to Stephen's prayer would be, therefore, the guilty renouncing the attitude making their sin unpardonable.

known to you then that this salvation of God has been sent to the Gentiles; they will listen." (Acts 28:25b–28)

The Jews, by their resistance, closed themselves and were not able *"to see with their eyes"* or *"to hear with their ears"* the works of the Spirit given to them to *see* and *hear* (Acts 2:33b). Thus, the Spirit in the community is an evident presence, but a person whom one can resist and whom the Jewish people effectively resisted.

However, more than ever, the Spirit is "the deciding authority" of the community. In fact, it is his authority that Luke wants to bring out more particularly. Pfitzner is correct in writing:

> . . . nowhere in Acts will we see an apostle, not even Peter or Paul, claim his apostolic authority as coming from the Spirit. Nowhere is apostleship described as a special charisma. Acts leaves the immediate impression that the apostles are filled with the Spirit and under his direction, in the same manner that the entire community is filled and led by the Spirit.[106]

It is again the Spirit that says to Philip to meet the Ethiopian eunuch: "Then the Spirit said to Philip, 'Go over to this chariot and join it'" (Acts 8:29), and it is the Spirit who carries him away when his work with the eunuch is ended. It is the Spirit who says to Peter to follow those sent by Cornelius:

> While Peter was still thinking about the vision, the Spirit said to him, "Look, three men are searching for you. Now get up, go down, and go with them without hesitation; for I have sent them." (Acts 10:19–20)

Peter remembers this command of the Spirit, in Acts 11:12, before the Jerusalem community to justify his action toward the Gentiles. *He* did not decide—it was the Spirit: "The Spirit told me to go with them and not to make a distinction between them and us" (Acts 11:12). It is also the Spirit who decides to send Paul and Barnabas on their mission: "While they were worshiping the Lord and fasting, the Holy Spirit said, 'Set apart for me Barnabas and Saul for the work to which I have called them. . . .' So being sent out by the Holy Spirit . . ." (Acts 13:2, 4).

---

[106] Pfitzner, pp. 214–15.

At the Jerusalem Assembly, it is the community and the Spirit who decide the requirements to which the Gentile Christians will be submitted: "For it has seemed good to the Holy Spirit and to us to impose on you no further burden than these essentials" (Acts 15:28). And, during a missionary journey, the Spirit of Jesus keeps Paul from following the itinerary that he had chosen:

> They went through the region of Phrygia and Galatia, having been forbidden by the Holy Spirit to speak the word in Asia. When they had come opposite Mysia, they attempted to go into Bithynia, but the Spirit of Jesus did not allow them. (Acts 16:6–7)

It is evident then that the orientations of the community come under the authority of the Spirit. Those who are "filled" with the Spirit and who are submitted to him become, therefore, his collaborators.[107] However, owing to their faithfulness and their submission to the Spirit, their actions become the actions of the Spirit.[108]

The Spirit and Church Expansion

The final words of the Resurrected One before disappearing behind the cloud (Acts 1:9) were to define the mission of the church: "You will receive power when the Holy Spirit has come upon you; and you will be my witnesses in Jerusalem, in all Judea and Samaria, and to the ends of the earth" (Acts 1:8).

Once again, it is the power of the Spirit that will assure the growth of the church.[109] Even the geographic plan of intervention is well-traced: "*Jerusalem, all Judea, Samaria and to the ends of the earth.*"[110] The rest of

---

[107] The disciples remain, nevertheless, free and autonomous agents. Bonnard's remark is pertinent in this regard: "The Spirit is not conceived as a divinizing power stripping the Twelve of their humanity but a help brought to the heart of their infirmity" ("L'Esprit Saint et l'Église selon le Nouveau Testament," p. 82).

[108] See Pfitzner, p. 214.

[109] Trocmé is probably correct when he writes, ". . . for Luke the missionary function of the divine Spirit is the central idea of pneumatology" ("Le Saint-Esprit et l'Église d'après le livre des Actes," p. 24).

[110] Schwartz's thesis wanting "the extremities of the earth" of Acts 1:8 not to go beyond the limits of Palestine does not seem convincing. Schwartz defends his position with two stylistic arguments: (1) the listing (Jerusalem, Judea and Samaria) preceding "to the ends of the earth" seems to limit the extension to the Palestinian categories; (2) the history of Christian mission such as described in Acts never witnesses a mission

the book of Acts demonstrates that this plan was remarkably well-respected, and this, of course, in conformity to the will of the Holy Spirit.[111]

It all begins in Jerusalem, the day of Pentecost. Under the action of the Spirit, the transformed disciples speak and explain the event of salvation accomplished by God in Jesus Christ. A multitude of hearers are convinced: "So those who welcomed his message were baptized, and that day about three thousand persons were added" (Acts 2:41). The authorities of the church were established thus solidly in Jerusalem. And to convince the reader of the solidarity of this first community, Luke presents, in a summary, the activities which are in a way a model of community life: "They devoted themselves to the apostles' teaching and fellowship, to the breaking of bread and the prayers" (Acts 2:42).

The book of Acts devotes seven chapters exclusively to the Jerusalem Church. Then, consecutively, describes the persecution of the Jerusalem Hellenistic Christians, for which Stephen, the martyr, seems to have been the launching; the Christians "scattered throughout the countryside of Judea and Samaria" (Acts 8:1); Philip, one of the Seven (see Acts 6:5), proclaimed the Christ in Samaria (Acts 8:5). His preaching, accredited by signs, had great success: "The crowds with one accord listened eagerly to what was said by Philip, hearing and seeing the signs that he did" (Acts 8:6). Once again, the works of the exalted Christ were audible and visible (Acts 2:33b). For it was certainly the Spirit's will that this Samaritan community be birthed and grow: the Spirit himself confirmed this community as an extension of the Jerusalem community.[112] He "falls" upon

---

led by the apostles outside of the land of Israel. Acts 1:8 would only correspond thus to the first phase of the Christian mission, i.e., to the first part of the book of Acts ("The End of the ΓH [Acts 1:8]: Beginning or End of the Christian Vision?" pp. 669–76). To counter Schwartz, one needs only recall, on the contrary, that the missionary expansion that the entire book of Acts recounts took place exactly according to the announced geographic plan in Acts 1:8.

[111] See on this subject Pfitzner, p. 233.

[112] Why had the intervention of the apostles Peter and John been necessary for the Spirit to be conferred on the Samaritans? Most likely it was to mark the unity of the faith of the Samaritan and Jerusalem communities. In this respect, Pfitzner, writes: "The Samaritan episode is not narrated to illustrate some special power inherent in the apostolic laying on of hands. Its purpose is rather to show that the apostles, who first received the Spirit and who are continually under the guidance of the Spirit, must confirm every new stage in the extension of the church, in the mission of Israel," (p. 225). This is also the opinion of Giblet, p. 168, and Sauvagnat, p. 84. But Bruce also brings an interesting point of view when he suggests that Peter and John's intervention could

the Samaritans when the Jerusalem Church emissaries, Peter and John, impose their hands on them:

> Now when the apostles at Jerusalem heard that Samaria had accepted the word of God, they sent Peter and John to them. The two went down and prayed for them that they might receive the Holy Spirit (for as yet the Spirit had not come upon any of them; they had only been baptized in the name of the Lord Jesus). Then Peter and John laid their hands on them, and they received the Holy Spirit. (Acts 8:14–17)

Peter and John, returning to Jerusalem, proclaim "the good news to many villages of the Samaritans" (8:25).

Thus, the Christian faith, at first birthed in a purely Jewish milieu, is now welcomed by this group formed from a mix of Jews and Gentiles. It seems that Luke wants to gradually mark the passage of the Christian message from the Jewish territory to the Gentile territory by passing through this "hybrid" group. In the episode of the Ethiopian eunuch (Acts 8:26–39), to whom the Spirit sends Philip (v. 29), we are not yet in a purely Gentile context; for the eunuch, quite obviously, is a proselyte since he is returning from a pilgrimage to Jerusalem (v. 27) and he is found reading the prophet Isaiah (v. 28). Soon, however, the message will reach the north of the country:

> Meanwhile the church throughout Judea, Galilee, and Samaria had peace and was built up. Living in the fear of the Lord and *in the comfort of the Holy Spirit, it increased in numbers*. (Acts 9:31)

Thus, all of the country of Palestine had been met by the Christian witness through the guidance of the Holy Spirit. It will now be the time to turn to the Gentile world. And the credit will go to Peter for integrating the first converts to the church, that is, Cornelius and his family.[113]

---

have been necessary to help overcome the attitudes of reproach that divided the Jews and Samaritans for so long. He writes, "It may be that the Samaritan converts, so long the objects of Jewish disapproval, needed this special gesture from the leaders of the Jerusalem church to incorporate them into the Spirit-possessed fellowship of the new people of God" ("The Holy Spirit in the Acts of the Apostles," p. 174).

[113] In crediting Peter with the opening of the church to the Gentiles, Luke most likely wanted to show the authenticity of the faith of the Gentiles and to situate it in continuity with the faith of Jerusalem. But, as Pfitzner explains, the initial missionary work in the Gentile milieu belongs to the Hellenists (see Acts 11:19–21): "Historically, it may have been the Hellenists who were the first real missionaries of the early church, but it

Cornelius is a "man who feared God" (Acts 10:2), that is, a converted Gentile to the faith of the God of Israel, without, however, having been circumcised. From Joppa, Peter has a vision about the true notion of purity and impurity (Acts 10:9ff.), where God teaches him "not to call anyone profane or unclean" (Acts 10:28). Then, the Spirit commands him to go to Cornelius's house (10:19). While he is telling again about the events of salvation in Jesus Christ, "the Holy Spirit fell upon all who heard the word" (10:44). And "The circumcised believers who had come with Peter were astounded that the gift of the Holy Spirit had been poured out even on the Gentiles" (Acts 10:45).

Here is the Pentecost of the Gentile nations. It is not to be mistaken; the manifestations do not deceive: "For they heard them speaking in tongues and extolling God" (Acts 10:46). The effects of the gift of the Spirit are the same as the Jewish Pentecost. The recipients are made prophets and bear witness to the grandeur of God.

But Peter's original scruples, even his resistance (see Acts 10:14; 11:5ff.), the astonishment of Peter's Jewish companions (10:45), as well as the necessity to convince the Jerusalem Church (11:1ff.), show with great clarity that the initiative to the Gentiles expressly belongs to the Holy Spirit.[114] Peter, in his faithfulness and obedience to the Spirit, can only, therefore, conform himself to the divine decision: "Can anyone withhold the water for baptizing these people who have received the Holy Spirit just as we have?" (Acts 10:47).

And when he relates the event to the Jerusalem community, he adds to his argument even the Lord's declaration:

> And I remembered the word of the Lord, how he had said, 'John baptized with water, but you will be baptized with the Holy Spirit.' If then God gave them the same gift that he gave us when we believed in the Lord Jesus Christ, who was I that I could hinder God? (Acts 11:16–17)

---

was the apostles, led by the Spirit, who still had to confirm the Gentile mission. Continuity in salvation history is thus one of the major themes of Luke in Acts" (p. 233).

[114] ". . . this community [in Jerusalem] finds itself driven to universality by the free gift, without the discrimination of the Holy Spirit," writes Borremans, p. 106. In the same vein, Trocmé: "Here, the gift of the Holy Spirit has the objective of forcing the hand of the Jewish-Christians so that they consent to baptize the believing Gentiles" ("Le Saint-Esprit et l'Église d'après le livre des Actes," p. 25). Also Tugwell, p. 272.

The frontiers are, therefore, abolished by the Spirit himself. The Spirit is responsible for the propagation of the Christian faith in the Jewish world first, and then in the Gentile world. He imposes universalism.[115]

The event at Cornelius's house takes on capital importance in the book of Acts. Furthermore, Luke highlights its importance by the allotted space that he accords to the narration of the event—it is the longest account of Acts (Acts 10:1—11:18); by the detailed repetition of the sequence from the vision in Joppa up to the outpouring of the Spirit in Caesarea; by the insistence on the fact that the decision to baptize the Gentiles was not his. But more so, to the Jerusalem assembly (Acts 15:1ff.), Luke justifies again the evangelization of the Gentiles (vv. 7–11) by having Peter tell once again the account of the conversion of Cornelius and his household:

> After there had been much debate, Peter stood up and said to them, "My brothers, you know that in the early days God made a choice among you, that I should be the one through whom the Gentiles would hear the message of the good news and become believers. And God, who knows the human heart, testified to them by giving them the Holy Spirit, just as he did to us. (Acts 15:7–8)

The key to interpreting the event at Cornelius's house is given in Acts 11:15–17a:

> And as I began to speak, the Holy Spirit fell upon them just as it had upon us at the beginning. And I remembered the word of the Lord, how he had said, "John baptized with water, but you will be baptized with the Holy Spirit." If then God gave them the same gift that he gave us when we believed in the Lord Jesus Christ . . .

What happens to the Gentiles is the repetition of the event of the Jewish Christians' Pentecost (Acts 2:2–4); it is the baptism in the Spirit, as Peter explains. God's decision regarding the Gentiles is exactly the same regarding the Jews. Also important is how the literary schemas of the two accounts remarkably correspond to one another. The table below illustrates this.[116]

---

[115] On this subject, see Borremans, pp. 107–8.

[116] I am indebted to Samain for the parallel he established ("Le récit de la Pentecôte," p. 231, note 9).

Jews	Gentiles
The Coming of the Spirit	
2:4: [They] were filled with the Holy Spirit	10:44; 11:15: The Holy Spirit fell upon them . . .
Divine Character of the Outpouring	
2:17: In the last days it will be, God declares, that I will pour out my Spirit	10:45: the gift of the Spirit had been poured out
	11:17: If then God gave them the same gift . . .
Charismatic Manifestations	
2:4b: . . . began to speak in other languages	10:46: They heard them speaking in tongues and extolling God.
2:11b: . . . in our own languages we hear them speaking about God's deeds of power	
Reactions of Astonishment	
2:7: Amazed and astonished, they asked . . .	10:45: The circumcised believers who had come with Peter were astounded
2:12: All were amazed and perplexed saying to one another . . .	

The door was thus opened to the Gentile world, but always in the interior of the frontiers of Palestine. However, following Stephen's martyrdom, the Hellenists had to flee Judea. This was the occasion to carry the Christian message into their new, welcoming lands; so much so that we soon learn that at Antioch, the word had been addressed to the Greeks (Acts 11:20) and that these had welcomed it: "The hand of the Lord was with them, and a great number became believers and turned to the Lord" (Acts 11:21).

Informed of this fact, the Jerusalem community delegates Barnabas, "a good man, full of the Holy Spirit and of faith" (11:24), to inquire about the events of Antioch. Barnabas remarked that such growth in this church required that he have the help of Saul's service, whom he finds and brings from Tarsus (vv. 24–25). This was the beginning of their collaboration:

"So it was that for an entire year they met with the church and taught a great many people" (Acts 11:26).

Under the directives of the Spirit, Paul and Barnabas undertake carrying the Christian message throughout the Roman Empire: "While they were worshiping the Lord and fasting, the Holy Spirit said, 'Set apart for me Barnabas and Saul for the work to which I have called them. . . .' So, being sent out by the Holy Spirit, they went down to Seleucia . . ." (Acts 13:2, 4). Once again, Luke is careful to mark the initiative of the Spirit at the origin of this missionary thrust. And once again as well, he will see that the Jerusalem Church, which submits to the decisions of the Spirit, sanctions this missionary work: "It has seemed good to the Spirit and to us . . ." (Acts 15:28).

Then, on a second journey, Paul and Barnabas will pursue (but separately) the missionary work throughout the Roman Empire. Moreover, it is always under the direction of the Spirit that the itinerary is traced:

> They went through the region of Phrygia and Galatia, having been forbidden by the Holy Spirit to speak the word in Asia. When they had come opposite Mysia, they attempted to go into Bithynia, but the Spirit of Jesus did not allow them. (Acts 16:6–7)

Finally, it is at Rome where Paul is at the end of his life; there, he is "proclaiming the kingdom of God and teaching about the Lord Jesus Christ with all boldness and without hindrance" (Acts 28:31). What the Jews refused to *see* and *hear*, the Gentiles, receive: "Let it be known to you then that this salvation of God has been sent to the Gentiles; they will listen [αὐτοὶ καὶ ἀκούσονται: *they will hear*]" (Acts 28:28). They will *hear* and *see* what the prophets would have wanted to *see* and *hear* (Luke 10:24)—what had not been given to them but was given to the believers at Pentecost and which is now given to the Gentiles.

Thus, from Jerusalem, the Jewish capital, the Spirit guides his church up to Rome, the capital of the Gentile world.[117] But "Rome symbolizes a new springboard,"[118] for Rome opens up to all the roads that lead to the extremities of the earth.

Conclusion

It was foundational for Luke to demonstrate the unity between Jesus's prophetic message and the prophetic message of the church. It was neces-

---

[117] And as Pfitzner expresses it, p. 233: "Every decisive step in the extension of the church from Jerusalem to Rome is marked by the Spirit's guidance and direction as he works through the apostles as those who represent the risen Lord himself."

[118] Bovon, "L'importance des médiations dans le projet théologique de Luc," p. 28.

sary, in this perspective, to establish that the Christians were the true witnesses of Jesus Christ. How then is the authenticity and the faithfulness of the witness guaranteed? By the Spirit.[119] In fact, by showing that it is in and by the Spirit of Christ that Christians announce the gospel, the validity of the witness is assured: the Spirit of Christ can only spread the Truth of Christ.[120]

But it was necessary that the believers first be endowed with this Spirit. This necessity is met in a picturesque way by the event of Pentecost (Acts 2:1–4). This event would, however, not have been possible if Jesus had not first himself received the plenitude of the Spirit. Luke is careful to explain that this prerequisite had also been met: God raised Jesus and exalted him (Acts 2:32–33). He communicated to him his Spirit and made him sit at his right hand. Jesus becomes, from this fact, suitable to transmit the Spirit. Pentecost takes, therefore, its explanation from the exaltation of Christ.[121] Acts 2:33 explains how the outpouring of the Spirit was made possible.

The report of the active presence and efficacy of the Spirit is, however, not the fruit of a dialectic deduction, but the fruit of experience.[122] The presence of the Spirit was felt and proven at the heart of the community; his works were *seen* and *heard*. This is what Luke affirms first in Acts 2:33 and does not cease to show by what follows. The works of the Spirit

---

[119] McPolin, p. 126, writes: ". . . in Luke (the Spirit is) the link between the ministry of the proclaiming Church and the ministry of Jesus; he is the personal link for the believer with the Incarnate and glorified Jesus." See also Guillet, "Saint Esprit: Luc–Actes," col. 190.

[120] In this sense, Bruner, *A Theology of the Holy Spirit*, p. 156, affirms: "The Spirit is not to be dissociated from Jesus. The Spirit is Jesus at work in continuation of his ministry." In the same sense Hill, "The Spirit and the Church's Witness," p. 24: "The Spirit is the power and presence of Jesus released from the constrictions of place and time to be with and among his followers everywhere and always." And finally, Guillet, "Saint-Esprit," col. 190: "Everywhere the Spirit intervenes, it is Jesus who intervenes."

[121] In this sense, Franklin writes: "The gift of the Spirit and the universal mission are closely related to the eschatological event of the Ascension in so far as they are derived directly from it, are the earthly result of it, and realize it by making it effective in the lives of men" (p. 196).

[122] The previously cited article of Borremans correctly aims to make it understood how much the Holy Spirit is a concrete reality in the life of Christians. It is their experience of the Spirit which permits this retrospective process leading to the history of Jesus, making them "seize this history as the always actual origin of their present experience" (p. 104).

at the heart of the community are so concrete and palpable that to deny them is to sin against the Holy Spirit (Luke 12:10).[123]

It comes out clearly, therefore, that, thanks to the exaltation of Christ, his work is perpetuated. The eschatological event proclaimed in Acts 2:33 is the essential cause of the birth and development of the church. Luke can, in effect, speak of the inspired witness of the believers and of the church expansion under the thrust of the Spirit because he already declared its causative principle in Acts 2:33. The entire account of Acts is rendered possible because Jesus received the Spirit and poured him out. The whole narrative of the book, therefore, takes its emphasis from Acts 2:33.

I use the word *event* without, however, asking the question of historicity. It is at a literary level that we situate ourselves; as a consequence, what is important is to evaluate the place and the role of the account in the entire narrative of Acts.

---

[123] See Borremans, p. 119.

THE EXALTATION OF JESUS—ACTS 2:33—LEADS TO THE OUTPOURING OF THE SPIRIT, CONTINUING THE WORKS OF JESUS IN HIS CHURCH

Jesus (Luke)	Pentecost (Acts)
Baptism: Jesus receives the Spirit from the Father (Luke 3:21–22)	Pentecost: The disciples receive the Spirit from Jesus Christ (Acts 2:2–4)
Jesus presents the anointing of his baptism as prophetic investiture (4:16ff.)	Peter presents Pentecost as the inauguration of the prophetic community (2:14ff.)
Soon afterwards, Jesus performs miracles, verifying his proclamation (4:33ff., the demoniac; 4:38ff., Peter's mother-in-law, etc.)	Soon afterwards, Peter and John heal a paralytic, verifying their preaching (3:1–10)
Description of Jesus's power (6:18–19)	Description of Peter's power (5:15–16)
The third Gospel shows the works of Jesus, which can be seen and heard (See Luke 10:24)	The book of Acts shows the works of the disciples, which can be seen and heard (2:33b), works illustrated in the account of Pentecost (2:1–13)

CHAPTER 7

CONCLUSION

At the time Luke produced his literary work, from all evidence, he already had in mind the plan of the whole of the two parts that compose it—Luke-Acts. The theological unity of the work—a unity which is woven around the theme of the history of salvation—shows, in effect, that Luke wanted his two volumes as one whole. Moreover, this examination has proven that the contents of Acts 2:33 is the meeting point between the two parts of the work. It is the recognition of the lordship of the Christ, expressed in Acts 2:33, that is the origin of this two-part work. The Christ acts with force; the Christian faith has an expansion that goes beyond all human capacity, but it is through the believers that everything happens. How was that made possible?

Luke is certain that it is the power of the Spirit that is at work. He draws the obvious conclusion:

> Being therefore exalted at the right hand of God, and having received from the Father the promise of the Holy Spirit, he [Jesus] has poured out this that you both see and hear. (Acts 2:33)

He then does a retrospective reading of Jesus's history in order to explain how the events of his earthly life could lead him to sit at the right hand of God. If God confided to him the government of the world, it is because Jesus lived up to expectations from his birth to his death. In order to get there, he had to be under the protection of the Spirit from his conception and exercise his ministry under the action of the same Spirit. It is in order to be able to proclaim the content of Acts 2:33 that Luke thus shows the Spirit intervening at Jesus's conception, and it is always in view of Acts 2:33 that he places the Spirit as the guarantor of Jesus's prophetic testimony beginning with his baptism. His total faithfulness to God merits, therefore, that he be raised from the dead (Acts 2:24) and that he receive the plenitude of the Spirit of God necessary for him to reign (Acts 2:33a).

However, since it is through the believers that the powerful works of the Christ are made concrete, it is thus that they also are animated by the same force that animated Jesus. The resurrected Christ poured out on them the Spirit that he received (Acts 2:33b), and they become capable of perpetuating his work. All of the church activity comes from the fact that Jesus received the Spirit and poured him out. All of church life is understood in the light of Acts 2:33.

In brief, it is the Spirit of God in Jesus who made way for the realization of the promises of salvation; it is through the Spirit that Luke marks the continuity between the Old Testament and the New (Luke 1–2); it is the same Spirit who perpetuates the works of Christ in the church. The Spirit is the principle of unity of Luke's entire theological work.

The hypothesis given from the beginning—that the contents of Acts 2:33 is the key to the interpretation of Lukan pneumatology—is verified throughout the study. However, the exercise of the verification of the hypothesis also made way for unfolding the great characteristics of the pneumatology of Luke-Acts, which will now be shown in the following pages.

1. LUKAN PNEUMATOLOGY:
A PNEUMATOLOGY IN THE TRADITION OF THE OLD TESTAMENT

Étienne Trocmé can give a person a start when he declares that Luke "did not possess a very elaborate and well thought out[1] pneumatology," or when he qualifies Luke's pneumatology as "rudimentary."[2] "But isn't the theme of the Spirit central to Acts?" one might answer back.

Indeed, it is not an exaggeration to speak of the Spirit in Acts as an essential element in the account.[3] If one dared to take out from the book all the times the Spirit is mentioned and intervenes, one would be left with

---

[1] Trocmé, "Le Saint-Esprit et l'Église d'après le livre des Actes," p. 21.
[2] Ibid., p. 24.
[3] Guillet, "Saint-Esprit: Luc-Actes," col. 184, will even affirm: "He is in fact the essential agent of the entire story told in Acts."

an account deprived of its skeletal structure. However, in spite of the indispensable role of the Spirit, Trocmé's affirmation, nevertheless, contains a great deal of truth.[4] The Lukan conception of the role of the Spirit reflects in fact, and in many ways, the language and the pneumatological patterns of the Old Testament.[5]

In the Old Testament perspective,[6] the Spirit is first and above all God's force of intervention in the world.[7] He is essentially God's effective

---

[4] If I concede to Trocmé that Luke can perhaps not have a very elaborate pneumatology, I categorically object to the explanation that he proposes for this statement: according to him ("Le Saint-Esprit," p. 21), "The author of the book of Acts especially spoke of the Holy Spirit as his sources did." On the contrary, Luke has a very personal manner of making use of the concept of the Spirit, and, in general, the passages where he makes the Spirit intervene are the most Lukan.

[5] Other than Trocmé, also of this opinion is Bonnard, "L'Esprit Saint et l'Église selon le Nouveau Testament," p. 84; Gillièron, "L'Esprit au service de la Parole (Luc)," p. 126; Lampe, "The Holy Spirit in the Writings of St. Luke," p. 160; Haya-Prats, pp. 22ff. (ET: pp. 4ff.). For Haya-Prats, the influence of the Old Testament is, however, limited; Luke drew from there his themes and several of his expressions, but this heritage, he would say, will only serve as a cultural milieu to a more precise concept that Luke seeks to give to the Holy Spirit (p. 24 [ET: p. 7]); Chevallier, "Luc et l'Esprit Saint," p. 12. As for Marsh, p. 103, he has this thought which appears very pertinent: "The writer who to my mind forms the best introduction to the New Testament Theology of the Spirit is St. Luke."

[6] To shed light on the characteristics and the actions of the Spirit in the Old Testament, I principally refer to Lys's exhaustive study, *"Rûach": le Souffle dans l'Ancien Testament*. This work, even if it is more than twenty-five years old, remains still today the fundamental study on the subject. Other than Lys, see Baumgärtel, pp. 56–72; Cazelles et al., "L'Esprit de Dieu dans l'Ancien Testament," *Le Mystère de l'Esprit Saint*, pp. 17–43; Cripps, "The Holy Spirit in the Old Testament," pp. 272–80; Guillet, *Thèmes bibliques*, pp. 208–55; Haulotte, "L'Esprit de Yahvé dans l'Ancien Testament," pp. 25–36; Heron, *The Holy Spirit: The Holy Spirit in the Bible, the History of Christian Thought and Recent Theology*; van Imschoot, "L'action de l'Esprit de Yahvé dans l'Ancien Testament," pp. 553–87; "L'Esprit," *Théologie de l'Ancien Testament*, pp. 183–200; Jacob, pp. 98–103; Maertens, *Le soufflé et l'esprit de Dieu*; Montague, pp. 3–124; Neher, pp. 85–101; Neve, *The Spirit of God in the Old Testament*; A. Richardson, pp. 103–24; Schweizer, *The Holy Spirit*.

[7] Neve describes in these terms the concept of *RUAH* in the Old Testament: "In the Old Testament literature ruah is only used to express God's activity *as he relates himself* to his world, his creation, his people. It was Israel's way of describing God, not as he is in himself, but as he communicates to the world his power, his life, his anger, his will, his very presence" (p. 2). In the same perspective: Baumgärtel, pp. 61ff.; Cazelles, "L'Esprit de Dieu dans l'Ancien Testament"; Haulotte, p. 32; Heron, p. 11; van Imschoot, "L'action de l'Esprit de Yahvé," pp. 557ff.; Jacob, pp. 98ff.; Lys, p. 345; Neher, p. 87; A. Richardson, p. 120; Schweizer, *The Holy Spirit*, pp. 12–13.

power, a constraining power against which no other force would know how to resist, a directive power that presides over the people's destinies.

Moreover, as one can observe throughout this study, the most adequate descriptive term of the Spirit in Luke is *power* (Luke 1:35; 24:49; Acts 1:8; etc.). *Spirit* and *power* have synonymous value (see Luke 1:35) in the perspective of the author. And this power has ways of acting which strangely resemble what is found in the Old Testament. Therefore, when Luke writes that "the Spirit of the Lord snatched Philip away" (Acts 8:39) after he had finished instructing the Ethiopian eunuch, the association is easily made with 1 Kgs 18:12, where Obadiah, chief of Ahab's palace, says to Elijah: ". . . as soon as I have gone from you, the Spirit of the Lord will carry you I know not where"; or again, in 2 Kgs 2:16, where questions are being asked on Elijah's disappearance: "It may be that the spirit of the LORD has caught him up and thrown him down on some mountain or into some valley." We think again of the violent way the Spirit of Yahweh lifts and snatches away Ezekiel (3:14): "The spirit lifted me up and bore me away . . . ." Just like Ezekiel saw himself being transported by the Spirit to where Yahweh wanted him to intervene, thus "Philip found himself at Azotus, and as he was passing through the region, he proclaimed the good news to all the towns until he came to Caesarea" (8:40).

In the Old Testament, it was also frequent that the Spirit of Yahweh would unexpectedly seize an individual to make him accomplish a particular act in favor of Israel. The chosen person, in this case, seems placed in a situation where he cannot remove himself from the divine will. It is the case of Samson who must combat the Philistines (Judg 14:6, 19; 15:14) and of Gideon who by himself must defend his tribe against the pillaging Midianites (Judg 6:34). In a different context, but also in an authoritative and irresistible way, the Spirit obliges Peter to go to the home of the Gentile Cornelius (Acts 10:19–20; 11:12); he reserves Paul and Barnabas (13:2) to send them on a mission (13:4); he keeps Paul from announcing the word in Asia (16:6) and he changes his itinerary (16:7); etc.

Luke does not hesitate either to refer back to some primitive practices when it is a matter of verifying the prophetic investiture of new converts. The appeal to speaking in tongues (Acts 10:46; 19:6; see 2:4) as the sign of the gift of the Spirit recalls the ecstatic behavior of the old prophets (1 Sam 10:6; 10–12; 19:23–24; Num 24:2) who entered into trances in order to pronounce their oracles. Luke, in the same way, assimilates the unusual language of speaking in tongues to the gift of prophecy (see Acts 2:17; 11:8).

But what is especially striking is the Old Testament tone of the descriptive vocabulary of the gift and of the action of the Spirit in Luke. One, in fact, finds in Luke-Acts, a verbal nomenclature that is clearly the reflection of the Old Testament terminology.[8] The inventory which follows, although just a summary, seems to be rather convincing.[9]

Send

Ps 104:30: God sends (ἐξαποστελεῖς) his spirit and the Earth is renewed. (Also Isa 48:16).	*Luke 24:49*: Jesus is going to send (ἀποστέλλω) the promise of the Father.

Clothe

Judg 6:34: The Spirit of the Lord clothes (ἐνέδυσε) Gideon. (Also 1 Chr 12:19; 2 Chr 24:20).	*Luke 24:49*: The disciples will be clothed (ἐνδύσησθε) with power.

Come upon

Ezek 2:2: The Spirit came on (ἦλθεν ἐπί) Ezekiel (See Num 24:2).	*Acts 1:8*: The Spirit will come on (ἐπελθόντος) the disciples (Also Luke 1:35).

Fall upon

Ezek 11:5: The Spirit falls on (ἔπεσεν ἐπί) Ezekiel (see Judg 14:6, 19; 1 Sam 10:6).	*Acts 8:16*: The Spirit falls on (ἐπιπεπτωκός) the Samaritans (also Acts 10:44; 11:5).

Pour out

Ezek 39:29: God will pour out (ἐξέχεα) his Spirit on Israel (also Joel 2:28–29; see Isa 32:15; 44:3; Prov 1:23).	*Acts 2:33*: The Spirit poured out (ἐξέχεεν) on the believers.

---

[8] See the list of verbs describing the interventions of the Spirit in the Old Testament noted by van Imschoot, "L'action de l'esprit de Yahvé," pp. 576–79; also, Baumgärtel, pp. 61ff. Also, on the Lukan use of traditional vocabulary of the Old Testament, see the list drawn up by George, "L'Esprit Saint dans l'oeuvre de Luc," pp. 528–29.

[9] The parallel is established with the text of the Septuagint.

Fill

Exod 31:3: Uri's son is filled (ἐνέπλησα) with the Spirit. (Also Exod 28:3; 35:31; See Isa 42:1; 48:16; 63:11).

Acts 2:4: The disciples were filled (ἐπλήσθησαν) with the Spirit. (Also Luke 1:15, 41, 67; Acts 4:31; etc.).

Say

Ezek 11:5: the Spirit says (εἶπεν) to Ezekiel ...

Acts 13:2: The Spirit says (εἶπεν) to the community (Also Acts 8:29; 10:19; 11:12; 19:1; 21:11).

Other verbs can be listed that do not exactly correspond in Greek, but carry the same idea:

Snatch away/Carry away:	Acts 8:39 / 1 Kgs 18:12; 2 Kgs 2:16; Ezek 3:14
Rest on:	Luke 3:22 / Num 11:25; Isa 11:2; 2 Kgs 2:15
Pour out:	Acts 2:17; 10:45 / Isa 29:10
Provoke/Test the Spirit:	Acts 5:9 / Isa 63:10ff.
Be on someone:	Luke 2:25 / Judg 3:10; Num 24:2

Other actions attributed to the Spirit in Luke-Acts equally betray an ancient conception of the movement of the Spirit:

- The Spirit leads Simeon to the temple: Luke 2:27

- One speaks by the Spirit: Acts 11:28; 28:25

- The Spirit prevents the announcement of the word from going into Bithynia: Acts 16:6–7

Note again these Old Testament examples where God, in "filling" with His Spirit, also communicates wisdom: Exod 28:3 (those skilled in making the sacred vestments); Exod 31:3 (Uri's son is filled with the Spirit so that he has wisdom); Isa 11:2 (the descendant of David will be filled with the spirit of wisdom). Likewise, in Acts, they look for in the group of the Seven, men full of the Spirit and of wisdom (6:3); Stephen is full of the Spirit and of wisdom (6:10); Barnabas was "a good man, full of the Holy Spirit and of faith" (11:24).

It appears evident that Luke's choice of words remain within the limits of the metaphor, faithful to the Old Testament conception from which they are inspired. The concrete character of the verbs used by the hagiographers of the Old Testament—"come on," "clothe," "pour out," "fill," etc.—must not lead to the conclusion that the Spirit was represented in a "material and fluid" manner, explains van Imschoot; it is a matter rather of a literary device aiming to "express the abundance of the divine gifts."[10] Besides, it must be said that Hellenistic Judaism, in making the Greek concept of *pneuma* holy, was very careful not to integrate this pantheistic dimension recognizable as Greek philosophy, one that effectively perceived it as the vital principle, at the same time spiritual and material, which moved as a fluid in the human organism.[11] Thus the Lukan appeal to a picturesque terminology to describe the roles of the Spirit aims quite simply, as in the Old Testament and in Judaism, to recognize the power and the richness of his interventions.

But undoubtedly the example most typical of the Old Testament character of the Lukan perception of the Spirit is Acts 8:26, 29, where Luke substitutes the Spirit with the Angel of the Lord. In effect, it is first the Angel of the Lord who calls out to Philip in verse 26. In verse 29, without any justification for the change, the Spirit now assumes the role of the Angel—the same alternation Angel/Spirit is in Peter's vision at Joppa (Acts 10:3, 19). Moreover, clearly in biblical language, the Angel of the

---

[10] Van Imschoot, "L'action de l'Esprit de Yahvé," p. 579; see also, Neher, p. 87; against Schweizer, "Le Nouveau Testament," pp. 145ff., who, in fact, sees the Spirit in Luke as "a fluid that fills man." He explains: "This conception fits much better to describe the Spirit as a reality that permeates the entire existence of man." However, to perceive the Spirit "as a reality that permeates the entire existence of man" is more descriptive of the Pauline vision than of the Lukan. George, pp. 528–29, also sees the Spirit "as fluid matter," but according to George's perception, contrary to that of Schweizer, this fluid does not permeate the human being but is outside of him: "One is 'plunged into'; it is 'poured'; one is 'clothed' in it; one is 'filled' with it; one is 'anointed' by it." George specifies, moreover, that these formulations in Luke, as in the Old Testament, are "largely metaphorical."

[11] On the subject, see the excellent study of Verbeke, *L'évolution de la doctrine du pneuma du stoïcisme à saint Augustin*. See also Kleinknecht, "Pneuma en grec," pp. 14ff.

Lord signifies God himself active in Creation.[12] His use as an intermediary figure aims to guard God's transcendence. The Spirit of God is also an intermediary figure in the same way as the Angel.[13] In the context of Acts, when Luke "interchanges" these designations, he illustrates then that he conceives the roles of these individuals according to the patterns of the Old Testament tradition. In this case, he wants to signify the divine origin of the decision to baptize the eunuch. Whether this decision is attributable to the Angel or to the Spirit, its significance remains the same.

From this last observation, one can deduce in corollary that, in Luke's perspective, one must not perceive the Spirit as a distinct entity of God any more than one so perceives the Angel of the Lord. For never did Israel want to make the Angel of the Lord a personal being different from God. On the contrary, when he evokes his acts and gestures, he simply translates his perception of the movement of God, thus it is when he evokes the acts and gestures of the Spirit.[14] Besides, it is remarkable that the purer the image of God becomes in biblical thought, the more refined the characteristics of his Spirit are and the more they merge with God's. Guillet writes:

---

[12] Some examples where the designations "Angel of the Lord" and "Yahvé" are "interchanged" within the same account show that the same value is accorded to the designations. Thus it is in the episode of the burning bush (Exod 3:2, 4) and again in the call of Gideon (Judg 6:11–12, 14).

[13] Van Imschoot, "L'Esprit," pp. 199–200, recalls this very biblical tendency to appeal to intermediary figures to avoid speaking of Yahvé as a direct participant. Thus, he explains, the use of the idioms "the hand of Yahvé," "the mouth of Yahvé," as well as "the spirit of Yahvé" mean to indicate the personal intervention of Yahvé. Neve, p. 127, recognizes the same relationship between the different idioms.

[14] The specialists are generally of the opinion that the texts of the Old Testament did not personalize the Spirit. This is what Lys brings out throughout his work. Of the same opinion: Cripps, p. 273, affirmed it in a categorical and terse sentence: "There is no recognition of the Person of the Holy Spirit from Genesis to Malachi"; Guillet, *Thèmes bibliques*, p. 250; Heron, p. 11; van Imschoot, "L'Esprit," p. 200; Neve, p. 127; A. Richardson, p. 120, whose remark renders with pertinence the most correct vision of the personal status of the Spirit in the Old Testament: "The Spirit of God is, of course, personal; it is God's δύναμις in action. But the Holy Spirit is not a person existing independently of God; it is a way of speaking about God's personally acting in history, or of the Risen Christ's personally acting in life and witness of the Church." Cazelles, "L'Esprit de Dieu dans l'Ancien Testament," p. 22, exhibits, however, an opposing point of view when he writes: ". . . in the Old Testament, the Spirit is never identified [with] God." He adds: ". . . also it is slowly that his personality is revealed." In the same thought, Bruce, "The Holy Spirit in the Acts of the Apostles," p. 179; Haya-Prats, pp. 89–90 (ET: 92–93).

> ... the greater the role of the spirit of God and significance in the world and in history, the more precise his characteristics become, one could say, and the less they appear distinct from those of God.[15]

Thus, as observed, Luke, who draws largely from the Old Testament patterns to speak of the Spirit, did not want to personalize[16] him either. On the contrary, he chose this category of language for what it already evoked: the powerful and effective action of God in the world.

The first conclusion, therefore, is that Luke did not elaborate an original pneumatology, but that he used almost slavishly—dare say—an already approved linguistic and conceptual network for which references are well established. In doing so, he indicated to his reader the interpretative framework of the related events.

2. A CHRISTIANIZED PNEUMATOLOGY

Luke appropriated the Old Testament pneumatological language, *but he Christianized it*. The experience of Christ's exaltation profoundly marked all of the newly birthed Christian community, as numerous literary witnesses attest: Rom 1:4–5; 8:34; Eph 1:19b–23; Col 3:1; Heb 1:3, 13; 10:12–13; etc. This experience does not uniquely point back to the initial christophanies; on the contrary, it persists in the life of the community. The presence of the Resurrected One, as the force directing the church, is not doubted at all by the Christians. The Living One acts with such power

---

[15] Guillet *Thèmes bibliques*, p. 216.

[16] George devoted a good part of his article "L'Esprit Saint dans l'oeuvre de Luc," pp. 527ff., to the question of the "personality of the Holy Spirit." The only possible method, he says, to know if Luke perceived the Spirit as a distinct person of God, is "to seek to recognize the most constant traits and the characteristics of his presentation of the Holy Spirit" (p. 527). According to George, it is a matter of seeing how Luke describes the action of the Spirit and his relations with the people who intervene in the history of salvation: men, Jesus, God. After the study of the texts, he arrives at the conclusion that "no text of Luke allows us to judge with certainty if he went beyond the ancient conception of the metaphorical personification of the Spirit" (p. 532). But George concedes, nevertheless, that if "one cannot . . . say that Luke clearly sees the Holy Spirit as a divine person similar and equal to the Father and the Son, . . . his presentation of the Spirit is open for subsequent developments" (p. 533). As to Chevallier, "Luc et l'Esprit," p. 12, he does not believe that Luke went beyond the Old Testament and Judaism concerning the personalization of the Holy Spirit. According to Knox, p. 92, there would be personalization of the Spirit in the same manner that one personalized Wisdom in the wisdom literature.

and effectiveness that one comes to understand that in him God established his Reign.

Jesus crucified was made Christ and Lord (Acts 2:36). God exalted him at his resurrection. The New Testament hagiographers proclaim this fact unanimously, but Luke is the only one to explain in an explicit way how Jesus was established in this messianic function: *"Being therefore exalted at the right hand of God, and having received from the Father the promise of the Holy Spirit . . ."* (Acts 2:33a).

The Spirit of God thus became the Spirit of Christ. Nevertheless, in his behavior, all the Spirit's power and effectiveness are retained and his direct actions remain essentially oriented toward salvation. It is the same Spirit. Luke, consequently, does not see any disadvantage, to speak of them, in reusing the Old Testament patterns and vocabulary describing the Spirit of God, as observed. However, the actions of the Spirit will be from now on in the continuation of Jesus's earthly mission. They will perpetuate his actions, his options, his ideals, his perception of God and of the human being, briefly, i.e., his existence as the Chosen One of God. The Spirit will be, according to the terms of R. E. Brown, "the presence of Jesus when Jesus is absent."[17]

The Spirit becomes, in this perspective, the response to the delay of the Parousia. Not that Luke had necessarily renounced the hope of the return of the Christ, for, he says, "This Jesus, who has been taken up from you into heaven, will come in the same way as you saw him go into heaven" (Acts 1:11b). However, it is no longer the time for speculation about the moment of the return: "It is not for you to know the times or periods that the Father has set by his own authority" (Acts 1:7). And especially, the delay must not be an excuse for inertia.: "Men of Galilee, why do you stand looking up toward heaven?" (Acts 1:11a). On the contrary, since the Spirit is poured out, energy must be mobilized to give testimony to the Christ "in Jerusalem, in all Judea and Samaria, and to the ends of the earth" (Acts 1:8b). Thus, the time of the end is more and more uncertain, but the Spirit of the Christ is there and his work continues. The Spirit is

---

[17] *The Gospel according to John (xiii–xxi)*, p. 1141. For John, however, the role attributed to the Advocate will be different from the one attributed to the Spirit in Luke-Acts. In Luke-Acts, the Spirit is essentially linked to testimony, in view of the expansion of the church. In John, he fills a triple role: (1) he is the presence of Jesus: "But the Advocate, the Holy Spirit, whom the Father will send in my name . . ." (John 14:26); (2) he is the defender of Jesus: "When the Advocate comes . . . he will testify on my behalf" (15:26); (3) he is the living memory of the church: "The Advocate . . . will teach you everything, and remind you of all that I have said to you" (14:26b).

God's response to the eschatological hopes.[18] It is in the gift of the Spirit that the promise is fulfilled:

> ... and you will receive the gift of the Holy Spirit. For the promise is for you, for your children, and for all who are far away, everyone whom the Lord our God calls to him. (Acts 2:38b–39)

The time of the Spirit has thus begun. But for Luke, it is Christ himself who pursues his work. That is because God, in resurrecting him, communicated to him his own Spirit. The Spirit of God becomes the Spirit of the Christ. *The Spirit is Christianized.* That is what Luke explains in Acts 2:33.

3. THE SPIRIT—GUARANTEE OF CONTINUITY

For Luke, the Spirit is the principle of unity of the entire history of salvation. He is the guarantee of continuity, not only between Jesus and the church, but also between the Old Testament and Jesus. Luke, in effect, structured the first two chapters of his Gospel in such a way as to make known the Old Testament anchoring of the Jesus event.[19] The characters surrounding the birth of the Savior are from the purest Jewish tradition: Joseph is from the Davidic line (Luke 1:27); Elizabeth and Zechariah are of priestly descent (Luke 1:5) and faithful observers of the Law (1:8–9, 59); Simeon is a Jew "righteous and devout, looking forward to the consolation of Israel" (2:25); Anna is a prophet from the tribe of Asher (2:36). These characters (with the exception of Joseph of whom Luke tells nothing) recognized, in the birth of the infant, the fulfillment of the announced salvation. Moreover, it is under the inspiration of the Spirit that they do it (this is, however, not explicit in Anna's case):

---

[18] The gift of the Spirit is not, however, the definitive eschatological fulfillment; the kingdom is not yet, as Franklin expresses it, p. 198: ". . . the gift of the Spirit . . . is neither a substitute for, nor an embodiment of the Kingdom, but a pledge of its reality and present existence." Maddox, "The Lukan Eschatology," *The Purpose of Luke-Acts,* p. 137, writes: "Luke clearly regards the coming of the Holy Spirit upon the disciples of Jesus at Pentecost as an 'eschatological' event." Haya-Prats, pp. 63ff., 70 (ET: 60ff.), adheres to Maddox's perspective. For Conzelmann, *Theology of St. Luke,* p. 95, the gift of the Spirit is the beginning of a long epoch, the period of the church, but not an eschatological gift.

[19] On this subject, see Chevallier, *Souffle de Dieu,* p. 163.

- Elizabeth was filled with the Holy Spirit. . . . "And why has this happened to me, that the mother of my Lord comes to me?" (Luke 1:41, 43)

- Zechariah was filled with the Holy Spirit and prophesied in these terms: "Blessed be the Lord God of Israel, for he has looked favorably on his people and redeemed them. He has raised up a mighty savior for us in the house of his servant David." (1:67–69)

- ". . . and the Holy Spirit rested on him [Simeon]. It had been revealed to him by the Holy Spirit that he would not see death before he had seen the Lord's Messiah." (2:25ff.)

- "At that moment she [Anna] came, and began to praise God and to speak about the child to all who were looking for the redemption of Jerusalem." (2:38)

- But, especially, it is under the protection of the Spirit that the child is conceived: "The Holy Spirit will come upon you . . ." (1:35).

- Finally, John the Baptist, the one who will prepare the way in preaching to Israel the baptism of repentance, is "filled with the Holy Spirit in his mother's womb." (1:15)

It is, therefore, the Spirit who verifies the prophetic oracles attesting that Jesus is the promised Savior. It is in the Spirit that the continuity between the Old and the New Testaments is assured.

Luke also insisted on establishing Jesus's ministry in the Spirit. The inaugural events of his public life are marked with the seal of the Spirit:

- He is empowered with the Spirit at baptism (3:22);
- He faces testing in the Spirit (4:1);
- He returns to Galilee in the Spirit (4:14);
- He begins preaching by affirming being anointed of the Spirit (4:18).

Luke thus wanted to show, with great insistence, that the Spirit of God is at the origin of Jesus's mission and that he is the guarantor of his success. One could be astonished, however, that Luke no longer speaks of the Spirit in relation to Jesus's ministry for the remainder of the Gospel.[20]

---

[20] There will still be some mention of the Spirit, but in relation to the formation of the disciples: at their return from mission (Luke 10:21); to speak of the excellent fruit of prayer (11:13); and to exhort the disciples to courageously confess their faith (12:10, 12).

This abstention manifestly aims to respect the autonomy of the central character, Jesus.[21]

It was important, for Luke, to establish the pneumatological anchor of Jesus's mission. But it was just as important to show that, as a free and autonomous man, Jesus corresponded in all ways to God's expectations.

On the other hand, before being lifted up to heaven, the Resurrected One promises his disciples that he will confer power on them (Luke 24:49), that of the Holy Spirit (Acts 1:4–5, 8), in order that they may be *his witnesses* (Acts 1:8), i.e., so that they perpetuate his message. The Spirit is, therefore, the evidence of continuity between Jesus's mission and that of the church,[22] but with the difference, this time, that the Spirit who animates the believers is the very Spirit of Christ (Acts 2:33), the Christianized Spirit poured out at Pentecost (Acts 2:2–4).

Luke had structured, with minute detail, the first two chapters of his gospel in order to mark the continuity between the Old and New Testaments, thus he will do with the first two chapters of Acts. But in Acts, the references to the Spirit are many more numerous than in the gospel (56 mentions as compared to 18). The Spirit intervenes constantly; the community is essentially under his movement. What Luke seeks to convey is clear: *it is the Christ himself who continues to act*.[23] It is he who directs his church and presides over its expansion. From a man of the Spirit during his earthly life, he became Lord of the Spirit in his resurrection.[24]

---

[21] This is the opinion of Chevallier, *Souffle de Dieu*, pp. 171, 215. However, one can ask why the Spirit is not named in Luke 24:49, since it is Jesus himself who must send the power promised by the Father and that consequently, on the contrary, the mention of the Spirit would not affect Jesus's autonomy. It is very likely that Luke simply wanted to orient his reader in this way toward the second volume of his work (see Haya-Prats, p. 245, endnote 2 [ET: 30n2]), where the power thus will be clearly identified with the Spirit (Acts 1:4–5, 8; 2:2–4, 16ff.). His silence, in Luke 24:49, would then be a skillful transition technique.

[22] Pfitzner brings out with great clarity this relation of continuity between Jesus's ministry and that of the disciples through the Spirit in his article "'Pneumatic' Apostleship? Apostle and Spirit in the Acts of the Apostles."

[23] A. Richardson makes this remark that proves to be particularly pertinent in the case of Acts: "NT writers do not attempt to distinguish between the operation of the Risen Christ and the operation of the Holy Spirit. Christ himself comes in the coming of the Holy Spirit" (p. 121).

[24] For this remark, see Dunn, "Spirit, Holy Spirit," p. 698; also Stravinskas, p. 265, who writes: "In Luke's Gospel, Jesus is a man of the Spirit 'par excellence.' After the resurrection, however, he is the Lord of the Spirit as he becomes God's agent in 'unleashing' the Spirit." This vision goes counter to that of Schweizer, "Le Nouveau Testament," p. 143, who considers that Jesus is Lord of the Spirit from his earthly life on.

Thus the Spirit is the principle of unity between the different periods of the history of salvation. And it is in the prophetic tradition that his action[25] is principally exercised: the characters surrounding Jesus's birth pronounce prophetic oracles bringing light to the meaning of the event; Jesus's mission is presented in prophetic terms; the Christians constitute the prophetic community[26] which perpetuates the work of the Christ.[27]

4. THE SPIRIT IN SERVICE OF CHURCH EXPANSION

The last chapter observed the critical importance of the Spirit concerning the expansion of the primitive church. The Spirit is, in Luke's point of view, the essential cause of the propagation of the faith. It is the Spirit who guides the first steps of the Pentecostal community in Jerusalem (Acts 2–7); it is by the initiative of the Spirit that the message is carried into Samaria (Acts 8) and to Cornelius (Acts 10–11); it is again under the impulse of the Holy Spirit that, with Paul and Barnabas, the church opens up to the pagan world, ultimately reaching the heart of the Roman Empire (Acts 13–28).

In spite of its poor numbers, the church experienced prodigious growth. For Luke, the Spirit is the explanation of the phenomenon. He is the agent responsible for the diffusion of the gospel throughout the world. He pursues there where Jesus left. And the believers, through whom he works, are the chosen witnesses to spread the Good News. They hold their letter of credibility from the fact that they were "filled with the Spirit."

It is in effect the characteristic trait of the witnesses to be "full"—the Seven (Acts 6:3); Stephen (6:5; 7:55); Barnabas/Paul (11:24)—or "filled" with the Spirit—Peter (4:8); the community (4:31); Paul/Barnabas (9:17); Paul (13:9), but this gift of the Spirit to believers is essentially in view of ministry. Contrary to what one finds in Paul, Luke does not speak of the Spirit as the cause of spiritual transformation (Rom 8:5) or as the principle of new life in Christ (Rom 8:10–11, 13ff.), but rather as a power enabling the believers to fulfill their prophetic function. In fact, the Spirit, in Luke's perspective, is more functional that relational.

---

[25] This is how George sees it, "L'Esprit Saint dans l'oeuvre de Luc," p. 515; also Gilliéron, p. 125.

[26] Jesus became Lord of the Spirit, which the disciples will never be. As Pfitzner explains, p. 226, "The apostles are not guarantors of the Spirit; they do not have the Spirit at their disposal, but are under the direction of the Spirit."

[27] In this regard Marsh, p. 104, writes: "The Spirit given to and abiding in the Church is a continuation and expansion of the Spirit-filled ministry of Jesus."

It is significant, also, that Luke refers to the text of Joel 2:28ff. to shed light on the event of Pentecost instead of the text of Ezek 36:26–27. Ezekiel's prophecy envisions the gift of the Spirit in view of a spiritual metamorphosis, which would render the human being capable of living according to God's plans.[28] But for Luke, it is in regard to testimony that the Spirit of Pentecost is poured out (Luke 24:49; Acts 1:8). Therefore, it is the vow formulated by Joel that finds its fulfillment. The dimension conveyed by Ezekiel's text cannot, of course, simply be ousted, for the testimony of faith in Christ presupposes conversion. But the Spirit in Acts first generates an enabling power for the prophetic function.

* * *

The predominant trait of the Spirit in Luke's writings is power. He is the source of dynamism that brings God's works to fulfillment. He is, in the Old Testament manner, the constraining force. His modes of intervention are not so different from what can be observed in the Old Testament. Luke's preoccupation was not to develop a pneumatology, but to appeal to the concept of the Spirit for what he already represents in biblical thought (neither did he intend to develop an ecclesiology; it was the expansion of the church that interested him).

However, in conserving the Spirit's Old Testament traits, Acts 2:33, nevertheless, confers to the Spirit a radically new nature. The newness revealed in Acts 2:33 is that the force constituting the lordship of God, i.e., the Spirit, is given in fullness to Jesus Christ, resurrected. Jesus is made Lord of the Spirit and pours him out so that all the believers become in their turn men and women of the Spirit.

Acts 2:33 is the culminating point of Luke's writings. All that is said of Jesus, in the gospel, leads toward it; all that is said of the church, in Acts, flows from it. It is the interpretative axis of Luke's christological and ecclesiological discourse.

---

[28] It is certainly in the line of Ezek 36:26–28 and of Jer 31:31–34 that the Pauline concept of the action of the Spirit in the believer must be considered; the Spirit is the agent of spiritual transformation. In Luke, it is the charismatic dimension that predominates; the manifestations of the Spirit of Pentecost are interpreted in the light of Joel 2:28–32. See Haya-Prats, p. 28 (ET: 10–11).

Bibliography

Adamson, J. *The Epistle of James*. The New International Commentary of the New Testament. Grand Rapids: Eerdmans, 1976.

Adler, N. *Das erste christliche Pfingstfest. Sinn und Bedeutung des Pfingstberichtes Apg 2:1–13*. Münster: Aschendorff, 1938.

Allard, M. "L'annonce à Marie et les annonces de naissances miraculeuses de l'Ancien Testament." *NRTh* 78 (1956): 730–33.

Antoniadis, S. *L'évangile de Luc. Esquisse de grammaire et de style*. Paris: Les Belles Lettres, 1930.

Argyle, A. W. "The Ascension." *ExpTim* 66 (1954–55): 240–42.

Audet, J.-P. "L'annonce à Marie." *RB* 63 (1956): 346–74.

Bachmann, H. *Computer-Konkordanz zum Novum Testamentum Graece*. 3rd ed. Nestle-Aland, 26. Auflage und zum Greek New Testament. Berlin: W. de Gruyter, 1985.

Baer, H. von. *Der Heilige Geist in den Lukasschriften*. Stuttgart: Kohlhammer, 1926.

Barrett, C. K. *A Commentary on the Epistle to the Romans*. Black's New Testament Commentary. London: A. & C. Black, 1957.

———. *Luke the Historian in Recent Study*. London: The Epworth Press, 1961.

———. *The Gospel according to St. John: An Introduction with Commentary and Notes on the Greek Text*. London: SPCK, 1960.

———. *The Holy Spirit and the Gospel Tradition*. 1947. Repr., London: SPCK, 1966.

———. *The Second Epistle to the Corinthians*. Harper's New Testament Commentaries. New York: Harper's & Row, 1972.

Bauer, W., W. Arndt, F. W. Gingrich, and F. W. Danker. *A Greek-English Lexicon of the New Testament and Other Early Christian Literature*. 2nd ed. Chicago, Ill.: University of Chicago, 1979.

Bauernfeind, O. *Die Apostelgeschichte*. Leipzig: A. Deichert, 1939.

———. *Kommentar und Studien zur Apostelgeschichte*. WUNT 22. Tübingen: J. C. B. Mohr, 1980.

Baumgärtel, F. "Esprit dans l'Ancien Testament." Pages 56–72 in *Esprit*. DBGK. Translated by Etienne de Peyer. Edited by Gerhard Kittel. Geneva: Labor et Fides, 1971.

Beasley-Murray. G. R. *Baptism in the New Testament.* London: Macmillan & Co., 1963.
Benoit, P. "L'Annonciation." Pages 197–215 in *Exégèse et théologie.* Vol. 3. Paris: Cerf, 1968.
———. "L'Ascension." Pages 363–416 in *Exégèse et théologie.* Vol. 1. Paris: Cerf, 1961.
Benoit, Pierre, M. E. Boismard, and A. Lamouille. *Synopse des quatre Évangiles en français, avec parallèles des apocryphes et des Pères.* Paris: Editions du Cerf, 1981.
Bertram, G. "Die Himmelfahrt Jesu von Kreuze aus und der Glaube an seine Auferstehung." Pages 187–217 in *Festgabe für Adolf Deissmann zum 60. Geburtstag 7. November 1926.* Edited by K. L. Schmidt, G. A. Deissmann, et al. Tübingen: J.C.B. Mohr (P. Siebeck), 1927.
———. "ὕψιστος." Pages 614–20 in *TDNT*, VIII. Translated by Geoffrey W. Bromiley. Edited by G. Kittel and G. Friedrich. 10 vols. Grand Rapids: Eerdmans, 1964–1976.
Best, E. "Spirit-Baptism." *NovT* 4 (1960): 236–43.
Blass, F., and A. Debrunner. *A Greek Grammar of the New Testament and Other Early Literature.* Chicago: University of Chicago Press, 1961.
Bock, D. L. *Proclamation from Prophecy and Pattern: Lucan Old Testament Christology.* JSOT 12. Sheffield: JSOT Press, 1987.
Boismard, M. E., and A. Lamouille. *Le texte occidental des Actes des Apôtres: reconstitution et réhabilitation.* Paris: Editions Recherche sur les civilisations, 1984.
Bonnard, P. *Épitre de saint Paul aux Philippiens.* Neuchâtel: Delachaux et Niestlé, 1950.
———. "L'Esprit Saint et l'Église selon le Nouveau Testament." *RHPR* 37 (1957): 81–90.
———. *L'Évangile selon saint Matthieu.* 1970. Repr., Geneva: Labor et Fides, 1982.
Boor, W. de. *Die Apostelgeschichte.* Wuppertal: R. Brockhaus, 1965.
Borremans, J. "L'Esprit Saint dans la catéchèse évangélique de Luc." *LumV* 25 (1970): 103–22.
Bovon, F. "Le Saint-Esprit." Pages 211–54 in *Luc le théologien.* Neuchâtel: Delachaux, 1978.
———. "Le Saint-Esprit, l'Église et les relations humaines selon Actes 20:36—21:16." Pages 339–58 in *Les Actes des Apôtres. Traditions, rédaction, théologie.* Edited by J. Kremer. Gembloux: Duculot, 1974.

———. "L'importance des médiations dans le projet théologique de Luc." *NTS* 21 (1974–75): 23–39.

———. *L'œuvre de Luc: Études d'exégèse et de théologie*. Lectio Divina 130. Paris: Cerf, 1987.

———. *Luc le théologien: Vingt-cinq ans de recherches* (1950–75). Neuchâtel: Delachaux, 1978.

Brisbois, M., see Guillemette.

Brown, F., et al. *A Hebrew and English Lexicon of the Old Testament*. 1907. Repr., Oxford: Clarendon Press, 1962.

Brown, R. E. "Gospel Infancy Narrative Research from 1976 to 1986: Part I (Matthew)." *CBQ* 48 (3, 1986): 468–83; "Part II (Luke)." *CBQ* 48 (4, 1986): 660–80.

———. "Luke's Description of the Virginal Conception." *ThSt* 35 (1974): 360–62.

———. "Luke's Method in the Annunciation Narratives of Chapter One." Pages 126–38 in *Perspectives on Luke-Acts*. Edited by C. H. Talbert. Special Studies Series 5. Edinburgh: T. & T. Clark, 1978.

———. *New Testament Essays*. Milwaukee: Impact Books-Bruce Pub. Co., 1965.

———. *The Birth of the Messiah: A Commentary on the Infancy Narratives in Matthew and Luke*. New York: Image Books-Doubleday, 1977.

———. *The Gospel according to John (i–xii), Introduction, Translation and Notes*. The Anchor Bible 29. Garden City, N.Y.: Doubleday & Co., 1966; *xiii–xxi*. The Anchor Bible 29A, 1970.

———. "The Problem of the Virginal Conception of Jesus." *ThSt* 33 (1972): 3–34.

Brown, S. "'Water-Baptism' and 'Spirit-Baptism' in Luke-Acts." *AThR* 59 (1977): 135–51.

Brox, N. *Der Erste Petrusbrief*. EKKNT XXI. Zürich: Benziger/ Neukirchener, 1979.

Bruce, F. F. *The Acts of the Apostles: The Greek Text with Introduction and Commentary*. 1951. Repr., Grand Rapids: Eerdmans, 1986.

———. *The Epistle to the Hebrews: The English Text with Introduction, Exposition and Notes*. The New International Commentary on the New Testament. Grand Rapids: Eerdmans, 1964.

———. "The Holy Spirit in the Acts of the Apostles." *Int* 27 (1973): 166–83.

———. *The Speeches in the Acts of the Apostles*. London: Tyndale, 1943.

Bruner, F. D. *A Theology of the Holy Spirit: The Pentecostal Experience and the New Testament Witness*. Grand Rapids: Eerdmans, 1970.

Buis, P. "Joël annonce l'effusion de l'Esprit." *Spiritus*, 2 (1961): 145–52.

Bultmann, R. *History of the Synoptic Tradition*. 1921. Repr., New York: Harper & Row, 1963.

———. *L'histoire de la tradition synoptique*. 1921. Repr., Paris: Seuil, 1973.

———. *Theology of the New Testament, Vol. 1*. New York: C. Scribner's Sons, 1951.

Bussche, H. van den. *Jean. Commentaire de l'Évangile spirituel*. Bible et Vie chrétienne. Bruges: Desclée de Brouwer, 1967.

Busse, U. *Die Wunder des Propheten Jesus. Die Rezeption, Komposition und Interpretation der Wundertradition im Evangelium des Lukas*. Forschung zur Bibel 24. Stuttgart: Katholischer Bibelwerk, 1979.

Cabie, R. *La Pentecôte. L'évolution de la cinquantaine pascale au cours des cinq premiers siècles*. Tournai: Desclée & Co., 1965.

Cadbury, H. J. *The Making of Luke-Acts*. 1927. Repr., London: SPCK, 1968.

———. "The Speeches in Acts." Pages 402–27 in *The Beginnings of Christianity. Part I: The Acts of the Apostles*. Volume 5. Edited by F. Jackson and K. Lake. London: Macmillan, 1933.

Callan, T. "Psalm 110:1 and the Origin of the Expectation That Jesus Will Come Again." *CBQ* 44 (1982): 622–36.

Cantinat, J. *Les Actes des Apôtres, traduits et commentes*. Tours: Mame, 1966.

———. *Les Épitres de saint Jacques et de saint Jude*. Sources Bibliques. Paris: Gabalda, 1973.

Caquot, A., and M. Philonenko, "Introduction générale." Pages xv–cxli in *La Bible. Écrits intertestamentaires*. Bibliothèque de la Pléiade. Tours: Gallimard, 1987.

Carruth, T. R. "The Jesus-as-Prophet Motif in Luke-Acts," Dissertation, Baylor University, 1973.

Cazelles, H. "L'Esprit de Dieu dans l'Ancien Testament." *QF* 9 (1979): 5–22; cols. 17–43, *Le Mystère de L'Esprit-Saint*. Tours: Mame, 1968.

Cazelles, H., ed. *Introduction à la Bible: Vol. II. Introduction critique à l'Ancien Testament*. Paris: Desclée, 1973.

Cerfaux, L. "Le symbolisme attaché au miracle des langues." Pages 183–87 in *Recueil L. Cerfaux II*. BETL VI–VII. Gembloux: Duculot, 1954.

Ceroke, C. P. "Luke 1:34 and Mary's Virginity." *CBQ* 19 (1957): 329–42.
Charlier, J. P. *L'Évangile de l'enfance de l'Église: Commentaire de Actes 1–2*. Études religieuses 722. Bruxelles: La Pensée Catholique, 1966.
Chevallier, M.-A. *L'Esprit et le Messie dans le bas-judaïsme et le Nouveau Testament*. Paris: Presses Universitaires de France, 1958.
———. "Luc et L'Esprit Saint. À la mémoire du P. Augustin George (1915–1977)." *RSR* 56 (1982): 1–16.
———. *Souffle de Dieu. Le Saint-Esprit dans le Nouveau Testament, Vol. I*. Le Point théologique 26. Paris: Beauchesne, 1978.
Congar, Y. *Je crois en l'Esprit Saint: révélation et expérience de l'Esprit*. Paris: Cerf, 1979.
Conzelmann, H. *Acts of the Apostles*. Hermeneia. 1963. Repr., Philadelphia: Fortress Press, 1987.
———. *An Outline of the Theology of the New Testament*. New York: Harper & Row, 1969.
———. *Théologie du Nouveau Testament*. Nouvelle série théologique 21. Paris: Éditions du Centurion, 1969.
———. *The Theology of Saint Luke*. 1954. Repr., New York: Harper & Row, 1961.
Coppens, J. "L'imposition des mains dans les Actes des Apôtres." Pages 405–38 in *Les Actes des Apôtres. Traditions, rédaction, théologie*. Edited by J. Kremer. Gembloux: Duculot, 1979.
Creed, J. M. *The Gospel according to St. Luke: The Greek Text with Introduction, Notes and Indices*. London: Macmillan and Co., Limited, 1930.
Cripps, R. S. "The Holy Spirit in the Old Testament." *Theol* 24 (1932): 272–80.
Cullmann, O. *Christologie du Nouveau Testament*. 1955. Repr., Neuchâtel: Delachaux et Niestlé, 1966.
———. "La signification du baptême dans le Nouveau Testament." *RTP* 30 (1942): 120–34.
Dahood, M. *Psalms III (101–150): Introduction, Translation and Notes*. The Anchor Bible 17A. Garden City, N.Y.: Doubleday, 1970.
Dalmann, G. *The Words of Jesus*. Edinburgh: Clark, 1909.
Daniélou, J. *Études d'exégèse judéo-chrétienne: Les Testimonia*. Paris: Beauchesne, 1966.
———. *Les évangiles de l'enfance*. Paris: Seuil, 1967.
Danker, F. W. *Jesus and the New Age according to St. Luke: A Commentary on the Third Gospel*. St. Louis: Clayton Publishing House, 1972.
Davies, J. G. "Pentecost and Glossolalia." *JTS* 3 (1952): 228–31.

Delcor, M. "Pentecôte (Fête de la)." *DBSup* 8 (1965): col. 858–79.
Delebecque, E. "Ascension et Pentecôte dans les Actes des Apôtres selon le codex Bezae." *RThom* (1982): 79–89.
———. *Études grecques sur l'Évangile de Luc*. Paris: Belles Lettres, 1976.
———. *Les Actes des Apôtres*. Paris: Société d'édition "Belles Lettres." 1982.
———. *Les deux Actes des Apôtres*. Paris: Gabalda, 1986.
Delobel, J. "La rédaction de Lc., IV, 14–16a et le 'Bericht vom Anfang.'" Pages 203–23 in *L'évangile de Luc. Problèmes littéraires et théologiques. Mémorial Lucien Cerfaux*. Edited by F. Neirynck. Gembloux: J. Duculot, 1973.
Dibelius, M. *Die Werdende Kirche. Eine Einführung in die Apostelgeschichte*. 1951. Repr., Hamburg: Furche-Verlag, 1967.
———. "Jungfrauensohn und Krippenkind. Untersuchung zur Geburtsgeschichte Jesu im Lukasevangelium." Pages 1–78 in *Botschaft und Geschichte: Gesammelte Aufsätze von Martin Dibelius*. Edited by M. Dibelius et al. 1932. Repr., Tübingen: Mohr (Siebeck), 1953.
———. *Studies in the Acts of the Apostles*. German, 1951. ET: London: SCM Press, 1956.
Dillon, R. J. *From Eye-Witnesses to Ministers of the Word: Tradition and Composition in Luke 24*. Analecta Biblica 22. Rome: Biblical Institute Press, 1978.
Dillon, R. J., and J. A. Fitzmyer. "Acts of the Apostles." Pages 165–214 in *The Jerome Biblical Commentary: Vol. II*. Edited by R. E. Brown et al. Englewood Cliffs: Prentice-Hall, 1968.
Dodd, C. H. *The Apostolic Preaching and Its Developments*. 1936. Repr., London: Hodder & Stoughton, 1963.
———. *The Interpretation of the Fourth Gospel*. London: Cambridge University Press, 1965.
Dömer, M. *Das Heil Gottes. Studien zur Theologie des lukanischen Doppelwerkes*. Bonner Biblische Beiträge 51. Bonn: P. Hanstein Verlag, 1978.
Dumais, M. *L'actualisation du Nouveau Testament*. Lectio Divina 107. Paris: Cerf, 1982.
———. *Le langage de l'évangélisation. L'annonce missionnaire en milieu juif (Actes 13:16–41)*. Montreal: Bellarmin, 1976.

Dunn, J. D. G. *Baptism in the Holy Spirit. A Re-examination of the New Testament Teaching on the Gift of the Spirit in Relation to Pentecostalism Today*. 1970. Repr., London: SCM Press, 1973.

———. *Christology in the Making. A New Testament Inquiry into the Origins of the Doctrine of the Incarnation*. Philadelphia: Westminster Press, 1980.

———. "Feast of Pentecost." Pages 783–88 in *The New International Dictionary of New Testament Theology*. Vol. 2. Edited by C. Brown. German, 1967. ET: Grand Rapids: Zondervan, 1980.

———. *Jesus and the Spirit. A Study of the Religious and Charismatic Experience of Jesus and the First Christians as Reflected in the New Testament*. London: SCM Press, 1975.

———. "Jesus, Flesh and Spirit: An Exposition of Romans 1:3–4." *JTS* 24 (1973): 41–68.

———. "Spirit, Holy Spirit." Pages 693–707 in *The New International Dictionary of New Testament Theology*. Vol. 3. Edited by C. Brown. German, 1967. ET: Grand Rapids: Zondervan, 1976.

Dupont, J. *Nouvelles études sur les Actes des Apôtres*. Lectio Divina 118. Paris: Cerf, 1984.

———. *Études sur les Actes des Apôtres*. Lectio Divina 45. Paris: Cerf, 1967.

———. "Jésus Fils de Dieu dans l'évangile selon saint Luc." *RB* 72 (1965): 185–209.

———. "La nouvelle Pentecôte (Ac 2:1–11)." *AsSeign* 30 (1970): 30–34.

———. "La première Pentecôte chrétienne." *AsSeign* 51 (1963): 39–62.

———. "Les tentations de Jésus dans le récit de Luc (Lc 4:1–13)." *ScEs* 14 (1962): 7–29.

Dupont-Sommer, A., M. Philonenko, A. Caquot, and J.-M. Rosenstiehl. *La Bible. Écrits intertestamentaires*. Bibliothèque de la Pléiade. Paris: Gallimard, 1987.

Ellis, E. E. *The Gospel of Luke*. Century Bible. London: T. Nelson & Sons, 1966.

Enslin, M. S. "The Ascension Story." *JBL* (1928): 64–66.

Epp, E. J. "The Ascension in the Textual Tradition of Luke-Acts." Pages 131–45 in *New Testament Textual Criticism: Its Significance for Exegesis. Essays in Honour of Bruce M. Metzger*. Edited by E. J. Epp and G. D. Fee. Oxford: Clarendon Press, 1981.

Ernst, Josef. *Das Evangelium nach Lukas*. Regensburg: Friedrich Pustet, 1977.

Evan, C. F. "Speeches in Acts." Pages 287–302 in *Mélanges bibliques en hommage au R. P. Beda Rigaux*. Edited by A. Descamps, et al. Gembloux: Duculot, 1970.

Feuillet, A. *Jésus et sa mere d'après les récits lucaniens de l'Enfance et d'après saint Jean*. Paris: Gabalda, 1973.

———. "Le baptême de Jésus." *RB* (1964): 321–52.

———. "Le récit lucanien de la tentation (Lc 4:1–13)." *Bib* 40 (1959): 613–31.

Fitzmyer, J. A. "David, 'being therefore a prophet . . .'" (Acts 2:30)" *CBQ* 34 (1972): 232–39.

———. "The Ascension of Christ and Pentecost." *ThSt* 45 (1984): 409–40.

———. "The Contribution of Qumran Aramaic to the Study of the New Testament." *NTS* 20 (1973–74): 382–407.

———. *The Gospel according to Luke (I–IX)*. The Anchor Bible 28. 1981. Repr., Garden City, N.Y.: Doubleday & Co., 1985.

———. *The Gospel according to Luke (X–XXIV)*. The Anchor Bible 28A. Garden City, N.Y.: Doubleday & Co., 1985.

———. "The Virginal Conception of Jesus in the New Testament." *ThSt* 34 (1973): 541–75.

Flender, H. *St. Luke Theologian of Redemptive History*. 1965. Repr., London: SPCK, 1967.

Franklin, E. *Christ the Lord: A Study in the Purpose and Theology of Luke-Acts*. Philadelphia: Westminster Press, 1975.

———. "The Ascension and Eschatology of Luke-Acts." *SJT* 23 (1970): 191–200.

Fuller, R. H. *The Foundations of New Testament Christology*. New York: Scribner, 1965.

———. *The Formation of the Resurrection Narratives*. New York: Macmillan, 1971: 94–130.

Furnish, V. H. *II Corinthians*. The Anchor Bible 32A. Garden City, N.Y.: Doubleday & Co., 1985.

Gaechter, P. "Der Verkündigungsbericht Lk 1:26–38." *ZKT* 91 (1969): 322–63; 567–86.

———. *Maria im Erdenleben. Neutestamentliche Marienstudien*. Innsbruck: Tyrolia, 1953.

Geldenhuys, N. *Commentary on the Gospel of Luke*. 1950. Repr., London: Marshall, Morgan & Scott, 1961.

Gelin, A. "L'Annonce de la Pentecôte (Joël 3:1–5)" *BVC* 27 (1959): 15–19.

George, A. *Études sur l'œuvre de Luc*. Paris: Gabalda, 1978.

———. "L'Esprit Saint dans l'œuvre de Luc." *RB* 85 (1979): 500–42.

———. "Note sur quelques traits lucaniens de l'expression 'par le doigt de Dieu.'" *ScEccl* 18 (1966): 461–66.

Geweiss, J. "Die Marienfrage Lk 1:34." *BZ* 5 (1961): 221–54.

Giblet, C. J. "Baptism in the Spirit in the Acts of the Apostles." *OiC* 10 (1974): 162–71.

Gillièron, B. *Le Saint-Esprit. Actualité du Christ*. Essais Bibliques 1. Geneva: Labor et Fides, 1978.

Gilmour, S. M. "Easter and Pentecost." *JBL* 81 (1962): 62–66.

Gils, F. *Jésus Prophète d'après les évangiles synoptiques*. Louvain: Publications Universitaires, 1957.

Goguel, M. *La naissance du christianisme*. Paris: Payot, 1946.

Gourgues, M. *À la droite de Dieu. Résurrection de Jésus et actualization du Psaume 110:1 dans le Nouveau Testament*. Paris: Gabalda, 1978.

———. "'Exalté à la droite de Dieu' (Ac 2:33; 5:31)" *ScEs* 27 (1975): 303–27.

———. "Lecture christologique du psaume CX et fête de la Pentecôte." *RB* 83 (1976): 5–24.

Graystone, G. *Virgin of All Virgins: The Interpretation of Luke 1:34*. Rome: Pontifical Biblical Commission, 1968.

Grelot, P. "La naissance d'Isaac et celle de Jésus. Sur une interprétation 'mythologique' de la conception virginale." *NRTh* 94 (1972): 462–87; 561–85.

———. *L'Espérance juive à l'Heure de Jésus*. JJC 62. Paris: Desclée, 1978.

Grundmann, W. *Das Evangelium nach Lukas*. THKNT 3. 1934. Repr., Berlin: Evangelische Verlagsanstalt, 1971.

———. *Das Evangelium nach Matthäus*. THKNT 1. 1968. Repr., Berlin: Evangelishe Verlagsanstalt, 1971.

———. "Der Pfingsbericht der Apostelgeschichte in seinem theologischen Sinn." Pages 584–94 in *Studia Evangelica*. Vol. II. Edited by F. L. Cross. Berlin: Akademie-Verlag, 1964.

———. "δεξιός." Pages 37–40 in *TDNT*, II. Translated by Geoffrey W. Bromiley. Edited by G. Kittel and G. Friedrich. 10 vols. Grand Rapids: Eerdmans, 1964–1976.

———. "δύναμις." Pages 284–317 in *TDNT*, II. Translated by Geoffrey W. Bromiley. Edited by G. Kittel and G. Friedrich. 10 vols. Grand Rapids: Eerdmans, 1964–1976.

Guillaume, J. M. *Luc interprète des anciennes traditions sur la résurrection de Jésus.* Paris: Gabalda, 1979.

Guillemette, P. *The Greek New Testament Analysed.* Kitchener, Ont.: Herald Press, 1986.

Guillemette, P., and M. Brisebois. *Introduction aux méthods historico-critiques.* Héritage et Project 35. Montreal: Fides, 1987.

Guillet, J. *Thèmes bibliques. Études sur l'expression et le développement de la Révélation.* Théologie 18. Paris: Aubier, 1954.

———. "Saint Esprit—Luc—Actes des Apôtres." *DBSup* 60 (1986): 179–92.

Haenchen, E. *The Acts of the Apostle: A Commentary.* Translated by Bernard Noble et al. 1965. Repr., Oxford: Basil Blackwell, 1971.

Hahn, F. *The Titles of Jesus in Christology: Their History in Early Christianity.* London: Lutterworth Press, 1969.

Hanna, R. *A Grammatical Aid to the Greek New Testament.* Grand Rapids: Baker Book House, 1985.

Hanson, R. C. P. *The Acts.* Oxford: Clarendon Press, 1967.

Harnack, A. von. *Luke the Physician.* London: William & Norgate, 1907.

———. "Zu Lk 1:34–35." *ZNW* 2 (1901): 53–57.

Haroutunian, J. "The Doctrine of the Ascension: A Study of the New Testament Teaching." *Int* 10 (1956): 270–81.

Hastings, A. *Prophet and Witness in Jerusalem: A Study in the Teaching of St. Luke.* London: Longmans, Green, 1958.

Haulotte, E. "L'Esprit de Yahvé dans l'Ancien Testament." Pages 25–36 in *L'homme devant Dieu. Mélanges offerts au Père Henri de Lubac.* Théologie 56. Edited by J. Guillet et al. Paris: Aubier, 1963.

———. "L'impact du baptême de Jean sur la vie de l'Église primitive selon les Actes des Apôtres." *FoiVie* 68 (1969): 56–67.

Havener, I., and A. Polag. *Q, the Sayings of Jesus.* Wilmington, Del: M. Glazier, 1987.

Hay, D. M. *Glory at the Right Hand: Psalm 110 in Early Christianity.* Society of Biblical Literature Monograph Series 18. Nashville: Abingdon Press, 1973.

Haya-Prats, G. *L'Esprit force de l'Église. Sa nature et son activité d'après les Actes des Apôtres.* Lectio Divina 81. Paris: Cerf, 1975. ET: *Empowered Believers: The Holy Spirit in the Book of Acts.* Translated by Scott A. Ellington. Edited by Paul Elbert. Eugene, Oreg.: Cascade Books-Wipf and Stock Publishers, 2011.

Hayes, J. H. "The Resurrection as Enthronement and the Earliest Church Christology." *Int* 22 (1968): 333–45.

Hendriksen, W. *New Testament Commentary: Exposition of the Gospel according to Luke*. Grand Rapids: Baker Book House, 1978.

Heron, A. I. C. *The Holy Spirit: The Holy Spirit in the Bible, the History of Christian Thought and Recent Theology*. Philadelphia: Westminster Press, 1983.

Heuthorst, G. "The Apologetic Aspect of Acts 2:1–13." *Scr* 9 (1957): 33–43.

Hilgenfeld, A. "Die Geburt-und Kindheitsgeschichte Jesu." *ZWT* 40 (1901): 177–235.

Hill, D. *New Testament Prophecy*. Atlanta: John Knox Press, 1979.

———. "The Spirit and the Church's Witness: Observations on Acts 1:6–8." *IBS* 6 (1, 1984): 16–26.

Hillmann, J. "Die Kindheitsgeschichte nach Lukas." *JPT* 16 (1891): 213–31.

Hoffmann, P. *Studien zur Theologie der Logienquelle*. Münster: Verlag Aschendorff, 1972.

Hooke, S. H. "'The Spirit was not yet.'" *NTS* 9.4 (1962–63): 372–80.

Hruby, K. "La fête de la Pentecôte dans la tradition juive." *BVC* 63 (1965): 46–64.

Hughes, P. E. *Paul's Second Epistle to the Corinthians*. The New London Commentary on the New Testament. London: Marshall, Morgan & Scott, 1962.

Hull, J. H. E. *The Holy Spirit in the Acts of the Apostles*. Cleveland: The World Publishing Co., 1967.

Hutton, W. R. "Considerations for the Translation of Greek *en*." *BT*, 9 (1958): 163–70.

Imschoot, P. van. "Baptême d'eau et baptême d'Esprit Saint." *ETL* 13 (1936): 653–66.

———. "L'action de l'Esprit de Yahvé dans l'Ancien Testament." *RSPT* 23 (1934): 553–87.

———. *Théologie de l'Ancien Testament; Tome 1, Dieu*. Tournai: Desclée & Cie, 1956.

Jackson, F. J. F., and K. Lake, eds. *The Beginnings of Christianity. Part I: The Acts of the Apostles*. 5 volumes. London: Macmillan, 1933.

Jacob, E. *Théologie de l'Ancien Testament*. Neuchâtel: Delachaux & Niestlé, 1955.

Jaubert, A. *La notion d'Alliance dans le judaïsme aux abords de l'ère chrétienne*. Patristica Sorbonensia 6. Paris: Éditions du Seuil, 1963.

Jeremias, J. *Die Sprache des Lukasevangeliums. Redaktion und Tradition im Nicht-Markusstoff des dritten Evangeliums*. Göttingen: Vandenhoeck & Ruprecht, 1980.

———. *New Testament Theology: The Proclamation of Jesus*. Translated by John Bowden. London: SCM Press, 1971.

Jervell, J. *The Unknown Paul: Essays on Luke-Acts and Early Christian History*. Minneapolis: Augsburg 1984.

Jones, D. L. "The Title 'Christos' in Luke-Acts." *CBQ* 32 (1970): 69–76.

Juel, D. "Social Dimensions of Exegesis: The Use of Psalm 16 in Acts 2." *CBQ* 43 (1981): 543–56.

———. *Luc-Actes. La promesse de l'histoire*. 1983. Repr., Lire la Bible 80. Paris: Cerf, 1987.

Käsemann, E. *Commentary on Romans*. London: SCM Press, 1980.

———. "The Problem of the Historical Jesus." *Essays on New Testament Themes*. 1960. Repr., London: SCM Press, 1964.

Kern, W. "Das Fortgehen Jesu und das Kommen des Geistes oder Christi Himmelfahrt." *GL* 41 (1968): 85–90.

Kèrrigan, A. "The 'Sensus Plenior' of Joel III,1–5 in Act. II,14–36." Pages 295–313 in *Sacra Pagina: Miscellanea Biblica Congressus Internationalis Catholici De Re Biblica*. Edited by J. Coppens. Gembloux: J. Duculot, 1959.

Kittel, G., and G. Friedrich, eds. *Theological Dictionary of the New Testament*. Translated by G. W. Bromiley. 10 vols. Grand Rapids: Eerdmans, 1964–1976.

Kleinknecht, H. "Pneuma en Grec." Pages 7–55 in *Esprit*. DBGK. Translated by d'Etienne de Peyer. Edited by Gerhard Kittel. Geneva: Labor et Fides, 1971.

Kloppenborg, J. S. *The Formation of Q*. Studies in Antiquity & Christianity. Philadelphia: Fortress Press, 1987.

Knox, W. L. *The Acts of the Apostles*. Cambridge: Cambridge University Press, 1948.

Kremer, J. "Die Voraussagen des Pfingstgeschehens in Apg 1:4–5 und 8." Pages 145–68 in *Die Zeit Jesu. Festschrift für Heinrich Schlier*. Edited by G. Bornkamm & K. Rahner. Freiburg: Herder, 1970.

———. *Les Actes des Apôtres. Traditions, rédaction, théologie*. BETL 48. Louvain: Gembloux Duculot, 1979.

———. *Pfingstbericht und Pfingstgeschehen. Eine exegetische Untersuchung zu Apg 2:1–13*. Stuttgarter Bibelstudien 63/64. Stuttgart: KBW Verlag, 1973.

———. "Was geschah Pfingsten? Zur Historizität des Apg 2:1–13 berichteten Pfingstereignisses." *WuW* III (1973): 195–207.

Kretschmar, G. "Himmelfahrt und Pfingsten." *ZKG* 66 (1954–55): 209–53.

La Potterie, I. de. "L'Onction du Christ." *NRTh* 80 (1958): 225–52.

Ladd, G. E. *A Theology of the New Testament*. London: Lutterworth Press, 1975.

Lagrange, M.-J. *Évangile selon saint Luc*. 1921. Repr., Paris: Gabalda, 1948.

———. *Évangile selon saint Matthieu*. 1922. Repr., Paris: Gabalda, 1948.

Lampe, G. W. H. "Acts." Pages 882–926 in *Peake's Commentary on the Bible*. Edinburgh: T. Nelson & Sons, 1962.

———. "Luke." Pages 820–43 in *Peake's Commentary on the Bible*. Edinburgh: T. Nelson & Sons, 1962.

———. "The Holy Spirit in the Writings of St. Luke." Pages 159–200 in *Studies in the Gospels. Essays in Memory of R. H. Lightfoot*. Edited by D. E. Nineham. Oxford: B. Blackwell, 1957.

———. "The Lucan Portrait of Christ." *NTS* 2 (1956): 160–75.

Lang, F. "πῦρ." Pages 928–48 in *TDNT*, VI. Translated by Geoffrey W. Bromiley. Edited by G. Kittel and G. Friedrich. 10 vols. Grand Rapids: Eerdmans, 1964–1976.

Larranaga, V. *L'Ascension de Notre-Seigneur dans le Nouveau Testament*. Scripta Pontificii Instituti Biblici. Rome: Biblical Institute, 1938.

Laurentin, R. *Les évangiles de l'enfance du Christ: vérité de Noël au-delà des mythes; exégèse et sémiotique, historicité et théologie*. Paris: Desclée de Brouwer, 1982.

———. *Structure et théologie de Luc 1–11*. Paris: Gabalda, 1957.

———. "Traces d'allusions étymologiques en Luc 1–2." *Bib* 37 (1956): 435–56.

Lavallée, F. *L'Esprit Saint et l'Église: Une analyse des Actes des Apôtres pour aujourd'hui*. Montreal: Éditions Paulines, 1987.

Le Deaut, R. "Pentecôte et tradition juive." *Spiritus* 2 (1961): 127–44.

Leany, A. R. C. *A Commentary on the Gospel according to St. Luke*. 1959. Repr., London: A. & C. Black, 1966.

———. "The Birth Narratives in St. Luke and St. Matthew." *NTS* 8 (1961–1962): 158–66.

Leenhardt, F. J. *L'épitre de saint Paul aux Romains*. Commentaire du Nouveau Testament. 2nd ed. Vol. 6. Geneva: Labor et Fides, 1981.

Legault, A. "Le baptême de Jésus et la doctrine du Serviteur souffrant." *ScEccl* 30 (1961): 147–166.

Legrand, L. "Fécondité virginale selon l'Esprit dans le Nouveau Testament." *NRTh* 84 (1962): 785–805.

———. *L'Annonce à Marie*. Lectio Divina 106. Paris: Cerf, 1981.

———. "L'arrière-plan néo-testamentaire de Luc 1:35." *RB* 70 (1963): 161–92.

Lentzen-Deis, F. *Die Taufe Jesu nach den Synoptikern, Literarkritische und gattungsgeschichtliche Untersuchungen*. Frankfurt: J. Knecht, 1970.

L'Eplattenier, C. *Les Actes des Apôtres*. Geneva: Labor et Fides, 1987.

Leuba, J. L. "Le rapport entre l'Esprit et la Tradition selon le Nouveau Testament." *VCaro* 50 (1959): 133–150.

Lindars, B. *New Testament Apologetic: The Doctrinal Significance of the Old Testament Quotations*. Philadelphia: Westminster Press, 1961.

Loader, W. R. G. "Christ at the Right Hand—Ps CX.1 in the New Testament." *NTS* 24 (1977/78): 199–217.

Lohfink, G. *Die Himmelfahrt Jesu: Erfindung oder Erfahrung*. Stuttgart: KBW Verlag, 1972.

———. *Die Himmelfahrt Jesu: Untersuchungen zu den Himmelfahrts-und Erhöhungstexten bei Lukas*. SANT 26. Munich: Kösel, 1971.

———. *La Conversion de saint Paul, démonstration de la méthode récente des sciences bibliques à propos des textes (Actes 9, 1-19; 22, 2-21; 28, 9-18)*. Paris: Cerf, 1967.

Lohse, E. "Die Bedeutung des Pfingstberichtes im Rahmen des lukanischen Geschichtswerk." *EvT* 13 (1953): 422–36.

———. "Lukas Theologe der Heilsgeschichte." *EvT* 14 (1954): 256–75.

———. "πεντηκοστή." Pages 44–53 in *TDNT*, VI. Translated by Geoffrey W. Bromiley. Edited by G. Kittel and G. Friedrich. 10 vols. Grand Rapids: Eerdmans, 1964–1976.

Loisy, A. *L'Évangile selon Luc*. Paris: Minerva, 1924.

———. *Les Actes des Apôtres*. Paris: Minerva, 1915.

Lyonnet, S. "L'Annonciation et la mariologie biblique: ce que l'exégèse conclut du récit lucanien de l'Annonciation." Pages 59–72 in *Maria in Sacra Scriptura*, IV, *Acta Congressus Mariologici-Mariani in Republica Dominicana anno 1965 Celebrati*. Rome: Pontificia Academia Mariana Internationalis, 1967.

———. "Le récit de l'Annonciation et la Maternité divine de la Sainte Vierge." *Ami du Clergé* 66 (1956): 33–48.

Lys, D. *"Rûach": le Souffle dans l'Ancien Testament*. Paris: Presses Universitaires de France, 1962.

Machen, J. G. "The Origin of the First Two Chapters of Luke." *PTR* 10 (1912): 212–77.

———. "The Hymns of the First Chapter of Luke," *PTR* 10 (1912): 1–38.

Maddox, R. L. *The Purpose of Luke-Acts*. Edinburgh: Clark, 1982.

Maertens, T. *Le soufflé et l'esprit de Dieu*. Bruges: Desclée de Brouwer, 1959.

Mann, C. S. "Pentecost in Acts." Pages 271–75 (Appendice III) in J. Munck, *The Acts of the Apostles. A New Translation with Introduction and Commentary*. The Anchor Bible 31. 1967. Repr., Garden City: Doubleday, 1978.

Manson, W. *The Gospel of Luke*. Moffatt New Testament Commentary. 1930. Repr., New York: R. R. Smith, 1963.

Marsh, T. "Holy Spirit in Early Christian Teaching." *ITQ* 45 (1978): 101–16.

Marshall, A. *The Interlinear Greek-English New Testament*. Grand Rapids: Zondervan, 1975.

Marshall, I. H. *Luke: Historian and Theologian*. 1970. Repr., Grand Rapids: Zondervan, 1976.

———. *The Acts of the Apostles: An Introduction and Commentary*. 1980. Repr., Grand Rapids: Eerdmans, 1984.

———. *The Gospel of Luke: A Commentary on the Greek Text*. New International Greek Testament Commentary. Grand Rapids: Eerdmans, 1986.

———. "The Significance of Pentecost." *SJT* 30 (1977): 347–69.

Martin, A. D. "The Ascension of Christ," *Exp* 16 (1918): 321–46.

McHugh, J. *The Mother of Jesus in the New Testament*. Garden City, N.Y.: Doubleday & Co., 1975.

McPolin, J. "Holy Spirit in Luke and John." *ITQ* 45 (1978): 117–31.

Ménard, J. E. "'Pais Theou' as Messianic Title in the Book of Acts." *CBQ* 19 (1957): 83–92.

Menoud, P. H. *Jésus-Christ et la foi: recherches néotestamentaires*. Paris: Delachaux & Niestlé, 1975.

Metzger, B. M. *A Textual Commentary on the Greek New Testament: A Companion Volume to the United Bible Societies Greek New Testament*. 3rd ed. London: United Bible Societies, 1971.

———. *Historical and Literary Studies: Pagan, Jewish, and Christian*. NTTS 8. Grand Rapids: Eerdmans, 1968: 77–81.

———. *The Text of the New Testament: Its Transmission, Corruption, and Restoration*. New York: Oxford University Press, 1964.

Michaeli, F. *Les livres des Chroniques, d'Esdras et de Néhémie*. Commentaire de l'Ancien Testament XVI. Paris: Delachaux & Niestlé, 1967.
Milik, J. T. *Ten Years of Discovery in the Wilderness of Judaea*. Naperville: Allenson, 1959.
Minear, P. S. "Luke's Use of the Birth Stories." Pages 111–30 in *Studies in Luke-Acts*. Edited by L. E. Keck and J. L. Martyn. Nashville: Abingdon Press, 1966.
———. "The Interpreter and the Nativity Stories." *ThTo* 7 (1950): 358–75.
———. *To Heal and to Reveal: The Prophetic Vocation according to Luke*. New York: The Seabury Press, 1976.
Mitton, C. L. *The Epistle of James*. London: Marshall, Morgan & Scott, 1966.
Mollat, D. "The Role of Experience in the New Testament Teaching on Baptism and the Coming of the Holy Spirit." *OiC* 10 (1974): 129–47.
Montague, G. T. *The Holy Spirit: Growth of a Biblical Tradition*. New York: Paulist Press, 1976.
Moule, C. F. D. "The Ascension—Ac i. 9." *ExpTim* 68 (1956–57): 205–09.
Müller, P. G. *Lukas-Evangelium*. Stuttgarter Kleiner Kommentar Neues Testament 3. 1984. Repr., Stuttgart: Verlag Katholisches Bibelwerk, 1986.
Munck, J. *The Acts of the Apostles*. The Anchor Bible 31. Garden City, N.Y.: Doubleday & Co., 1967.
Murphy-O'Connor, J. "Christological Anthropology in Phil. 2:6–11." *RB* 83 (1976): 25–50.
Murray, J. *The Epistle to the Romans: The English Text with Introduction, Exposition and Notes*. New London Commentary on the New Testament. London: Marshall, Morgan and Scott, 1967.
Mussner, F. *Apostelgeschichte*. Würzburg: Echter-Verlag, 1984.
———. "'In den lezten Tagen' (Apg 2:17a)." *BZ* 5 (1961): 263–65.
Myre, A. *Un souffle subversif. L'Esprit dans les lettres pauliniennes*. Recherches nouvelle série 12. Montreal: Bellarmin, 1987.
Neher, A. *L'essence du prophétisme*. 1955. Repr., Paris: Calmann-Levy, 1972.
Neil, W. *The Acts of the Apostles*. New Century Bible Commentary. 1973. Repr., Grand Rapids: Eerdmans, 1981.
Neirynck, F., ed. *L'Évangile de Luc. Problèmes littéraires et théologiques. Mémorial Lucien Cerfaux*. BETL 32. Gembloux: Duculot, 1973.

———. "The Miracle Stories in the Acts of the Apostles. An Introduction." Pages 169–213 in *Les Actes des Apôtres: Traditions, rédaction, théologie*. Edited by J. Kremer. Louvain: Gembloux, Duculot, 1979.

Nestle, E., and K. Aland. *Novum Testamentum Graece*. Stuttgart: Deutsche Bibelgesellschaft, 1985.

Neve, L. *The Spirit of God in the Old Testament*. Tokyo: Seibunsha, 1972.

Oliver, H. H. "The Lucan Birth Stories and the Purpose of Luke-Acts." *NTS* 10 (1963–1964): 202–26.

O'Reilly, L. *Word and Sign in the Acts of the Apostles: A Study in Lucan Theology*. Rome: Editrice Pontificia Università Gregoriana, 1987.

Osty, E., and J. Trinquet. *La Bible. Le livre des Psaumes*. Paris: Éd. Rencontres, 1971.

O'Toole, R. F. "Acts 2:30 and the Davidic Covenant of Pentecost." *JBL* 102.2 (1983): 245–58.

Packer, J. W. *The Acts of the Apostles*. Cambridge Bible Commentary. Cambridge: Cambridge University Press, 1966.

Parent, R. *L'Esprit vous rendra libres en ces temps de Pentecôte*. Foi et liberté. Montreal: Fides, 1974.

Parratt, J. K. "The Holy Spirit and Baptism." *ExpTim* 82 (1971): 266–71.

Parsons, M. C. *The Departure of Jesus in Luke-Acts: The Ascension Narratives in Context*. Sheffield: JSOT, 1987.

———. "The Text of Acts 1:2 Reconsidered." *CBQ* 50 (1988): 58–71.

Paul, A. *Intertestament*. CE 14. Paris: Cerf, 1975.

Perkin, N. "Mark xiv.62: The End Product of Christian Pesher Tradition?" *NTS* 12 (1965–66): 150–55.

Perrot, C. *Les récits de l'enfance de Jésus. Matthieu 1–2—Luc 1–2*. CE 18. Paris: Cerf, 1976.

———. "Les récits d'enfance dans la Haggada antérieure au 2e s. de notre ère." *RevScRel* (1967): 481–518.

Pesch, R. *Die Apostelgeschichte, Volume I, Apg 1–12; Volume II, Apg 13–28*. EKKNT. Zürich: Benziger Verlag, 1986.

Pfitzner, V. C. "'Pneumatic' Apostleship? Apostle and Spirit in the Acts of the Apostles." Pages 210–35 in *Wort in der Zeit*. Edited by W. Haubeck and M. Bachmann. Leiden: Brill, 1980.

Plummer, A. *The Gospel according to S. Luke*. 1896. Repr., Edinburgh: Clark, 1960.

Potin, J. *La fête juive de la Pentecôte: Étude des text liturgiques*. Lectio Divina 65. Paris: Cerf, 1971.

Quesnel, M. *Baptisés dans l'Esprit. Baptême et Esprit Saint dans les Actes des Apôtres*. Lectio Divina 120. Paris: Cerf, 1985.
Rahlfs, A., ed. *Septuaginta*. 1935. Repr., Stuttgart: Deutsche Bibelgesellschaft, 1979.
Ramsey, M. *Holy Spirit: A Biblical Study*. London: SPCK, 1977.
Reiling, J., and J. L. Swellengrebel. *A Translator's Handbook on the Gospel of Luke*. Leiden: Brill, 1971.
Rengstorf, K. H. "ἀποστέλλω." Pages 398–447 in *TDNT*, I. Translated by Geoffrey W. Bromiley. Edited by G. Kittel and G. Friedrich. 10 vols. Grand Rapids: Eerdmans, 1964–1976.
Rese, M. "Die Aussagen über Jesu Tod und Auferstehung in der Apostelgeschichte. Ältestes Kerygma oder lukanische Theologumena?" *NTS* 30 (1984): 335–53.
Richard, J. "Conçu de Saint-Esprit, né de la Vierge Marie." *ET* 10 (1979): 291–321.
Richardson, A. *An Introduction to the Theology of the New Testament*. London: SCM Press, 1958.
Richardson, N. *The Panorama of Luke: An Introduction to the Gospel of Luke and the Acts of the Apostles*. London: Epworth Press, 1982.
Rigaux, B. *Témoignage de l'évangile de Luc*. Bruges: Desclée de Brouwer, 1970.
Roloff, J. *Die Apostelgeschichte*. Das Neue Testament Deutsch 5. Göttingen: Vandenhoeck & Ruprecht, 1981.
Sabourin, L. *L'Évangile de Luc. Introduction et commentaire*. Rome: Editrice Pontificia Università Gregoriana, 1985.
Sahlin, H. *Der Messias und das Gottesvolk. Studien zur protolukanischen Theologie*. Uppsala: Almquist, 1945.
Samain, E. "Le récit de la Pentecôte, Ac 2:1–13." *La foi et le temps* 1 (1971): 227–56.
———. "Le discours-programme de Jésus à la synagogue de Nazareth. Luc 4:16–30." *FoiVie* (11, 1971): 25–43.
Sanders, J. A. *The Psalms Scroll of Qumrân Cave 11 (11 Q Ps^a)*. Oxford: Clarendon, 1965.
Sauvagnat, B. "Se repentir, être baptisé, recevoir l'Esprit. Actes 2:37ff." *FoiVie* 80 (1981): 77–89.
Schedl, C. *Als sich der Pfingsttag erfüllte. Erklärung der Pfingstperikope Apg 2:1–47*. Wien: Herder, 1982.
Schelkle, K. H. "Christi Himmelfahrt." *GL* 41 (1968): 81–85.

Schenk, W. *Synopose zur Redenquelle der Evangelium. Q-Synopse und Rekonstruction in deutschen Übersetzung mit kurzen Erläuterungen.* Düsseldorf: Patmos Verlag, 1981.

Schille, G. *Die Apostelgeschichte des Lukas.* Berlin: Evangelische Verlasganstalt, 1983.

———. "Die Himmelfahrt." *ZNW* 57 (1966): 183–99.

Schillebeeckx, E. "Ascension and Pentecost." *Worship* 35 (1960–61): 336–63.

Schlier, H. "Jesu Himmelfahrt nach den lukanischen Schriften." *GL* 34 (1961): 91–99.

Schmithals, W. *Das Evangelium nach Lukas.* Züricher Bibelkommentare NT 3/1. Zürich: Theologischer Verlag, 1980.

———. *Die Apostelgeschichte des Lukas.* Züricher Bibelkommentare NT 3/2. Zürich: Theologischer Verlag, 1982.

Schmitt, A. "Ps 16:8–11 als Zeugnis des Auferstehung in der Apg." *BZ* 17 (1973): 229–48.

Schmitt, J. "La prédication apostolique. Les formes, le contenu." Pages 107–33 in *Où en sont les études bibliques? Les grands problèmes actuels de l'exégèse.* Edited by J. J. Weber and J. Schmitt. Paris: Centurion, 1968.

———. "Le milieu baptiste de Jean le Précurseur." *RSR* 47 (1973): 391–404.

———. "Les discours missionnaires des Actes et l'histoire des traditions prépauliniennes." *RSR* 69 (1981): 165–80.

Schnackenburg, R. *Der Brief an die Epheser.* EKKNT. Neukirchen: Neukirchener Verlag, 1982.

———. *The Gospel according to St. John, Volume 1.* New York: Herder & Herder, 1968.

Schneider, G. *Das Evangelium nach Lukas: Kapitel 1–10.* Würzburg: Echter-Verlag, 1977.

———. *Die Apostelgeschichte: Teil 1, 1:1–8:40.* Freiburg: Herder, 1980; *Volume 2, 9:1–28:31.* 1982.

———. *Lukas, Theologe der Heilsgeschicht: Aufsätze zum lukanischen Doppelwerk:* Bonn: P. Hanstein Verlag, 1985.

———. "Lk 1:34, 35 als redaktionelle Einheit." *BZ* 15 (1971): 255–59.

Schnider, F. *Jesus der Prophet.* Orbis Biblicus et Orientalis 2. Göttingen: Vandenhoeck & Ruprecht, 1973.

Schubert, K. *Jésus à la lumière du Judaïsme du premier siècle.* Lectio Divina 84. Paris: Cerf, 1974.

Schubert, P. "The Final Cycle in the Speeches in the Book of Acts." *JBL* 87 (1968): 1–16.

Schulz, S. *Q: Die Spruchquelle der Evangelisten*. Zürich: Theologischer Verlag, 1972.

Schürer, E. *Geschichte des jüdischen Volkes im Zeitalter Jesu Christi*. Volume 3. Leipzig: J. C. Hinrich, 1909.

Schürmann, H. *Das Lukasevangelium: Kommentar zu Kap. 1:1–9:50*. Herders theologischer Kommentar zum Neuen Testament. Freiburg: Herder, 1969.

Schwartz, D. R. "The End of the ΓΗ (Acts 1:8): Beginning or End of the Christian Vision?" *JBL* 105 (4, 1986): 669–76.

Schweizer, E. "Concerning the Speeches in Acts." Pages 208–16 in *Studies in Luke-Acts*. Edited by L. E. Keck and J. L. Martyn. Nashville: Abingdon Press, 1966.

———. "Le Nouveau Testament." Pages 126–233 in *Esprit*. DBGK. Translated by d'Etienne de Peyer. Edited by Gerhard Kittel. 1959. Repr., Geneva: Labor et Fides, 1971.

———. "πνεύμα." Pages 389–455 in *TDNT*, VI. Translated by Geoffrey W. Bromiley. Edited by G. Kittel and G. Friedrich. 10 vols. Grand Rapids: Eerdmans, 1964–1976.

———. "The Concept of the Davidic 'Son of God' in Acts and Its Old Testament Background." Pages 186–93 in *Studies in Luke-Acts*. Edited by L. E. Keck and J. L. Martyn, Nashville: Abingdon, 1966.

———. *The Good News according to Luke*. Atlanta: John Knox Press, 1984.

———. *The Good News according to Matthew*. Atlanta: John Knox Press, 1975.

———. *The Holy Spirit*. Philadelphia: Fortress Press, 1980.

Sieber, J. H. "The Spirit as the 'Promise of My Father' in Luke 24:49." Pages 271–78 in *Sin, Salvation and the Spirit*. Edited by D. Durken. Collegeville, Minn.: The Liturgical Press, 1979.

Sjöberg, E. "RouaH dans le judaïsme palestinien." Pages 73ff. in *Esprit*. DBGK. Translated by d'Etienne de Peyer. Edited by Gerhard Kittel. Geneva: Labor et Fides, 1971.

Sleeper, C. F. "Pentecost and Resurrection." *JBL* 84 (1965): 389–99.

Smail, T. S. *Reflected Glory: The Spirit in Christ and Christians*. London: Hodder, 1975.

Smalley, S. S. "Spirit, Kingdom and Prayer in Luke-Acts." *NovT* 15 (1973): 59–71.

Smith, R. H. *Easter Gospels: The Resurrection of Jesus according to the Four Evangelists*. Minneapolis: Augsburg, 1983.
Spicq, C. S. *Les Épitres de saint Pierre*. Sources Bibliques. Paris: Gabalda, 1966.
Stempvoort, P. A. van. "The Interpretation of the Ascension in Luke and Acts." *NTS* 5 (1958–59): 30–42.
Stöger, A. *L'évangile selon saint Luc*. Paris: Desclée & Co., 1968.
Stone, M. E., ed. *Jewish Writings of the Second Temple Period*. Philadelphia: Fortress Press, 1984.
Stravinskas, P. M. J. "The Role of the Spirit in Acts 1 and 2." *TBT* 18 (1980): 263–69.
Sullivan, F. A. "'Baptism in the Holy Spirit': A Catholic Interpretation of the Pentecostal Experience." *Greg* 55 (1984): 48–68.
Surgy, P. de., "Langue." Col. 654–55 in *Vocabulaire de théologie biblique*. Edited by X. Léon-Dufour. 1970. Repr., Paris: Cerf, 1981.
Talbert, C. H. *Acts*. Atlanta: John Knox Press, 1984.
———. *Literary Patterns, Theological Themes and the Genre of Luke-Acts*. Missoula, Mont.: Scholars Press, 1974.
Tatum, W. B. "The Epoch of Israel: Luke I–II and the Theological Plan of Luke-Acts." *NTS* 13 (1966–67): 184–95.
Taylor, V. *The Historical Evidence for the Virgin Birth*. Oxford: Clarendon Press, 1920.
———. *The Names of Jesus*. London: Macmillan & Co., 1962.
Thompson, G. H. P. *The Gospel according to Luke*. Oxford: Clarendon Press, 1972.
Thüsing, W. "Erhöhungsvorstellung und Parusieerwartung in der ältesten nachösterlichen Christologie." *BZ* 11 (1967): 95–105; 12 (1968): 54–80; 223–40.
Tiede, D. L. *Prophecy and History in Luke-Acts*. Philadelphia: Fortress Press, 1980.
Tinsley, E. J. *The Gospel according to Luke*. Cambridge: Cambridge University Press, 1965.
Townsend, J. T. "The Speeches in Acts." *AThR* 42 (1960): 150–59.
Trocmé, E. *Le "livre des Actes" et l'histoire*. Paris: Presses Universitaires de France, 1957.
———. "Le Saint-Esprit et l'Église d'après le livre des Actes." Pages 19–44 in *L'Esprit-Saint et l'Église*. Edited by Académie internationale des sciences religieuses. Paris: Fayard, 1969.
Tugwell, S. "Relections on the Pentecostal Doctrine of 'Baptism in the Holy Spirit.'" *HeyJ* 13 (1972): 268–81; 402–14.

Turner, M. B. "Jesus and the Spirit in Lucan Perspective." *TynBul* 32 (1981): 3–42.
Turner, N. "The Preposition *en* in the New Testament." *BT* 10 (1959): 113–20.
———. "The Relation of Luke I and II to Hebraic Sources and the Rest of Luke-Acts." *NTS* 2 (1955–56): 100–09.
Vanhoye, A. *Structure littéraire de la letter aux Hébreux*. Paris: Desclée de Brouwer, 1963.
Vaux, R. de. *Les Institutions de l'Ancien Testament*. 2 vols. 1960. Repr., Paris: Cerf, 1982.
Verbeke, G. *L'évolution de la doctrine du pneuma du stoïcisme à saint Augustin*. Étude philosophique. Paris/Louvain: Desclée de Brouwer, 1945.
Vermes, G. *Jesus the Jew: A Historian's Reading of the Gospels*. Glasgow: Collins, 1973.
Vesco, J.-L. *Jérusalem et son prophète*. Paris: Cerf, 1988.
Vielhauer, P. "On the 'Paulinism' of Acts." Pages 33–50 in *Studies in Luke-Acts*. Edited by L. E. Keck and J. L. Martyn. Nashville: Abingdon Press, 1966.
———. "Zur Frage der Christologishe Hoheitstitel." *TLZ* 90 (1965): col. 576–79.
Voss, G. *Die Christologie der lukanischen Schriften in Grundzügen*. Studia Neotestamentica 2. Paris: Desclée de Brouwer, 1965.
———. "'Zum Herrn und Messias gemacht hat Gott diesen Jesus' (Apg 2:36)" *BibLeb* 8 (1967): 236–48.
Vouga, F. *L'Épitre de saint Jacques*. Commentaire du Nouveau Testament. 2nd series. Geneva: Labor et Fides, 1984.
Weeden, T. J. *Mark—Traditions in Conflict*. Philadelphia: Fortress Press, 1971.
Weiser, A. *Die Apostelgeschichte: Kapitel 1–12*. ÖTK 5.1. Würzburg: Gütersloh und Echter, 1981.
———. "Die Pfingstpredigt des Lukas." *BibLeb* 14 (1973): 1–12.
Weiss, B. *Die Quellen des Lukasevangeliums*. Stuttgart: J. G. Cotta, 1907.
Weiss, J. *Earliest Christianity*. Vol. 1. 1917. Repr., New York: Harper & Brothers, 1959.
Westcott, B. F., and F. J. A. Hort. *The New Testament in the Original Greek*. London: Macmillan, 1896.
Wilckens, U. *Der Brief an die Römer*. EKKNT. Neukirchen: Neukirchener Verlag, 1980.

———. *Die Missionsreden der Apostelgeschichte. Formund Traditionsgechichtliche Untersuchungen.* WMANT 5. Neukirchen-Vluyn: Neukirchener Verlag, 1963.

Williams, C. S. C. *A Commentary on the Acts of the Apostles.* Edinburgh: Clark, 1957.

———. *The Acts of the Apostles.* London: A. & C. Black, 1957.

Wilson, S. G. "The Ascension: A Critique and an Interpretation." *ZNW* 59 (1968): 269–81.

———. *The Gentiles and the Gentile Mission in Luke-Acts.* Cambridge: Cambridge University Press, 1973.

Wintermute, O. "Jubilees." Pages 35–142 in *The Old Testament Pseudepigrapha.* Volume 2. Edited by J. H. Charlesworth. Garden City, N.Y.: Doubleday & Co. 1985.

Yates, J. A. "Luke's Pneumatology and Luke 11:20." Pages 295–99 in *Studia Evangelica: Vol. II.* Edited by F. L. Cross. Texte und Untersuchungen 87. Berlin: Akademie-Verlag, 1964.

Zehnle, R. F. *Peter's Pentecost Discourse: Tradition and Lukan Reinterpretation in Peter's Speeches of Acts 2 and 3.* Society of Biblical Literature Monograph Series 15. Nashville: Abingdon Press, 1971.

Zerwick, M., and M. Grosvenor. *A Grammatical Analysis of the Greek New Testament.* Vol. 1. Rome: Biblical Institute Press, 1974.

Ziesler, A. "The Name of Jesus in the Acts of the Apostles." *JSNT* 4 (1979): 28–41.

Zimmermann, H. "Evangelium des Lukas 1–2." *TSK* 76 (1903): 247–90.

Index of Persons

Adamson, J. 55
Adler, N. 180
Allard, M. 115, 116
Antoniadis, S. 170, 179
Audet, J. 115, 116, 129
Baer, H. von 12, 13, 26
Barrett, C. 55, 56, 57, 63, 84, 133, 149, 168, 189, 190, 191, 221
Bauer, W. 31, 51, 52, 72, 89, 98, 119, 169, 171
Bauernfeind, O. 31, 45, 180, 182
Baumgärtel, F. 239, 241
Beasley-Murray, G. 191, 193
Benoit, P. 80, 88, 114, 115, 151, 192
Bertram, G. 32, 52, 53, 61, 119
Best, E. 190
Blass-Debrunner 31, 179
Bock, D. 149
Boismard, M. 151, 192
Bonnard, P. 54, 59, 189–90, 226, 239
Boor, W. de 31, 42, 43, 45, 93
Borremans, J. 12, 18, 19, 26, 205, 211, 213–14, 229, 230, 233, 234
Bovon, F. 8, 14, 181, 232
Brisebois, M. 5
Brown, F. 52
Brown, R. 56, 58, 111–12, 112, 113, 114, 115, 116, 121, 128, 129, 130, 133–34, 135, 136, 137, 143, 144, 149, 189, 246
Brown, S. 192, 199, 201
Brox, N. 54
Bruce, F. 31, 35, 37, 65, 99, 199, 209, 228, 244
Bruner, F. 233
Buis, P. 44
Bultmann, R. 76, 104, 113, 123, 127, 129, 192
Bussche, H. van den 58
Busse, 156
Cabie, R. 181, 182, 183
Cadbury, H. 5, 36, 113, 114
Callan, T. 28, 66
Cantinat, J. 31, 55
Caquot-Philonenko 183, 189
Carruth, T. 156
Cazelles, H. 43, 239, 244
Cerfaux, L. 209
Ceroke, C. 129
Charlier, J. 181
Chevallier, M. 12, 23, 24, 26, 104, 113, 134, 135, 140, 143, 145, 148, 163, 169, 184, 185, 189, 190, 191, 192, 193, 197, 205, 208, 210, 239, 245, 247, 249
Congar, Y. 1
Connor, D. xvii

Conzelmann, H. 5, 6, 7, 8, 10, 11, 14, 16, 21, 31, 32, 34, 37, 43, 45, 47, 64, 75, 90, 112, 122, 123, 143, 159, 169, 181, 186, 199, 209, 210, 214, 247
Coppens, J. 192, 206, 211
Creed, J. 90
Cripps, R. 239, 244
Cullmann, O. 150, 152, 155, 164
Dahood, M. 60
Dalmann, G. 123
Daniélou, J. 66, 111
Danker, F. 118, 143
Davies, J. 181, 209
Delcor, M. 43, 181, 209
Delebecque, E. 31, 73
Delobel, J. 173
Denny, J. 17
Dibelius, M. 6, 35, 36, 37, 113, 181
Dillon, R. 71, 76, 98, 102
Dodd, C. 35, 36, 38, 58, 113
Dömer, M. 6, 8, 10, 11
Dumais, M. 35, 155, 205, 216
Dunn, J. 14, 57, 63, 99, 104, 105, 149, 153, 181, 184, 189, 190, 197, 205, 249
Dupont, J. 31, 32, 35, 36, 38, 61, 62, 66, 168, 169, 171, 181, 182
Dupont-Sommer et al. 123, 125,
Elbert, P. 20
Ellington, S. 20
Ellis, E. 128, 129, 186
Enslin, M. 85
Epp, E. 68
Ernst, J. 71, 90, 99, 112, 117, 144, 150, 169, 187, 188
Evan, C. 35
Feuillet, A. 111, 151, 164, 168, 171
Fitzmyer, J. 31, 47, 68, 69, 70, 72, 76, 81, 90, 98, 100, 101, 111, 112, 113, 116, 117, 118, 120, 122, 123, 130, 131, 133, 134, 136, 143, 150, 153, 154, 160, 163, 164, 169, 174, 181, 186
Flender, H. 8, 9
Fohrer, G. 43
Franklin, E. 8, 10, 83, 158, 212, 215, 233, 247
Fuller, R. 28, 68, 76, 77
Gaechter, P. 114, 115
Geldenhuys, N. 142, 150
Gelin, A. 43
George, A. 12, 21, 22, 23, 26, 111, 112, 121, 141, 142, 147, 151, 169, 171, 221, 241, 243, 245, 250
Gewiess, J. 130
Giblet, C. 190, 198, 228
Gillièron, B. 99, 171, 211, 239, 250
Gils, F. 154, 155, 158, 160
Goguel, M. 5

Gossett, S.	xvii	Hoffman, P.	187
Gourgues, M.	32, 33, 34, 41, 61, 63, 66, 181	Hruby, K.	182, 184
		Hughes, P.	55
Graves, R.	xvii	Hull, J.	12, 16, 17, 26, 184
Graystone, G.	116, 128, 129, 130		
		Hutton, W.	170
Grelot, P.	117, 132	Imschoot, P. van	15, 188, 189, 190, 239, 241, 243, 244
Grundmann, W.	60, 71, 89, 127, 140, 151, 164, 169, 173, 174, 181, 188		
		Jacob, E.	239
		Jaubert, A.	184
Guillaume, J.	69, 74, 78, 79, 80	Jeremias, J.	70, 72, 155, 160, 163, 166
Guillemette, J.	5	Johnson, S.	xvii
Guillet, J.	12, 24, 25, 26, 100, 174, 224, 233, 238, 239, 244, 245	Juel, D.	150, 161
		Käsemann, E.	7, 63
		Kerrigan, A.	43, 45
Gunkel, H.	xi	Kleinknecht, H.	243
Haenchen, E.	5, 31, 42, 43, 75, 76, 94, 180, 181, 182, 184, 208	Kloppenborg, J.	193
		Knox, W.	181, 245
		Kremer, J.	41, 49, 184, 196, 199, 208, 209
Hahn, F.	28, 62, 144, 149, 158		
		Kretschmar, G.	181
Hanna, R.	171	La Potterie, I. de	24, 25, 152, 155, 157, 159, 161, 205, 214
Hanson, R.	31		
Harnack, A.	112, 114, 127		
		Ladd, G.	123
Hastings, A.	156	Lagrange, M.	135, 168, 189
Haulotte, E.	201, 239		
Havener, I.	187	Lake, K.	73
Hay, D.	66	Lampe, G.	12, 13, 14, 25, 26, 99, 154, 158, 211, 215, 239
Haya-Prats, G.	xvii, 7, 12, 20, 21, 25, 99, 155, 169, 181, 189, 205, 239, 244, 247, 249, 251		
		Lang, F.	189, 193
		Larranaga, V.	85
Hayes, J.	104	Laurentin, R.	111, 113, 116, 119, 121, 129, 132, 142
Heron, A.	239, 244		
Hilgenfeld, A.	112		
Hill, D.	ix, 158, 205, 209, 210, 212, 223, 233	Lavallée, F.	31
		Le Deaut, R.	181, 182, 183
Hillman, J.	127		

Leany, A.	112, 151, 187	Ménard, J.	155
Leenhardt, F.	62	Menoud, P.	70–71, 72, 73, 84, 85, 88, 184
Legrand, L.	111, 112, 115, 116, 117, 120, 121, 122, 127, 132, 134, 141, 144, 148, 150, 151	Menzies, R.	xiii, xvii
		Metzger, B.	67, 68, 69, 70, 76, 150
Legault, A.	151, 155	Michaeli, F.	125
Lentzen-Deis, F.	157	Minear, P.	111, 112, 113, 156, 205
L'Eplattenier, C.	181	Mitton, C.	54
Lindars, B.	104	Mollat, D.	155, 214
Loader, W.	32, 62, 66	Montague, G.	239
		Morgenthaler, R.	113
Lohfink, G.	35, 36, 38, 71, 76, 78, 80, 83	Moule, C.	81
		Müller, P.	153
Lohse, E.	6, 180, 182, 184	Murphy-O'Connor, J.	58
		Murray, J.	63
Lys, D.	43, 239, 244	Mussner, F.	31, 39, 180
Lyonnet, S.	115, 132, 142	Myre, A.	xv, 145
		Neher, A.	239, 243
Machen, J.	112	Neil, W.	209
Maddox, E.	8, 11, 44, 247	Neirynck, F.	217
		Nestle-Aland	27, 68, 150
Maertens, T.	239	Neve, L.	239, 244
Mann, C.	184	Nineham, D.	13
Manson, W.	5, 173, 188	Oliver, H.	99, 112, 113
Marsh, T.	211, 212, 239, 250	O'Reilly, L.	155, 157, 182, 199, 205, 209, 218, 221, 222
Marshall, A.	115		
Marshall, I.	8, 9, 37, 42, 68, 70, 72, 73, 76, 82, 86, 90, 100, 105, 112, 130, 136, 142, 150, 163, 168, 169, 181, 184, 185, 187, 188, 189, 197, 199	Osty, E.	60
		O'Toole, R.	31, 100, 103, 184
		Packer, J.	31
		Parsons, M.	69, 71, 81, 82, 83, 84, 87
Martin, A.	69	Paul, A.	123
McHugh, J.	129	Perkin, N.	28
McPolin, J.	99, 233		

Index of Persons

Perrot, C. — 111
Pesch, R. — 31, 33, 37, 39, 45, 75, 77, 181, 182, 208
Petroff, L. — xv
Pfitzner, V. — 99, 205, 211, 212, 215, 225, 226, 227, 228, 232, 249, 250
Plummer, A. — 5, 80, 81, 100, 113, 129, 135, 169, 188, 189
Polag, A. — 187
Potin, J. — 182, 209
Quesnel, M. — 193
Reiling-Swellengrebel — 115, 119, 131, 168
Richard, J. — 105, 142
Richardson, A. — 182, 209, 239, 244, 249
Rinaldi, G. — 43
Roloff, J. — 31, 37, 43, 45, 76, 77, 181
Romilly, J. de — 36
Sabourin, L. — 68, 71, 76, 147, 151, 163, 186, 189, 193
Sahlin, H. — 73, 113,
Samain, E. — 156, 157, 159, 182, 205, 207, 209, 230
Sanders, J. — 47
Sauvagnat, B. — 207, 228
Schedl, C. — 31, 47, 49
Schenk, W. — 187
Schille, G. — 31, 33, 43, 76, 77, 87
Schillebeeckx, E. — 184, 199
Schlier, H. — 71
Schmithals, W. — 31, 112

Schmitt, J. — 35, 42, 190, 207
Schnackenburg, R. — 56, 57, 63–64
Schneider, G. — 6, 8, 31, 33, 45, 76, 77, 93, 112, 130, 131, 143, 150, 154, 164, 180, 185, 209, 218
Schnider, F. — 159, 160
Schubert, P. — 35
Schulz, S. — 187, 192
Schumacher, S. — xvii
Schürer, E. — 79
Schürmann, H. — 115, 118, 130, 136, 144, 149, 150, 154, 155, 173, 187, 188, 189, 190, 193
Schwartz, D. — 226, 227
Schweizer, E. — 12, 14, 15, 22, 35, 38, 89, 115, 119, 123, 130, 132, 141, 142, 150, 164, 169, 187, 190, 192, 209, 239, 243, 249
Sellin, E. — 43
Sieber, J. — 98, 99
Sjöberg, E. — 104
Sleeper, C. — 181, 184, 199
Smalley, S. — 211
Smith, R. — 68, 71, 99, 156
Spicq, C. — 55
Spolarich, S. — xi, xvii
Stempvoort, P. van — 68, 71, 76, 87
Stevenson — 43
Stöger, A. — 130, 142, 151, 153
Stone, M. — 183

Stravinskas, P.	99, 182, 249	Williams, C.	31, 93, 181
Stronstad, R.	xii	Wilson, S.	75, 76, 77, 88, 209
Sullivan, F.	190, 197, 199, 200	Wintermute, O.	183
Surgy, P. de	209	Wolff	43
Talbert, C.	8, 9, 10, 76, 83, 87, 163, 164	Yates, J.	20
		Zehnle, R.	35, 41, 43
Tatum, W.	99		
Taylor, V.	123, 127	Zerwick-Grosvenor	31, 114, 115
Thompson, G.	129		
Thüsing, W.	62	Ziesler, A.	223
Tinsley, E.	187	Zimmermann, H.	112
Townsend, J.	35		
Trinquet, J.	43, 61		
Trocmé, E.	5, 12, 17, 18, 37, 73, 181, 184, 209, 226, 229, 238, 239		
Tugwell, S.	191, 229		
Turner, M.	99		
Turner, N.	114, 170		
Vanhoye, A.	64		
Vaux, R. de	184		
Verbeke, G.	243		
Vermes, G.	130		
Vesco, J.	156		
Vielhauer, P.	5, 62		
Voss, G.	31, 32, 33, 106, 156		
Vouga, F.	54		
Weeden, T.	28		
Weiser, A.	31, 35, 43, 45, 77, 182, 208		
Weiss, B.	113		
Weiss, J.	61, 104,		
Welchbillig	43		
Wescott-Hort	68		
Wilckens, U.	32, 35, 37, 38, 63		

Index of Ancient Sources

Old Testament

Genesis
1:2	141
1:26	163
2:7	142
4:1	129
4:17	129
5:24	77, 82
6:2	122
11:4	82
14:18	120
15:6	136
16:11	138
17:1–15	116
17:15–22	116
17:19	118, 138
19:8	129
21:2	137
38:1	70
40:13	56
40:19	56

Exodus
3:2	243
3:4	243
4:22	122
6:23	137
13:12	141
15:6	60
19:16–19	182
19:16ff.	185
19:20	181
23:16	182
25:20	132
28:3	242
31:3	242
32:1	70
35:31	242
40:35	132

Leviticus
9:22	70
23:2	141
23:37 LXX	141

Numbers
5:14	131
6:3–4	138
10:34	132
11:25	135, 242
11:29	23, 135
24:2	240, 241, 242
24:22	240

Deuteronomy
5	185
14:1	122
16:9–10	182
16:9–11	182
32:43	65
33:12	132
33:26	82

Judges
3:10	242
6:11–12	244
6:11–18	117
6:11ff.	116
6:14	244
6:34	240, 241
11:39	129
13	116
13:1–25	117
13:4	138
13:5	118
13:14	138
13:20	82
14:6	240, 241
14:19	240
15:14	240

1 Samuel
1–2	116
1:11	138
2:7	53

1 Samuel (cont.)

2:10	52
7:14	148
10:6	240, 241
10:10–12	240
16:13	139
19:23–24	240

2 Samuel

7	104
7:9–16	121
7:11	123
7:12	123
7:12–13	47, 103
7:13	123
7:14	65, 122, 123, 125
7:14–16	124, 125

1 Kings

2:19	60
13:2	138
17:8–24	159
17:9–10	160
17:10–24	160
17:20–22	161
17:23	160
18:12	240, 242
19:3ff.	161
19:4–8	162
19:19–21	161

2 Kings

2	79
2:9–10	78, 185
2:11	74, 82, 161
2:11–12	77
2:15	78, 242
2:16	240, 242

1 Chronicles

12:19	241
17:11–14	103
17:13	122
17:13–14	125
22:10	122
28:6	122

2 Chronicles

24:20	241

Job

1:6	122
1:19	131
2:1	122
4:15	131
5:11	53
27:3	141
33:4	141

Psalms

2:2	154
2:7	64, 104, 105, 122, 143, 151, 152, 153, 154
6:18	29
7:7	52
8:7	64
16	48
16:7–8	60
16:8–11	46
16:10	146
17:7	60
17:49	52
19:15	93
20:7	60
21:9–10	60
25:7	104
25:14	104
29:1	122
33:6	141
36:34	52
37:35	58
45:7–8	65
45:10	60
45:11	52
48:2	119
51:13	189
63:9	60
73:15	164
74:5–6	192
74:11	60
76:2	119
80:16	60

Psalms (cont.)	
82:1	122
82:6	121
86:10	119
89:3–4	103
89:4–5	121
89:30	121
89:37	121
91:4	132
96:4	119
97:9	58
98:5	52
102:26–28	65
104:2ff.	82
104:4	65
104:30	141, 241
109:31	60
110	66, 32
110:1	28, 32, 48, 60, 61, 63, 64, 65, 66, 91, 104
115:16	82
118	32
118:16	32
121:5	60
132:11	47
132:11–12	121
132:12	103
135:5	119
145:3	119
147:5	119
147:18	141
148:13–14	52
149:4	53

Proverbs	
1:23	242
3:34	53
29:23	53

Isaiah	
1:2	122
4:3	141
4:4	189, 191
4:5	132
5:16	52
5:24	188
6:6–7	198
6:9–10	30
6:10	29
7:14	118, 129, 138
9:6	121
11:1–2	104
11:2	23, 104, 121, 154, 242
11:3 LXX	154
11:13	58
11:14	190
14:13	53
14:13ff.	82
14:15	53
29:10	242
32:15	23, 100, 131, 192, 241
34:4	65
35:8	141
39:29	100
41:14	93
41:16	191
42	153
42:1	23, 104, 151, 153, 154, 155, 157, 164, 242
42:1ff.	55
42:7	157
44:3	23, 100, 192, 242
44:6	93
45:23	59
47:14	188
48:13	60
48:16	241, 242
49:1	138
49:5	138
49:7	93, 151
49:26	93
52—53	57
52:13	52, 53
53	164
55:3	121
59:20	93

Isaiah (cont.)

61:1	23, 135, 156, 157, 158, 167, 174, 206, 214
61:1–2	21, 207
61:1–3	104
62:2	141
62:8	60
63:10–11	189
63:10ff.	242
63:11	242
63:16	93
63:19	153
66:15	189
66:24	189

Jeremiah

10:6	119
15:7	191
17:12	52
20:9	198
23:5	121
23:29	198
30:9	104
31:31–34	20, 182, 251
33:15	121
33:21	103
50:34	93
51:2	191

Ezekiel

1:1	153
2:2	241
3:14	240, 242
11:5	135, 241, 242
17:24	53
34:23–24	121
34:23ff.	103
34:24	103
36:24–28	20
36:26–27	xvii, 182, 192, 198, 251
36:26–28	251
36:27	43
37:14	141
37:24–25	121

39:29	23, 43, 241
48:1	70

Daniel

4:10	82
4:14	120
4:34	58
7:13	28, 62, 66
11:12	58

Hosea

11:1	122
13:4	93

Joel

2:28	25, 29, 100, 192
2:28ff.	xvii, 23, 251
2:28–29	43, 100, 196, 198, 241
2:28–32	20, 22, 42, 99, 182, 200, 207, 210, 251
2:32	44

Amos

1:4	188–89
9:11	121

Micah

5:8	52
6:8	54

Zechariah

6:12	121
12:10	100

Malachi

2:6	159
3:1	159
3:2	188, 193
3:3	189
3:19	188
3:21	188
3:24	159

New Testament

Matthew
1:1–16	163
1:18	133
1:21	118
1:29	129
3:1–6	186
3:4	159
3:7	186
3:7–10	186
3:10	186, 187
3:10–14	186, 187
3:11	186, 188, 193, 194
3:12	188
3:17	151, 155
4:1	166
4:12	172
5:29	61
5:39	61
6:3	61
7:11	221
8:19	167
8:19–22	161
9:17	29
11:7–19	159
11:9	159
11:11	159
11:14	159
11:23	28, 53
11:23ff.	55
12:3	213
12:18	154
12:28	20
12:32	213
12:34	186, 187
13:14	29
13:54–58	156
13:57	157
14:20	166
15:37	166
16:1	187
17:5	128, 133, 151
17:10–13	159
19:28	65
22:43–44	65
22:44	28
22:70	90
23:12	54, 55
23:33	186, 187
25:31	89
25:33	61
26:64	28, 65, 89
27:35	180
27:54	147, 165
28:2	75
28:18	89

Mark
1:1–6	186
1:6	159
1:8	186
1:11	151, 155
1:12	166
1:14	172
1:39	166
3:26	166
3:29	213
4:12	29
4:28	166
5:7	120
6:1–6	156
6:4	157
8:19	166
9:7	128, 133, 151
9:11–13	159
12:36	28
14:62	28, 65, 89
15:20	70
15:24	180
15:39	147, 165
16:5	61, 75
16:19	72, 82

Luke
1—2	45, 110ff., 139, 215, 238
1:5	247
1:5ff.	136

Luke (cont.)

1:6	136	1:52	28, 54, 55
1:8	179	1:56	83
1:8–9	247	1:59	247
1:11	61, 137	1:67	134, 135, 167, 180, 242
1:11–20	119, 128, 137		
1:13	114	1:67–79	135, 248
1:15	138, 167, 180, 242, 248	1:68	120
		1:76	120, 159
1:15–17	138	2:4	187
1:16	120	2:6	179
1:16–17	159	2:11	104
1:17	170	2:15	83
1:18	128	2:20	83
1:21	179	2:25	135, 242, 247
1:22	154	2:25ff.	248
1:25–27	180	2:26	136
1:26–35	115	2:27	136, 170, 179, 242
1:26–38	111, 128, 154	2:36	247
1:27	130, 247	2:36–38	136
1:31	114, 118	2:38	248
1:31–35	107, 110, 111–36	2:39	83
1:32	114, 120, 123, 145, 147, 148	2:43	179
		3:1–6	186
1:32–33	34, 82, 118, 121, 124, 129, 142, 144, 145, 149	3:3	152
		3:6	6
		3:7–9	186
1:32–35	149	3:9	188
1:33	114, 148	3:10–14	188
1:34	115, 129, 130, 133	3:12	187
1:34–35	119, 126, 127, 128	3:15	188
1:35	14, 99, 115, 120, 123, 127, 128, 129, 130, 131, 132, 133, 134, 140, 140–41, 141, 142, 144, 145, 146, 147, 148, 149, 240, 248	3:16	110, 170, 185, 186, 188, 190, 191, 193, 194, 196–97, 198, 199, 200, 202, 203, 204
		3:17	188, 190,
		3:20	83, 152, 173–74
1:36–37	143	3:21	152
1:38	83	3:21–22	107, 110, 150, 153, 235
1:39–56	134		
1:41	134, 139, 167, 180, 242, 248	3:22	48, 152, 153, 155, 163, 242, 248
1:41–44	139	3:23	163
1:42–43	134	3:38	140
1:43	248		

Luke (cont.)	
4:1	110, 154, 165ff., 166, 167, 168, 170, 171, 205, 248
4:1–13	140, 157
4:1ff.	107
4:3	146, 172
4:5	171
4:8	120
4:9	146, 172
4:12	120
4:14	17, 99, 110, 154, 157, 170, 172ff., 205, 214, 248
4:14–16	173
4:14ff.	107
4:16	156, 157
4:16–21	42, 156
4:16ff.	157, 235
4:17	156
4:18	11, 24, 110, 157, 172ff., 175, 206, 214, 248
4:18–19	22, 156, 158
4:18–21	42
4:24	157, 161, 206
4:25–26	157, 161, 206
4:27	157
4:27–28	161
4:31	112
4:31ff.	214
4:33ff.	235
4:34	146
4:37	179
4:38ff.	235
4:41	147
5:1	179
5:10	187
5:12	179
5:17–26	217, 219–20
5:36	187
6:12	152
6:18–19	235
6:20	70
6:21	156
6:35	120, 164
7:11	160
7:11–12	160
7:11–17	159, 160
7:13–15	160
7:14	161
7:15	160
7:16	215
7:16–17	160
7:22–23	215
7:24–28	159
7:33	138
7:16	157, 160
7:26	159
7:28	159
7:39	157, 162
8:5	179
8:10	29, 30
8:23	179
8:28	120, 147
8:40	179
8:42	179
8:43	170
9:7–8	162
9:14	128
9:18	152, 179
9:19	157, 162
9:28–29	152
9:29	179
9:33	179
9:36	179
9:51	69, 161, 179
9:54	161
9:57–62	161
9:61	187
9:61–62	161
10:15	28, 53
10:21	110, 214, 248
10:24	30, 215, 232, 235
10:27	120
10:32	187
10:35	179
10:58	179
11:1	179
11:2	152
11:9–13	221
11:13	221, 248

Luke (cont.)		22:41–44	152
11:17	180	22:43	162
11:18	180, 187	22:44	170
11:21	170	22:59	72
11:20	20	22:64	162
11:21–22	131	22:67	90, 147
11:22	127	22:67–68	90
11:27	70, 179	22:69	28, 62, 66, 89, 90, 91, 94
12:10	110, 213, 224, 234, 248	22:69–70	65
12:11–12	212	22:70	147
12:12	110, 248	23:11	75
12:15	179	23:12	28, 170
12:35–59	193	23:34	180
12:52	180	23:40	170
12:53	180	23:46	152
12:54	187	24	71
12:57	187	24:1–12	82
13:17	215	24:4	75, 76, 179
13:33	157, 162	24:7	88
14:11	28, 54, 55	24:13–35	82
14:31	170	24:15	179
14:34	170	24:19	157, 158, 170
15:12	187	24:21	88
16:1	187	24:26	46, 83, 91
16:15	170	24:29	81
16:16	8	24:33	81
16:22	170, 187	24:36	83
16:23	70	24:36ff.	88
17:11	179	24:41–42	194
17:14	179	24:44	81
17:23–37	193	24:44–46	83
17:24	160	24:44–49	83
18:9	187	24:45	101
18:13	70	24:46	46, 88
18:14	54	24:46–47	101
18:35	179	24:47	84, 147
19:19	187	24:47–49	83
20:37	120	24:48	84, 101
20:42	28	24:49	xvii, 14, 25, 68, 73, 84, 92, 97, 98, 99, 100, 101, 102, 194, 194ff., 195, 196, 197, 198, 199, 203, 204, 240, 241, 249, 251
21:25	170, 179		
21:26	131		
21:36	127		
22:12	187		
22:17	180		
22:22	46		

Luke (*cont.*)

24:50	70, 71
24:50–53	51, 66, 67, 69, 70, 72, 73, 81, 82, 83, 87, 95, 101, 195
24:51	68, 69, 70, 72, 76, 91
24:51–53	80
24:52	70, 71, 72
24:53	71

John

1:14	166, 167
2:5	29
3:7	58
3:9	58
3:13	57, 82
3:14	28, 57, 58
3:14–15	56, 57, 58
3:15	57, 58
6:33	82
6:38	82
6:42	82
8:28	28, 56, 57
8:28–29	57
10:3	70
12:31	56
12:32	28, 56, 57
12:34	56, 57
13:1	56
13:34	28, 56
14:26	246
15:26	101, 2246
16:7	101
16:11	56
19:24	180
20:17	56, 67, 82
21:6	61

Acts

1–2	113, 185
1:1	84
1:1–2	87
1:1–3	101, 102
1:1–5	84, 85
1:1–12	88
1:2	68, 69, 72, 74, 81, 84
1:3	68, 80, 84, 85, 87, 88
1:3–11	69
1:4	29, 84, 101, 196
1:4–5	84, 88, 98, 99, 102, 195, 196, 198, 199, 203, 204, 249
1:5	101, 194, 197, 198, 200
1:6	73, 85, 88, 126
1:6–14	74
1:7	85, 246
1:7–8	86
1:8	xvii, 17, 29, 86, 86, 88, 99, 102, 127, 131, 194, 195, 197, 198, 199, 203, 204, 211, 216, 226, 227, 239, 241, 246, 249, 251
1:8–11	76
1:9	68, 74, 78, 86, 88, 226
1:9–11	51, 66, 67, 68, 69, 73, 74, 78, 79, 80, 84, 87, 94, 95, 100, 102, 126
1:10	75, 86, 94
1:10–11	86
1:11	69, 72, 74, 86, 94, 246
1:12	88
1:14	152
1:22	72, 74, 85
2—7	250
2	25
2:1	152, 179
2:1–4	29, 41, 87, 100, 102, 126, 178, 180, 185, 199, 208, 233
2:1–13	95, 185, 211, 235
2:2	179, 180, 201
2:2–3	49, 182, 185

Acts (cont.)		2:19–21	45
2:2–4	176, 196, 199, 203, 204, 208, 216, 230, 235, 249	2:21	44
		2:22	41, 45, 48, 109, 198, 212, 214
2:2ff.	198	2:22–24	92
2:3	180, 193, 206, 209	2:22–32	42, 102
2:3–4	211	2:22–36	42, 49, 104
2:4	134, 168, 179, 180, 195, 201, 203, 208, 231, 240, 242	2:23	48, 109, 199, 212
		2:23–24	45
		2:24	39, 46, 48, 109, 199, 212, 238
2:4–13	48		
2:5	208, 209, 211	2:25	28
2:5–13	208	2:25–28	46, 48
2:6	208	2:25–36	91
2:6ff.	206	2:26	46
2:7	231	2:26–36	41
2:8	208	2:27	39, 46, 146
2:9–11	209	2:29	39, 47, 48, 92
2:11	208, 209, 209, 211, 231	2:29–39	40
		2:30	34, 47, 48, 103, 104
2:12	231	2:30–31	46, 47, 105, 109, 124
2:13	208		
2:14	41, 70	2:30–36	111
2:14–15	42	2:30ff.	97
2:14–20	41	2:31	34, 47, 104
2:14–21	104–05	2:31–33	175
2:14–28	39	2:31–39	63
2:14–36	27, 38, 109	2:32	28, 34, 48, 85, 105, 106, 126, 145, 199, 212
2:14–41	216		
2:14ff.	235		
2:15–21	41	2:32–33	24, 94, 148, 233
2:15–22	48	2:32–36	105, 126
2:16	42	2:33	xv, 2, 3, 12, 14, 17, 22, 25, 26, 27, 28, 29, 30, 31, 33, 42, 48, 49, 51, 52, 53, 59, 62, 63, 66, 67, 91, 94, 96, 97, 98, 100, 102, 103, 105, 106, 109, 111, 113, 126, 127, 145, 146, 148, 149, 165, 174, 175, 176, 177, 195, 196, 198, 199, 200, 201, 204, 212, 215, 225, 227, 233, cont.
2:16–17	102, 211		
2:16–18	198		
2:16–21	22, 42		
2:16–36	95		
2:16ff.	206		
2:17	10, 25, 29, 44, 100, 103, 168, 231, 240, 242		
2:17–18	196		
2:17–36	177		
2:17ff.	79, 102		
2:18	29, 44		
2:19	45		

Acts (cont.)

	234, 235, 237, 238, 242, 246, 247, 249, 251
2:33–35	42
2:33ff.	84
2:34	28, 32, 33, 48, 82, 91
2:34–35	48, 106, 126, 128
2:35	127, 148
2:36	14, 42, 48, 90, 106, 109, 113, 126, 127, 149, 175, 199, 216, 246
2:38	15, 24, 200
2:39	29
2:38–39	27, 38, 41, 49, 93, 109, 195, 200, 247
2:41	227
2:42	215, 227
2:43	215, 222
2:45	180
2:47	215
3:1–9	212
3:1–10	215, 217, 219–20, 235
3:1–11	216
3:2	215
3:6	215, 222
3:9–12	212
3:10	212
3:11	215
3:12	215
3:12–26	38
3:13	146, 215
3:14	146, 165
3:15	215
3:16	179, 217, 222
3:18	46
3:22	158
3:24	158
4:1ff.	216
4:7	217, 222
4:8	134, 169, 180, 212, 250
4:8–10	216
4:8–12	38
4:10	222
4:16–17	224
4:17–18	223
4:18	214, 217
4:18ff.	158
4:19–20	38
4:24–31	22
4:27	146, 154, 214
4:28	46
4:29–30	221
4:30	146, 179, 222
4:31	25, 99, 169, 180, 213, 221, 222, 242, 250
4:33	85, 99
5:3	223
5:9	223, 242
5:12	215
5:15	128, 133, 222
5:15–16	235
5:19	70
5:19–32	38
5:28	92
5:29	92
5:29ff.	92
5:30	28, 92, 222
5:31	28, 31, 59, 62, 66, 84, 91, 92, 93, 223
5:31–32	93
5:32	15, 28, 93, 222, 223
5:41	223
5:42	223
6:3	167, 168, 242, 250
6:5	167, 168, 213, 222, 227, 250
6:8	222
6:10	213, 243
7:1—8:3	222
7:22	158
7:25	158
7:35	32, 93, 158
7:36	70
7:37	158
7:40	70
7:48	120

Acts (cont.)

7:51	213, 224	10:28	229
7:52	146, 165	10:30	75
7:54	213	10:31	85
7:55	28, 167, 213, 250	10:34–43	38
7:55–56	62, 66, 91, 94	10:36	206
7:55ff.	84	10:38	24, 99, 157, 214
7:56	28, 90	10:44	229, 231, 241
7:60	224	10:44–45	22
8	250	10:44–47	25
8:1	227	10:45	229, 231
8:5	227	10:45–46	208
8:6	179, 227	10:46	180, 210, 229, 231, 240
8:14	228		
8:15–18	22, 24	10:47	229
8:16	201	10:47–48	200
8:24	127, 132	11:1ff.	229
8:25	228	11:5	241
8:26	243	11:5ff.	229
8:26–39	228	11:8	240
8:27	228	11:12	225, 240, 242
8:28	228	11:15	22
8:29	225, 228, 242, 243	11:15–17	230
8:39	240, 242	11:16	194, 197, 199, 203, 204
8:40	240		
9:1–19	217	11:16–17	229
9:3	179	11:17	231
9:16	217	11:19–21	228
9:17	134, 169, 180, 213, 250	11:20	231
		11:21	231
9:17–18	217	11:24	167, 168, 213, 222, 231, 243, 250
9:19–20	213		
9:20	147, 217	11:24–25	231
9:21	147	11:26	213, 232
9:22	147	11:28	242
9:31	228	12:10	83
9:51	179	12:17	70
10—11	250	12:21	75
10:1—11:18	230	13—28	250
10:2	229	13:1ff.	217
10:3	243	13:2	225, 232, 240, 242
10:7	83	13:4	225, 232, 240
10:9ff.	229	13:7	28
10:14	229	13:9	134, 169, 180, 213, 250
10:19	229, 242, 243		
10:19–20	225, 240	13:16–41	38

Acts (cont.)	
13:16–42	217
13:17	32, 70
13:27	46
13:32–33	105
13:33	14, 104, 105, 113, 123, 151
13:34	39
13:35	39, 146
13:36	39
13:40	127, 132
13:46	224
14:3	221
14:8–11	217, 219–20
14:10	217
14:11	70
14:19	127, 132
15:1ff.	230
15:7–8	230
15:7–11	230
15:8	222
15:12	221
15:28	226, 232
16:6	240
16:6–7	226, 232, 242
16:7	212, 240
16:17	120
16:25	179
16:26	179
16:37	70
16:39	70
17:14	70
17:25	180
17:26	140
19:1	179, 242
19:4	201
19:5	201
19:5–6	201
19:6	25, 201, 208, 210, 240
20:16	179
21:5	70
21:11	242
21:28	70
21:38	70
22:14	146, 165
22:22	70
23:47	165
26:11	70
26:22	46
27:28	72
28:6	179
28:25	242
28:25–28	224–25
28:26–28	30
28:28	6, 232
28:31	232

Romans	
1:3	145
1:3–4	75, 143, 144, 145, 149
1:3f.	104
1:4	104, 144
1:4–5	245
3:15	29
5:12–21	140
5:14	163
8:5	xii, 250
8:10–11	xii, 250
8:13	xii
8:13ff.	250
8:14	164
8:34	27, 62, 75, 245
14:9	75

1 Corinthians	
15:22	163–64
15:24–28	66
15:45–49	140, 164
16:8	179

2 Corinthians	
11:7	28, 55

Galatians	
1:17	166
3:14	28
3:26	164
4:6	164

Ephesians

1:13	28
1:19–20	63, 75
1:19–23	245
1:20	27, 63
1:21	64
1:21–23	63, 66
1:22	64
2:5–6	75
2:7	127, 131
4:8–10	75
4:9–10	82
4:10	67
4:22ff.	140

Philippians

2:6–8	58
2:6–11	53, 140
2:8	65
2:9	28, 53, 58, 75
2:9–10	59
2:10–11	63, 66

Colossians

3:1	27, 64, 75, 245
3:9ff.	140

1 Thessalonians

1:10	143

1 Timothy

2:8	70
3:16	67, 72, 75
4:1–2	43

2 Timothy

3:1	43

Titus

3:6	29

Hebrews

1:3	64, 65, 75, 245
1:4	64
1:5	64, 65
1:6	65
1:8	27
1:8–9	65
1:10–12	65
1:12	65
1:13	27, 64, 65, 245
2:18	62
4:14–16	62
7:1	120, 166
7:25	62
8:1	27, 65
8:9	70
10:12	27
10:12–13	65, 245
12:2	27, 65
12:19	179

James

2:2	75
2:3	75
4:10	54, 55
5:1	127, 131

1 Peter

3:4	28
3:9	28
3:22	27–28, 64, 66, 75
5:5–6	54, 55

2 Peter

2:21	166
3:22	82

1 John

2:25	28

2 John

8	166

3 John

8	74

Revelation

16	29
16:6	29

Extra-Biblical Sources

Old Testament Apocrypha

2 Esdras
7:29	125
12:10–26	79
12:10–50	77, 79
13:10	189

1 Maccabees
2:58	78
5:27	121

Sirach
2:1–18	53
4:10	122, 164
47:11	121
48:9	78
50	71
50:20	70
50:20ff.	72
50:21	71
50:23	71

Wisdom of Solomon
2:18	122, 164
18:13	122

Dead Sea Scrolls

1QapGn 12:17	120
1QapGn 20:12	120
1QapGn 20:16	120
1QapGn 21:2	120
1QapGn 21:20	120
1QapGn 22:15	120
1QapGn 22:16	120
1QapGn 22:21	120
1QS 4:20ff.	190
1QS 4:22	120
1QS 65:24	190
1QSb 5:27–28	120
4QFlor 1:10–11	125
4QFlor 1:11–12	125
4QFlor 10–13	121, 123
4QPsDnA[a]	122

Other Ancient Sources

Aeschylus
Eumenides
28	119

Apocalypse of Ezra
7:6	78

Ambrose
Sermon 36	209

Aquila
OT Translation	154

Augustine
Sermon
266	209
271	209

2 Baruch
40:3	125
76	77, 79

1 Enoch
9:3	120
10:1	120
46:7	120
60:1	120
60:22	120
62:2	104
91:8–9	192
93:8	78

2 Enoch
67	78

Ez Rabba
48:102	141

Genesis Rabba
96:60	141

Gregory of Nazianzus
"On Pentecost"	209

Gregory of Nyssa
in context	131

John Chrysostom
Hom. 2 On Pentecost	209

Irenaeus
Against Heresies
5.5.1	78

Josephus
Antiquities
4.8.48	79
6.8, 2 #166	47
9.2, 2	78

Jubilees
1:1	183
6:17	183
16:18	120

Marcion
in context	112

Philo
The Decalogue
46–47	185

Pindar
Nemean Odes
1.60 [90]	119
11.2	119

Psalms of Solomon
15:4–5	189
17:21	121, 125
17:37	104
18:7–8	104

Rabbi Jose ben Halafta
Seder Olam	182

Rabbi Eleazar ben Pedat
[Pentecost/Torah]	183

Sibylline Oracles
3:47–50	121, 125

Symmachus
OT Translation	154

Tacitus
Annals
10.24	36

Tertullian
De Anima
50	78

Testament of Judah
24:2	104

Testament of Levi
4:2	123
4:4	123
18:7	104

Theodotion
OT Translation	154

Thucydides
History of the Peloponnesian Wars
1.22.1	36

www.ingramcontent.com/pod-product-compliance
Lightning Source LLC
Chambersburg PA
CBHW030230170426
43201CB00006B/167